YOKNAPATAWPHA BLUES

Southern Literary Studies
Scott Romine, Series Editor

YOKNAPATAWPHA BLUES

FAULKNER'S FICTION AND SOUTHERN ROOTS MUSIC

TIM A. RYAN

LOUISIANA STATE UNIVERSITY PRESS BATON ROUGE

Published by Louisiana State University Press

Manufactured in the United States of America
First printing

Designer: Barbara Neely Bourgoyne
Typeface: Ingeborg
Printer and binder: Maple Press

Library of Congress Cataloging-in-Publication Data
Ryan, Tim A., 1971–
Yoknapatawpha blues : Faulkner's fiction and southern roots music / Tim A. Ryan.
pages cm
Includes bibliographical references and index.
ISBN 978-0-8071-6025-1 (cloth : alk. paper) — ISBN 978-0-8071-6026-8 (pdf) — ISBN 978-0-8071-6027-5 (epub) — ISBN 978-0-8071-6028-2 (mobi) 1. Faulkner, William, 1897–1962—Criticism and interpretation. 2. Music and literature—United States—History—20th century. I. Title.
PS3511.A86Z965276 2015
813'.52—dc23

2014038730

The paper in this book meets the guidelines for permanence and durability of the Committee on Production Guidelines for Book Longevity of the Council on Library Resources. ♾

IN MEMORIAM:

Stuart Kidd
James M. Mellard
Johanna Rushing
Leslie Scott and Mary Winterson Scott
Alisa Smith-Riel
Jake Adam York

CONTENTS

ACKNOWLEDGMENTS

The ideas underlying this book date back to my undergraduate years at the University of Reading in England in the early 1990s, a place quite unlike Mississippi between the two world wars, but where I nonetheless first encountered both William Faulkner and the country blues. By day, I became enchanted with the history, literature, and culture of the modernist era, the Great Depression, and the Deep South, courtesy of the brilliance and passion of those monumental professors in the (now sadly defunct) American Studies Department, particularly Christine MacLeod, Lionel Kelly, and the late, great Stuart Kidd. In the evenings, outside the classroom, Pete Mitchell opened up a wealth of vital musical avenues to me—not least the blues—through his extensive record collection and performances with contemporary R&B ensemble Crawfish Thompson. It was, then, in a gray, suburban, and unimpeachably English commuter town that I began to imagine the interconnections between the works and worlds of Faulkner and Charley Patton.

My first journey below the Mason-Dixon Line in 1992 contributed further to my appreciation of the relationship between southern vernacular music and fictional Yoknapatawpha County, particularly when I visited Elvis Presley's alleged birth-house in Tupelo and Faulkner's home at Rowan Oak on the same Saturday. I am grateful to Julian Pettifer (long before he became Julian Barratt or Howard Moon) and Sherone Rogers for being such sterling companions on that excursion. On my most recent sojourn in Oxford, Mississippi, in 2013, Larry Wells proved to be the very essence of southern hospitality and collegiality, as well as the heart and soul of the Faulkner family tradition.

During seven years of research and writing I have benefited greatly from the input, guidance, and encouragement of many talented and knowledgeable scholars, writers, and artists, both on the conference circuit and via e-mail. My sincere and profound thanks to everybody who moderated or participated in panels at which I presented my research, made pertinent comments, asked searching questions, provided opportunities to publish articles, performed invaluable editorial work, supplied information of which I was unaware, helped make me a better writer, or who was just willing to talk about Faulkner and/or the blues. Of particular note in a very long list are Ann Abadie, Ted Atkinson, Seth Berner, Martyn Bone, Stacy Burton, Scott Casper, Eurie Dahn, Thadious Davis, David Evans, Robert Fox, Tom Freeland, T. Austin Graham, Jürgen Grandt, Robert Hamblin, John Herceg, Jennie Joiner, Donald Kartiganer, Martin Kreiswirth, Kyle Kretzer, John Lowe, Daniel Margolies, Ana Moreno, Dustin Morrow, Drew Mullen, Erich Nunn, Charles Peek, Christopher Rieger, Ben Robbins, Owen Robinson, Mary Sefferly, Amritjit Singh, Theresa Towner, Dawn Trouard, Irene Visser, Jay Watson, Randall Wilhelm, Dai Xiaoli, and the late Jake Adam York.

Two people played a particularly important role in the writing of this book. Since I discovered her essay on Faulkner and the blues, Jane Isbell Haynes has been a valued electronic pen friend, whose knowledge, observations, questions, and incisive commentary on portions of the manuscript significantly improved it. The scholarship of Adam Gussow, meanwhile, has been a constant inspiration to me as a student of the blues. More than that, Adam provided crucial feedback on the opening chapters and has been an incredibly generous supporter of my work and career.

I am delighted that this book continues a rewarding association with Louisiana State University Press. John Easterly's early enthusiasm kick-started the project, and Margaret Lovecraft brought it home. Patricia Schroeder and Scott Romine provided admirably comprehensive and judicious reviews of the manuscript, encouraging me to produce both a more succinct study and a more developed central argument. Stan Ivester—who recalls seeing Willie Dixon, John Lee Hooker, and Muddy Waters perform in Chicago—was an incomparable copyeditor; Lee Sioles has done a wonderful job of transforming a manuscript into a book; and Jennifer Keegan is spreading the word with great aplomb.

I also owe a profound debt of gratitude to those exceptional graduate students at Northern Illinois University who have shared my love of Faulkner, particularly Jose Fernandez, Amy Glaves, Bonnie Miller, Justin Ness, Jessica Smith, Toby Veeder, and the late Alisa Smith-Riel. I am especially indebted to Chia-feng Chang for his tireless work collating "race records" advertisements from the pages of the *Chicago Defender*. Kudos as well to Elizabeth Bowman and Christina Gilleran, who did a magnificent job organizing the 2008 Midwestern Conference on Literature, Language, and Media at NIU in the wake of an appalling campus shooting. Miraculously—given the circumstances—that conference proved a wonderful venue for the first public airing of the ideas from which this book eventually developed.

The Graduate School at NIU generously supported my endeavors with a 2011 Summer Research and Artistry Grant. Chris Jones provided me with an opportunity to teach a class on American literature and music in a Themed Learning Community, while his successor in the Honors Program, J. D. Bowers, invited me to talk about Faulkner and the blues to visiting students and faculty from China. I am also grateful for the collegiality of my Department of English friends, especially Scott Balcerzak, Susan Edwards, Mark Van Wienen, and, above all, Amy Levin and Jan Vander Meer, who arranged a much-needed subvention at a crucial moment. Finally, I salute the thousands of undergraduates who have studied with me at NIU since 2007, and who have enriched my life by listening to the blues of Patton, Geeshie Wiley, Robert Johnson, and Howlin' Wolf every bit as seriously as they read the novels of Faulkner.

Despite the distance that separates us, I could not have completed this book without the love and support of my extended families in England, Idaho, and California: my parents, Tom and Susan Ryan; my siblings, Garry Ryan and Paula Crawford, and their families: Kathryn, James, Grace, Sinead, Adam, Vanessa, and Jean; my lifelong friend Neil Humphries; Daniel Doornbos and Gillian Flato; Gary Mayall, Kathy, and all the Grandys; and the late Johanna Rushing. My love of modernist American culture is partly an inheritance from my maternal grandfather, Leslie Scott, who never once stepped foot on U.S. soil but whose swing quintet wowed the GIs stationed in Bath during World War II. He and his wife, Mary Winterson Scott, were contemporaries of Faulkner and the heroes of the blues, and they inspired my interest in an era that predated my birth.

I must not overlook the contribution of a close companion who entered my life at the very moment that I began researching this project and who has been at my side ever since, sitting quietly while I read and type, accompanying me on many lengthy hikes during which I have worked through numerous ideas and problems, and—from time to time—enlivening my literature classes with his presence. From a ten-week-old rascal to a seven-year-old furry best friend, my loyal Tennessee pup, Kipper, has followed this monograph from inception to completion, although I suspect he will be rather more interested in smelling the final product than reading it. I should offer a shout-out, as well, to Kipper's human and canine companions, who have enriched our neighborhood walks through the cold of January and the humidity of July alike, especially Jan, Ray, and Jake Nelson.

Although this book has been germinating for many years, I could never have written it without Dee Anna Phares, whose acuity, expertise, imagination, humor, and love inform every page. She provided meticulous commentary on multiple drafts of the manuscript, contributed numerous ideas, shared her knowledge of textual editing, and developed the crucial concept of amphitextual studies to explain the nature and purpose of our work. She has also patiently endured Charley Patton songs on endless iPod rotation, as well as my stubborn sifting through gargantuan piles of dusty 78s at myriad garage and estate sales in vain hopes of finding a long-lost Skip James among all the Bing Crosbys and Sammy Kayes. More importantly, Dee Anna enabled me to find myself, and she always encourages me to be myself. Without her, I would not have rediscovered the magic of American culture of the twenties, thirties, and forties, nor the wonder of the world around me.

YOKNAPATAWPHA BLUES

INTRODUCTION

THE RISE OF THE BOLL WEEVIL

In popular memory, 1929 is synonymous with disaster and ruin. The Wall Street Crash in October—prelude to a devastating, decade-long economic depression—signaled the abrupt end of a legendary era of social revolutions, modernist creativity, and unbridled hedonism: the Jazz Age. Curiously, this year of tumultuous endings also marked the unpredictable flowerings of two immensely significant and influential American artists. Their shared point of geographical origin, furthermore, was no less improbable than the inauspicious historical moment of their emergence. Both hailed from the South, a region H. L. Mencken had famously dismissed as being "almost as sterile, artistically, intellectually, culturally, as the Sahara Desert" (370). Their native Mississippi was one of the most marginal territories in that supposedly irredeemable cultural wasteland, boasting "few natural resources" as well as "a bad climate and a backward population," while being "deficient in decent hospitals, colleges, newspapers, and libraries" (Angoff and Mencken 371). As Ted Gioia concludes, it was "as if a Third World country had been abandoned in the heart of the United States, left to fend for itself, with its simple rural staples of cotton and catfish, in the midst of a booming, modern economy whose benefits it did not share" (2). In 1929, however, two Mississippians—in the face of national catastrophe and the Magnolia State's myriad disadvantages—did nothing less than redefine modern music and fiction.

* * *

In June, just four months before the stock market collapse, a guitarist and singer from the Delta traveled by train to Richmond, Indiana, to record some of his blues songs for the Paramount company.[1] Charley Patton had long enjoyed local fame in Sunflower County, particularly on Joe Dockery's plantation, where he lived from time to time. For close to twenty years Patton had performed his broad musical repertoire—including popular ballads, religious anthems, country tunes, rhythmic blues, and old-time rags—for diverse audiences, black and white, in an array of Mississippi venues, from picnics and "jook" joints to street corners and fish fries.[2] It was not until he was almost forty, however, that Patton had a chance to reach a much larger audience.

In the Indiana studio, the bluesman discovered that making a phonograph record was a complicated process, quite distinct from his usual manner of performance. He had to hold his head almost completely still while he sang so that his voice would register at a consistent level for the microphone. Since a single side of a ten-inch 78-rpm phonograph disc could not accommodate more than 200 seconds of music, none of his performances could much exceed three minutes. If a train rumbled past on the nearby tracks, he would have to stop and begin his song over again once the intrusive noise had dissipated. Finally, Patton, an inveterate and flamboyant crowd-pleaser, had to perform without an audience to energize and inspire him.[3] Undaunted by these circumstances, the bluesman began pressing his guitar strings with a metal slide and started singing an idiosyncratic version of an old country reel: "It's a little boll weevil, see it movin' in a[n] empty [square], Lordy. . . ."

Far from his home and despite all the technical obstacles before him, Patton committed more than a dozen of his songs to wax before the day was done. Two of them appeared the following month on the bluesman's first "hot record," which Paramount promoted in the *Chicago Defender,* the nation's foremost black newspaper ("Pony Blues" n.p.). Sales were sufficient for Paramount's agent to invite Patton for a second studio visit in October—this time at the company headquarters in Grafton, Wisconsin—where he produced almost twenty-five sides in another marathon session.[4]

Patton was by no means the first country blues singer, nor even the first Mississippi blues performer, to preserve his work for posterity,[5] but he was, as William Barlow avers, "the heart and soul of the early Delta blues tradition" (33). Although Patton died in relative obscurity in 1934, his recordings and acolytes took the Mississippi blues far beyond Dockery

Plantation: to Memphis, Chicago, and, ultimately, the world. If, as Gioia suggests, the Delta blues is "the underlying heartbeat of all styles of popular music" (6), then the works of Patton—and those of such peers, protégés, and successors as Son House, Robert Johnson, "Bukka"[6] White, Howlin' Wolf, Muddy Waters, and B. B. King—are now widely recognized as being among the quintessential expressions of the form.

Patton's specific influence is more visible in the twenty-first century than ever. Bob Dylan's acclaimed 2001 album, *Love and Theft,* includes "High Water (For Charley Patton)," a free-associating flight of fancy inspired by the bluesman's song about the 1927 Mississippi flood. The blues is also central to the music of one of the most critically acclaimed rock bands of the first decade of the new millennium, the White Stripes, who covered such songs as House's "Death Letter Blues" and Blind Willie McTell's "Southern Can Is Mine." A 2007 photograph captures guitarist Jack White and drummer Meg White in the studio with a picture of Patton conspicuously pasted upon the wall behind them, the bluesman looking down impassively upon his upstart musical descendants.[7] In fact, the White Stripes often ended shows with a ringing version of the very song about the boll weevil with which Patton began his recording career.

Patton's choice of "Mississippi Boweavil [*sic*] Blues" as his introduction to the larger world was, in some respects, a curious one for a man subsequently renowned—if a little hyperbolically—as the "Founder of the Delta Blues."[8] Given Patton's status as one of the architects of modern American music, it is strange that his first recorded song was not an aggressively contemporary blues number but an archaic "agricultural pseudo-lament" that had been performed around the South in one form or another for years (Spottswood 60).[9] Even though it was the bluesman's maiden recording, present-day anthologies of Patton's work typically avoid opening with the boll weevil song, beginning instead with more characteristic performances from the same session, such as "Down the Dirt Road Blues" or "Pony Blues."[10]

Nonetheless, "Mississippi Boweavil Blues" was an entirely appropriate song to mark Patton's emergence as a recording artist. The musician's choice of a well-known ballad implies neither a lack of confidence nor an attempt to pander to listeners; instead, Patton's first recording demonstrates how an accomplished artist can take a tired popular song and recycle it into something strange, unrecognizable, and compelling. Most recorded versions of the boll weevil ballad are catchy singsong pieces, like Lead Belly's folksy versions or Brook Benton's slick 1961 cover. Patton's rendition is an entirely different beast, a radically minimalist deconstruction of the song that offers only the barest suggestion of the traditional melody and lyrics. Instead of an infectious tune, Patton provides an uncompromisingly repetitive and hypnotic one-chord drone which gradually builds to a dizzying tempo.

So familiar are we with the blues today that its conventions often cannot help but seem formulaic and predictable; yet, many decades after its creation, Patton's "Mississippi Boweavil Blues" vividly embodies the alien qualities of the genre and suggests how avant-garde such music must have sounded in its infancy. W. C. Handy's description of his first encounter with the blues emphasizes above all its fundamental strangeness. In his 1941 autobiography, the renowned bandleader and composer recalls an evening very early in the century that he spent dozing at Tutwiler station in the Delta while waiting for a train. In this legendary and oft-cited tale,[11] Handy reports being jolted into consciousness by a curious noise, waking to discover a black guitarist pressing a knife against the strings of his instrument so as to manipulate and alter its tones, producing "the weirdest music I had ever heard," accompanied by a stark and repetitive lyric (74). Handy might as well be describing "Mississippi Boweavil Blues," in which Patton exploits the same slide technique, bending notes into exotic sounds, as he intones his circular verses. One blues scholar even speculates that the Tutwiler guitarist *was* Patton (Evans, *Big Road Blues* 174–75).[12] At the very least, as Stephen Calt and Gayle Dean Wardlow suggest, Patton's take on the boll weevil song—like the music Handy heard in Tutwiler—"implies a broad exposure to sounds, and an urge to upgrade the music about him" (95).

Literary criticism provides a useful way of conceptualizing the unorthodox virtues of Patton's "Mississippi Boweavil Blues." In 1917, the Russian scholar Victor Shklovsky argued that, in literature and art, familiarity breeds indifference. As "perception becomes habitual, it becomes automatic," he observed. "Habitualization devours works, clothes, furniture, one's wife, and the fear of war." Consequently, the purpose and "technique of art is to make objects 'unfamiliar,' to make forms difficult"—to use unorthodox artistic approaches to render familiar things strange and surprising (19, 20). Shklovsky thus echoes Ezra Pound's famous modernist dictum, "Make It New!" If, for a twenty-first-century listener, habitualization has devoured the power of the blues to the extent that a conventional twelve-bar, three-line AAB verse is often apt to sound pedestrian and hackneyed, Patton's weird recording from 1929 is still fresh and arresting. The Delta bluesman took the most conventional text imaginable—an antiquated country ballad—and turned it into music that is uncompromisingly modern, radically experimental, and utterly gripping, a textbook fulfillment of Shklovsky's theories.

"Mississippi Boweavil Blues" is as notable for its content as its form. Although the song concerns the agricultural blight caused by the eponymous insect—which had emerged from Mexico in the 1890s and had been decimating Mississippi cotton crops since the early years of the twentieth century[13]—Patton's recording is no mere lament. For all the apparent simplicity of its repetitive words—couched in pithy two-line stanzas—"Mississippi Boweavil Blues" is a complex and multifaceted song that is as much concerned with humorous triumph as grim ruin. In the first verse, the speaker warns that, because of the boll weevil infestation, "[y]ou can plant your cotton and you won't get half a cent." Throughout the song, the weevil inexorably spreads—moving from Louisiana and Texas into Arkansas and Mississippi—and it multiplies at an alarming rate: the single weevil of the opening stanza produces an increasingly large family whose "native home," by the final verse, is "[m]ost anywhere they raise cotton and corn." The music's pace becomes ever more frenetic as the pest proliferates, and then the song ceases with jarring abruptness, ending with a terrifying vision of insects swarming "in the air" all across the southern states, as if a biblical plague has suddenly rained down upon modern America. For all the frenzied horror of the song, however, "Mississippi Boweavil Blues" is also, paradoxically, a jolly romp. Its skillfully controlled accelerating tempo is as joyously thrilling as it is unsettling, and there is palpable glee in Patton's voice when he assumes the role of the mischievous boll weevil itself, announcing that he's "going down to Mississippi, gonna give Louisiana hell, Lordy." Calt and Wardlow even go so far as to characterize the song as a "waggish work; the weevil is construed as a funny fellow, making the rounds like a blues singer" (111).

The song's self-contradictory tone reflects the South in which Patton lived, a world of apparently impregnable white supremacy, exploitative labor practices, and brutal racial injustice. Any assault upon this status quo was a cause for celebration by black Americans, however harshly it may have affected them as well. Barlow acknowledges that "black farm workers were themselves victimized by the boll weevil's insatiable appetite for cotton," but adds that "they still felt a kinship with the weevils' dogged determination in 'just looking' for a home. Furthermore, they viewed the misfortunes that the boll weevil brought the white plantation owners as retribution for the exploitation of black farm workers" (23).[14] Carl Sandburg—who published a version of the song in 1927, two years before Patton's recording—similarly notes its "paradoxical blend of moods": "quickstep and dirge, hilarious defiance and bowed resignation" (8). The famous poet adds that, if white southern planters "felt the multiplied myrmidons of the boll weevil to be as terrible as one of the Four Horsemen of the Apocalypse," then the "imagination of the negro field workers played shrewdly and whimsically on the phantom that came so silently to destroy the work of man on the land that man claims to own" (252).

Patton's recording does not merely include paradox, but revels in it. "Mississippi Boweavil Blues" emphasizes contradiction, fluidity, and even chaos over absolutism, stability, and the status quo. The lyrics embrace a world of multiple truths, in which the tragedy of agricultural blight is also a source of uproarious comedy, a relentlessly destructive pest is also a revolutionary hero, devastation is also a kind of triumph, and the roles of oppressor and oppressed can be reversed in a moment.

"Mississippi Boweavil Blues" was, then, a resonant choice for Patton's first recording. Just as the boll weevil—a tiny and apparently insignificant insect—spread across the South, despite all efforts to repress and arrest its progress, so did the recording session in June 1929 give Patton—an obscure black man from rural Mississippi—the opportunity to speak far beyond the Delta, unimpeded by the white authorities and social barriers that customarily restricted the lives and movements of African Americans. The initial release of "Mississippi Boweavil Blues"—on the bluesman's third record in September—did not even need to include Patton's name. Attributing the song to "The Masked Marvel," Paramount offered a prize to any listener who could correctly ascertain the performer's identity, a clear indication of the renown that Patton had achieved within a few months of his first recording session.[15] In this instance, the blues clearly represents "the emerging consciousness of a younger generation of African Americans living in a new historical era—seeking personal freedom, social mobility, and better compensation for their labor" (Barlow 6). Patton's boll weevil may indeed be a destructive pest, but it is also a symbol of the unquenchable spirit of the black community, the music of the rural South, and, above all, the bluesman himself: an uncontainable force, poised to make its name known across America and the globe.

In early October—four months after Patton's landmark recording session, just a week or two after the release of "Mississippi Boweavil Blues," and mere days before Wall Street began its monumental collapse—Jonathan Cape and Harrison Smith published a novel by a white Mississippian in which the boll weevil also makes an appearance. It was entitled *The Sound and the Fury,* and its author, William Faulkner, hailed from the state-university town of Oxford, barely seventy miles from Patton's locale.

Up until 1929, Faulkner's literary career had been somewhat spotty, if sporadically promising. His apprenticeship involved a volume of callow poetry and two fairly undistinguished novels, one a bleak tale of disoriented war veterans and the other an arch satire about bohemian artists. Then, the author stumbled upon his core subject: the decline of the old plantation order and the rise of a vigorously modern South. Even in the editorially butchered *Sartoris,* published in January 1929, the pieces are clearly beginning to fall into place, the book's feverishly idiosyncratic style conveying the writer's excitement upon discovering that his own marginalized and parochial locality possessed all the materials necessary for an immortal literary mythology.

Faulkner's fourth novel changed everything. Thoroughly fulfilling the frustrated promise of *Sartoris, The Sound and the Fury* portrays modern southern society in uncompromisingly experimental terms, telling the story of the once-aristocratic Compson family's disintegration from the distorted perspectives of its three brothers: the cognitively disabled Benjy, the disillusioned romantic intellectual Quentin, and the cruelly materialistic Jason. Akin to Patton's radical reinvention of the boll weevil song, *The Sound and the Fury* takes the conventional materials of a melodramatic southern family saga and renders them in startlingly innovative terms.[16] The opening chapter, told from Benjy's viewpoint, is a modernist *tour de force*: a tale narrated by an individual without any sense of sequential time, past and present blurring into an almost-incomprehensible kaleidoscope of impressionistic images.

Like Patton's blues, Faulkner's stories showed the world that great things could come out of Mississippi, even if the world at large took some time to acknowledge the fact. As the author doggedly expanded and developed the chronicle of his fictional Yoknapatawpha County throughout the 1930s, his stock gradually rose, and, by the 1950s, his work was enjoying popular recognition and a slew of awards as well as critical plaudits. Faulkner's reputation has continued to evolve since his death, and his influence now permeates southern, American, and global fiction, from the works of Flannery O'Connor, Cormac McCarthy, and Toni Morrison to those of Jean-Paul Sartre, Gabriel Garcia Márquez, and Mo Yan.

The Sound and the Fury—one of Faulkner's central achievements—has inspired thousands of pages of critical commentary, explanation, analysis, and interpretation, but nobody has ever acknowledged that its use of the boll weevil is uncannily similar to that in "Mississippi Boweavil Blues." If the novelist may not have known Patton's particular recording, he was undoubtedly aware of the boll weevil's presence in southern vernacular music. In 1928—the year that Faulkner composed his tale of the Compsons—the author's former teacher and family friend, Professor Arthur Palmer Hudson, published a version of the song—entitled "Mister Boll Weevil"—in *Specimens of Mississippi Folk-Lore* (56).[17] What is more, Faulkner had quoted directly from Handy's "Yellow Dog Blues" in his 1926 debut novel, *Soldiers' Pay* (157), and *The Sound and the Fury* invokes a satirical observation from the same song: "Down there the boll weevil works while the darkies play" (Handy 83).

The boll weevil episode in *The Sound and the Fury* highlights the profound differences between white and black perspectives on southern society.[18] The splenetic Jason—the narrator of the novel's third section—is obliged to work in a hardware store because of his family's declining fortunes. Here, he relentlessly harasses a black employee known as Uncle Job. If Jason's view of the world, particularly with regards to race, is inflexible and absolutist, Job's canny responses to the white man's bullying reveal a complex worldview that—like Patton's "Mississippi Boweavil Blues"—acknowledges multiple truths and incorporates conflicting perspectives simultaneously. Where Jason's narrative is comically repetitive in its unending reiteration of shallow complaints and unconscious contradictions, Job's pithy observations are layered and nuanced, mobilizing paradox with unerring skill and conveying multiple meanings in very few words, just like a blues lyric.

In a particularly telling passage, Jason describes his annoyance at Job's tardiness in uncrating a shipment of agricultural cultivators.

> "You ought to be working for me," I says. "Every other no-count nigger in town eats in my kitchen."
>
> "I works to suit de man whut pays me Sat'dy night," he says. "When I does dat, it dont leave me a whole lot of time to please other folks." He screwed up a nut. "Aint nobody works much in dis country cep de boll-weevil, noways," he says.
>
> "You'd better be glad you're not a boll-weevil waiting on those cultivators," I says. "You'd work yourself to death before they'd be ready to prevent you."
>
> "Dat's de troof," he says, "Boll-weevil got tough time. Work ev'y day in de week out in de hot sun, rain er shine. Aint got no front porch to set on en watch de wattermilyuns growin and Sat'dy dont mean nothin a-tall to him." (189–90)

Here, Jason articulates his standard resentments, constructing Job as a lazy and worthless individual who complacently leeches off those white patriarchs—like Jason—who supposedly do all the real work, just as the boll weevil exploits the planter. Jason believes that he has been cruelly deprived of everything his race and heritage ought to have guaranteed him: he is merely a white-collar employee when he should be a leisured white landowner. Nonetheless, he views himself as a beleaguered paternalist, doomed to be host to multiple parasites—family dependents, black servants, demanding mistresses, and exploitative northern bankers—who absorb all the money that he considers his rightful reward. In his barbed exchange with Job, Jason essentially asserts, like Handy's lyric—but without any of its implicit irony—that "the boll weevil works while the darkies play" (Handy 83).

Job dismantles Jason's empty and self-deluding rhetoric with impressive acuity and concision. When the African American man declares that "nobody works much in dis country cep de boll-weevil," his specific implication is that people no longer work the *land* as the hardy insect now does. Jason's father was heir to a substantial farming estate, but, in an age of drastic social, economic, and technological change, the Compson family has gradually sold its holdings, acre by acre, until the ancestral home is no longer a site of agricultural production. Equally, the increasing mechanization of farming and the disruption and damage caused by the flood of 1927, as well as the blight of the boll weevil, displaced black laborers and further stimulated the ever-growing migration to northern cities. Job, then, makes an incisive statement about substantial economic and social transitions occurring in Mississippi that affect white and black people alike.

Job's comments specifically emphasize that Jason is no less an exile from the traditional southern plantation system than the displaced black sharecropper, and that the privileges once bestowed by that system upon landowning whites are no longer privileges that the Compsons realistically can claim. Although Jason thinks of himself as a traditional white patriarch, who feeds "no-count nigger[s]" at his table and who has the authority to bark orders at Job, there is no meaningful distinction between the two employees in economic terms: neither has access to the means of production, and both work for the boss who pays them. The white man with the aristocratic ancestors is no less a wage-slave than the African American whose forefathers were literal slaves. Job emphasizes, in other words, that he—like Jason—is one of the lucky ones to be employed in a paying job when the alternatives are to work relentlessly under oppressive conditions as a sharecropper or to be thrown off the land altogether. It is no coincidence that the black character's name has the same spelling as the word "job": the only individual mentioned in the passage that is working for himself or working the land, never mind working industriously, is the boll weevil.

Jason is unable or unwilling to comprehend the substance of Job's remarks or the contradictions inherent in his own assertions. All he hears when Job makes his comment about the boll weevil is the surface observation that the insect toils hard, which merely provokes Jason to assert that Job is lazy in comparison to the assiduous agricultural pest. Jason, however, also thinks of people of color and boll weevils as being equally parasitic, resulting in a torturous construction in which Jason casts Job simultaneously as the personification and antithesis of the insect. He says that the human Job is uncrating the cultivators so slowly that they will not be mobilized in time to save the cotton, and, thus, if Job were also a boll weevil, he would work himself to death, compulsively consuming all the cotton before tardy humans—like Job—could cultivate it.

Job wins the debate, whether or not Jason realizes it, by turning the white man's words against him. Echoing Jason's reference to the boll weevil tirelessly working in the fields, Job invokes the conditions of agricultural labor that African Americans had endured since the days of slavery and that they continued to perform in the twentieth century, even in an age of burgeoning mechanization, insect plagues, mass migration, disastrous flooding, and the evolution of a service economy. The black man exposes the racial ideologies that underpin Jason's rhetorical division of Job into two: the parasitical insect who rapidly consumes the white planter's crop and the lazy worker who fails to do his job with sufficient alacrity. Job's words expose the disparity between the southern stereotype of the lazy black worker and the historical actuality that people of color have performed much of the region's backbreaking agricultural toil. The boll weevil may be working, but neither Job, nor any other member of his racial community, has either the leisure time or the resources to "play" like the "darkies" in Handy's song. Job's conclusion that "Sat'dy dont mean nothing a-tall" to the boll weevil implies that the black sharecropper's work is similarly ceaseless, yet is without remuneration at the week's end.

Because Jason refuses to accept the blunt fact that Job is his economic equal in a wage system, the best riposte he can offer is that "Saturday wouldn't mean nothing to you, either . . . if it depended on me to pay you wages" (190). Jason projects his anachronistic notions of the racial hierarchy onto modern economic organization by imagining himself not as Job's fellow employee, but as his boss: the white man ruling over the black man once more. As Thadious Davis puts it, Jason "has inherited, and accepted, membership (physical and psychological) in a social order once based upon wealth and class, but degenerated into empty rituals and manners—the external trappings of an old order" (*Faulkner's "Negro"* 86). Certainly, Jason's flimsy fantasies are much less persuasive than the complex analysis of reality articulated by Job—or by Charley Patton.

Faulkner and Patton were neighbors, contemporaries, and fellow artists. Between them, they made Mississippi one of the most important sites of cultural activity in the nation: the state that produced some of modern America's most canonical literature as well as nurturing its foundational form of popular music. In one of Faulkner's last novels, *The Mansion* (1959), salesman V. K. Ratliff appropriately muses that, "even though the rest of the world, at least that part of it in the United States, rates us folks in Mississippi at the lowest rung of culture, what man can deny that . . . we too grope toward the stars?" (466). In fact, the Magnolia State's finest artists of the twentieth century did much more than grope toward the stars; they made unparalleled contributions to world culture.

Neither Faulkner nor Patton, however, was aware of the accomplishments of the other. The bard of Dockery Plantation and the storyteller from Oxford stood on either side of the racial chasm that divided the South in this era. The two never met, and it is doubtful they would have had very much to say to each other if they had, given the permissible standards of discourse between white and black men in this time and place. Nonetheless, they both used revolutionary formal techniques to describe, explore, and reimagine the same world and themes. Their common use of the boll weevil as a subversive symbol for the African American people of the South is but one of a multitude of parallels, correspondences, connections, and echoes between their two bodies of work. Faulkner and Patton may not have been able to hear each other across the racial and social gap, but, in the present day, we have the privilege of being able to listen to them together.

1

HOMERS OF THE COTTON FIELDS

WILLIAM FAULKNER AND THE BLUES IN TWENTIETH-CENTURY AMERICA

In their film *O Brother, Where Art Thou?* (2000), the Coen Brothers present the blues and Faulkner's Yoknapatawpha mythology as smoothly intersecting elements in an imaginary pre–World War II South. Best known for translating Homer's *Odyssey* into a postmodern pastiche of classic Hollywood hayseed comedies, *O Brother* also borrows situations from the "Old Man" narrative of Faulkner's *If I Forget Thee, Jerusalem* (1939), including an escape from the state penitentiary, a great flood, and a protagonist who loses his sweetheart to a shady character named Vernon T. Waldrip. Equally prominent in this eclectic mix is the tale of historical Delta blues singer Tommy Johnson (ably played by contemporary blues artist Chris Thomas King), who makes a Faustian pact in hopes of musical success. "Oh, son," says one of the escaped convicts to Tommy in horrified reaction, "for that you traded your everlasting soul?" "Well," the pragmatic bluesman responds, "I wasn't usin' it."[1]

If this quirky cinematic fantasia plays upon the provocative geographical and temporal proximity of the blues to Faulkner's world, literary scholars and music critics have found it difficult to establish concrete or meaningful connections between the novelist and the music. After all, no canonical Mississippi blues artist ever gave any indication of having read Faulkner's works or even having heard of him, while the Oxford author included the blues in his novels and stories only rarely and in brief vignettes. Furthermore, Faulkner published dense, sophisticated modernist fiction, whereas the bluesmakers played for raucous dances and recorded three-minute pop songs. Patton and Faulkner may have been neighbors and contemporaries, but, for that matter, so are New Yorkers Don DeLillo and 50 Cent—and few would claim that there is much artistic common ground between the works of this latter pair. It is hardly surprising, then, that there never has been a book-length study of Faulkner and the blues before now.

As the parallels between the boll weevil passage in *The Sound and the Fury* and Patton's "Mississippi Boweavil Blues" suggest, however, the relationships between Faulkner and the blues—historical, regional, and thematic—are substantial and specific, rather than vague or tenuous. The apparent chasm between the works of Patton and Faulkner—and between music criticism and literary scholarship—is, in fact, easily bridgeable, requiring only that listeners attend to the complex modernism of blues records and that readers look beyond direct references to the music in Faulkner's fiction.

Very few articles in the vast and ever-expanding body of Faulkner criticism address the blues, and those that do are almost exclusively concerned with the author's demonstrable awareness of the music: with what Faulkner knew about the blues and when he knew it (Gussow, "Plaintive Reiterations" 53). Thadious Davis and Adam Gussow provide the most comprehensive and illuminating assessments of popular music in Faulkner's fiction, from the performance by a jazz band in *Soldiers' Pay* to the singing of a black street musician in *Flags in the Dust.*[2] Erich Nunn draws attention to the importance of both black and white popular music to the design of *Sanctuary.* Charles Peek, Carol Gartner, and Ken Bennett examine blues elements in "That Evening Sun" (1931), a story that takes its title from the lyrics of Handy's "St. Louis Blues," while H. R. Stoneback suggests that the characters and situations of 1940's "Pantaloon in Black" derive from another Handy song, "Easy Rider." Finally, Jane Isbell Haynes identifies striking similarities between blues ballads about "Stagolee," and the brief scene in *The Hamlet* in which V. K. Ratliff imagines Flem Snopes defeating the Devil.

Although each of these studies highlights the presence of the blues in Faulkner's world, collectively they cannot help but suggest that vernacular music does not play a particularly significant role in the author's fiction. Of Faulkner's nineteen novels and dozens of short stories, scholars have identified references to the blues in only five books and three tales—virtually all of them fleeting, and, with a couple of exceptions, all appearing in works published before 1932. Gussow judiciously concludes that Faulkner's "place in the blues literary tradition is . . . closer to the margins than the center" ("Plaintive Reiterations" 53). One prominent blues scholar goes even further, suggesting that occasional references to the music in the works of an author who lived in Mississippi in the early decades of the twentieth century are far less notable than their relative "scarcity of blues description" (Evans qtd. in Gussow, "Plaintive Reiterations" 54).

Blues criticism, meanwhile, tends to say little about Faulkner, unless mentioning him in passing for a little historical context or local color. Patton's biographers quote the description in *The Mansion* (1959) of the Delta at the turn of the century in order to paint a picture of the environment in which the singer and guitarist was born and raised (Calt and Wardlow 71). Ted Gioia, meanwhile, describes Will Dockery—the founder of the plantation on which Patton sometimes lived—as a "Faulknerian character come-to-life" (47), an evident reference to Thomas Sutpen in *Absalom, Absalom!,* who similarly wrests a plantation out of a swampy wilderness. Likewise, Francis Davis invokes the protagonist of *Light in August* in his description of the enigmatic Patton as "such a riddle that he might himself be a fiction, a Faulkner creation, a Joe Christmas" (99).

Occasionally, music writers acknowledge thematic parallels between the Mississippi blues and Faulkner's fiction. Greil Marcus was one of the first to compare Faulkner's writings to the blues tradition when he observed that Robert Johnson recorded his eerie songs about a "world without salvation, redemption, or rest" at virtually the same time that Faulkner wrote in *Absalom, Absalom!* of "*that dream-state in which you run without moving from a terror in which you can not believe, toward a safety in which you have no faith*" (Marcus, *Mystery Train* 24, 33; Faulkner, *Absalom, Absalom!* 113). Up until now, however, writers have been content to identify such parallels in passing rather than to explore them in any depth or detail.

Essentially, disciplinary differences discourage music critics and literary scholars alike from comprehensive examination of the intersections between Faulkner's fiction and the blues. Just as the writer from Oxford and the creators of the blues inhabited entirely distinct spheres within a single region, so are the Faulkner expert and the blues enthusiast likely to share parallel but sometimes surprisingly dissimilar knowledge and interests. Although some people are as enamored of Howlin' Wolf's "The Natchez Burning" as they are of Faulkner's "Barn Burning," many who are familiar with "Dry Spell Blues" may never have glanced at "Dry September," and those who know all about the Holston House may not even have heard of Son House.[3] Habitual emphasis upon Faulkner's overt depictions of the music diverts literary critics from investigation of broader thematic parallels between fiction and song. Equally, although studies of the blues often discuss lyrics as a literary form, they do not characterize them as being at all like the kind of literature that Faulkner produced.

Those few studies by Faulkner critics that acknowledge the blues conventionally address the music as just one more cultural background for illuminating the works of the writer, without exploring the corresponding possibility that it might be equally enlightening to interpret blues songs in relation to the Yoknapatawpha fiction. Literary critics sometimes risk reducing a diverse musical form with a complex history to a few broad abstractions, and Faulkner scholars typically invest particular blues songs or artists with significance only when they are identifiable as direct sources for the author's fictional characters or scenarios. Patrick McHugh's analysis of blues elements in *If I Forget Thee, Jerusalem* provides a useful illustration of both the evident potential and the conventional pitfalls of literary scholarship's treatment of African American music. McHugh draws attention to the contrast between the novel's "feeling of stasis" and the common emphasis in the blues upon "impending change" ("The Birth of Tragedy" 73). This analysis, however, is ultimately rooted in rather hazy generalizations about the nature of "the blues"—generalizations that appear to derive from a single theoretical study of the music rather than from consideration of specific songs or recordings.[4] This article, furthermore, does not acknowledge that some of the subjects of Faulkner's novel—such as the Mississippi State Penitentiary at Parchman Farm and the 1927 flood—are also the topics of numerous blues songs. Finally, McHugh's interpretation neglects the fact that *If I Forget Thee, Jerusalem* includes among its minor characters a blues guitarist. For all the promise of its insights, this scholarly investigation of "the spirit of the blues" in relation to Faulkner's work is not very attentive to the very musical form it is so concerned to invoke.[5]

Such limitations are not exclusive to Faulkner criticism, for literary scholars in general are prone to stumble when addressing vernacular or commercial music. *Call and Response: The Riverside Anthology of the African American Literary Tradition* (1997) is a notable collection of black writing that is especially valuable for its emphasis upon oral and musical traditions as well as literary forms. Even so, this anthology is often bewildering in its categorization of specific blues texts. It defines Handy's commercial

"St. Louis Blues" as "rural blues" and Delta musician Willie Brown's 1930 "Future Blues" as "urban blues." It also includes Billie Holiday's "God Bless the Child" in a section on "classic blues"—a term that conventionally refers to the music of female singers of the 1920s—even though Holiday was a jazz vocalist, "God Bless the Child" is a pop song, and it was recorded in 1941. If complaints about such categorizations risk seeming pedantic, imagine, as an equivalent, an anthology of American literature that presented *The Scarlet Letter* as realist, *Moby-Dick* as naturalist, and *Adventures of Huckleberry Finn* as modernist.

Scholarly writing about the blues, meanwhile, tends to be historical, cultural, musicological, sociological, and anthropological at least as often as it employs the philosophies and strategies of literary criticism. The multiple disciplines involved in blues studies define the genre's lyrics variously as oral history, autobiographical musings, vernacular poetry, social critique, oral-formulaic tradition, or pop novelty—but usually not as modernist narrative.[6] Since Faulkner was a man of letters rather than an oral storyteller, and an aesthetic experimenter, not a writer of popular, sociological, or protest fiction, conventional scholarly approaches to the blues do not establish any firm basis for comparative analysis of the author's works and the music of the rural South.[7]

Not only are the dominant approaches in blues studies quite distinct from prevalent strategies in Faulkner criticism, but, while students of the Mississippi author are hardly likely to question the interpretive possibilities and subtextual depths of his work, lovers of popular music often wonder if scholars are inclined to "read too much" into song lyrics.[8] Music fans—and even professional music critics—are sometimes unreceptive to academic studies that characterize blues songs as something more than uncomplicated musical entertainment, or which suggest that lyrics contain anything other than lightly dramatized autobiography.[9] Even Peter Guralnick—an astute music writer and devotee of the blues—once bluntly declared that the idea of "Blues as poetry" is nothing more than "well-intentioned romance" (*Feel Like Going Home* 39). When Gussow first suggested the presence of a recurrent subtext of lynching in prewar blues songs, outraged music enthusiasts accused him of "flagrant projection." "The blues were about a lot of things, they protested—broken hearts, bad luck, going to Kansas City, hungering for love—but lynching wasn't one of them" (*Seems Like Murder Here* xiii). Had Gussow been making such claims about the subtexts of canonical poems or novels instead of popular blues songs, it is unlikely that he would have encountered such strenuous objections. As John J. Sullivan notes, the writings of blues aficionados often involve a "reflexive swerving between ecstatic appreciation and an urge to minimize the aesthetic significance of the country blues." There is only slight exaggeration in Sullivan's observation about hardcore blues fans that, "when the music was all but unknown, they hailed it as great, invincible American art; when people . . . caught on and started blabbering about it, they rushed to remind everyone it was just a bunch of dance music for drunken field hands" ("Unknown Bards" 88).

It is undeniable that blues songs often do not appear to be very purposefully designed constructions. Guralnick's observation that many traditional blues lyrics seem to "consist of no more than a series of unrelated verses strung together at random" highlights the genre's emphasis upon casual extemporization (*Feel Like Going Home* 40). Singers customarily conjured up ad hoc stanzas by dipping—with apparent arbitrariness—into a common storehouse of formula lines and phrases; consequently, blues songs were rarely fixed entities, but could change dramatically from performance to performance. Even to some informed devotees, the idea of coherent textual meaning in prewar country blues verses is dubious, if not altogether absurd. A few blues artists agree: Mississippi guitarist Eddie "Son" House once complained that Patton, his occasional playing partner, would "sing a lot of monkey-junk in a record" (qtd. in Calt and Wardlow 264).

It is hardly surprising that blues aficionados struggle to imagine Patton—that clowning, guitar-thrashing showman—painstakingly crafting lyrics with complex and nuanced meanings. As John Fahey firmly emphasizes, "Patton used his musical abilities, as well as his ability to dance and do tricks with the guitar, in order *to please an audience*." In his initial survey of Patton's recordings, Fahey—a talented musician as well as a perceptive blues lover—even suggests that the "outstanding characteristic of these songs is the disconnection, incoherence, and apparent 'irrationality' of the stanzas" (*Charley Patton* 29, 60).[10] Similarly, in their biography of Patton, Calt and Wardlow skillfully delineate the guitarist's sophisticated musical innovations while thoroughly dismissing his artistry as a lyricist, observing that the "Patton couplet frequently had no dimension beyond its presentation of a petty experience." Calt and Wardlow essentially characterize Patton as an illiterate, drunken, womanizing braggart who also just happened to be an inventive guitarist (53, 35–37, 51).

Increasingly, critics and specialists have questioned the assumption that prewar blues musicians were lacking in conscious artistry or professionalism, or that they were incapable of composing coherent lyrics. Evans disputes stereotypical representations of Patton as a lazy and hedonistic roué," arguing to the contrary that the Delta bluesman was "an artist who was serious about his work and whose work should be taken seriously" ("Charley Patton" 118). Michael Taft, meanwhile, suggests that the studio—precisely because of its technical constraints on performance, as well as the freedom it offered musicians to read lyric sheets as they recorded—"compelled singers to produce concise, coherent, forceful songs. Energy otherwise spent on 'stage presence' went into lyric writing" (*Blues Lyric Formula* 301). Blues performer Rubin Lacy—a contemporary of Patton—even declared that the "blues is sung not for the tune. It's sung for the words mostly. A real blues singer sings a blues for the words" (qtd. In Taft, *Blues Lyric Formula* 8).

Nonetheless, blues journalists and music scholars alike are sometimes reluctant to engage in the kind of analysis of song lyrics that is *de rigueur* in studies of literature precisely because, to a greater or lesser degree, consciously or unconsciously, they are skeptical about the capacity or inclinations of the genre's singer-songwriters to craft verses with substantial or intricate meanings. Faulkner scholarship is renowned for its meticulous textual analysis and rigorous scrutiny of what lies between the author's lines, from the traditional interpretive philosophies of the New Criticism in the 1950s to the theoretically inflected approaches of the twenty-first century. Conversely, it has always been uncommon in blues writing for discussion of a single song to exceed a couple of pages—or even a couple of paragraphs. This is true even of such notable scholarship as Sterling A. Brown's "The Blues as Folk Poetry" (which cites lines and verses from dozens of songs in 16 pages), Paul Oliver's *Blues Fell This Morning* (which deals with 350 songs in 289 pages), Samuel Charters's *The Poetry of the Blues* (which discusses a mixture of isolated verses and complete lyrics from well over 100 songs in 173 pages), Guido van Rijn's *Roosevelt's Blues* (which addresses 128 songs in 211 pages), and Evans's analysis of songs about the 1927 flood (which considers more than 20 complete lyrics in 66 pages).[11]

Faulkner's artistry obviously is not in doubt, but, if it is debatable how much care was involved in the design of many prewar blues songs, it would be a profound mistake to underestimate their potential as integrated and interpretable texts. The beauty of the blues lyric resides in its capacity to say a great deal without apparently saying very much. Oliver emphasizes that formula phrases in the blues possess "a shorthand significance with a wealth of unstated associations permitting a maximum of content with a strict economy of means" ("Blues as an Art Form" 4). Evans concludes from his fieldwork that, if the average country blues song may initially appear to be a random assemblage of unrelated stanzas, it actually possesses "a remarkably cohesive and symmetrical structure" and an "underlying logic or structural unity" (*Big Road Blues* 69, 146). Angela Davis avers that the "realism of the blues does not confine us to literal interpretations. On the contrary, blues [lyrics] contain many layers of meanings and are often astounding in their complexity and profundity" (24).

Despite the appearance of Charters's exploratory *The Poetry of the Blues* as early as 1963, it was not until the 1990s that blues scholarship began to explore the richness of the genre's lyrics in earnest. In answer to his critics, Gussow produced the seminal *Seems Like Murder Here* (2002), demonstrating through incisive study of specific verses and related writings how "black southerners evolved blues song as a way of speaking back to, and maintaining psychic health in the face of, an ongoing threat of lynching" (xii). Equally notable are Evans's astute exploration of Patton's songs about hybrid racial identity ("Charley Patton" 181–83), Luigi Monge's exhaustive interpretation of "the dichotomy between sacred and secular" in the lyrics of Son House (224), Steven C. Tracy's nuanced analysis of the traditional "Red River Blues" in *Langston Hughes and the Blues* (185), Eric Rothenbuhler's perceptive take on Robert Johnson's songs, Angela Davis's feminist readings of verses sung by Bessie Smith and Ma Rainey, and M. G. McGeachy's comparative analyses of medieval English poetry and prewar country blues lyrics.

Like such scholars, I proceed from the assumption that, whatever the circumstances of their creation or the immediate purposes of their creators, blues lyrics possess multiple levels of meaning. The theoretical turn in literary studies has made any lingering doubts about the poetic inclinations of blues lyricists essentially irrelevant. Scholars now habitually embrace interpretive approaches that supplement or even transcend the traditional critical mission to decode "what the author is trying to say," and the discipline of English no longer assumes that a writer is the sole or ultimate arbiter of textual meaning. Contemporary literary scholarship is as much inclined to address a text's capacity to generate endlessly proliferating meaning as to delineate an author's conscious purposes. As Faulkner once put it, "The artist is of no importance. Only what he creates is important" (*Lion in the Garden* 238). The illiteracy of some of the bluesmakers, their mobilization of stock formula lines, and the circumstances in which they created their recorded works—sometimes plied with whiskey and forced to halt abruptly if a performance threatened to exceed the three-minute mark—do not particularly matter. Although the canonical blues artists worked in a highly formulaic popular medium and many of them lacked formal education, they nonetheless created works that beguile and provoke the listener no less than Faulkner's fiction captivates and stimulates the reader.

The simple notion that blues songs are not just oral poetry but also a kind of modernist verse or even nonlinear narrative is all that is required to establish a firm foundation for comparative analysis of Faulkner's published fiction and the recordings that serve as the permanent texts of the blues tradition. Faulknerians tend to characterize the blues as a monolithic cultural or folk phenomenon, rather than as a modern recorded art form that boasts a wide variety of schools and practices, as well as a clearly defined canon of major artists and key works. As Gussow notes, although Faulkner critics sometimes suggest that the author "can sing the blues just as convincingly as his darker-skinned brothers across the tracks . . . [f]ew commentators feel a similar need to reassure us that Muddy Waters, Robert Johnson, and B. B. King were urbane modernists and self-conscious aesthetic innovators—and Faulkner's peers in that regard—even though that's exactly what Waters, Johnson, and King were" ("Plaintive Reiterations" 58). In Edward Comentale's formulation, "the blues mobilizes the very excess of modern life—its extreme feelings, its stark formalism—for its own ends" (32).[12] For all the apparent minimalism, fragmentation, and free-association of the lyrics of any prewar blues record, it is evident that it ultimately has a coherent story to tell, just as the most obscure, experimental, and disjointed modernist poem or novel—such as E. E. Cummings's paean to Buffalo Bill or *The Sound and the Fury*—has a coherent story to tell.

My goal is to institute a dynamic intertextual dialogue between Faulkner and the blues, not to discuss the author's knowledge of the music, or, for that matter, how familiar blues singers might have been with modernist literature. Only a few, brief passages in Faulkner's canon depict blues musicians, but there are numerous thematic and formal parallels between the Yoknapatawpha chronicle and blues records. What is more, the singers of the Delta were no less artists than the novelist from Oxford, and a canonical prewar country blues recording—such as Patton's "High Water Everywhere," Geeshie Wiley's "Last Kind Words Blues," or Robert Johnson's "Dead Shrimp Blues"—is as complex and redolent with meaning as *If I Forget Thee, Jerusalem,* "That Evening Sun," or *Sanctuary.*

It is easy to lapse into banal abstractions or blithe suppositions about the superficial geographic, temporal, and thematic proximities of Faulkner to the blues. Gussow is rightly skeptical of the tendency of today's culture industry to commodify the author and the music as twin Mississippi exemplars of "dirty-South authenticity" and "icons of the Real: rough-hewn, but subtle, not to everybody's taste." Any meaningful comparison of the Mississippi novelist and the blues first has to transcend the trite notion that "Faulkner *must* be bluesy" because "he lived just around the corner from all those famous blues guys." Gussow interrogates an equally problematic assumption—as articulated in a publication of the Mississippi Valley Blues Society—that Faulkner's fiction and blues songs similarly address such issues as "love/loss," the "effects of the past," and "movement." As Gussow notes, these "are indeed themes shared by *Light in August, Absalom, Absalom!,* and any number of Charley Patton songs, but they're also the themes of such novels as *Anna Karenina* and *Portrait of a Lady*"—and just about any work of art or literature. Such vague abstractions hardly establish any true kinship or genuinely revealing intersections between the works of Faulkner and the country blues tradition ("Plaintive Reiterations" 55, 56, 57).

Nonetheless, Faulkner's fiction and the recorded blues *did* emerge at the same time and in the same place, and there are many substantial historical and thematic similarities between them. Both, for example, negotiate between the traditional/parochial and the experimental/cosmopolitan in their designs, techniques, and structures. Both, moreover, address such specific shared topics as the flooding of the Mississippi, relationships between paternalist white planters and black sharecroppers, male sexual impotence, incarceration at Parchman Farm, and racial violence, as well as the effects of the boll weevil upon southern agriculture.

Comparative analysis of the blues and the fiction of one of the twentieth century's most sophisticated American writers demonstrates the capacity of vernacular song to withstand and reward intensive textual scrutiny, but this is not to suggest that the importance of African American music is dependent upon its similarities to Faulkner's work. Just as *Light in August,* "A Rose for Emily," and *Go Down, Moses* possess characteristics that no popular song could possibly embody, so do such classic blues pieces as "Hard Time Killin' Floor Blues," "Hellhound on My Trail," and "Skinny Leg Blues," boast qualities for which there are no conceivable equivalents in any work of literature.

If the bluesmakers contributed no less to American modernist culture than Faulkner, even erasure of the traditional "great divide" between high art and popular culture does not establish an entirely level playing field between literature and the blues.[13] Since it requires considerably greater space to discuss a novel of several hundred pages than it takes to address a song that may contain only 150 words, it is inevitable that a greater number of the pages that follow are devoted to Faulkner's writings than to music. What is more, the Oxford author enjoyed social and cultural advantages routinely denied his African American neighbors, including greater opportunities to pursue his creative vocation. Despite his heavy drinking, interludes as a Hollywood screenwriter, and reckless horse riding in later life, Faulkner enjoyed a lengthy literary career, producing hundreds of works, short and long, over a period of forty years. Many of the great Mississippi blues artists had much shorter lives and significantly briefer musical or recording careers. Patton was born only six years ahead of Faulkner, but died a full twenty-eight years before him. Although he performed for local audiences on plantations for years, Patton's opportunities to record his works for posterity were limited to just four brief sessions between 1929 and 1934. The total studio output of the mysterious Geeshie Wiley is even sparser, numbering a mere six songs. Meanwhile, Robert Johnson—the most canonical of the Delta blues singers—died in his twenties, having participated in only two recording sessions. Even Howlin' Wolf—who ultimately surpassed Faulkner in age by two years—devoted much less of his life to music than he would have liked. Hubert Sumlin, Wolf's longtime guitarist, recalls the singer bemoaning the fact that he "started at 40, and that was 40 years too late" (qtd. in Trynka 43). While Faulkner might complain about his periodic creative servitude as a Hollywood scriptwriter, Wolf spent much of the first half of his life engaged in genuine hard labor, plowing cotton fields. He ultimately crammed all his vital recorded musical work into a career virtually half the length of Faulkner's. A long-range comparison between Faulkner's fiction and the blues thus necessitates discussion of more than one musician.

Even so, this study focuses upon just six songs by canonical singer-songwriters: Patton's "High Water Everywhere," Wiley's "Last Kind Words

Blues," Johnson's "Dead Shrimp Blues," Wolf's "Moving" and "Can't Stay Here," and—briefly in the conclusion—Bukka White's "Parchman Farm Blues" and Lead Belly's "The Midnight Special." Four of these artists hailed from Faulkner's Mississippi, while the other two—Wiley and Lead Belly—are associated with such nearby regions as Texas and Louisiana. Equally, I discuss only a few of the Oxford author's works—essentially the novella "Old Man," the short story "That Evening Sun," and the novel *Sanctuary,* along with brief consideration of *The Reivers* and *The Mansion.* I hope that other scholars will investigate further Faulkner novels and stories in relation to the works of other Mississippi bluesmakers, such as Skip James, Sid Hemphill, Fred McDowell, Mississippi John Hurt, Muddy Waters, John Lee Hooker, and B. B. King, as well as such musicians from other states as Blind Lemon Jefferson, Bessie Smith, Peetie Wheatstraw, Memphis Minnie, and Blind Willie McTell.

One benefit of such a focused critical approach to Faulkner and the blues is its potential accessibility to literary scholars and music fans alike, and, for the same reason, I largely eschew specialist theoretical terminology. Suffice it to say that this book blends elements of cultural studies, new historicism, and identity studies with the kind of close textual analysis commonly associated with the New Criticism: a multivalent and eclectic approach for which Dee Anna Phares has coined the term "amphitextual studies" (n.p.). This critical viewing "from all sides" is attentive to the ways in which culture creates and shapes textual meaning, while also emphasizing the inherent value and complexities of the text itself—whether literary or popular cultural. It is an approach that is simultaneously "intratextual, intertextual, contextual, and metatextual" (n.p.).

For the sake of further orientation for readers from different disciplines, we begin with a brief historical survey of the blues for the Faulknerian and a potted narrative of the author's life and career for the blues lover. This joint history of the writer and the music demonstrates that Faulkner's literary career and the development of the blues—particularly the recorded Mississippi blues—paralleled each other at every stage. Both the country blues and Faulkner's work divide into two clear phases. Before World War II, the author and the musicians of the South produced significant work, if with relatively limited recognition. After the war, Faulkner's stories and vernacular music moved into the national mainstream, even as the aging author and the elders of the blues struggled to assert themselves in a rapidly shifting cultural environment.

The blues and Faulkner came into the world almost simultaneously: the author was born in 1897, around the time of the earliest rural beginnings of the music in various parts of the South.[14] The names of the late-nineteenth-century originators of this musical genre are largely lost to history, but the 1890s witnessed the births of many of the first generation of iconic blues recording artists, including Patton.[15]

The blues first achieved cultural prominence in the opening decades of the twentieth century, as Faulkner was growing up. If the rural architects of the music enjoyed only local renown within black communities in this era, popularized adaptations of the genre became a national and multiracial craze. African American bandleader W. C. Handy made a fortune from compositions derived from songs he had heard in and around the Delta, beginning with "Memphis Blues" (1912) and "St. Louis Blues" (1914). As a young man, Faulkner danced to the music of Handy's orchestra, both at private parties and social functions in the halls of Ole Miss.[16] For most Americans in the 1910s, in fact, the blues meant Handy's sheet-music publications and performances by such white artists as Bee Palmer, Gilda Gray, Marion Harris, Morton Harvey, and Margaret Young.[17] As T. Austin Graham points out, one of the central paradoxes of blues history is that "a music synonymous with blackness in the national imagination and perhaps the most recognizably African American song form ever created, was taken up by and made popular among whites almost from the moment it became commercially available" (137).

There was no commercial American recording of a black artist singing the blues until 1920. Mamie Smith's "Crazy Blues" paved the way for a series of records by African American vocalists—mostly female and usually backed by full jazz bands—that commonly owed as much to pop and Tin Pan Alley as to the black musical traditions of the rural South. Prominent members of this "urban," "classic," or "vaudeville" blues scene included Ma Rainey and Bessie Smith, the "Empress of the Blues."[18]

It was not until the spring of 1926 that Blind Lemon Jefferson "shocked the music world" with his pioneering recordings of "the raw, unfiltered blues of rural America" (Gioia 42). Jefferson's songs certainly presented a dramatic alternative to the polished productions of the urban singers. There was no piano, no trumpet, no clarinet, just the singer accompanying his sparse verses by strumming his guitar "in real southern style," as one advertisement put it ("Booster Blues" 7). If Jefferson's was not quite the first country blues record,[19] it nonetheless heralded a new era in American music, as phonograph companies—hoping to replicate the commercial success of the Texan's disc—swiftly recruited other guitar-toting purveyors of down-home songs.[20]

Although blues records in this era may have sold in six-figure quantities,[21] their consumers were predominantly African American. Robert Dixon and John Godrich overstate the case when they assert that "Race Records" in this period "sold to an entirely black market" (245). Evidence suggests that a variety of listeners enjoyed the popular blues of Handy and the recordings of the urban blueswomen, but it is true that the country blues records of Jefferson—and, later, Patton—found their way mostly into the homes of lower-class people of color. Few white consumers were aware of the recorded country blues in the 1920s and 1930s, and the culture at large remained all but oblivious to its significance.

If 1926 was an important year in blues recording history, it also marked a watershed in Faulkner's literary career, with the author's debut novel appearing in February, just five weeks before Jefferson's first blues record arrived in stores. In one scene in *Soldiers' Pay,* the white protagonists attend a private party at which an African American band performs for the revelers. Among the "reiteration of wind and strings warm and troubling as water," a few fragments of lyrics are briefly discernible, including, "I wonder where my easy rider's gone" and "shake and break it, dont let it fall" (156, 157). This first line derives from Handy's "Yellow Dog Blues" and the second from a bawdy old "country rag" (Spottswood 60), a version of which would be recorded by none other than Patton just three years later. The novel ends with white characters listening to the singing of a black church choir (256). Faulkner's first novel thus cemented the writer's oblique relationship with African American, southern vernacular, and popular music.

Although *Soldiers' Pay* and its successor, *Mosquitoes* (1927), are tentative journeyman works, the aspiring author soon found his literary form. Spurred by an editor's rejection of his third novel, *Flags in the Dust,* Faulkner, as one biographer puts it, "exploded into brilliance" (Williamson, *William Faulkner* 220). With a friend's help, the writer swiftly adapted *Flags* into the shorter *Sartoris,* retaining the passage celebrating "Some Homer of the cotton fields" (*Flags* 780; *Sartoris* 226), as if announcing the emergence of the southern country blues singer as national poet. Then, between 1928 and 1932, Faulkner did nothing less than produce four of the most significant novels in American literature. Hot on the heels of *The Sound and the Fury* came *As I Lay Dying* (1930), a darkly comic tale of a poor white family's efforts to transport the coffin of its matriarch to the town of Jefferson, Faulkner's fictional version of Oxford. Like its predecessor, *As I Lay Dying* is a work of experimental bravado, its narration consisting of fifty-nine interior monologues from the divergent perspectives of fifteen different characters. In sharp contrast to this self-consciously avant-garde masterpiece, Faulkner dismissed his next novel, *Sanctuary* (1931), as a cheaply sensationalist potboiler that he had cynically produced purely for the money. For all its lurid elements, however, the narrative's quintessentially Faulknerian style—elliptical, indirect, and obscure—ingeniously reconciles populist pulp fiction and modernist high art. Finally, *Light in August* (1932) is the multilayered story of the Yoknapatawpha community and its torturous attitudes toward race, racial identity, and racial history. If these four monuments of modern fiction were not sufficient achievement, the five-year period in which they were written and published also saw the appearance of almost thirty of Faulkner's short stories, including such enduring pieces as "A Rose for Emily," "Dry September," "Spotted Horses," and "That Evening Sun." Unlike such accessible tales, Faulkner's novels of this period were too challenging, too innovative, and too overwhelming to garner immediate recognition or widespread appreciation. Nonetheless, as Noel Polk says of the author's output in the late 1920s and early 1930s, "In quantity alone, this record is astounding; in quality, it is perhaps unparalleled in the literature of the English language" (*Children of the Dark House* 40).

Faulkner was not the only artist to enjoy a Golden Age between 1928 and 1932; these years also constitute the classic era of the country blues—especially the Mississippi blues—on record. In the late twenties, a slew of rural musicians emerged to compete with Lemon Jefferson for the attentions of the black record-buying public. Although Georgia boasted such prominent singer-songwriters as Willie McTell and Blind Blake, Mississippi was the indisputable heart of the blues in this era. The northern hill country—the blues center closest to Faulkner's Oxford—was home to such significant figures as Sid Hemphill and Fred McDowell, but its denizens made very few recordings of their work until after World War II.[22] During Faulkner's flowering as a writer in the late twenties and early thirties, the landmark records of the Mississippi blues primarily came from artists associated with the Delta, notably House, Tommy Johnson, Skip James, Mississippi John Hurt, and, of course, Patton.[23]

Paramount released Patton's songs almost as quickly as he recorded them, issuing more than twenty records between mid-1929 and early 1932, numerous monuments of popular music among them. "A Spoonful Blues," for example, is a remarkable depiction of cocaine addiction and its impact upon a community, with Patton adopting multiple voices to dramatize his tale: the gruff tone of the narrator, the impassive rumble of the addict, the plaintive keening of an abused woman, and even the voice of the guitar, which "speaks" the conspicuously unsung word "spoonful" as a menacing refrain. With its multiple voices and perspectives, the song is a musical analogue of Faulkner's modernist narrative strategies in *As I Lay Dying*.

Even the titles of Patton's records and Faulkner's publications frequently echoed each other. In 1925, the author published a sketch inspired by and named after a folk ballad, "Frankie and Johnny," a song that Patton recorded as "Frankie and Albert" at the end of the decade.[24] In October 1929, one could listen to Patton's latest record, "Screamin' and Hollerin' the Blues," while reading Faulkner's new novel, *The Sound and the Fury*. *As I Lay Dying* arrived in stores in October 1930, at the very same time as Patton's "Jesus Is a Dying-Bed Maker." One of Patton's last great records, "Moon Going Down," appeared at the beginning of 1931, shortly before the publication of Faulkner's "That Evening Sun Go Down"—as it was then called—in H. L. Mencken's *American Mercury* magazine.

Not only did both Faulkner's and Patton's first major works emerge in 1929, but their most productive periods ended almost concurrently as well. When the Great Depression all but demolished the American music industry—devastating the market for "race records" in particular—music companies abandoned the country blues as rapidly as they had embraced it just a few years previously.[25] The rural singers who had recorded so fruitfully for a few years quickly disappeared back into local obscurity. Patton continued to perform in and around Sunflower County, but after recording forty-two sides between June 1929 and the summer of 1930, did not set foot in a studio again for more than three years. Once the Depression took hold, the recordings from his earlier sessions appeared ever more intermittently on phonograph discs, and to smaller and smaller sales, finally tapering off altogether early in 1932. The bluesman participated in only one more studio session—in New York in 1934—just a few months before his death.

Equally, the publication of *Light in August* in the summer of 1932 drew a line under Faulkner's most prolific period as a writer. For several years afterwards, the novelist seemed to tread water, producing an uncharacteristic and rapidly written novel about disillusioned stunt pilots entitled *Pylon* (1935) and overseeing two collections of short stories that had already appeared in such periodicals as the *Saturday Evening Post.*[26] With financial security a concern, he tried his hand at screenwriting, working for MGM from 1932 to 1933, Universal in 1934, and Twentieth Century Fox in 1935, but little of his work made it to the screen.

After these comparatively unremarkable intervals in their respective careers, the Mississippi country blues and Faulkner bounced back—at least briefly—in 1936. In October, the author published the magisterial *Absalom, Absalom!,* a dense historical epic about a monomaniacal planter and slaveholder. One month later, a young Delta singer named Robert Johnson traveled to Texas to make his first recordings. A second session followed in June 1937, but an untimely death by poisoning in August 1938 abruptly ended Johnson's promising career.

Had Johnson not met a premature end, he would have achieved national recognition at John Hammond's public celebration of black music, the first "Spirituals to Swing" concert at Carnegie Hall in December 1938. In Johnson's absence, Hammond played the audience a couple of the bluesman's records on a phonograph. *Time* magazine covered the event in its edition of January 2, 1939, observing, "What the concert did demonstrate is that the best U.S. Negro music is not all produced in Harlem and on Broadway, but that some of it comes from towns of the South and Middle West" ("Music" 23). This comment indicates that white America was at last beginning to catch onto the importance of the rural blues, but the article does not deign to mention Johnson's posthumous pseudo-appearance at the event.[27] Faulkner fared somewhat better, gracing the front cover of the same magazine just three weeks later, with the accompanying feature describing him as "the grim chronicler" of the South's decay, and, potentially, "the grim humorist of her transformation" ("When the Dam Breaks" 48). Despite *Time*'s acknowledgment, however, both Faulkner's fiction and the Mississippi blues were already caught up in periods of uncertainty, stagnation, and transition by 1939.

By the mid-thirties, in fact, the blues was clearly moving out of the country and into the city, even if the music would not achieve its most fully realized urban sound until the 1950s. For all their expanded instrumentation, the Chicago-made records of such stalwarts as Memphis Minnie (Lizzie Douglas), Peetie Wheatstraw, Big Bill Broonzy, and John Lee "Sonny Boy" Williamson are often slicker and more prone to novelty and commercialized formula than the southern blues of their predecessors.[28]

Rural blues became increasingly marginal in this era, at least as far as commercial recordings were concerned. Bukka White's renowned 1940 session after his release from the penitentiary at Parchman Farm is a notable exception to this rule. In just a couple of days, White recorded twelve songs, several of them powerful meditations on the experience of incarceration, including "District Attorney Blues" and "Parchman Farm Blues." In many respects, however, White's session represents one of the last gasps of the country blues tradition on record, at least before the blues revival of the 1950s and 1960s. It did not help that military mobilization and two musicians' union strikes severely restricted the activities of the recording industry for much of the forties.[29]

The rural blues was far from dormant in this period, however, as the field recordings made by folklorists John and Alan Lomax for the Library of Congress in the late thirties and early forties amply demonstrate. The Lomaxes preserved music by such marginalized or forgotten figures as Son House, Willie Brown, and David "Honeyboy" Edwards, as well as songs by a talented bootlegger on Stovall's Plantation in Coahoma County. Born McKinley Morganfield, but calling himself Muddy Waters, he would go on to become a crucial figure in the postwar electric renaissance of the blues.

Just as the commercially recorded blues was relatively stagnant in the late thirties and early forties, Faulkner's published work in the same period rarely scaled the heights of his previous accomplishments. Increasingly, the author assembled novels out of short stories he had previously printed in periodicals. *The Unvanquished* (1938) was cobbled together from tales about the Civil War and Reconstruction that originally appeared in the *Saturday Evening Post* and *Scribner's* between 1934 and 1936. Similarly, *The Hamlet* (1940)—the first installment in Faulkner's slow-burning trilogy about the rise of the grasping Snopes family—cheerfully rehashes several of its set pieces from stories the author had published in magazines at the beginning of the 1930s and an incomplete manuscript from the same period. Even the one unqualified triumph in this era of Faulkner's career—

his powerful exploration of southern race relations in *Go Down, Moses* (1942)—was assembled from previously published material.[30] One of the few fully original novels that Faulkner produced in these years was *The Wild Palms,* a curious experimental work that follows two entirely separate narratives in alternating chapters. A fallow period followed this phase of Faulkner's career: after *Go Down, Moses,* six years would pass before the author published another book.

The decade after World War II witnessed the rebirth of the blues in a new context and the public revitalization of Faulkner's career. After a period of transition in the 1940s, a blues revolution occurred at the dawn of the fifties. Chester Burnett, the self-styled "Howlin' Wolf," had been playing the blues for so long that he had once been a protégé of Patton. It was not until 1951, however, that he made his first recordings. Wolf's eerie moaning and cavernous bellow, the discordant clanging of electric guitars, and horn-like blasts of wildly amplified harmonica sounded the dramatic beginnings of a new musical era.[31]

This era coalesced when Wolf moved to Chicago and began his musical rivalry with Muddy Waters, who had come north some years previously. In the clubs of the Windy City and on their singles for the Chess label, these two Mississippi expatriates produced an impressive canon of modern blues, wrenching the music from its acoustic country roots and making it into a national, electrically amplified postwar form. If Patton, Johnson, and other prewar artists were now largely forgotten, Wolf and Waters put the blues on the hit parade. The former placed five songs in the *Billboard* Rhythm and Blues top twenty in the 1950s, while Waters scored a trio of top ten songs in 1954 alone.[32] Other Mississippi expatriates experimenting with electric blues—including B. B. King and John Lee Hooker—regularly joined Wolf and Waters on the *Billboard* charts between the late forties and the mid-fifties. Despite the determinedly contemporary sound of the electric blues, these northern and urban recordings were often rooted in memories, materials, and even specific songs of the prewar rural South. Almost a quarter of a century after Patton first recorded it, Wolf made a version of "Pony Blues," while, as late as 1963—a full twenty years after he had moved to Chicago—Waters proudly sang, "My Home Is in the Delta."

Just as popular electric blues records were establishing a national audience for black musical traditions, an upstart white sibling emerged to eclipse them. In 1954, a young singer from Tupelo, Mississippi, exploded onto the scene with his first single, "That's All Right,"[33] and America was soon in thrall to Elvis Presley and rock 'n' roll.[34] Although the blues was central to the music of Presley, Chuck Berry, Little Richard, Jerry Lee Lewis, and Ray Charles, these artists' radical and eclectic experiments in synthesizing rhythm 'n' blues, gospel, and country made straightforward—and even electrified—blues seem almost instantly outdated to young record buyers. After 1956—the year of Presley's "Heartbreak Hotel"—Wolf never landed another new song on the *Billboard* charts.[35]

For Wolf and Waters—both on the verge of their fifties—it was the beginning of the end. Their recordings of the late 1950s and 1960s often lack the verve and freshness of their earlier work, even though Wolf made some infectious records in collaboration with imperious songwriter Willie Dixon—including "Red Rooster," a song with which the Rolling Stones would score a British number one. The success of the Stones cover version is telling: at the very moment that a new, young, white, and—increasingly—global audience was discovering the blues, its primary purveyors were beginning to burn out and lose their black listeners at home. William Ferris discovered from his research in the Delta in the 1960s that younger African Americans "associate blues with black accommodation and feel the music is inconsistent with their life-style" (45), while Ernest J. Gaines recalls sardonically of his college years in the mid-fifties that "very few of my African American friends . . . wanted to listen to it [the blues] at all because they wanted to forget what those ignorant Negroes were singing about" (27).[36] After 1964's "Killing Floor," Wolf's major artistic work, like that of Waters, was essentially behind him. Market forces and opportunistic studio executives pressured the aging bluesmen to record novelty dance numbers and lurching psychedelic blues-rock albums for the white youth market.

Faulkner's postwar career followed a pattern similar to those of the two Chicago-based bluesmen, in which critical plaudits and popular attention coincided with the author's unfashionable traditionalism and his struggle against waning artistry. Like the songs of Wolf and Waters, Faulkner's fiction continued to concern the South during the earlier decades of the twentieth century, and he similarly made new texts out of old materials and themes, such as his rewriting of both *Sanctuary* and "That Evening Sun" in *Requiem for a Nun* (1951).

Soon after World War II, a series of events made Faulkner a national literary giant, seemingly overnight, although mainstream recognition of his work had, in truth, been building slowly throughout the thirties. As late as 1946, the author was still toiling away in Hollywood and could complain to his agent of being a prophet without honor at home: "In France, I am the father of a literary movement. In Europe I am considered the best modern American and among the first of all writers. In America, I eke out a hack's motion picture wages" (qtd. in Blotner, *Biography* 1203). Malcolm Cowley's 1946 anthology, *The Portable Faulkner*—a highly accessible introduction to the author's complex fictional world—provided concrete confirmation of the author's importance and stimulated sales of his works in the United States. This collection even inspired Faulkner to declare, "By God, I didn't know myself what I had tried to do, and how much I had succeeded" (qtd. in Cowley 91). The author then began the 1950s with two important honors: the National Book Award for his *Collected Stories* and the Nobel Prize for Literature. Another National Book Award and a Pulitzer Prize soon followed for *A Fable* (1954).

Despite this new cultural visibility, popularity, and respect, Faulkner was in decline and he knew it. Granville Hicks spoke for many when he said of the author's later novels that "one feels in them strength of will and mastery of technique rather than the irresistible creative power that surged forth so miraculously in the earlier work" (qtd. in Blotner, *Biography* 1747). *A Fable* cost Faulkner years of frustrated effort and stands as one of his most laborious and awkward novels, its literary awards notwithstanding. He even acknowledged privately that he had "written myself out and all that remains now is the empty craftsmanship—no fire, force, passion" (qtd. in Blotner, *Biography* 1587).[37]

This was, after all, an era of glamorous young storytellers whose works engaged with the freshest trends of the Cold War world. They were the literary rock 'n' roll that threatened to eclipse Faulkner's down-home blues. Next to Norman Mailer, Truman Capote, Jack Kerouac, Grace Paley, James Baldwin, Mary McCarthy, and J. D. Salinger, Faulkner—like Wolf and Waters—could not help but appear to be a relic from a previous generation whose works remained stubbornly rooted in the prewar South. Although Faulkner's Yoknapatawpha chronicle begins in the earliest years of the Republic, long before the author's birth, its narrative arc barely extends beyond World War II, even though Faulkner continued to produce novels into the 1960s. *Requiem for a Nun* is set in the late thirties, *A Fable* during World War I, and *The Reivers* (1962) in the first decade of the twentieth century, while the Snopes trilogy, which concluded with *The Town* (1957) and *The Mansion* (1959), ends around 1946. As Thadious Davis observes, "Faulkner never seemed to move beyond the thirties in his general conception of the South" (*Faulkner's "Negro"* 5).

Despite his gradual decline and old-fashioned commitment to an earlier era, Faulkner was far from finished after World War II. If his novels of the 1950s hardly compare with his achievements of the 1920s and 1930s, they are hardly less notable than the works of any author of the postwar period. Furthermore, like the aging bluesmen, Faulkner was quite capable of pulling the occasional ace out of his sleeve in his later years. The prose interludes between the dramatic sequences in *Requiem for a Nun* are particularly memorable—providing a feverish, mythical retelling of the history of Yoknapatawpha County and the founding of Jefferson via its first public building, the Holston House—while some argue that *The Mansion* marks an impressive return to peak form.[38]

Equally, if Howlin' Wolf never recaptured the energy of his earlier years, a handful of his later recordings are substantial and enduring. "Ain't Goin' Down That Dirt Road" (1968)—his eerie, acoustic recasting of Tommy Johnson's "Big Road Blues"—and the endearingly sloppy career retrospective, "Moving" (1973), demonstrate that Wolf's fire had not entirely gone out. Waters fared better yet, giving a commanding performance of "Mannish Boy" as one of the guest artists in Martin Scorsese's film of The Band's final concert, *The Last Waltz* (recorded 1976, released 1978). This appearance set the scene for Waters's impressive autumnal comeback with the searing *Hard Again* album in 1977, recorded when he was in his early sixties.

If the elder Faulkner and the aging bluesmen were clearly past their primes by the end of the 1950s, their critical reputations quickly became secure. That decade saw the emergence of the first book-length scholarly studies of Faulkner's work, culminating in Olga Vickery's *The Novels of William Faulkner* in 1959. The author's death in 1962 only further stimulated the scholarly Faulkner industry, which now includes an annual conference at the University of Mississippi, a biannual journal, and a steady stream of critical monographs.

Just as literary scholars cemented the value of Faulkner's achievements, so did determined music aficionados stimulate a blues revival. The Rolling Stones allegedly refused to appear on the American TV show *Shindig* in

1965 unless Howlin' Wolf could perform too. It was the bluesman's only national television appearance during his lifetime. In the surviving footage, Jack Good, the show's host, banters inanely with Mick Jagger and Brian Jones of the Stones, and—unconsciously echoing Faulkner's complaint of achieving recognition abroad before receiving it at home—asks of the elderly Mississippi singer, "He's quite famous isn't he, in Britain?" Wolf then stalks onscreen to perform a stately "How Many More Years," jabbing his finger admonishingly at the camera throughout the song, while the youthful Stones sit reverently at his feet, and a bevy of glamorous studio dancers perched upon stools try to clap along and groove to this strange and unfashionable music.

The Stones and many other English and American youths who first discovered the blues in its electric form had an opportunity to trace the genre back to its rural roots when a series of LPs made the canonical works of the prewar country blues readily accessible for the first time since the 1930s. The watershed year in this process was 1961—the year when Faulkner was working on his last novel—which saw the appearance of two compilation albums, *The Immortal Charlie Patton*[39] and Robert Johnson's *King of the Delta Blues Singers*. The early sixties also saw the release of some of Wolf's classic singles of the previous decade in convenient LP form, notably on the eponymous *Howlin' Wolf* (1962), better known by the affectionate nickname, "The Rocking Chair Album," because of its cover illustration.

Such records brought the blues to a new and wider audience, achieving for the music what *The Portable Faulkner* had done for the novelist from Oxford. Waters even ruefully recalled, "Before the Rolling Stones, people over here didn't know nothing and didn't *want* to know nothing about me" (qtd. in Wald, *Escaping the Delta* 245).[40] The blues revival led to belated interest in surviving prewar black musicians as well as contemporary artists. Many long-forgotten Mississippi blues singers—including House, Hurt, James, and McDowell—enjoyed a brief renaissance, made new records, and performed for appreciative crowds at folk festivals and coffee houses, finally receiving the acclaim many of them had earned decades earlier.

If blues scholarship took some time to develop as a field, it was only because the task was so challenging. Faulkner scholars not only had the novels but also numerous other resources available to them, not least the author himself, who submitted to interviews and question-and-answer sessions at universities in locations as disparate as Virginia and Nagano,

Japan. In contrast, aside from his recorded music, there were few concrete signs that an individual called Charley Patton had ever existed. Furthermore, academia in this era was not as interested in rural black musicians as it was in esteemed white literary figures. Although professional folklorists had published studies of the blues since before World War I, there was still little critical interest in the blues—particularly the commercially recorded blues—as a modern art form.

In the absence of scholarly research, tenacious and enterprising blues aficionados took upon themselves the task of locating the documentary foundations for blues studies. On the basis of nothing more than the 1928 song title, "Avalon Blues," one fan tried writing to Hurt care of the Post Office in Avalon, Mississippi, and was astounded to receive word that the singer was still a denizen of the town.[41] Amateur sleuths unearthed marriage certificates, school records, death certificates, and photographs of long-forgotten country blues artists—including the few surviving pictures of Patton and Robert Johnson.[42] Mack McCormick even claimed to have found the man who killed Johnson, and reported the crime to the surprised Greenwood police thirty years after the fact.

Two important books in this era kick-started critical scholarship on the commercially recorded blues: Samuel Charters's *The Country Blues* (1959) and Paul Oliver's *Blues Fell This Morning* (1960).[43] By the time Wolf and Waters died, in 1976 and 1983 respectively, their status as major twentieth-century artists was at last beginning to be recognized, as were the achievements of their predecessors: the 1990 issue of a CD box set of Robert Johnson's recordings unexpectedly achieved platinum sales. The master of the Delta blues, whose songs had been heard by maybe a few thousand people during his lifetime, was now thrilling millions across the world.

Little more than thirty years separate the publication of Faulkner's first novels and the initial recordings of the country blues in the mid- to late twenties from the author's final book and Wolf's last major singles in the early sixties. As Calvin Coolidge's America morphed into John F. Kennedy's America, Faulkner's fiction and the recorded country blues—ostensibly so different in nature—emerged from a single locale, grew up alongside each other, achieved recognition together, and declined almost simultaneously. These two bodies of work tell of the same rapidly changing region and nation: a world of economic disarray, racial tensions, colossal natural disasters, unleashed sexuality, global conflicts, incarcerated lower-class populations, technological revolutions, gender anxiety, legal chicanery, and human frailty.

The comparative analysis in chapter 2 concerns representations of the Mississippi flood of 1927 in Patton's "High Water Everywhere" (1930) and Faulkner's "Old Man" (1939). The protagonist of the latter is unable to develop his heroic actions during the flood into the kind of meaningful narrative that numerous real-life blues singers constructed about the event. An unnamed guitarist who wanders briefly through a single scene in the story, however, provides an object lesson in how to speak truth to power that is reminiscent of Patton's lyric. "Old Man" marks a transitional moment in Faulkner's portrayal of African American characters and black oral culture at the end of the 1930s, and the following two chapters examine the author's implicit process of working toward this watershed moment in earlier works.

The twin subjects of chapter 3 are the 1931 short story "That Evening Sun" and Geeshie Wiley's cryptic "Last Kind Words Blues" (1930). Neither the song nor the story is simply about the abandonment of a female speaker by her male partner; each also concerns a woman who must exploit her creative powers to their utmost in order to narrate that abandonment, explain its possible implications, and mitigate its threatening consequences. Specifically, Nancy and Wiley's speaker similarly employ oral narrative in their efforts to exorcize the hideous specter of racial lynching.

Chapter 4 examines how Faulkner's *Sanctuary* (1931) and Robert Johnson's "Dead Shrimp Blues" (1936) exploit the same vivid symbol of male sexual dysfunction. Where Johnson's lyrics assert the singer's discursive power over the threat of impotence, Horace Benbow's frustrated and pathetic confession about his hatred for the chore of taking shrimp home to his wife—and the fear of female sexuality that this tale encapsulates—sets into motion a chain of violent events.

The fifth chapter jumps from prewar Mississippi to postwar America, applying critical ideas about Faulkner's swansong, *The Reivers* (1962), to the paradoxical treatment of rural nostalgia on *The Back Door Wolf* (1973), the last album by Howlin' Wolf. Both the novel and the record concern black mentors who tutor white youths in complex and multivalent worldviews.

Finally, for those devotees of Faulkner who cannot help but wonder precisely what the author knew about the blues and when he knew it, the Conclusion addresses the author's evolving knowledge of the blues as a young man, his dislike of music in middle age, and his growing appreciation of American vernacular songs in later life. Faulkner's penultimate novel,

The Mansion, reflects the writer's—and the nation's—belated recognition of the value and values of various genres of prewar southern roots music.

Together, these analyses demonstrate that self-narration and racial performativity are central to both Faulkner's fiction and blues verses. Theresa Towner notes that Faulkner's work consistently fuses "questions of racial and individual identity to examinations of voice," and that it "repeatedly investigates the always arduous process of how one learns to speak for oneself" (30). The characters of Yoknapatawpha County and the country blues often face a stark choice between asserting their control over language or being controlled by or through language. They similarly struggle to develop voices, forms of discourse, narrative strategies, and racially inflected personae that will allow them to articulate, define, and take command of their worlds.

Despite the inevitable limitations of a white modernist author's depictions of African American characters and cultures, Faulkner's fiction consistently portrays black people who—like the protagonists of blues songs—are able to snatch victory from the jaws of defeat through their mastery of language. From Job in *The Sound and the Fury* and the speaker of "Last Kind Words Blues" to Wolf's final songs and Uncle Parsham in *The Reivers,* the blues and the Yoknapatawpha fiction involve men and women of color who skillfully mobilize imaginative rhetoric in order to assert their individualism in the face of adversarial forces. In Houston A. Baker's terms, each of these characters talks his or her way out of "tight places," developing "a black voice that if it did not *transcend* the past would at least ameliorate, accommodate, and critique the past in ways confidently articulate with what the majority of black people require" (*Turning South Again* 15).

The ability of the author's white characters to define themselves through narrative, meanwhile, frequently depends upon the extent to which they are able to tap into the wellsprings of southern vernacular culture, commonly represented by the African American blues. If, in the earlier Yoknapatawpha fiction, the white characters—such as Jason Compson—remain largely oblivious to the power of blues discourse, Faulkner's 1930s protagonists at least struggle to engage with it, from Horace's failed attempt to sing his impotence blues in *Sanctuary* and Quentin's frustrated efforts to comprehend the significance of Nancy's blues tale in "That Evening Sun" at the start of the decade, to the tall convict in "Old Man" at the close of the thirties, who falls under the spell of a black guitarist. No less than their creator do such characters "try to express clumsily in words what the pure music would have done better" (*Lion in the Garden* 248);[44] they, too, seek a form of discourse that will liberate them from "tight places." For all their attempts to harness the agency and independence that modern African American culture articulates, their imaginary constructions or performances of blackness ultimately are rooted in inherited assumptions about the passive and static nature of people of color.

Like his white protagonists, Faulkner continually struggled with the implications of his black characters and the meanings of the blues. The Yoknapatawpha novels of the late 1940s and early 1950s regularly include elder African American characters who instruct youthful whites in a complex folk wisdom rooted in black vernacular culture. The growing social tensions of the emerging civil rights era, coupled with the author's growing concerns about his ability to represent black subjectivities, however, resulted in several novels in the 1950s in which the people of color are marginal.

In *The Mansion,* at the end of the decade, Faulkner achieved a new breakthrough in the figure of Mink Snopes, a white character implicitly associated with folk, country, and blues music. Mink's mastery of multiethnic southern vernacular discourses and his commitment to transracial lower-class rural values enable his triumph. It is as if Faulkner had to imagine Mink's transcendence of racial boundaries in order to engage fully with black characters again. The author's subsequent—and final—novel, *The Reivers,* restored people of color to the foreground of his fictional world and re-emphasized the value of black tutelage of white children. The evolution of Mink's character—from initial hostility to people of color to his unexpected involvement in a newly interracial South—parallels the larger cultural shifts of the late 1950s and 1960s. If Faulkner occasionally wrote about the blues in the 1920s, the characterization of Mink implies a more nuanced—if idealized—vision of the interconnectivity of various forms of southern roots music, and the role that such cultural expression might play in a truly multicultural America.

The author's ambivalent depictions of people of color and the attempts of his white protagonists to participate in black culture imply the artificiality and permeability of categories of racial identity. As Judith Sensibar observes, Faulkner's stories and novels consistently highlight "the innate instability of all kinds of social constructions" (*Faulkner and Love* 77). Sensibar identifies the author's complex relationship with his longtime

African American caregiver, "Mammy" Caroline Barr, as one of the central biographical sources of this recurrent fictional obsession. By watching Barr "switching roles and lifting and dropping her mask as she moved back and forth between her two worlds—[white] Oxford and [black] Freedman Town," Faulkner learned at an early age "that race, like culture, was performative and that its performance changed in response to place and audience." In Faulkner's world, the boundaries between black and white "were permeable; they could seep and leak, and, sometimes, even dissolve" (*Faulkner and Love* 81, 62, 77).

Echoes of blues themes in Faulkner consistently accompany acts of racial performativity, not just the multiple masks that Nancy assumes in "That Evening Sun," but also the attempts of white characters to construct themselves in terms of African American subject positions, whether the tall convict's flawed imitation of the blues guitarist in "Old Man" or Horace's vain attempt to emulate "Black Ulysses" in *Sanctuary*. Each, however, has very different implications. As Houston Baker notes, the "framing of *blackness* by black Americans in the United States is always, at least in part, a defense against clear liabilities of the black American body legally and juridically *framed*" (*Turning South Again* 36): a creative response to threats of incarceration, socially sanctioned violence, and institutionalized oppression, from the plantation to Parchman Farm. Those moments of "blackface" performance by whites in Faulkner—like the nineteenth-century minstrel tradition examined by Eric Lott—involve instead a "mixed erotic economy of celebration and exploitation," or "love and theft." Lott argues that the "very form of blackface arts—an investiture in black bodies—seems a manifestation of the particular desire to try on the accents of 'blackness' and demonstrates the permeability of the color line." Such desire is "less a sign of absolute white power and control than of panic, anxiety, terror, and pleasure" (*Love and Theft* 6). Faulkner's fiction and blues lyrics lay bare the complex racial dynamics of the pre–civil rights South, and gesture toward cultural possibilities not determined by the binary opposition between black double-consciousness, on one hand, and white minstrelsy, on the other.

The blues—initially a product of rural and marginalized African American communities—eventually exerted a powerful influence upon mainstream American society, and the general arc of Faulkner's fiction reflects the process by which white people in the twentieth century slowly learned to listen to black culture. This process is complex and ongoing, involving, as Lott suggests, simultaneous attraction and resistance, immersion and distance, exoticizing romanticism and genuine comprehension. Graham argues that, by engaging with popular music in their fiction, modernist authors sometimes were able to transcend "many of the Western world's most persistent cultural divisions, whether between author and audience, subject and object, material and ideal, black and white, or male and female" (3). In a 1927 essay, Rudolph Fisher even suggested that the "Nordics" enjoying African American music in Harlem nightspots "at last have tuned in on our wave-length. Maybe they are at last learning to speak our language" (qtd. in Graham 162).

Gesturing no less idealistically than such accounts or Faulkner's fiction to the notion of commercialized vernacular culture as the potential basis for a harmonious multicultural future, *O Brother, Where Art Thou?* ends with the escaped white convicts and blues guitarist Tommy Johnson—now comprising a hit-making country band called the Soggy Bottom Boys—performing at a political meeting. Gubernatorial reform candidate Homer Stokes—a tub-thumping segregationist and Klan leader—angrily calls for public repudiation of this newfangled "miscegenated" group, declaring, "These boys is not white. Hell, they ain't even old-timey." The townspeople, however, are so attracted to this vibrant and novel music—which is at once both folk tradition and modern commercial culture—they simply "don't mind" that the band is integrated, and run the dogmatic Stokes out of town on a rail. The incumbent governor, sensing which way the cultural wind blows, moves quickly to pardon the Soggy Bottom Boys for their "rough and rowdy past" and hires them as his new "brain trust," in which capacity they will be "the power behind the throne." Casual viewers might conclude that such a fantasy blithely glosses over the racial and social tensions that defined Mississippi during the Great Depression and well beyond. The film's resolution is so extravagantly convenient, however, and its subtly discordant notes so palpable—such as the ultimate preeminence of white hillbilly music over the blues, the painfully evident voicelessness of the African American guitarist in these key climactic scenes, and the governor's slick co-option of the band's popularity for his own ends—that the artificially satisfying Hollywood ending underlines rather than elides these tensions, dramatizing Lott's interracial "economy of celebration and exploitation."

Nonetheless, by the time Faulkner published his final novel, a new generation of listeners was discovering the value of the prewar country blues and the African American communities from which it had sprung. A single hit record could not turn racial reactionaries into progressive multiculturalists, but significant numbers of white people were for the first time listening seriously to Charley Patton, Robert Johnson, and Howlin' Wolf at the very moment that they were also encountering the challenging words and inspiring speeches of Fannie Lou Hamer, Malcolm X, and the Reverend Martin Luther King Jr. Although Patton had sung during his first recording session in 1929 of "going away to a world unknown," he could barely have imagined the world that was in the process of becoming just three decades later, as the boundaries between black and white began to seep, leek, and, sometimes, even dissolve.

2

BACKWATER RISING, MEN SINKING DOWN

THE GREAT MISSISSIPPI FLOOD IN "OLD MAN" AND "HIGH WATER EVERYWHERE"

In 1927's *Father Mississippi,* Lyle Saxon provides a pithy "postage-stamp" summary of that spring's unprecedented flooding: "Four hundred lives, seven hundred thousand persons made homeless, thirteen million acres engulfed, and three hundred million dollars' worth of destruction." Herbert Hoover was yet more succinct and dramatic, characterizing the deluge as "the greatest peace-time calamity in the history of our country." Eyewitnesses to the disaster, meanwhile, simply spoke of "a tan colored wall seven feet high, and with a roar as of a mighty wind" (Saxon 345, 372; Daniel, *Deep'n as It Come* 19).[1]

Given the magnitude of the Great Mississippi Flood and its impact upon the South in general, and the Mississippi Delta in particular, it is hardly surprising that musicians and singers immediately seized upon the topic. Bessie Smith recorded her "Backwater Blues" just prior to the catastrophe, but Columbia marketed the song as if it were a response to it. Numerous African American musicians quickly followed suit, with Blind Lemon Jefferson, Laura Smith, Sippie Wallace, Lonnie Johnson, Alice Pearson, Barbecue Bob, and many others producing records about the disaster. Charley Patton's two-part "High Water Everywhere"—released by Paramount in the spring of 1930—was one of the last musical accounts of the flood, but is now the most widely renowned.[2]

In stark contrast to this torrent of musical dramatizations, the flood inspired comparatively few literary treatments, either by white or African

American authors. Where Sterling A. Brown's poem "Children of the Mississippi" (1931) dramatizes the threat of the river in general terms, his "Cabaret" (1932) presents complacent whites enjoying stereotypes of exotic blackness at a Chicago nightclub while people drown in the South. Robert Frost's abstract verse, "The Flood" (1928), may be informed by the event, while Richard Wright's two flood stories, "Silt" (1937) and "Down by the Riverside" (1938), are more likely to have been inspired by the flooding of 1937 than that of the previous decade.[3] One of the rare fictional works to provide a direct and explicit account of the 1927 disaster is "Old Man," a story embedded in *The Wild Palms* (1939), an experimental novel that Faulkner had wanted to publish as *If I Forget Thee, Jerusalem.*

Similarities between "High Water Everywhere" and *If I Forget Thee, Jerusalem* transcend the shared subject matter of the 1927 flood. Both works also address a more abstract theme: the tension between self-actualization and an individual's obligations to the larger social group. They deal with this issue, furthermore, specifically in terms of voice, each exploring how an individual might mobilize vernacular discourses to challenge existing social hierarchies—as an act of individual self-assertion and in the name of communal justice.

Where the speaker of "High Water Everywhere" ultimately reconciles the tensions between individual autonomy and the demands of society, the central character in "Old Man" fails to craft a functional narrative about his experience and is unable to develop a voice that adequately represents either the individual or the group. A crucial—yet largely neglected—passage in Faulkner's tale suggests that its protagonist misunderstands a vital lesson provided by one of the story's minor figures: a man who proves entirely capable of expressing himself authoritatively and speaking truth to power on behalf of his marginalized community, just like the narrator-protagonist of Patton's song. This character in Faulkner's novel is an African American blues guitarist.

If I Forget Thee, Jerusalem is one of Faulkner's most eclectically allusive and richly intertextual—as well as intratextual—works. Critics identify it as a parody of Hemingway's *A Farewell to Arms,* as a dramatic dialogue between the philosophies of Schopenhauer and Nietzsche, and as a sly satire on Hollywood genre conventions. They discuss the book in relation to Psalm 137, the fiction of Stephen Crane, Dante's *Divine Comedy,* and even popular romance novels.[4] Scholars also read Faulkner's text in relation to itself, since *If I Forget Thee, Jerusalem* consists of two separate stories presented in alternating chapters. "The Wild Palms" is the tale of two tragic lovers, Harry Wilbourne and Charlotte Rittenmeyer, who turn their backs on society and its conventional values in order to pursue their wild passion across Depression-era America, ultimately to destruction. Charlotte dies after a botched abortion performed by Harry, an act for which the latter is incarcerated at Parchman Farm. "Old Man"—set a decade earlier—concerns a group of inmates from the same prison who are press-ganged into the relief effort during the 1927 flood. Its main character, an unnamed "tall convict," is washed away on the tide while seeking refugees. Surviving the waters, the convict cares for a pregnant woman while being constantly confounded in his attempts to surrender to the authorities. He helps deliver the baby on a snake-infested Indian mound and ensures that mother and infant return home safely before he is finally successful in giving himself up. In spite of the tall convict's heroism, the corrupt Parchman administration punishes him for his supposed escape attempt by adding ten years to his sentence.

If literary critics define *If I Forget Thee, Jerusalem* in terms of self-reflexivity and intertextuality, blues scholars conventionally interpret songs about the Mississippi flood as documentary records or works of protest. Certainly, the fact that the flood inspired works by numerous black blues singers but virtually none by white authors speaks volumes: like Hurricane Katrina almost eighty years later, the flood threw the racial inequalities of American and southern society into sharp relief.[5] During the 1927 disaster, the Mississippi National Guard herded refugees—90 percent of whom were black—into concentration camps, which, as David Evans notes, rapidly "turned into virtual prisons and slave labor markets" ("High Water Everywhere" 5, 6). Evans characterizes blues songs about the flood as subversive counter-narratives to official accounts of the event, in which the oppressed and silenced tell their side of the story and protest the injustices perpetrated by the white ruling class. He defines Patton's "High Water Everywhere" as the culmination of this trend, in which the singer indicts the conditions at the camps and critiques those rescuers who "either did not care or did not make as strong an effort as they might have" when it came to black victims of the flood ("High Water Everywhere" 64). Patton's song even depicts the waters consuming "fifty families and children" while a white onlooker callously comments, "Tough luck, they can drown."[6]

Faulkner's "Old Man"—which emerged in the same year as that great work of progressive literary protest, *The Grapes of Wrath*—contains no less pointed social commentary than any of the flood blues. Early in the narrative, a truck carrying the Parchman convicts to the flood zone passes a cabin with water "up to the window ledges" and an imperiled black family perching upon the roof, awaiting help: "The woman on the housetop began to shriek at the passing truck, her voice carrying faint and melodious across the brown water, becoming fainter and fainter as the truck passed and went on, ceasing at last, whether because of distance or because she had stopped screaming those in the truck did not know" (54). This scene is reminiscent of Patton's "Tough luck, they can drown": the white rescue mission does not pause for a moment to consider the plight of an African American family. There is an additional layer to the scenario in Faulkner's version, for the chained white convicts in the truck are virtually as helpless as the black victims of the flood, their welfare dependent upon the whims of the powerful.

Despite such explicit and provocative depictions of social inequality in "Old Man," Faulkner's reputation as a sophisticated experimental modernist is so thoroughly cemented that no scholar would be likely to characterize the story as didactic social protest. As Ted Atkinson notes, the Mississippi author was "too much the artist to run the risk of his fiction reading as propaganda," and critics commonly assume that "Faulkner's fiction was disengaged from the issues and concerns of the politically inflected literature prominent in the thirties" (8, 3).

Nonetheless, as the flood scenes in "Old Man" demonstrate, Faulkner's innovative modernist aesthetic and prosaic social commentary are not mutually exclusive categories. As Atkinson demonstrates, Faulkner evidently was not "tone deaf to the tenor of the times or preoccupied with formal experimentation to the point of obliviousness" (8). *Light in August, Absalom, Absalom!,* and *Go Down, Moses* all address such universal—and typically Faulknerian—issues as the tension between empty intellectual abstractions and meaningfully instinctive responses to the world, while also unflinchingly depicting the irrationality and destructive cruelty of both regional and national racial orthodoxies.[7]

Like "Old Man," "High Water Everywhere" is not reducible to a documentary record of the flood or a straightforward work of social protest, even though it powerfully depicts the conditions brought on by the catastrophe, as well as the racial discrimination involved in the rescue operation. No less than Faulkner's novel, Patton's song is a multifaceted work that explores grand artistic themes characteristic of its creator, as well as specific social issues.

The most striking complication of *If I Forget Thee, Jerusalem* is its unorthodox dual-narrative structure. Although "The Wild Palms" and "Old Man" unfold alongside each other, there is no concrete connection between the two tales, one a tragic love story and the other a mock-heroic comedy. The only evident intersection is that Harry, in "The Wild Palms," begins his sentence at Parchman in 1938, when the tall convict from "Old Man" is likely still serving time there, although the two never meet in the narrative. The strange design of the novel and the absence of any direct relationship between its two stories proved puzzling to a first generation of readers, with one bewildered reviewer even dubbing it a "Mississippi Frankenstein."[8] Since the original edition of 1939, publishers have often printed "Old Man" and "The Wild Palms" separately, as if they were discrete entities,[9] while recent editions have restored the book's original form and tentatively reinstated Faulkner's preferred title, derived from the biblical Book of Psalms.[10]

Although critical interpretations of Faulkner's text often focus upon one or another of its two narratives, scholars today are united in the view that *If I Forget Thee, Jerusalem* really *is* a novel—that it is an artistically coherent whole, and that there are substantial thematic relationships between its two stories. As the author himself acknowledged, the underlying organizational principle of the book is "like counterpoint in music" (*Lion in the Garden* 247). Scholars conceptualize the book's unity in terms of the parallels and disjunctions between its two narrative strands, noting, for example, that one of the central issues at stake in both of the tales is the complex relationship between the individual and society. In the tragic "Wild Palms," Harry and Charlotte's intense love affair is a radical assertion of personal desire and an absolute rejection of society and its oppressive demands. The protagonist of the comic "Old Man," in contrast, thinks little of love and—after the crime that sent him to Parchman in the first place—conforms to society and submits to authority willingly. As Doreen Fowler puts it, "If Harry and Charlotte are the high priest and priestess of love and freedom, the convict serves equally faithfully the opposite values—order and responsibility" ("Measuring Faulkner's Tall Convict" 280).

Critics often differ in their judgments of the central characters of each tale, sometimes elevating one narrative's protagonist(s) over the other(s).

Some commentators, as Fowler notes, hail Harry and Charlotte's "triumph over convention" and their quest for "perfect freedom," while viewing the tall convict as merely a "dull-witted countryman" who "throws away his freedom and sacrifices himself on the altar of convention" ("Measuring Faulkner's Tall Convict" 280). Contrarily, others see the book as "an annoyed reaction to the tendency in literature to romanticize love excessively." From this latter perspective, the convict is an embodiment of "man's functional relationship to nature and his fellows," whereas the lovers represent a "*reductio ad absurdum* of the romantic fallacy" in their foolish dedication to "an ideal, a mere abstraction" (Volpe, *Reader's Guide to Faulkner: The Novels* 214, 230, 227, 225).

Of course, any interpretation of Faulkner's book that chooses sides in such a fashion risks missing the point. As Michael Grimwood observes, "Such judgments illuminate the readers more than the novel. Critics who prefer Harry seem to value nonconformism and personal rebellion; those who favor the convict seem to value discipline and social responsibility" (*Heart in Conflict* 96). The critical habit of playing one story off against the other or preferring one tale's protagonist(s) to the other(s) tends to obscure rather than illuminate the book's meanings, since the point is that the convict and the lovers alike are simultaneously heroic *and* foolish. The tall convict's determination to fulfill his mission and return to prison is both a display of admirable integrity and a destructive denial of freedom. The lovers' rejection of society is a worthy act of individualism while also being dangerously isolating and wildly unrealistic. What complicates the issue is that Faulkner's book does not immediately appear to present a clear resolution to these tensions: an individual who can maintain personal integrity in the midst of society or square romantic impulses with the pragmatic quest for survival.

Like Faulkner's book, "High Water Everywhere" has a bipartite structure: it originally appeared in two parts on either side of a single phonograph record. It was customary for lengthy songs to be lopped in half in such a fashion—as with Bessie Smith's bawdy epic of 1928, "Empty Bed Blues[11]—but "High Water Everywhere" is an unusual case on two counts. It was the only two-part blues record by Patton released during his lifetime,[12] and, more significantly, it is evidently not one long song split in half simply because of the limited capacity of a 78 rpm disc. Blues scholars often overlook the implications of the song's division and commonly discuss "High Water

Everywhere" as if it were an uncomplicatedly uniform whole with a single narrative strand and a consistent mood. Paul Oliver, for examples, refers to "the six-minute *High Water Everywhere,*" and even presents his transcription of the lyrics as an unbroken unit, without identifying where Part I ends or Part II begins (*Blues Fell This Morning* 219–20).[13] In recent years, auditors have been more attentive to the distinctions between the two parts of the song. As Evans notes, the record entitled "High Water Everywhere" actually consists of "two separate songs about the 1927 flood. They differ in the events they describe, in mood, in tempo, melody, and to some extent in their guitar parts" ("High Water Everywhere" 60). Stephen Calt and Gayle Dean Wardlow even speculate that the first part was initially the whole song, and that the recording engineer was so impressed with Patton's spectacular performance that he asked for an immediate sequel, which the bluesman then improvised on the spot (203–5). New research even suggests that the second part may not depict the 1927 disaster at all, but might be about a later flood in a separate location (Evans, e-mail). The first, more dynamic, part of the song is a feverish account of the narrator's incessant wandering through various locations in the Mississippi flood zone. The second part is a somber and chilling dirge that concerns the drowning of fifty families in Arkansas. As Dick Spottswood puts it, "the momentum and passion" of the record's first part "seem to evolve towards resignation" in the second (63).

As with *If I Forget Thee, Jerusalem,* the parallels and contrasts between the two separate strands of "High Water Everywhere" illuminate the work as a whole. Given the fundamental differences between the two songs that comprise Patton's flood blues, Evans advocates reading them separately ("High Water Everywhere" 60), but the contrapuntal relationship between "The Wild Palms" and "Old Man" suggests that an equally appropriate critical approach is to address "High Water Everywhere" in similar terms: as a complete work organized around a call-and-response relationship between its two parts.

In light of the record's grave subject matter, critics tend to assume that both parts of Patton's flood blues are equally serious in tone and similarly tragic in content. Evans, for example, asserts that the first section is characterized by "fear and confusion," and the second by "stark terror" ("Charley Patton" 194). After all, how could a song about a massive natural disaster be anything other than a somber and horrified examination of human suffering? "High Water Everywhere," furthermore, is a blues song:

a genre defined by its tendency, in Ralph Ellison's famous words, "to keep the painful details and episodes of a brutal experience alive in one's aching consciousness, to finger its jagged grain" (78).

Although both songs concern lethal flooding, each part of "High Water Everywhere" is, in fact, quite distinct in both mood and meaning. As Ellison also says, the blues transcends pure tragedy through its transformation of "brutal experience" into "near-tragic, near-comic lyricism" (78). The second part of Patton's song, with its grim death toll, is indeed a tale of "fear, confusion, and compassion" (Palmer 75), but its vivid portrayal of the terrors of the flood has diverted modern listeners from considering the possibility that the first part of "High Water Everywhere" may be nothing less than a hymn to the power of the individual in the face of massive natural and social forces—that it is as much "near-comic" as "near-tragic," just like "Mississippi Boweavil Blues." The narrator's journey through the Mississippi flood zone is not exactly a happy tale, but the protagonist is ultimately triumphant, proudly telling the world how he survived the flood and escaped to safety.

Despite the trials that its protagonist faces, the first part of "High Water Everywhere" is a thrillingly dynamic performance. Its vibrancy is a significant clue to the celebration of individuality that is its central theme. As Ted Gioia says, "On part one, Patton casually juggles a foot-stomping ground tempo with a faster guitar-slapping counter-rhythm that spurs on his powerful six-string groove" (73). Patton's dynamic and infectious rhythms create a mood not of horrified urgency, but of boldly confident exuberance, or, as Gioia suggests, sheer "*funkiness*" (73).[14]

Rooted in a wealth of eyewitness testimony, Pete Daniel's study of the 1927 flood emphasizes that such exuberance, if not common during the disaster, is nonetheless a matter of historical record: "As calamitous as it was, the flood provided a break from routine; in some cases the tension of the emergency was welcome relief from the dull and repetitive life of the rural South, especially for young people. Rescue workers, enjoying the challenge of the river, invariably vowed that they would gladly volunteer again, for the rescue work was personally rewarding. In one way, then, the disaster was terrible—yet people remember not only the terror, but also more lighthearted moments" (*Deep'n as It Come* 10). If the first part of "High Water Everywhere" is hardly lighthearted, it is also not without humor, and it ultimately suggests that its protagonist's freedom from routine in the chaos of the flood is very rewarding indeed. Of all the critics to discuss the song, only Edward Comentale's brief, yet unorthodox, characterization captures this mood: "As the flood seeps across the region, dissolving everything in its path, the bluesman slips from site to site, hollerin' all the way with reckless glee" (50).

The song's first part begins as a tale of the river's immense power and frightening speed, but ultimately proves to be the story of the human speaker's agency and mobility. It concerns "poor Charley," who wanders throughout the Delta, the waters relentlessly rising everywhere that he goes. Beginning with objective observations about environmental conditions ("The backwater done rose around Sumner now" and "[the] river is ragin' high"), the song increasingly involves assertions of individual choice ("I am goin' out [of] high water" and "I'm goin' back to the hilly country"). In the early verses, the protagonist can describe only thwarted action, such as when he confesses, "I would go to the hill country" or "I would go down to Rosedale, but they tell me it's water there." A crucial shift occurs midway through the fifth stanza, when the narrator makes the spoken interjection, "Boy, I'm goin' to Vicksburg." From this point on, Charley ceases to tell of what he has been prevented from doing and instead firmly states what he will do: "Well, I'm goin' over the hill where water, oh it don't never blow."

Earlier in Part I, however, the speaker deliberately moves toward, not away from, the deadly floodwaters, traveling from Drew through Leland, Greenville, Shaw, Vicksburg, and Tallahatchie. As Evans observes, "Over the course of the song, he takes us into areas of the Delta that were much harder hit [by the disaster]. This is against all logic for someone fleeing the flood" ("High Water Everywhere" 62). Calt and Wardlow read the song's curious geographical trail as merely "unlikely" and as having "no basis in fact" (201, 202), whereas historical sources suggest that the journey of Patton's protagonist is not so improbable. Tucker Couvillon, one of Daniel's eyewitnesses, was sufficiently "young and interested in excitement" in 1927 to embark on a reckless exploration of the flood zone. Almost overtaken by the waters, Couvillon concluded, "I wanted a little bit of excitement, and I got it too. But I got a little too much" (*Deep'n as It Come* 39). Calt and Wardlow's complaint about the song's credibility, furthermore, is only meaningful as far as "High Water Everywhere" is a documentary or autobiographical statement. If the song is essentially a work of the imagination, questions about the feasibility of Charley's journey are quite irrelevant.

More than just "a dramatic device" (Evans, "High Water Everywhere" 62), the protagonist's curious trajectory is central to the song's meanings.

Charley's apparently deliberate pursuit of jeopardy suggests that he will not allow his movements to be dictated, not even by the greatest natural disaster to strike Mississippi in the twentieth century. Although he finally opts for the safety of higher ground, the protagonist's perverse wanderings suggest that he views this cataclysmic event as a personal challenge—as an opportunity to assert his individual agency in the face of immense and antagonistic forces.

It is not just nature against which Charley tests himself, and it is not only the flood that threatens to obstruct his movements. In the second verse of Part I, Patton's protagonist says he "would go to the hill country, but they got me barred." Critics conventionally read "they" as a thinly veiled reference to the white authorities that restricted the African American population to refugee camps and forced its members to work on levees against their will. In John Barry's description of the flood in Greenville, black people simply "were no longer free. The National Guard patrolled the perimeter of the levee camp with rifles and fixed bayonets. To enter or leave, one needed a pass. . . . The levee camp became a slave camp" (313, 315). Evans echoes this account: "In many places, black men who tried to leave the area, even those who were simply passing through, were arrested by white police and National Guard troops and forced to work on the levees. . . . Blacks, who had no stake in the physical or social order of these towns, who were valued merely for their labor, were forced to work in extremely dangerous conditions to save and rebuild the world that the white folks had made and ruled" ("High Water Everywhere" 51). Some flood songs openly refer to imprisonment and forced labor in the camps. The speaker of Lonnie Johnson's "Broken Levee Blues" (1928) angrily complains about having been taken from his home and made to work for the relief effort.[15] Histories of the flood suggest that such anger was widespread and that numerous black refugees actively sought their freedom from the camps, even though the price for trying to abscond could be high. As Barry notes, officials did not even bother to deny that soldiers who caught escapees whipped them with rifle straps (315).

Although Charley speaks of being "barred," the defining characteristic of Part I of "High Water Everywhere" is the speaker's constant motion. While drawing attention to those who would restrict his movements, the protagonist of the first part of Patton's song ultimately declares any efforts to arrest his mobility ineffectual. Although it would be a mistake to read most blues lyrics as straightforward linear narratives,[16] the litany of place names in Part I of "High Water Everywhere" invites such a reading and provides a clear geographical framework for it.[17] The first verse suggests that the narrator-protagonist initially has been driven "down the line" by the rising of the backwater at Sumner. He briefly takes refuge at Drew, before noting that "the water done struck" there too, implying that he has had to move on from this recently flooded location. He then states at the beginning of the second verse that "the whole round country" has "overflowed," indicating that he has seen more devastation since leaving Drew. At the end of the second verse, he concedes that he is barred from the hill country, but the beginning of the third verse finds him already in Leland and thinking of traveling on to Greenville. In the fourth verse, furthermore, he has arrived in Greenville, found it flooded, and is already planning on his next move. The speaker never seems to be an immobile prisoner in a refugee camp. Other people may be subject to imprisonment, but not Charley. He is not trying to slip through a white cordon in order to escape from a camp; instead, he seeks to elude white authorities in order to get to higher ground. Just as Charley challenges nature by traveling into the flood zone, so does he challenge the power of the white authorities by roaming freely through areas within which, or from which, they seek to restrict him.

The central theme of the first part of "High Water Everywhere," then, is self-assertion as defined by freedom of movement in the face of the most limiting forces imaginable. At the song's end, Charley asserts that the combined powers of the flood and the white South are insufficient to hinder him; he is "goin' back to the hilly country"—the forbidden, inaccessible ground—where he "won't be worried no more." Neither nature nor society can stop him going where he pleases. This final declaration might appear to be a pat and insufficient resolution to the conditions so vividly depicted elsewhere in the song. Versions of the phrase "Won't be worried no more" or "Won't be worried long" are such recurring formulae in the blues that this ending could seem clichéd and superficial, a trite anticlimax.[18] On a practical level, this abrupt conclusion may have resulted simply from the recording engineer signaling that Patton needed to wind up the song quickly because he was in danger of exceeding the three-minute mark. Such an ending, however, provides one more instance of the narrator's radical individualism, and is thus an appropriate finish to the first part of "High Water Everywhere." As he embarks on a journey during which he will face the twin challenges of armed authorities and an immense natural disaster, the protagonist genuinely believes that he will experience no further worry. This is a startling declaration of agency by a black southern artist of this era—as radical and idealistic a rejection of the dominant society as that performed by Harry and Charlotte in "The Wild Palms."

Like the lovers of "The Wild Palms," however, the protagonist of the first part of "High Water Everywhere" takes individualism to an extreme that is, finally, impossibly idealistic, potentially alienating, and even dangerously dysfunctional. In the middle of a devastating disaster, Charley seems virtually oblivious to the existence of others, except as sources of information regarding the progress of the flood as he escapes to safety—alone. This explains the bizarre rhetorical construction in the third verse of Part I: "I'm gonna move over to Greenville 'fore I bid you goodbye." In this sole reference to his partner in the song, Charley coldly tells her that he will abandon her and travel to Greenville before he so much as thinks to say farewell.[19] This is not the only indication in the song of its protagonist's relentless self-absorption. Some transcriptions of the fifth verse even suggest that Charley aims to get intoxicated at one of the stops on his journey: "I'm goin' to Vicksburg for a high of mine."[20] Finally, while suffering sweeps the country, Patton's protagonist indulges in sardonic humor, observing wryly that the floodwaters "starched my clothes."[21] This image is undeniably comic: the refugee's garments are first soaked by the river and then baked in the sun so that they are like over-starched clothes from the cleaners. In the midst of a disaster that killed hundreds, "poor Charley" finds time to complain about sartorial ruination. The speaker's self-absorption echoes some individuals' historical recollections of the flood. Daniel notes of one of his sources that, "[l]ike most young people caught up in the flood, she admits that she was afraid her mind 'was on having fun and not thinking (as I should have been) of all the destruction the flood was causing and had caused'" (*Deep'n as It Come* 45).

The first part of "High Water Everywhere" moves well beyond understandable self-absorption into the realm of near-solipsistic meditation. Patton's lyrics in general have proven an endless challenge to transcribers, given the poor sound quality of the available recordings and the singer's raw diction. As Robert Dixon and John Godrich put it, "Patton's deep rough voice blurred over the lyrics and often descended into incomprehensibility" (290). Even by Patton's standards, "High Water Everywhere" is unusually incomprehensible, as if the singer, while apparently concerned to "tell the world" what he has seen, is caught up in a private internal dialogue, as reflected in the constant shift between sung and spoken lines. In its own way, the song is as alienating and impenetrable as any of Faulkner's modernist literary experiments in subjective viewpoint and streams of consciousness.

Defiant assertions of self and radical subjectivity are, in fact, recurring issues throughout Patton's work, and "High Water Everywhere" uses a grand natural disaster as an occasion for the singer to explore this customary thematic concern. Robert Palmer argues that "Patton found public events truly meaningful only insofar as they impinged on his private world—his perceptions, his feelings. . . . The singer is so involved that in many cases his involvement becomes both the subject and substance of the work" (75). Evans suggests that the key to the bluesman's sense of individualism and personal freedom was the geographical mobility that he enjoyed as a successful roving entertainer:

> The triumph of Charley Patton over this environment and social system was that he was able to live at least as prosperously as his father . . . and have a maximum of physical mobility. A Negro landowner had no mobility in this potentially hostile environment, and a renter could only exercise his mobility once a year following his financial settlement with the "bossman." Charley was his own bossman. His niece described the situation by saying, "He just left when he got ready, because he didn't make no crops. . . . He was a *free man*." . . . The kind of ambiguous status that he sought, which would enable him to avoid the status of "nigger," could only be obtained through movement. ("Charley Patton" 143, 177)[22]

In Houston Baker's terms, Charley is the "purposefully fantastic . . . *black flâneur*" (*Turning South Again* 63), and Part I of "High Water Everywhere" dramatizes this figure in more grandiose terms than any other Patton song. Even during a monumental flood, when many members of the black community were restricted to refugee camps, Charley remains his own "bossman," and he expresses his autonomy through freedom of movement, despite all the obstacles in his path. Patton's protagonist thus embodies the potential mobility of the southern black population, which streamed north in vast numbers, in spite of the efforts of white planters to impede them.[23]

The confident independence of the protagonist of Part I of "High Water Everywhere," however, comes at the apparent cost of any meaningful connection to the people around him. Palmer observes of the speaker's attitudes that "[s]uch unflinching subjectivity may seem callous and self-involved, but in the context of its time and place it was positively heroic. Only a man who understands his worth and believes in his freedom sings as if nothing else matters" (75). Charley, however, acts as if nobody else matters too, including the lover that he abandons so flippantly in the third verse. While the African American community endures the horrors of the flood, Patton's protagonist merely jests about getting high and getting his clothes starched. This callous jokester strums as Mississippi sinks. Evans concludes that Patton pursued "a bold and potentially dangerous course," since his mobility and freedom "could leave him outside both organized white and black society" ("Charley Patton" 177). Part I of Patton's song, then, expresses an individual exceptionalism that is as much a trap as a triumph.

Faulkner's "Wild Palms" also concerns the pitfalls of excessive individualism. Just as Patton's protagonist defies social strictures and defines himself as a self-reliant hero who operates beyond human law and society, so do Harry and Charlotte flee the demands and responsibilities of the social world for the joys of romantic love. Ultimately, they pursue this idealistic vision to an uncompromising extreme, rigidly following Charlotte's dictate that "it's got to be all honeymoon, always. . . . Either heaven, or hell: no comfortable safe peaceful purgatory between for you and me" (71). What horrifies Charlotte—and, eventually, her loyal disciple Harry—is the prospect of becoming like everybody else and turning into a conventional, bourgeois married couple. Harry finally refuses to be "like any husband with his Saturday pay envelope and his suburban bungalow full of electric wife-saving gadgets and his table cloth of lawn to sprinkle on Sunday morning . . . the doomed worm blind to all passion and dead to all hope" (112).

Like Patton's protagonist in the first part of "High Water Everywhere," Harry and Charlotte's freedom depends upon physical movement. Every time conventional life threatens to engulf them, they hit the road—to Chicago, to a cabin in Wisconsin, back to Chicago, then to Utah, Texas, New Orleans, and, finally, the Gulf Coast. No less than Charley, they defy the world by deliberately seeking out challenging or even hazardous destinations—most dramatically, a profoundly inhospitable and rapidly declining mine in the frozen wastes of Utah. As Richard Godden puts it, the two "confuse mobility with freedom" (207).

Just as Charley's independence exacts a significant price, so does the lovers' unyielding dedication to the ideal of "all honeymoon, always" come at great cost. While some critics salute the couple's courage in giving up all certainty and security in an attempt to transcend the soul-destroying numbness of the modern world, Harry and Charlotte's detractors argue that their single-minded and self-destructive refusal to become "slave[s] to respectability" is, finally, unsettlingly juvenile (113). If their stand against conformity is bold and liberating, they take it to a dogmatic and dysfunctional extreme.

Although the story of Charlotte and Harry is a tragedy of wasted lives, there is an extent to which it is an unnecessary and even self-willed tragedy. Whatever the costs, Charley's individualism in Part I of "High Water Everywhere" is a triumph against the odds. In contrast, Harry and Charlotte actively court misery and defeat. Early in the story, as Charlotte prepares to abandon her husband and children in order to travel to Chicago with Harry, the latter muses, "*You are born submerged in anonymous lockstep with the teeming anonymous myriads of your time and generation; you get out of step once, falter once, and you are trampled to death*" (46). Right from the beginning, Harry has decided that the only way to prove his separation from the "teeming anonymous myriads" is to be destroyed by them. Later in the narrative, Harry reiterates that the choice he faces is "to conform, or die" (118). At the very end of the story, when the imprisoned Harry decides to devote his life to memorializing Charlotte, he famously avers, "*Between grief and nothing I will take grief*" (273). However touching this declaration, it once more reveals the imaginative poverty of the choices that Harry has assigned himself: either he must accept conformity, anonymity, and nothingness, or he must endure grief, destruction, and death. Harry conceives of the world in terms of rigid absolutes, of binary oppositions between which he must choose, with no sense of there being any additional options along the continuum between the two poles. Certainly, such possibilities as triumph, fulfillment, or happiness are not part of this limited equation. Patton's defiant "Won't be worried no more" is just not something that Harry or Charlotte can conceive. They have decided that the world is corrupt, and thus the way to demonstrate their virtue is to court disaster. For all their uncompromising courage, the couple willingly accepts the entirely clichéd roles of doomed, tragic lovers: a modern day Romeo and Juliet. Friar Laurence's warning to the reckless pair in Shakespeare's play is equally applicable to Faulkner's characters: "These violent delights have violent ends. . . . Therefore love moderately" (II.5 9, 14). Harry and Charlotte's idealistic and subversive choice to become romantic victims simultaneously involves their conforming to the most conventional and limiting literary tropes.

Like Charley in Part I of "High Water Everywhere," Harry and Charlotte's constant movement prevents them from becoming integrated into any kind of meaningful community that might leaven their unswerving dedication to romantic love. To be sure, many of the people that Harry and Charlotte encounter during their travels are poor candidates for membership in a community in which the two lovers might function productively. The vulgar and predatory Bradley at the lake house and the judgmental Gulf Coast doctor who attends the dying Charlotte are just two instances of the small-minded living death that the lovers seek to evade by leaving society behind. Nonetheless, Harry and Charlotte's failure to find a meaningful role in any larger group is also a sign of their profound spiritual poverty. The couple's apparent indifference to the oppressed and abandoned Polish miners in Utah finally reveals the complacent and empty self-absorption at the heart of their idealistic romance.[24]

In sum, "The Wild Palms" and the first part of "High Water Everywhere" reveal both the profound power and the inherent limitations that rejection of society's rigid strictures involves. Neither text, however, offers a coherent solution to the alienation from community that necessarily results from an individual's uncompromising dedication to self-actualization. It is the second part of Patton's song and "Old Man"—the parallel narrative in *If I Forget Thee, Jerusalem*—that provide enlightening counterpoints to these stories of radical individualism.

In both tone and theme, Part II of "High Water Everywhere" is the polar opposite of its predecessor. It begins at a funereal pace, in stark contrast to the dynamic, pulsing rhythms of the first part. The somber tempo matches the sobering content: where Part I does not refer to a single death, the second part opens with an appalling body count, describing how, when the backwater hit the town of Joiner, "[i]t was fifty families and children suffer to sink and drown." Furthermore, Patton's protagonist is no longer the mobile individual of the first part of "High Water Everywhere," but is trapped by the flood. There are no jokes about starched clothes and no boasts about individual freedom; the speaker just describes the water implacably rising up to his bed as he passively waits for a slow and capricious relief effort to rescue him. The song's second part does not ramble wildly across the Delta like the first, but stretches a single disastrous event in one location over six agonizing verses.

This is not, furthermore, just a tale of personal peril, for the song emphasizes that the narrator endures the same dangers as his neighbors. The depiction of the protagonist's situation in the opening line of the third stanza ("The water was risin,' got up in my bed"), clearly echoes the description of a comrade's jeopardy at the beginning of the second verse ("The water was risin' up in my friend's door"). "Friend" is not a word that appears in the self-absorbed narrative of Part I of "High Water Everywhere." No longer focused upon his own situation, the narrator of Part II presents a mournful portrait of the suffering of the larger black community, explicitly identifying his membership in it. The fifth and penultimate verse begins, "Oh, high the water risin,' *our* men sinkin' down" (my emphasis).[25] The final line reiterates the overall song's emphasis upon individual perception and solitude, but suggests that the protagonist is no longer disengaged, as in the song's first part, but feels deeply connected to those killed in the flood: "I couldn't see nobody home and was no one to be found."

To adapt Fowler's reading of *If I Forget Thee, Jerusalem,* the protagonist of the first part of Patton's song is the high priest of freedom, dismissing the rest of the world in order to pursue his own selfish goals and desires, whereas the speaker of the second part expresses his sense of social responsibility by recognizing and recording the suffering of those lost in the flood. In its entirety, "High Water Everywhere" is a plaintive portrayal of the victimization suffered by the southern black community, but Patton refuses to speak only as a passive victim. Before he sings a protest song, he first establishes his credentials as an active, potent, and socially subversive agent: the radical articulation of individual autonomy and black agency in the first part of the song is the necessary precondition for the second part. In this respect, the song is reminiscent of the nineteenth-century fugitive slave narratives, whose authors celebrated the individual ingenuity that enabled them to escape from servitude while protesting the oppression of the majority who remained enslaved.[26]

The point of "High Water Everywhere" is not so much the flood itself but Patton's ability to widely communicate its meanings for black Americans. The ending of the initial verse of the first part expresses the excitement of an artist who has recently discovered that the medium of recording can bring his words and music to a vast audience: "*I'll tell the world* the water done struck Drew'ses town" (my emphasis). Although the bluesman had to alter and adapt his works for the marketplace—coding his critiques of white society and cutting down songs that might last up to half-an-hour when performed before live audiences in jook joints to three-minute chunks[27]—he wholeheartedly seized the opportunity to express himself to the larger world. Through modern technology, a black man from rural Mississippi could assert his individualism and agency, articulate his culture, and bring attention to both the value and the plight of his community on phonographs across the country.

In Faulkner's story, the tall convict—another marginal and oppressed figure—must also develop a voice and achieve mastery over a bewildering series of events by forging them into a coherent narrative and performing it for an audience. Initially, the convict is taciturn and distrustful of language, but something changes as he begins to relate his adventures in the flood to his fellow prisoners upon his return to the Parchman bunkhouse: "Then, suddenly and quietly, something—the inarticulateness, the innate and inherited reluctance for speech, dissolved and he found himself, listened to himself, telling it quietly, the words coming not fast but easily to the tongue as he required them" (280).

The original biblical title of Faulkner's novel clearly alludes to the complexities of narration, audience, and context. As Karl Zender observes, the full verse of Psalm 137 from which the book's title derives is "If I forget thee, O Jerusalem, let my right hand forget her cunning" (137:5). Zender argues that "the cunning of which the psalmist speaks is specifically his ability to perform as an artist" (60). "Cunning" does not only connote artistic skill, however, for, as Vincent Allan King observes, the captive Jewish artist in Babylon "must balance his audience's need for a song of liberation with the reality that this song will not be kindly received by the Babylonians. . . . The psalmist, then, must sing two songs: the mirthful public song that his masters require and the more private and tragic song which reminds his people that they are never fully conquered as long as they can remember Jerusalem" ("The Wages of Pulp" 507). In other words, the psalmist must be able to provide a musical story that is at once innocuous entertainment for the master class and a subversive counter-narrative on behalf of an oppressed people.

Patton regularly performed for white audiences, providing both the mirth they demanded and subtle criticism that they may not have recognized.[28] The bluesman even presented a copy of his satirical record about local white authorities, "Tom Rushen Blues" (1929), to its eponymous subject (Evans, "Charley Patton" 186), apparently confident that it would be accepted as jocular parody rather than as pointed critique. Equally, "High Water Everywhere" is funkily energetic musical diversion as well as subversive social commentary. Patton used the popular medium of blues—controlled and recorded by white businessmen and marketed to the African American population as entertainment—for a tale of black self-actualization and an eloquent protest against the inequities of the flood relief effort.[29]

At stake in both Faulkner's story and Patton's song, then, is not only the survival of the protagonists but also their ability to weave potent narratives out of what they have witnessed and experienced—narratives that enable the oppressed to assert themselves and to challenge the status quo, while also fulfilling the requirements of the entertainment industry. In this respect, "Old Man" and "High Water Everywhere" echo the complex interrelationship between white police power and emerging modern black culture in the early twentieth century that Bryan Wagner describes in *Disturbing the Peace*. The triumph of self-expression in Patton's song, however, highlights the ultimate shortcomings of the tall convict's late-blooming eloquence. Although Faulkner's protagonist apparently asserts control over what he has endured by telling his story to an appreciative crowd, it is, finally, an inadequate tale told in a contrived manner to a restricted—and literally captive—audience.

Critical opinion on Faulkner's tall convict—and thus the meanings of his story—has shifted fundamentally over the years. Scholars now frequently emphasize the character's flaws, differing significantly from those earlier critics who celebrated his virtues. In one of the earliest books about Faulkner's fiction, William Van O'Connor even describes the tall convict as "one of the most admirable figures Faulkner has created" and as "a man of great courage and almost unbelievable endurance" (*Tangled Fire* 105, 107). Another critic in the mid-1950s spoke similarly of the convict as "one of Faulkner's most engaging heroes, a man of awesome integrity" (Stonesifer 255). It is hard to imagine such unconditional endorsement in contemporary criticism. For Patrick McHugh, the tall convict is anything but heroic, characterized by "complacency rather than *hubris,* fear rather than courage, and impotence rather than strength" ("William Faulkner" 31). Anthony Hoefer describes the convict as merely "a comic fool" (551), and Daniel Singal goes still further, dismissing the character as "a pitifully inadequate being" (*William Faulkner* 243).[30]

The differences between early and later critics concerning the tall convict are not as irreconcilable as they initially appear. The first generation of scholars commonly based its evaluations of the character upon his conduct during the flood, whereas critics in recent years tend to concentrate upon his behavior at the end of Faulkner's story, particularly his performance as storyteller in the prison bunkhouse. In later life, Faulkner himself observed, semi-admiringly, that the tall convict is "just stupid and ignorant enough to bull right on through" the perils of the flood (*Faulkner in the University* 176–77). The author might reasonably have added, however, that the convict is not astute or wise enough to make a meaningful tale out of his experiences.

Certainly, much of the recent scholarship on *If I Forget Thee, Jerusalem* emphasizes the protagonist's inability to convert his adventures and traumas into compelling rhetoric or empowering narrative. King suggests that the tall convict in "Old Man" and the two lovers in "The Wild Palms," are all "artist figures who refuse to respond creatively to their predicaments. They refuse to fashion their own life-stories. Instead, they confine themselves to pulp fictions, secondhand stories which are devoid of love and hope" ("The Wages of Pulp" 522). Similarly, Pamela Rhodes and Richard Godden argue that, after all his experiences, the convict has learned only how to "give his Parchman public what it wants—a verbal peep show . . . [an] oral tale of the proletariat as confined and impotent as Harry's reverie" at the end of "The Wild Palms" (110).[31]

It is true that the narrative's emphasis upon counterpoint is palpable in the striking contrast between the convict's dispassionate and perfunctory reportage, on one hand, and Faulkner's lush and vibrant literary art, on the other. "After a while," the convict tells his prison audience, "we come to a house and we stayed there eight or nine days then they blew up the levee with dynamite so we had to leave" (211). This stark and unpunctuated sentence's insufficiency is thrown into sharp relief by Faulkner's vivid eighteen-page dramatization of the same episode, in which the convict enters into a business partnership with a "Cajan" trapper and discovers for the first time how fulfilling work can be outside the restrictive environment of the prison farm. As Cynthia Dobbs puts it, "the convict's terse version of events remains so much less interesting than Faulkner's. . . . [T]he convict has created only a dull tale of circularity" (832).[32]

The problem is not that the tall convict cannot compete with Faulkner's sophisticated artistry. One does not have to be a literary writer to tell a powerful story, as vernacular blues songs confirm. There is no reason why the convict should not be able to weave his flood adventures into an oral narrative that is as simple and direct, yet as compelling and resonant, as "High Water Everywhere," but he does not. The fundamental limitation of the tall convict's narrative—characterized by cynical irony and radical understatement—is that it fails to express either the substance of his experiences or the nature of his responses to them. Unlike Patton's blues song, the convict's account deadens his adventures, draining them of all drama, emotion, detail, and meaning. When his fellow convicts ask what kind of trouble he got into on the outside, he simply says, "Woman. It was a fellow's wife." When they ask how much he won in a dice game, he says only, "Enough" (282, 284). His deadpan and minimalist narrative voice barely hints at his habitual psychological state: bitter outrage (21, 22, 123, 196). After all that he has endured and all he has seen, the only conclusion the tall convict can draw—his final statement in the book—is, at once, inarticulate, profane, misogynistic, and meaningless: "Women, shit" (287).

The convict's dispassionate narrative voice is not the natural, unmediated rhetoric of a stoic and laconic countryman, but an artificial construction, as mannered and contrived in its way as the rhetoric of the pulp crime stories that the convict curses for having inspired the outlaw behavior that brought him to Parchman in the first place. The numerous allusions to *A Farewell to Arms* throughout *If I Forget Thee, Jerusalem* suggest that the convict's narrative style is, in fact, an acid caricature of Hemingway's minimalist prose and a parody of that writer's taciturn male heroes.[33] Where Patton's protagonist ultimately learns that there is much more that needs to be said about the flood than that "it starched my clothes," the convict fails to move beyond a posture of sardonic understatement.

The tall convict's mask of deadpan sarcasm isolates him from community and society no less than Charley's oblivious self-absorption in the first part of "High Water Everywhere." The convict is continually curt with the pregnant woman whom he saves from the flood. They seem to talk more during their initial encounter than throughout their lengthy association in the rest of the book (125–29). When questioned by a sympathetic doctor at one point in his odyssey, the convict gives the most cursory answers possible, reducing his crime to five simple words: “I tried to rob a train” (208). He is at his most effusive when communicating with his business partner, the Cajan, and, because of the language barrier, they converse only through mime. While Patton will “tell the world” of his experiences, the convict finally elects to express himself only to the most insular audience imaginable: a small coterie of fellow prisoners, a passive and powerless community.

The convict’s adoption of the clichéd role of the terse, macho, and self-assured cynic prevents him from asserting himself, celebrating freedom, or questioning the status quo. As a form of rhetoric, sarcastic stoicism suggests that, lacking the power to change anything, people might as well find humor in the circumstances that they must endure. Although the convict achieves a kind of celebrity in the bunkhouse for the bland account of his adventures, he meekly accepts the unjust addition of ten years to his prison sentence as punishment for his unwitting disappearance during the flood. The story’s grimly humorous punch line is that, after enduring the perils of the flood, caring for a pregnant woman, and surviving a relentless series of frustrations, the tall convict readily embraces imprisonment over liberty.

It is not just that the convict accepts incarceration, but that he is twice imprisoned because of his inability to comprehend or to take control of narrative. His initial sentencing came about because he made the mistake of assuming that stories in pulp crime magazines could serve as reliable reference texts for the budding criminal. Following such examples “to the letter” led only to a disastrously inept attempt at a train robbery and to a prison cell, where he seethes with rage at the authors who misled him with “criminally false” information (21). At the end of the story, the tall convict loses his freedom again, but this time because of the lies of the Parchman authorities. Legally, the convict is a free man, since the state—presuming him dead after his disappearance during the flood—has officially discharged him. Following his unexpected return, the warden and his associates are quick to resolve the problem by assuring the convict that they have no choice but to punish him for his absence. Even if they narrate from a position of power, and with more purpose and creativity than their prisoner, this manipulation is still entirely dependent upon the tall convict’s complicity. Although he seems to understand that there is no substance to the dishonest bluster of the authorities, the convict is quite content for others to dictate his circumstances. Where he once cursed the pulp writers for inspiring his attempt at armed robbery, he does not question the Parchman authorities at all, nor does he criticize them, even privately, for returning him to prison.

In all these respects, the tall convict could not be less like Patton or his protagonist. Where the convict's story is emotionless, "High Water Everywhere" vividly portrays the horrors of the flood; where the convict's tale is self-effacing, Patton's lyric is a defiant assertion of self; where the convict's discourse is clichéd in its hardboiled, Hemingway-pastiche minimalism, Patton's rhetoric is uncompromisingly his own (sometimes incomprehensibly so); where the convict accepts his lot with bitter cynicism, Patton's song speaks out against injustice; where the convict tells his story to a profoundly limited audience, Patton spoke not only to the black community in the Mississippi Delta, but also sang eloquently on phonographs across the South and the urban North in his own time, and across ages and continents to a global audience in the twenty-first century.

The convict's ultimate inability to convert his experience into productive or empowering narrative is curious, given that "Old Man" initially appears to be a kind of *bildungsroman*—a story of experience and education—like that other great tale of a young man traveling down the Mississippi, *Adventures of Huckleberry Finn.* Ursula Brumm suggests that the river not only liberates the tall convict, but also "educates him to narrate his experience." The convict's journey through the flood turns him from a man who was "unable to express his thoughts and intentions" into "a creator, instead of an imitator of literature" (243, 245, 247).

It is true that Faulkner's story and the flood give the convict a second chance: an opportunity to wrestle with real-life adventures straight out of a pulp magazine and to become the narrator of his own exploits instead of remaining the victim of somebody else's stories of derring-do. As Brumm suggests, to some extent the passive consumer of misleading and sensationalist fiction becomes the authoritative reporter of unvarnished nonfiction after his experiences in the flood.

The ultimate limitations of the convict's narrative in the Parchman bunkhouse suggest, however, that something has gone awry with this education. Critics often attribute the convict's ultimate failure as a storyteller to such inherent character flaws as complacency, fear, or a "monumental lack of imagination" (McHugh, "William Faulkner" 31; Millgate, *Achievement of William Faulkner* 177).[34] What is ironic and tragic about the convict's story, however, is that it is not inevitable. It is precisely because he misunderstands the lessons of his flood experience that he ends up wresting failure from the jaws of the potential victory outlined by Brumm.

At the outset of "Old Man," the tall convict is sufficiently bitter about the consequences of his misplaced faith in pulp magazine fantasies that he refuses to trust language at all, and withdraws from self-expression and self-narration altogether. He is unable to explain his motives at his trial because "he could not tell them . . . did not know how to tell them" (22). The convict is similarly inarticulate and withdrawn at Parchman, except for those times "as he trod the richly shearing black earth behind his plow or with a hoe thinned the sprouting cotton and corn or lay on his sullen back in his bunk after supper" when "he cursed in a harsh steady unrepetitive stream" (22). This single reference to the tall convict's speaking aloud in the story's opening chapter reads like an unconscious parody of Alan Lomax's description of how prisoners maintained and expressed their individuality on southern prison farms through song: "A convict, by raising his holler from time to time during the long day of toil, could announce his existence and fend off the crushing weight of prison anonymity. His signature song voiced his individual sorrows and feelings. By this means, he located himself in the vast fields of the penitentiary, where the rows were often a mile long and a gang of men looked like insects crawling over the green carpet of the crops" (273). Faulkner's convict has considerable facility for language if he can curse in a steady stream apparently without repeating himself—an act of oral improvisation as impressive as any blues singer's extemporaneous invention. A stream of profanities, however, is an entirely meaningless form of expression, however artfully arranged. His "signature song" is inadequate to his individual sorrows and feelings, and does nothing to distinguish him in the anonymous environment of the prison farm.

The opening chapter of "Old Man" seems to promise a story in which the convict will recover his faith in language and discover more compelling forms of discourse, and the flood provides him with several crucial lessons about voice, narrative, and power. The first of these is that those in authority are apt to ignore raised and desperate voices, a lesson that the convict struggles to internalize. When the truck from Parchman fails to rescue—or even respond to—the shrieking Negro woman on the roof of the sinking shack, it is clear that even the loudest, most plaintive sounds are ineffective and, thus, essentially meaningless when uttered by those without power. This lesson is repeated almost immediately when one of the other convicts in the truck begins screaming for the guards to unlock their chains, but "for all the answer he got the men within radius of his voice might have been dead" (55). Twice in the story, the convict forgets this lesson and makes the mistake of raising his voice when trying to surrender to the authorities. After he gets lost in the flood, he begs a group of armed refugees to return him to prison, but they reject his pleas, assuming that he is insane or inebriated (140). Later, upon spying some soldiers, the convict runs towards them, shouting, "I want to surrender!" and receives only a burst of machine gun fire in reply (146). As someone without power, the tall convict must develop an alternative mode of expression to the sound and fury of desperate bellowing.

In the second chapter, the convict encounters two instances of highly effective understatement, both of which influence the form of discourse that he ultimately adopts. These examples similarly derive from African American sources, each involving or alluding to popular music. The convict's understanding of these forms of discourse, however, remains partial and incomplete.

The first instance is the moment when a Negro levee-worker identifies the "profound deep whisper" of the river as the voice of the "Ole Man." "He dont have to brag," another black character helpfully explains (61, 62). This observation clearly echoes the most famous song from Jerome Kern and Oscar Hammerstein's popular musical about theatrical folk on the Mississippi, *Show Boat.* In "Ol' Man River," Paul Robeson, the renowned African American bass-baritone, sings that the Mississippi "mus' know something / But don't say nothin'." The song was a national hit in 1928, and the first film version of *Show Boat*—also featuring Robeson—premiered in May 1936 during Faulkner's screenwriting tenure at Twentieth-Century Fox, not long before he began writing *If I Forget Thee, Jerusalem.*[35] The implication in both the song and Faulkner's story is that the most powerful do not have to shout or even speak above a whisper: the quietly murmuring Mississippi River has the capacity to wreak immense devastation.

The convict makes the mistake of assuming that, if the river is so mighty that it need only whisper, then he can appear strong by similarly refusing to boast. In the Parchman bunkhouse, the convict's terse style suggests that, like the Mississippi, he knows much more than he says and "dont have to brag."[36] Such a strategy, however, prevents him from incorporating into his narrative all the drama he has witnessed and all the heroism he has performed. In addition, nature has no actual speech, so for the convict to impersonate the river's "voice" is an implicit denial of his own humanity. Furthermore, his verbal approximation of the Ole Man's "whisper" is merely an imitation of the rhetoric of the powerful without possession of the substance of that power. In short, the convict's laconic cynicism may be inspired by the Mississippi, but it is as empty and meaningless as the character's earlier reliance upon streams of profanity, as well as being barely distinguishable from the spare, hardboiled dialogue of the pulp crime stories that he has already rejected.

Immediately after hearing about the Ole Man's whispering power, the convict encounters a more accessible and functional lesson in the potential of understatement from an African American musician. As boats loaded with refugees approach the levee, the convict hears "the faint plinking of a guitar" across the water, a sound that continues throughout the scene. When the boat's passengers disembark, the convict finally sees that the source of the sound is "a young, black, lean-hipped man, the guitar slung by a piece of cotton plow line about his neck. He mounted the levee, still picking it. He carried nothing else, no food, no change of clothes, not even a coat." The tall convict is utterly transfixed and is "so busy watching this that he did not hear the guard until the guard stood directly beside him shouting his name" (63).

Neither existing scholarship on Faulkner's story nor blues criticism has much to say about this guitarist or his function in the tale. Thadious Davis and Adam Gussow only briefly address him in their astute discussions of African American music in Faulkner's canon. Thomas McHaney's book-length study of *If I Forget Thee, Jerusalem* bypasses the black musician in a single sentence (69). McHugh's analysis of "the spirit of the blues" in Faulkner's novel, Peter Lurie's reading of its pop culture elements, and Phil Smith's discussion of aural cacophony in the text do not mention him at all. Cheryl Lester—one of few Faulkner scholars to have given any attention to the unnamed blues guitarist—characterizes his appearance as a "cameo," and focuses instead upon the metaphorical treatment of black migration elsewhere in the novel ("*If I Forget Thee, Jerusalem*" 196). Two blues scholars identify Faulkner's guitarist with Patton and "High Water Everywhere," but only in passing. Francis Davis imagines that, "[i]f the world was the creation of E. L. Doctorow, a novelist for whom history amounts to name-dropping and literature to rotogravure, Patton would have crossed paths with William Faulkner. The singer would have been the model for the 'young, black, lean-hipped man' who, still strumming his guitar, boards a skiff full of blacks rescued from the flood" (98). Evans, meanwhile, suggests—if without further elaboration—that Patton's flood blues provides a "mirror image" for the scenes on the levee in Faulkner's story ("High Water Everywhere" 12).

In fact, Faulkner's anonymous guitarist resembles Patton and his song's protagonist in several distinct ways. As a black refugee dependent upon a white rescue effort, the African American musician in "Old Man" could easily appear to be a passive victim, albeit one who is more fortunate than the doomed families in the second part of "High Water Everywhere." Yet he is also clearly akin to the assured and potent protagonist of the song's first part, his music ringing across the levee as a bold assertion of its creator's humanity and agency. In other words, the guitarist embodies and combines elements of the two contrasting parts of Patton's flood song.

Faulkner's guitarist provides an example of self-assertion that gives the convict serious food for thought: he is the antithesis of the screaming, desperate victims of the flood and strides confidently through the chaotic aftermath of an immense natural disaster. Despite his position in the social hierarchy, he is indeed a human equivalent of the Ole Man. He does not need to shout or brag to make his authority felt, nor even speak at all, for the strumming of his guitar is sufficient eloquence, providing the principal human presence and "voice" in the scene despite the prevalence of nominally more powerful figures. Even though the tall convict is no musician, the power of self-expression that the black guitarist demonstrates evidently strikes home—to the extent that he becomes as deaf to the shouts of the guard as those in authority are to the screams of powerless victims of the flood.

The irony is that the convict does not understand that his brief vision of the guitarist constitutes only half a lesson. There are only two scenes in "Old Man" in which the tall convict is not present, both of which are important precisely because of the absence of the story's central viewpoint character. These two scenes are connected, furthermore, by the presence of the Parchman warden. The second such episode is in the story's final chapter, when the prison authorities discuss how they will manipulate the convict into returning to his cell, reasserting their rhetorical authority while the protagonist surrenders his. The other scene in which the convict is not present is the exact opposite: it shows how the powerless can speak truth to power, a lesson that could have inspired the tall convict to choose a very different rhetorical and narrative style—and a very different outcome—if only he had witnessed it.

This crucial scene occurs early in the novel, when the convict has vanished while seeking two refugees trapped by the flood waters: the pregnant woman clinging to a cypress tree and a man stranded on the roof of a sinking cotton house. Investigating the prisoner's disappearance, the Parchman warden interviews the cotton-house man after his belated recovery. This unnamed white character, however, is too consumed with "impotence and rage" to provide useful testimony about the missing convict (66): "'I set there on that sonabitching cotton house, expecting hit to go any minute . . . and them boats come up and they never had no room for me. Full of bastard niggers and one of them setting there playing a guitar but there wasn't no room for me. A guitar!' he cried; now he began to scream, trembling, slavering, his face twitching and jerking. 'Room for a bastard nigger guitar but not for me—'" (67).

If the second part of "High Water Everywhere," suggests that white rescuers neglected black victims of the flood, here the tables are turned: a boat full of African American refugees floats serenely past an imperiled white man while one of them even serenades him with a tune. That the black man pleasantly strums his guitar—seemingly oblivious to the white man's fear of imminent drowning—is more than incongruous; the cotton-house man appears to read it as a deliberate affront. The object of the white man's anger shifts rhetorically from the people in the boat ("bastard niggers") to the instrument ("A guitar. . . . a bastard nigger guitar"), suggesting his rage over both people of color and an inanimate object apparently having priority over him, but also implying that the music itself is the crowning insult.

The cotton-house man's response to what he perceives to be a violation of conventional racial priorities is the same bitter and helpless rage displayed by the weakest and most vulnerable characters throughout the story. His loud and disjointed bawling is reminiscent of the black woman crying from the roof of the sinking house, the screaming of the prisoner in the truck, and the protagonist's stream of curses in prison, as well as the latter's pitiful attempts to surrender later in the narrative. Although the anonymous man's location during the flood associates him with the financial and social power of the white planter—he is literally on top of the cotton economy—his inarticulate shouting renders him as impotent as an abandoned flood victim or hapless lower-class convict.

This scene in Faulkner's story is the exact reverse of an event that took place during the 1927 flood. Barry's historical account demonstrates that, while black refugees in Greenville were forced to inhabit crude shelters and work on the levees, whites in the town were able to live almost as freely as usual, even traveling the river on steamboats. What is more, the white residents were not content to enjoy their privileged position silently: "Petty insults stirred more resentment. Whenever the steamer *Capitol* pulled away from the dock, its calliope routinely played 'Bye Bye Blackbird.' It was like a slap in the face to the blacks" (312).[37] The guitar-player episode in "Old Man" turns this insult around. Now a rescued black man plays a tune for a stranded white man, and—whether or not the guitarist's choice of melody is as sarcastic as in Barry's example—the rage of the cotton-house man suggests that the guitarist's strumming is no less a slap in the face than the sound of the *Capitol*'s calliope to Greenville's black community.

Music plays a prominent role in histories of the flood, both as plaintive lament and thinly veiled social commentary. Saxon's book about the event—which Faulkner evidently used as a reference source when writing "Old Man"[38]—describes a group of black refugees stranded on a levee singing the spiritual "Jesus Is a Dying-Bed Maker" (310). The quoted lyrics are virtually identical to those in the version of the song recorded by none other than Patton immediately following "High Water Everywhere." It is conceivable that the flood song's description of water creeping up to the speaker's bed brought this gospel song to Patton's mind. If the refugees in Saxon's account are closer to the forlorn black family trapped on the housetop in "Old Man" than to the proud African American guitarist, another historical example suggests the capacity of vernacular music to speak truth to power. Hoping to secure the government's commitment to social reform in the Delta after the disaster, Robert R. Moton, chairman of the Colored Advisory Committee, wrote of "a song that these people sang in the levee camps—that the flood had washed away the old account. They felt that the flood had emancipated them from a condition of peonage" (qtd. in Daniel, *Deep'n as It Come* 139–40).

Just like the narrator-protagonist of "High Water Everywhere," the guitarist in "Old Man" at first seems to speak only for himself as he struts across the levee, but the appearance of the cotton-house man—who has been reduced to gibbering rage by the black man's music—suggests that Faulkner's guitarist also speaks eloquently on behalf of the African American community. Like the poet of Psalms, the guitarist uses his artistic skills to entertain the powerful and powerless alike, while simultaneously using his art to subvert the status quo and to celebrate his people. In Faulkner's story, in contrast to the Jews in Babylon, it is the audience, not the artist, who is literally captive, while the guitarist's tune brings its listener not pleasure, but misery.

A solo black guitarist in rural Mississippi in 1927 was almost certainly a blues musician, and the cotton-house man's complaint is an awkward imitation of blues verse. This is not the only occasion in Faulkner's fiction in which speech resembles blues structures. Charles Peek notes that some of Nancy's dialogue in "That Evening Sun," when isolated from other characters' interjections, replicates the AAB pattern of the blues ("That Evening Sun[g]" (133–34). In "Old Man," however, the inarticulate rage of a white speaker distorts the elegant and economical AAB tradition of black folk music into an artless and redundant ABBB:

> I set there on that sonabitching cotton house, expecting hit to go any minute . . .
> [T]hem boats come up and they never had no room for me.
> Full of bastard niggers and one of them setting there playing a guitar but
> there wasn't no room for me . . .
> Room for a bastard nigger guitar but not for me.

The cotton-house man's "song" shares some elements with "High Water Everywhere," but where the former is characterized by garbled and repetitive hysteria, the latter is distinguished by its control and concision. The closest equivalent to the cotton-house man's complaint in "High Water Everywhere" is the penultimate stanza of the second part:

> Oh, high the water risin,' our men sinkin' down
> Sayin' the water was risin', airplanes is all around. . . .
> It were fifty men and children: "Tough luck, they can drown."

Patton's version amplifies the peril of the situation through the repetition of the A line ("Oh, high the water was risin.' . . . Sayin' the water was risin'"), and retains for its B line the devastating comment about the willingness of would-be rescuers to let certain individuals die. Patton's song is even more dramatically effective for assuming briefly—without editorialization—the voice of one of those responsible for the failure to save fifty people from drowning, rather than the voices of the victims, requiring that the listener infer why members of the relief effort might be so callously unconcerned about such an immense death toll in this particular instance. In contrast, the man on the cotton house in "Old Man" deals with his peril in a single A line and repeats his complaint about being neglected over three B lines, leaving nothing to his auditors' imaginations. His relentless focus on the guitarist—who is neither responsible for the white man's peril nor in any position to resolve it—is more a delusional digression from, than a compelling explanation of, his situation. In fact, Faulkner's guitarist goes one better than Patton, since his music alone—absent of lyrics—is sufficient to reduce the cotton-house man to blabbering hysteria and garbled imitation.

The disjunction between how the tall convict and the cotton-house man view the guitarist—the former as merely compelling entertainment, the latter as subversive counter-narrative—echoes critical debates about the social and political dimensions of the blues. The convict sees the guitarist speaking only for himself, commanding everyone's attention, but without apparently disturbing conventional hierarchies. In this respect, Faulkner's protagonist is like those earlier blues scholars who tended to define the blues as being essentially personal and rarely concerned with social commentary. Samuel Charters, for example, once declared that "[t]here is little social protest in the blues," and concluded that "the Negro in America . . . has turned to the blues as the expression of his personal and immediate experience" (*Poetry of the Blues* 152, 173). Similarly, Peter Guralnick asserted in 1971 that "blues for the most part confines itself to a very restricted range of subjects: women and whiskey but rarely social conditions; sexual but never political innuendo" (*Feel Like Going Home* 39). Like the man on the cotton-house, however, contemporary scholars are more attentive to the implications of apparently innocuous songs. The difference is that such studies—notably Gussow's analysis of blues songs as radical responses to lynching—celebrate the music's implicit rebellion rather than castigating it.

Following his semi-education, the convict adopts a laconic cynicism reminiscent of the first part of "High Water Everywhere," but, while using such potentially subversive language, he merely conforms to what the system demands of him. The tall convict never develops the compassion and humanist commitment demonstrated by the narrator of the second part of Patton's song, just as he never imbues his story with the implied social commentary of the black guitarist's playing in "Old Man."

As well as failing to understand the potential of discourse to subvert power, the tall convict continues to lack insight about the importance of context. His original imprisonment came about because of his inability to distinguish between fact and fiction, and the black musician's example leaves him none the wiser. The guitarist uses an understated rhetoric—music without words—because he is not powerful, unlike the Mississippi River, which whispers because it is all-powerful. In a situation in which it would be dangerous to speak openly, the black musician does not sing a lyric as overt as "High Water Everywhere," and appears to be doing nothing more than innocently strumming a guitar, even if his indulgence in entertainment while a white man is in danger of drowning is a subtly subversive act. The absence of vocals, furthermore, implies that there are lyrics the guitarist *could* sing, but chooses not to sing in this context. Similarly, Palmer speculates that Patton's recorded version of "High Water Everywhere" may be less overt in its social commentary than when the bluesman performed versions of the song for exclusively black audiences (75). Equally, in a verse critical of President Woodrow Wilson in his recording of "When the War Was On" (1929), Blind Willie Johnson conspicuously elides the final line, slyly allowing a guitar passage to replace the presumably incendiary lyrics (van Rijn, *Roosevelt's Blues* 8).

Just as many white listeners would not have picked up on the implications of Johnson's provocative omission, Faulkner's tall convict is a poor reader of popular culture. He adopts the guitarist's understated form of rhetoric, but without any apparent sense of its function, purpose, or how it is tailored for a specific situation and audience. The convict uses a minimalist style of discourse in all situations—even within the comparative safety of the bunkhouse with his fellow prisoners—that the guitarist mobilizes in dangerous circumstances and before potentially hostile listeners. The convict's experiences during the flood could have taught him that contexts can change radically—that a river can flow backward and that a prisoner can freely sail the waterways—but he never learns how to develop forms of vernacular discourse that can be mobilized effectively in a variety of situations or for different audiences. If the guitarist achieves agency through folk discourse, the convict's attempts to use vernacular rhetoric merely provide a narrative framework and philosophical rationale for his incarceration and disenfranchisement.

The black guitarist's musical triumph over the spluttering cotton-house man suggests that the chaos of the flood temporarily disrupts conventional racial hierarchies, even if the tall convict is unable to profit from such disruption. Where the white man from the cotton house temporarily becomes socially less important than a man of color, the tall convict symbolically becomes other than white. One early Faulkner scholar even mistakenly assumed that the protagonist of "Old Man" is "a Negro convict from the vicinity of Frenchman's Bend" (Miner 101). More recently, Lester claims that, although the convict clearly is not literally African American, his "marginal status in relation to the community and his experience of the flood code him as black" ("*If I Forget Thee, Jerusalem*" 201). More specifically, the tall convict takes on the characteristics of two particular black figures. He is a victim of the flood, like the woman screaming from the roof of the shack, and he is a survivor and narrator of the event, like the guitarist. Where the guitarist turns the breakdown of racial orthodoxies into cause for celebration, however, the convict's symbolic or performed blackness brings him no advantage; he merely becomes subject to the most negative of racial stereotypes.

Faulkner's story draws attention to the similar ways in which antebellum slavery and the modern prison farm construct African American subjectivities, dramatizing what Houston Baker calls the "carceral network that has continuously held the black-South body in a state of 'suspended rights'" (*Turning South Again* 93). Published just a decade before the Mississippi flood, *American Negro Slavery* (1918) by Georgia historian Ulrich B Phillips describes black Americans of the past as being characterized by "obsequious obedience, the avoidance of open indolence and vice, the attainment of moderate skill in industry, and the cultivation of the master's good will" (328). Even in the present, Phillips argues, "negroes . . . show the same easy-going, amiable, serio-comic obedience and the same personal attachments to white men, as well as the same sturdy light-heartedness and the same love of laughter . . . which distinguished their forebears" in slavery (xxiv). If, for Phillips, antebellum plantations had been "the best schools yet invented for the mass training of that sort of inert and backward people which the bulk of the American negroes represented" (343), then many whites thought of the state prison as taking up where antebellum slavery left off. As David Oshinsky notes in his study of incarceration in Jim Crow Mississippi, one white southerner even characterized time at Parchman Farm as "a smooth and simple extension of normal black life: 'They do the same work, eat the same food, sing the same songs, play the same games of dice and cards, fraternize with their fellows, attend religious services on Sunday morning and receive visitors on Sunday afternoon'" (136).[39]

African American commentators did not hesitate to reject the insidious notion that Parchman, any more than slavery, was a benevolent paternal institution. As Oshinsky observes, "black convicts took a rather different view. Their prison songs . . . portrayed Long-Chain Charlie [the traveling sergeant of Parchman] as an evil man who stole their freedom and brought them despair" (136). Certainly, no blues song about the Mississippi penitentiary likens servitude there to "normal black life." The protagonist of Bukka White's "Parchman Farm Blues" (1940) talks of being cruelly separated from his loving wife and of having to work daily from dawn to sunset. He concludes that, "If you wanna do good, you better stay off ol' Parchman Farm." In Baker's pithy summation, "From *plantation* to 'prison farm' is scarcely a liberating mobility toward *modernism*" (*Turning South Again* 92).

The symbolically black tall convict in "Old Man" thoroughly conforms to dominant white discourses about African Americans within such institutions as slavery and prison. Faulkner's Parchman clearly resembles the antebellum sites of slavery: "there is no walled penitentiary in Mississippi; it is a cotton plantation which the convicts work under the rifles and shotguns of guards and trusties." In every respect, the tall convict is a submissive, loyal, hard-working, and sober slave on this plantation, with an amiable line in ironic but unthreatening humor. During his ordeal in the flood, he thinks longingly of "the familiar fields where he did work he had learned to do well." He has also turned down the opportunity for higher station offered by the Parchman authorities for his loyalty and competence. The convict rejects the chance to be an armed "trusty," opining that he would prefer to stick to plowing and that he "already tried to use a gun one time too many" (21, 139, 140). According to the terms of the Jim Crow South, the tall convict is everything that a slave or person of color is supposed to be. Although he attempts to imitate the self-assured blackness of the guitarist, he ends up merely performing crude blackface, assuming a persona that is passive, obedient, serio-comic, immobile, incarcerated: his life a smooth and simple extension of African American enslavement.[40]

The tall convict slips into this role partly because, like other white auditors of his era, he mistakenly understands black music as a quaint folk tradition rather than as an expression of African American modernity—and, furthermore, as a tradition associated with immobility and incarceration, rather than with freedom and independence. Just as white folklorists in the nineteenth century collected slave songs, their successors in the mid-twentieth recorded prison songs. As Wagner observes, folklorist John Lomax even "made a case in 1933 to the Library of Congress that black music in its 'primitive purity' was obtainable 'as nowhere else from Negro prisoners,'" whose "tightly circumscribed conditions were 'practically ideal' for folklore collection." Arguing that "prisoners were the last folk singers and prisons were the only remaining repositories for black authenticity, Lomax transformed the legal imperatives that defined black tradition into cultural properties," making criminality a "baseline criterion for black cultural authenticity" (215, 216, 217). At the very historical moment that white people sought to prevent the African American population migrating from the South, they characterized blues songs as reassuring expressions of cultural continuity in southern life—even as tacit acceptance by black people of subservience, dependence, and circumscribed mobility.

If I Forget Thee, Jerusalem highlights the tensions between plaintive and subversive blues, folk tradition and commercial mass culture, white people's appreciation for black music and their blinkered misunderstanding of African American expression. Lester argues that the book torturously articulates "Faulkner's ambivalent recognition of the contradictions most urgently haunting the Jim Crow South," and that its stories of thwarted and defeated Caucasian rovers—Charlotte, Harry, and the tall convict—ultimately displace, deflect, and minimize white anxiety about black mobility more than they expose, analyze, or critique it ("*If I Forget Thee, Jerusalem*" 191,199, 200). Even as the novel represses and evades its racial and cultural implications, however, it flaunts and revels in them. Whether in the profound disjunction between the cotton-house man's rage at the guitarist's music and the convict's wide-eyed admiration of it, or the absurd distance between the convict's sincere emulation of the guitarist's style and his caricature performance of black carceral passivity at Parchman, Faulkner's novel complicates and satirizes reductive white responses to black vernacular culture.

Ostensibly constructing vibrant folk tradition and commercial popular culture as polar opposites, Faulkner's novel implicitly demolishes the apparent barriers between them. It may appear that, divorced from any tradition he can truly call his own, the tall convict first becomes subject to the mass-manufactured fantasies of pulp fiction and, later, a clueless emulator of African American vernacular expression: he is unable to define himself in relation to either consumer society's escapist entertainment (because it is essentially meaningless) or black America's musical traditions (because he does not understand their meanings). While the author seems to have harbored fairly old-fashioned notions about the differences between folk authenticity and mass culture, and between high literature and low popular culture, Erich Nunn identifies an evident "blurring of the boundaries between folk and popular" throughout 1931's *Sanctuary* (83). In "Old Man," the guitarist's music—and its multiple effects on different audiences—similarly erases the distinctions between such categories as art and mass culture, folk and pop, personal and political.

From a twenty-first-century viewpoint, furthermore, "Old Man" operates as a dramatization of two conflicting conceptions of mass media. The spell that pulp fiction casts over the convict suggests a crudely Marxist notion of popular culture, in which the masses are simply helpless subjects of a dominant hegemony. In contrast, the black guitarist's command of musical rhetoric reflects a more contemporary view of popular culture as having the potential to resist or evade the power of socially sovereign forces and ideologies. The tall convict is a classic stooge of the ruling class, whereas the guitarist subverts the status quo, demonstrating that, as John Fiske suggests, popular culture "is made by the people, not imposed upon them. . . . Popular culture is the art of making do with what the system provides" (25).[41]

The limitations of the convict's rhetoric in contrast to that of the guitarist also suggest that "Old Man" represents a transitional moment in Faulkner's depiction of black people.[42] In the author's earlier fiction that engages directly with issues of race, African American or mixed-race characters tend to be doomed tragic victims (such as Joe Christmas in *Light in August* and Charles Bon in *Absalom, Absalom!*), or models of patient endurance (most notably, Dilsey in *The Sound and the Fury*). Faulkner's few overtly subversive black characters prior to the guitarist of "Old Man"—such as Caspey in *Flags in the Dust* or Loosh in *The Unvanquished*—are often both unsympathetic and ridiculous. However, Faulkner's major work of the 1940s, *Go Down, Moses,* conceptualizes a much broader range of possibilities for black characters—from the victimization of Rider in "Pantaloon in Black" to the rebellious antics of the proud and confident Lucas Beauchamp in "The Fire and the Hearth." Indeed, the contrast between the guitarist's triumphant mobilization of discourse and the impoverished rhetoric of the tall convict in "Old Man" parallels Beauchamp's manipulation of landowner Roth Edmonds and his canny exploitation of a hapless white salesman in *Go Down, Moses.* Equally, the convict's thwarted imitation of the guitarist's understated style paves the way for Beauchamp's more effective tutelage of the young Chick Mallison in *Intruder in the Dust.*[43]

In *If I Forget Thee, Jerusalem,* however, the convict's vision of the African American guitarist is not sufficient to overcome his ingrained assumptions about blackness. As a consequence, he is incapable of constructing a vernacular tale that might invest his experience with meaning—a tale that conceptualizes the majestic chaos of the flood, the tragedy of the family abandoned to the rising waters, the terror of a snake-infested Indian mound, the patient courage of his pregnant female companion, the joy of working for himself in the Louisiana swamps, or the hypocrisy of the prison system. For all his heroism, the convict cannot sing a song of himself as empowering or dramatic as either "High Water Everywhere" or the wordless tune of Faulkner's bluesman.

3

SEE MY BABY FROM THE OTHER SIDE

THE GHOSTS OF LYNCHING IN "THAT EVENING SUN" AND "LAST KIND WORDS BLUES"

Echoes of the blues in Faulkner's biography and fiction often coincide with violence—particularly racial violence. Rider, who falls victim to a white mob in "Pantaloon in Black," takes his name from W. C. Handy's "Easy Rider," and, although Faulkner may not have heard of Charley Patton, the ghost of one Nelse Patton looms over depictions of lynching in "Dry September" (1931) and *Light in August* (1932). In September 1908, Nelse—a black bootlegger who apparently slit the throat of a local white woman after supposedly making improper advances to her—was taken from the Oxford jail by a mob, repeatedly shot, and hanged from a pole in the town square. As Joel Williamson observes, "Faulkner was almost eleven on the night of the lynching, and his bed was not more than a thousand yards from both the jail and the square" (*William Faulkner* 159).[1] These grim events also obliquely inform the 1931 story, "That Evening Sun," the title of which derives from the opening line of Handy's "St. Louis Blues" (1914): "I hate to see de eve'-nin sun go down" (Handy 143).[2] Just as the female protagonist of Handy's song cannot sleep for thinking of her departed lover, Nancy in Faulkner's tale obsesses over her mysteriously absent partner: a razor-scarred "badman" who is reminiscent of Nelse but bears the incongruous name "Jesus."[3] Although both story and song are about a woman's fear of the impending dark, what distinguishes them is the specific reason for Nancy's trepidation about sundown: she is convinced that Jesus plans to return and kill her with his razor under cover of dark.

Although the title of Faulkner's tale ironically references "St. Louis Blues," Nancy's isolation, her expectation of a gruesome fate, the mood of terror that infuses "That Evening Sun," its invocation of supernatural presences, and its subtle implications of racial violence share rather more in common with one of the most mysterious and haunting country blues records: Geeshie Wiley's "Last Kind Words Blues" (1930). The lyrics of this song, furthermore, suggest an alternative reading of Nancy's situation and ultimate fate. In "Last Kind Words Blues," the female speaker first speculates about the reasons for her lover's absence and then finds consolation and agency through the narrative that she constructs in response to and about that absence. Where critics tend to read Nancy as a passive victim, Wiley's song raises the possibility that Jesus is not hiding in a ditch waiting to commit murder after all, and that the woman's apparent terror of her former lover is, in reality, an outward manifestation of her process of coming to terms with what actually may have happened to him. The parallels between "Last Kind Words Blues" and "That Evening Sun" suggest that Nancy does not fear Jesus, but fabricates a story about being haunted by him precisely because—like Wiley's narrator—she is exploring the possibility that her lover may be dead, or, at least, that he might as well be. In a desperate situation, Nancy—no less than the protagonist of the blues song—uses her tale to achieve a subtle victory over the white community that has exploited, oppressed, and abused her. Without mentioning lynching, "That Evening Sun" and "Last Kind Words Blues" implicitly concern black women who respond boldly and creatively to the threat of racial violence.

"That Evening Sun" is unexpectedly accessible, even straightforward, for a Faulkner work, but is simultaneously bewildering in its ambiguity and open-endedness. It takes the form of a childhood reminiscence by Quentin Compson, who also appears in *The Sound and the Fury, Absalom, Absalom!,* and two other short stories.[4] Following the sophisticated diction of the tale's opening section, the mature Quentin's reveries reflect the childlike perspective of his youth: sentences become plain and short, and the narrative increasingly consists of little more than reported dialogue. For all this superficial simplicity, however, Quentin's tale glosses over crucial information, and its ending is radically inconclusive.[5]

The story revolves around the troubled Nancy, who lived and worked on the Compson place during Quentin's youth. In one of Quentin's recollections, Nancy accosts Stovall, a respected white citizen, on the streets of Jefferson, and accuses him of repeated failure to pay her for certain unnamed services.[6] Stovall's response to these allegations is to kick Nancy in the teeth. Consigned to the local jail, a distraught Nancy tries unsuccessfully to hang herself in her cell. Another of Quentin's memories involves Nancy goading Jesus, her common-law husband, by denying his paternity of her unborn child. Jesus responds by uttering dark threats concerning the unidentified father within the hearing of the Compson children, an act that results in his expulsion from the white family's household, after which he abruptly disappears from Jefferson altogether.

The central action of the story concerns Nancy's panic upon hearing a rumor that Jesus has returned to town, for she now apparently believes that her former lover means to slaughter her. Nancy seeks refuge in the Compson house, but her white employers soon forbid her from sleeping there. She responds by taking the three young Compson children—Quentin, Caddy, and Jason—to her cabin at night to serve as the only kind of shield available to her. She tries telling a story to keep them occupied, but an annoyed Mr. Compson comes to bring the children home, bluntly dismissing Nancy's fears of Jesus as absurd, given the absence of any concrete evidence of the man's presence. Quentin's narrative abruptly breaks off as the Compsons leave Nancy—who now appears to be resigned to what she believes is her inevitable fate—alone in her cabin in the dark. The story never confirms if her fear of Jesus's vengeance is well founded or entirely irrational, for Quentin never reveals if Nancy lives to see the sun rise.

"That Evening Sun" is complicated not only because of its many lacunae and its absence of resolution, but also by dint of its torturous relationships with other Faulkner works. Rather than illuminating the story, additional appearances by Quentin and Nancy in the author's tales and novels only serve to make it yet more confusing.[7] For example, Caddy's memory in *The Sound and the Fury* of "when Nancy fell in the ditch and Roskus shot her and the buzzards came and undressed her" inspired some early critics to conclude that Jesus must have slit the throat of his partner in "That Evening Sun," and that another Compson servant put her out of her misery (33). As Stephen Whicher persuasively argues, however, the Compson adults would not permit a murder victim to rot in a ditch in full sight of their children (253). The "Nancy" of Caddy's recollection is evidently one of the Compsons' animals: an injured horse or dog, not a human being.[8]

Some readers consider the appearance of Nancy Mannigoe in *Requiem for a Nun* (1951) as decisive evidence that Jesus does not kill his common-law wife in the earlier story. Like her predecessor, the Nancy of *Requiem* once endured a brutal assault by a white banker after she demanded money from him (554–55). Faulkner openly acknowledged that this Nancy is "the same person actually. These people I figure belong to me and I have the right to move them about in time when I need them" (*Faulkner in the University* 79). The novelist's caveat here, however, is crucial: this may be the same Nancy, but Faulkner also firmly asserts his authorial right to reinvent and remobilize characters, regardless of inconsistencies in the larger narrative of Yoknapatawpha County.[9] Consequently, *Requiem for a Nun* does not confirm anything at all about the Nancy of "That Evening Sun," including her ultimate fate.

A classic instance of Faulkner's habit of rewriting characters according to his particular purposes at any given moment is the very different ways in which the author deploys Quentin in several works. The second section of *The Sound and the Fury* concerns the events immediately preceding Quentin's suicide at Harvard in 1910, which is to say several years before his retrospective narration about Nancy in "That Evening Sun" at the age of twenty-four.[10] Malcolm Cowley questioned this glaring inconsistency while editing *The Portable Faulkner,* but the novelist was so untroubled by the contradiction that he refused to remedy it, confessing that he had "never made a genealogical or chronological chart" for his characters, "perhaps because I knew I would take liberties with both—which I have" (qtd. in Cowley 53).[11] As Hans Skei concludes, "Despite the temptation to read it in the light of *The Sound and the Fury* or *Requiem for a Nun,* or even more cautiously in comparison with 'A Justice' [another story narrated by Quentin], one should insist on the autonomy" of "That Evening Sun" (179–80).

Regardless of inevitable inconsistencies across multifarious stories and novels written over a thirty-five-year period, it is provocative that, if only in terms of its relationship to the larger chronology of Yoknapatawpha County, "That Evening Sun" is a story told by a phantom.[12] In fact, Faulkner's tale resembles a ghost story in several respects. Even the seemingly mundane opening paragraph constructs everyday life in Jefferson in supernatural terms, with "iron poles bearing clusters of bloated and ghostly and bloodless grapes" having replaced the trees of Quentin's childhood, and where laundry is no longer gathered by human servants but "flees apparitionlike" in motor vehicles (289).[13] The comfortingly real world of the past has become the inhospitably ghostly realm of the present. The eerie language in the introduction is an appropriate prelude to a chilling tale about a lone woman's terror of a mysterious and deadly force in the dark that nobody but she can see. Although Jesus appears directly in only a single short scene preceding the main action, his threatening presence pervades the tale: in Robert Hamblin's words, he is "a spectral figure linked with forebodings of doom" ("Before the Fall" 87). Nancy even claims that her former lover has magically deposited a horrifying symbol of his homicidal intentions—a bloody hog-bone—in her cabin, but this object inexplicably vanishes before any of the white characters see it (307).[14] In many respects, "That Evening Sun" is a literary version of the spooky stories that the author loved to tell local children.[15]

Although Faulkner's tale revels in the conventions of the ghost or horror story, it also consistently undermines and even parodies them. For one thing, the narrative withholds the ghastly killing that it goes to such lengths to suggest is an inevitable conclusion. In addition, there is nothing within the story itself to imply that Quentin is speaking from beyond the grave; it is only knowledge of other Faulkner works that permits such a reading.[16] In short, "That Evening Sun" is a horror story without an ultimate horror, a ghost story that lacks an explicit appearance by a ghost.

The notion of "That Evening Sun" as an abstruse or perverse ghost story may seem a long way from "St. Louis Blues," but enigmatic tales of haunting are a central part of the blues tradition. The narrator of Walter Davis's "Blue Ghost Blues" (1932) is terrified by the specter of sheer loneliness: he describes himself as "a poor broken-hearted bachelor" whom "the blue ghost . . . haunts all night long." In the same year that Faulkner published "That Evening Sun," Lonnie Johnson similarly sang, "Blues, you only a ghost, you sleeps all day and worry me all night long."[17] Bessie Smith's "Haunted House Blues" (1924) is particularly reminiscent of Nancy's situation: the speaker's home is "haunted" because "my mistreating daddy hangs around me day and night" and "makes me swear I'll have no other man but him." The song's opening stanza suggests that male jealousy has filled the house with the ghosts of multiple men, presumably the female protagonist's former and/or imagined lovers. The speaker is finally driven to such despair by her partner's possessiveness and paranoia that, like Nancy in Faulkner's tale, she even embraces the prospect of death, declaring, "Go tell the undertaker to fix that old coffin of mine."[18]

"Last Kind Words Blues," meanwhile, was one of only six recordings made by Wiley, a figure so enigmatic that she might as well have been a ghost herself. As John J. Sullivan says of Geeshie—or maybe Geechie, or even Geetchie[19]—Wiley and her collaborator L. V.—or "Elvie"—Thomas, "despite more than 50 years of researchers' efforts to learn who the two women were or where they came from, we have remained ignorant of even their legal names" ("Ballad of Geeshie and Elvie" 26). Critics often assumed that Wiley was from Mississippi, with some rumors even locating surviving family members and the singer's grave in Faulkner's Oxford (Gioia 125), but, in his later years as a literary celebrity, the white author could only fantasize about the kind of anonymity that enshrouded the blues singer: "It is my ambition to be . . . abolished and voided from history, leaving it markless, no refuse save the printed books" (qtd. in Blotner, *Biography* 1276). Although her records survived, Wiley seemed to have evaporated from history as mysteriously and completely as Jesus disappears from Jefferson in "That Evening Sun." Not until 2014—almost eighty-five years after they made their recordings—did Sullivan locate hard information about Wiley and Thomas. It turns out that Lillie Mae Wiley was probably born in Louisiana and lived in Thomas's hometown of Houston for many years—where she acquired her nickname—before disappearing into western Texas and Oklahoma. Although Sullivan spoke to relatives of Thomas and located a photograph of her, he acknowledges that Wiley still remains essentially a mystery: "L. V. comes out of it all an indelible character, but Geeshie we don't know." The lone surviving person who knew Wiley claims that "there was something funny about her background. He said that she'd been 'maybe Mexican or something'" ("Ballad of Geeshie and Elvie" 49)—an uncanny echo of the rumors surrounding the origins of the racially ambiguous Joe Christmas in *Light in August* (374, 377).[20]

No less than its mysterious creator, "Last Kind Words Blues" is a kind of ghost itself, a revenant of an earlier musical era. It conforms to very few of the familiar musical conventions of the blues, including the AAB three-line structure and the regular twelve-measure form. Much of it, furthermore, is in A minor, an unusual key for a blues of that period.[21] Critics characterize Wiley's song as "a lone survival of an older, already vanishing, minstrel style," or "an old melody, an old lyric with a modern, blues sentimentality and vocal style," or even as an embodiment of "the moment when black secular music was coalescing into blues" (Sullivan, "Unknown Bards" 86; Cordeiro 64; Kent qtd. in Cordeiro 68).

* * *

Like Quentin's narrative in "That Evening Sun," the lyrics of Wiley's song are deceptively simple. The minimalist, enigmatic, and open-ended language clearly dramatizes a woman's mourning for deceased family members and, possibly, her encounter with the ghost of a partner who disappeared during World War I. The song also implicitly concerns the causes and consequences of racial violence, obliquely addressing such issues as white economic power, black migration, and lynching.

Just like Nancy in Faulkner's tale, the female speaker of "Last Kind Words Blues" is haunted by loss. At its most basic level, Wiley's song concerns the narrator's recollection of the "last kind words" of her "daddy"—evidently a term of endearment for a lover or husband instead of a reference to a biological father—before he left for "the German War." The narrator cites the instructions for burial left by the man in case of his death, but she also recalls his assurance that he would return from the conflict with a gift for her. The speaker then acknowledges her restless character, recalls her mother's deathbed advice, and expresses her feelings of dejection.[22] Sullivan argues that Wiley's lyrics also describe the return of her "ghost lover"—that the man's parting words are not "kind," in the sense of loving, but instead carry the archaic connotation of "natural." Anything he says afterwards is thus supernatural or preternatural. Bereft of the material presence of her lover and haunted by his spectral shadow, the female speaker has "nothing to look forward to but the reunion death will bring" ("Unknown Bards" 87, 88).

Although the speaker of "Last Kind Words Blues" apparently embraces death, she also seeks to forestall this eventuality, giving her something else in common with Faulkner's Nancy. Greil Marcus observes that the narrator of Wiley's song cannot help but wish to live a little longer even as she expresses a desire to die: "every time she sings the word 'I' or 'me' or 'my' it stretches out, takes over whole lines of meter, drowns the words around it, as if the singer believes she may never get a chance to say another word. . . . [It is] as if like Scheherazade she knows she may not outlive her tale" (*Invisible Republic* 202, 203). Nancy similarly fights to avoid the fate to which she also seems resigned. When she attempts to hang herself in her jail cell, Nancy uses her dress for a noose, but, with no other item of clothing available, "she didn't have anything to tie her hands with and she couldn't make her hands let go of the window ledge" (291). As Mark Coburn describes this chilling scene, "Nancy is unwilling to live but unable to die"

(213).[23] One critic's analysis of the scene in which Nancy makes a futile effort to distract the Compson children with an improvised fairytale carries an even more direct echo of Marcus's reading of Wiley's song: Skei says that Nancy "tells her story for the same reasons stories have been told since Scheherazade: to stay alive, to keep the darkness at bay, though without much hope that the telling of something has the power to magically change it" (189). John Gerlach similarly observes of this scene that, when "facing what she regards as an inevitable end, she chooses to prolong the moment of its arrival as long as possible" (136), much like Wiley's protagonist.

It is not only that the narrator of Wiley's song postpones the moment of her passing; her language also blurs the boundary between life and death, represented in each of the song's last two stanzas by a body of water: "one of the oldest death metaphors" in African American music (Sullivan, "Unknown Bards" 87). In the first of these stanzas—the most perplexing in the song—the speaker enigmatically says: "The Mississippi River, you know it's deep and wide, / I can stand right here, see my baby from the other side." Here, Wiley adapts a standard blues formula. In "Lonesome Day Blues" (1932), Rube Glaze sings it as "The Mississippi River, so deep and wide / I can't see my good man on the other side," while it appears in Big Bill Broonzy's "Mississippi River Blues" (1934) as "Missi'ppi River is so long, deep, and wide / I can see my good gal standing on that other side." It is even possible that Faulkner knew some variant of the formula, since he uses essentially the same idea and image in "Old Man." When the prisoners first approach the flooded Mississippi, the tall convict strains his eyes to see the levee on the opposite bank, and ponders, "*That's what we look like from there. That's what I am standing on looks like from there*" (62).

Compared to the versions by Broonzy, Glaze, and even Faulkner, Wiley's particular use of the formula is obscure and unsettling in the way that it dismantles and erases boundaries, whether between river banks or between life and death. As Sullivan observes, "there's something spooky happening to the spatial relationships" in the eccentric construction in "Last Kind Words Blues": "If I'm standing *right here,* how am I seeing you *from* the other side? The preposition is off. Unless I'm slipping out of my body, of course, and joining you *on* the other side" ("Unknown Bards" 87). The speaker may indeed slip over to "the other side," as Sullivan suggests, either in her imagination or in spirit, as a kind of preparation for death, temporarily leaving her physical body in the material world. Once in the realm of the dead, however, she may not necessarily discover her lover beside her. If Sullivan's invaluable reading clarifies the location of the song's speaker, the placement of her husband remains ambiguous. It may be that from her imaginative or spiritual vantage point on "the other side" the speaker can clearly see her man because he is over there too, or it may be that what she specifically sees "*from* the other side" is that he is back across the water in the material world. The final line of the song leaves either possibility open. Some auditors render it as "I believe I'll see ya after I cross the deep blue sea," whereas others hear "I may not see you after I cross the deep blue sea."[24] Although these are conflicting readings, both suggest uncertainty: whether the speaker hopes she will see her partner in the afterlife or doubts he is there, she simply does not know for sure whether he is dead or alive.

"Last Kind Words Blues," then, is more than a song about mourning the dead; it is specifically about the difficulty of mourning an individual whose fate is unknown. The man who departed for the war has clearly not returned, but the speaker makes no mention of receiving official confirmation of his death in combat. In just two lines elsewhere in the song, the speaker clearly describes her mother's unambiguous passing and plain deathbed advice:

> My mama told me, just before she died,
> "Lord, precious daughter, don't you be so wild."

Earlier, however, the same narrator spends four whole stanzas discussing her lover's last words without ever verifying that he has actually passed on. Critics usually just assume that the male protagonist is deceased. In Sullivan's reading, he "has died as he seems to have expected—the first three verses establish this, in tone if not in utterance" ("Unknown Bards" 87). The lack of specificity here, however—tone, not utterance—reduces certainty to possibility. If her lover is dead, the speaker no longer wants to live, but what if she were to die only to discover in the afterlife that he has not passed on after all? This doubt explains the conflicting impulses of the song's narrator: like Nancy, she is "unwilling to live" without her man, "but unable to die" because he may still be alive and simply has not returned to her (Coburn 213), in which case her death obviously would not bring about their reunion.

The speaker is no more certain about *how* her lover may have met his fate than she is about the fact of his demise. Although the man departed for war, the apparent absence of official notification of his death and the contradictory instructions he left for the disposal of his remains imply that there is more than one way in which he could have met his end:

> "If I die, if I die in the German War,
> I want you to send my body, send it to my mother-in-law."
> . . . .
> "If I get killed, if I get killed, please don't bury my soul.
> I cry, just leave me out, let the buzzards eat me whole."

Some scholars have sidestepped the problems presented by the apparently inconsistent nature of these instructions by transcribing the second line of the first of these stanzas as a request for the man's "money," not his "body," to be dispatched to his relative.[25] This rendering makes more immediate literal sense than two conflicting sets of instructions about bodily disposal, but Wiley's delivery sounds distinctly like "body," and the apparent contradiction is not necessarily as nonsensical as it first appears. If the female speaker's mother is already dead (and there is no evidence of when this event—described in the fifth stanza—occurs in the chronology), then the man's first instruction could simply suggest his wish to be buried alongside his wife's family, a touching declaration of his closeness to his partner and his sense of kinship with her.[26] Alternatively, the statement could be mordantly ironic, an instruction to send his corpse to someone who has already passed over to the other side. As Barry Lee Pearson and Bill McCulloch point out, there is a long tradition of blues songs containing "sarcastic or comic burial instructions" (81).[27]

The issue is further complicated by the question of whom the man is addressing: after all, these are not "the last kind words my daddy said to me," but "the last kind words I heard my daddy say," a construction which makes it feasible that the song's female protagonist is reporting words that she heard addressed to someone else. One possibility is that, when the man enlists—or is drafted into—the services, the military authorities ask what arrangements he would like to make in case he falls in combat. He considers the question essentially meaningless since he knows that if he dies on the battlefield he will be buried there. He subtly satirizes the phony compassion of the military bureaucrats by making a request that cannot be fulfilled: send my body to my mother-in-law. If this relative is—unknown to the military recruiters—already dead, it is an even more craftily sarcastic answer. When the authorities confirm that there is no possibility of shipping a body home from overseas, the man, having made his point, revises his answer, saying that he simply does not care what happens to his remains if they cannot be returned to his family. After these declarations to the military officials, however, the man privately assures his wife in the song's fourth stanza—the last spoken by him—that he will come back to her from the war bearing gifts. Although this reading is appealing for its comprehensive and coherent explanation of the song's lyrics, it is necessarily hypothetical.

Such speculation aside, it is provocative that the two versions of the husband's last request clearly echo each other ("If I die, if I die . . ." / "If I get killed, if I get killed . . .") while being entirely inconsistent in their details. Although the male protagonist of "Last Kind Words Blues" seems to be talking repetitively about the possibility of dying in battle, the stark differences between his two descriptions of death also imply perishing in the German War by choice, on one hand, and suffering an obscure but violent demise against his will in some anonymous location, on the other. Regardless of whom the male protagonist is addressing, and whether he is asking to send his "money" or his "body" home, "Last Kind Words Blues" emphasizes that the prospect of violent death is nothing new to an African American man in this era. The speaker's husband implies that, should he die in the war, it would be appropriate for the military authorities to dispose of him overseas as ruthlessly as the white citizenry regularly disposes of lynching victims at home.

In the first of the two instruction stanzas, the man imagines a death that leaves his corpse sufficiently undamaged that it could—in theory, at least—be shipped home to his extended family rather than being disposed of overseas among strangers. In the second, the man envisages a devastating form of death that would leave nothing but his soul and a few scant remnants upon which carrion birds might feast. The first stanza describes a time-honored arrangement for treating a deceased person, whereas the second involves a violation of human decency and a shockingly public display of physical dissolution. The instructions in the first stanza are presented in an active construction, "If I die," whereas the second uses the passive "If I get killed." This distinction implies that death in combat is a possible consequence that the man has consciously accepted or even chosen, but that something which happens to him or is done to him, over which he has no control, is another form of death entirely. Finally, the first set of instructions refers specifically to death in war and in a particular location, whereas the second is not specific about either the place or cause of death.

The man's contradictory words obviously suggest his anxiety about the disjunction between eager wartime patriotism and the visceral realities of battlefield slaughter. The second of the two stanzas even echoes Hemingway's renowned World War I novel, *A Farewell to Arms,* published the year before Wiley recorded her song. Frederick Henry, the book's protagonist, says of the carnage he has witnessed in combat that "the sacrifices were like the stockyards at Chicago if nothing was done with the meat except to bury it" (185).

On another level, the rhetorical differences between the two sets of instructions suggest the man's ambivalence, as a person of color, about his participation in World War I: he elects to serve his country while also being aware that he risks sacrificing himself on behalf of a nation that will continue to discriminate against him on racial grounds. Even as many members of the African American community hoped that black contributions to the war effort would reap social rewards, others remained skeptical that military service by people of color would change entrenched racial hierarchies in any substantial way. One orator hopefully declared that, "when we have proved ourselves men, worthy to work and fight and die for our country, a grateful nation may gladly give us the recognition of real men, and the rights and privileges of true and loyal citizens of these United States" (qtd. in Barbeau and Henri 7). In contrast to such optimism, James Weldon Johnson recalled hearing one man of color dismiss the idea of serving in the military with the rationale that the "Germans ain't done nothin' to me" (233).[28] The evident reservations of the male protagonist of "Last Kind Words Blues" echo in the ambivalent words of another black American, J. Henry Hewlett, which shift from proud patriotism to profound doubt within a single sentence: "I am a full-blooded American; every time I hear a band play a national air my blood steams up to the boiling point and I feel as much buoyed up as anyone else, but when it is all over and I begin to meditate and reflect, cold chills sweep over me" (qtd. in Barbeau and Henri 11).[29]

Beyond the anxieties of soldiers in general and the concerns of African American recruits in particular, "Last Kind Words Blues" also implies a resemblance between the damage inflicted upon the human body in war and another kind of carnage perpetrated in peacetime. In the half-century before Wiley recorded "Last Kind Words Blues," lynching almost certainly claimed more African American lives in the South and Midwest than were lost in the Great War.[30] Between 1880 and 1930, there were 3,220 confirmed lynchings in the United States, nearly 1 per week, and the vast majority of the victims were black and male (Gussow, *Seems Like Murder Here* 45). The Mississippi Delta—the heartland of the blues—was a particular hotspot for racial violence, where, according to the NAACP, there were at least 66 lynchings during the first three decades of the twentieth century, an average of 1 every five-and-a-half months (James Cobb 114). Just one year before Wiley recorded "Last Kind Words Blues," Charley Shepherd of the Delta's Bolivar County was tortured and killed in a particularly sadistic and grotesque manner (Oshinsky 141–43). In *Caste and Class in a Southern Town,* his 1937 sociological study of Indianola in Sunflower County, John Dollard concluded from interviews that lynching was "one of the major facts in the life of any Negro," and that its threat was "likely to be in the mind of the Negro child from earliest days" (358, 330).[31]

"Last Kind Words Blues" is not a rarity among blues songs if its depiction of a black corpse preyed upon by vultures is a subtle allusion to the similarities between battlefield destruction and lynch-mob annihilation. Gussow's seminal study, *Seems Like Murder Here,* persuasively demonstrates that lynching is a central—if covert—subtext of the blues between the two world wars. Given the obvious dangers of recording explicit protests about white-on-black violence in this era, blues singers tended to address the subject in coded, metaphorical, or even unconscious language. As Gussow observes, "lynching is inscribed in the blues lyric tradition in a variety of ways: as anxieties about encirclement, torture, and dismemberment; as a blues nightmare about Hell's 'dragons'; as direct address to an oppressive phantasmic presence . . . that stops at the black subject's front door, chases him from tree to tree and does him many sorts of harm; as songs of romantic loss." In his reading of Bessie Smith's "Haunted House Blues," for example, Gussow looks beyond the surface tale of a woman's fear of an obsessively jealous lover to suggest that it is also an expression of "the trauma suffered . . . by the black female blues subject whose bed has been emptied not by infidelity, but by death"—the brutal handiwork of psychotic white mobs (*Seems Like Murder Here* 22, 186).

Gussow's reading of Smith's song raises the possibility that any blues about spectral haunting might harbor a subtext about racial violence. In Lonnie Johnson's "Blue Ghost Blues" (1938), for example, the phantoms surrounding the speaker's house in the night brandish "shotguns and pistols," accoutrements not normally associated with supernatural apparitions, but which members of lynch mobs customarily carried. Of course, the purpose of the white sheets worn by the most notorious organized group of racial vigilantes was to evoke avenging southern ghosts. Faulkner's African American caregiver, Caroline Barr, or "Mammy Callie," used to tell stories about "the days after the [Civil] War, about frightening riders in the white of the Ku Klux Klan who claimed they were dead Confederates burning in hell but riding at night for brief periods" (Blotner, *Biography* 76).

For a modern listener, furthermore, the projected scenario in "Last Kind Words Blues"—in which buzzards peck at the exposed corpse of the male protagonist—cannot help but sound disturbingly familiar. Specifically, it anticipates the words of a very famous song recorded nine years after Wiley's blues: Billie Holiday's "Strange Fruit" (1939)—the first hit record to include an overt description of racial lynching—in which human victims are reduced to "fruit for the crows to pluck."

The implicit parallel in "Last Kind Words Blues" between the deaths of soldiers on European battlefields and the wave of racially motivated torture-murders in Jim Crow America reflects the historical fact that the number of lynchings in the United States increased drastically after World War I. Black men who had served their country were particularly vulnerable to racist violence. In Pete Daniel's words, "After fighting to make the world safe for democracy, blacks returned to find it unsafe for themselves" (*Standing at the Crossroads* 81). R. A. Lawson notes that, "In 1919, the year many of the soldiers returned home, ten African American veterans were lynched, and at least four of them were murdered while wearing their U.S. armed forces uniforms" (*Jim Crow's Counterculture* 125). For whites determined to reassert the racial status quo after the end of hostilities, a black soldier was a particularly problematic phenomenon: his uniform represented both his individual courage and his status as American patriot, whereas the purpose of existing social conventions was to deny that people of color could be heroes, individuals, or citizens. As Carter Woodson pithily observed, "The very uniform on a Negro was to the southerner like a red rag thrown in the face of a bull" (326).[32]

Wartime service and the denial of social equality in its aftermath—especially given prior hopes to the contrary—stimulated an openly militant attitude on the part of some African American veterans. As Gussow notes, "Du Bois's ringing declension in the May 1919 issue of *Crisis* set the summer's tone: 'We return. / We return from fighting. / We return fighting'" (*Seems Like Murder Here* 180). That year witnessed a surge of race riots in American cities—at least thirty-eight in number—as black people fought back against attempts by white communities to reassert racist norms. One uniformed veteran, Daniel Mack, was beaten to death by a mob after he "allegedly told a white that he had fought in France and did not intend to take mistreatment from white people" (Barbeau and Henri 177). A Mississippian named Joe Pullen similarly refused to bow to intimidation after leaving the military. In 1923, he killed his white landlord in a fight over the year's monetary settlement. A posse of a thousand men pursued Pullen through the swamps, eventually shooting him, but not before four of its number had also fallen prey to the ex-soldier's gun. Soon after Pullen's killing, white authorities instituted a curfew in the area, which included Dockery Plantation, one of the centers of local blues activity. David Evans theorizes that the aftermath of the Pullen incident was one of the factors responsible for the decline of the vibrant blues scene in the vicinity (*Big Road Blues* 190–91).[33]

Written in 1927 but set in 1919, Faulkner's *Flags in the Dust* presents a satirical picture of the returning black veteran and his increasingly outspoken desire for equality in the figure of Caspey. This character's war service may have consisted only of dockyard labor,[34] but he returns from Europe full of absurdly exaggerated stories about battlefield heroism. He also tells his family members that he is disinclined to resume his role as servant to the white Sartoris clan: "I dont take nothin' fum no white folks no mo'. . . . War done changed all dat. If us cullud folks is good enough ter save France fum de Germans, den us is good enough ter have de same rights de Germans is. . . . War unloosed de black man's mouf. . . . Kill Germans, den do yo' oratin', dey tole us. Well us done it" (589). When Caspey recklessly expresses such attitudes within the hearing of Old Bayard Sartoris, however, the white patriarch "reached a stick of stove wood from the box at his hand and knocked Caspey through the opening door and down the steps" (607)—a bluntly forceful reminder that the war has not affected racial orthodoxies after all.

In this early work, predating the more sophisticated portrayals of African American characters in some of Faulkner's later fiction, Caspey is a stereotypical and ridiculous figure whose militant attitudes are built on a weak foundation and whose comeuppance is inevitable, even warranted.[35] For a twenty-first-century reader, however, Caspey's assertion that black wartime service demands racial equality at home stands as an eloquent call for justice. Regardless of the character's flaws or the implied ideologies of the text, Caspey is a striking example of those returning black veterans who "bridled at the thought of reinhabiting their expected 'place' within the lacerating indignities of Jim Crow" (Gussow, *Seems Like Murder Here* 179–80).

The male protagonist of Wiley's song is prescient in his observation that, should he survive the Great War, he will find himself barely more secure in the cotton fields of the South than he was in the trenches of France. The very language in which he expresses his hopes of returning home implies a belief that, while African American involvement in the war effort might make no appreciable difference to racial orthodoxies, it will encourage a militant attitude to social justice on the part of black veterans: "When you see me comin' look 'cross the rich man's field, / If I don't bring you flour, I'll bring you bolted meal."

The first line of this verse signals the persistence of traditional socioeconomic arrangements. The land that the man must cross to return to his lover does not belong to either of them: it is "the rich man's field." Furthermore, if the female protagonist lives in sufficient proximity to this field that she must look across it in order to see her man returning, it is likely that she is a tenant farmer or agricultural worker for a wealthy white landlord.

The second line of the stanza suggests that the black veteran will no longer be willing to accept a system that privileges the white planter and impoverishes the African American laborer. For years, critics puzzled over the final words in this line, struggling to understand just what the man was promising to bring the song's narrator—a "boutonnière," or "Beaujolais" from France, perhaps? With John Fahey's help, Sullivan came to the realization that the line refers to "bolted meal" or "finely sifted meal"—"the rich man's flour" ("Unknown Bards" 88). The black soldier, then, envisions a postwar future in which either he will be in a position to purchase not just flour, but finely sifted meal, or, if economic inequality persists and his earnings are insufficient for him to be able to provide for his wife, he will be inclined to redress the injustice by stealing it from the white planter.

As the fates of Joe Pullen and Daniel Mack suggest, African American soldiers who returned from Europe with such rebellious attitudes were often subject to swift and brutal repression, and the male protagonist of "Last Kind Words Blues" is quite aware that he is vulnerable to various kinds of violence. Even if he does not die in the war, the Jim Crow South is less likely to reward him for having served his country than to brutalize or murder him for his expectation of social justice. His provocative "last kind words" suggest that he is too intelligent, too principled, and too outspoken to thrive in a world in which black men routinely endured the honorific "boy," the agrarian dream of self-sufficient farming had degraded into a rigid feudal system of white planters and black serfs, and returning military heroes were killed by mobs for being "uppity." The man in Wiley's song wants to believe in a better future, but his graphic visions of a violent end eclipse such hopes.

If the first half of Wiley's song focuses upon the ambiguous fate of the man, the second half concerns the woman he left behind and her efforts to cope with abandonment and bereavement. Geographical mobility does little to remedy the pain that the speaker feels, and the only solace she finds is in constructing a story about her painful experiences.

The fifth stanza of "Last Kind Words Blues" suggests that the female speaker's response to her partner's failure to return from war has been to participate in the Great Migration to the North in search of better prospects: "I went to the depot, I looked up at the sun, / Cried, 'Some train don't come, gon' be some walkin' done.'" Here, Wiley's lyrics echo the language and sentiments of a poem printed in 1917 in the *Chicago Defender,* a publication renowned for its tireless promotion of the benefits of leaving the South: "Some are coming on the passenger, / Some are coming on the freight, / Others will be found walking, / For none have time to wait" (qtd. in Lawson, *Jim Crow's Counterculture* 86–87).[36] As Isabel Wilkerson notes, "555,000 colored people left the South during the decade of the First World War—more than all the colored people who had left in the five decades after the Emancipation Proclamation" (161–62).

The single-minded determination of Wiley's speaker to make a fundamental change in her life in the fifth stanza, however, shades into regret in the sixth when she recalls that her mother advised, "don't you be so wild." Although the North promised to be a relative haven of opportunity in comparison to the South, the abrupt shift from a traditional rural lifestyle to a modern urban environment could be both disorienting and arduous. As Lawson puts it, "[t]he southern blacks' relocation was also a dislocation." Northern cities, furthermore, often proved to be almost as inhospitable to African Americans as the repressive Jim Crow South. Many blues songs look back fondly to "a romanticized and familiar South, contrasted against the less-friendly, colder North" (Lawson, *Jim Crow's Counterculture* 107, 112). The narrator of "Last Kind Words Blues" seems to be wondering if she left the South rather too abruptly after her lover failed to return from the war—that maybe her decision was rash, or even "wild."

Alternatively, it may be that the protagonist's "wild" nature is what makes her migration necessary in the first place. Whether she has always shared her absent husband's militant attitudes about racial justice or is driven to bitter rage by his disappearance, the woman's fierce opinions or uncompromising conduct are likely to earn her a reputation as being unruly in the eyes of whites—a reputation that could result in brutal repression.

In Faulkner's fiction, as well as in blues songs, African American women sometimes warn family members about the dangers of overt resistance to white supremacy. Thadious Davis highlights a passage in *The Sound and the Fury* in which Dilsey "attempts to curb [her grandson] Luster's conduct because, in the traditional order of things in the South, such conduct can only lead to suffering or perhaps even death" (*Faulkner's "Negro"* 80). As an outspoken black woman, the protagonist of "Last Kind Words Blues" may understand that the only way to guarantee her well-being is to leave home quickly—by train or on foot.

Even if the song's protagonist does not travel north or does not leave home specifically because of the threat of white violence, she clearly feels cut off from any meaningful human connection. Her mother has died, her lover has never returned, and she has left her home. Alone and bereft, all she can do is wonder incessantly about her husband's fate: Was he killed in the war? Could he have been lynched? Might he have met some other violent or untimely death? Is he still alive somewhere, and should she have waited longer for him to return? Unwilling to live without him and yearning for reconciliation in the afterlife, but afraid to die in case he is still alive somewhere, all she has is her song.

Wiley's protagonist shares much in common with one of the central female characters in Langston Hughes's novel, *Not without Laughter,* which also appeared in 1930. Like the speaker of "Last Kind Words Blues," Annjee Rodgers is heartbroken when her husband leaves to serve in World War I, and she becomes increasingly concerned about his unknown fate. In a letter to her son, Sandy, she mourns, "I do not know what has happened to your father in France. The war is awful and so many mens are getting killed. Have not had no word from Jimboy for 7 months from Over There and am worried till I'm sick" (275). In the final chapter, the female family members that the soldier left behind find some comfort—like Wiley's heroine—in the blues. Harriet—Anjee's daughter and a professional blues singer—moves her mother to tears with her performance of a song about how "*Ma heart is breakin'—ma baby's gone away*" and "*if you lose yo' man, you'd just as well be dead!*" Sandy notes that Harriet's performance is "[j]ust like when papa used to play for" his mother (298). In other words, Harriet's song resurrects Jimboy's spirit, just as "Last Kind Words Blues" seems to resurrect the speaker's lost husband.

Although, like Annjee, the narrator of "Last Kind Words Blues" cannot resolve her situation, she can at least tell her story, just as Harriet sings her mother's story, and just as Nancy in "That Evening Sun" tells her story "for the same reasons stories have been told since Scheherazade: to stay alive, to keep the darkness at bay, though without much hope that the telling of something has the power to magically change it" (Skei 189). Although she feels despair, power over narration provides the speaker of Wiley's song with some solace and agency. In the realms of her imagination, the protagonist is even able to project herself across the deep waters between life and death and "see my baby from the other side."

Like "Last Kind Words Blues," "That Evening Sun" is a story about an African American woman's obsession with the mystery of an absent lover. Of course, Jesus does not depart for service in World War I, there is no overt suggestion that he has died, and Nancy displays no intention of leaving town. Nonetheless, the numerous gaps, absences, and unspoken implications in Faulkner's story—and the interpretive possibilities that they open up—are strongly reminiscent of Wiley's song. No less than "Last Kind Words Blues," "That Evening Sun" alludes to lynching and concerns a black woman who tells her story as a way of coping with—and even overcoming—the racial oppression and feelings of isolation that threaten her.

Just as any detailed analysis of the minimalist and ambiguous "Last Kind Words Blues" necessarily involves conjecture and supposition, so is "That Evening Sun" sufficiently open-ended as to invite—even demand—speculative readings. Laurence Perrine characterizes the story as a "skein of uncertainties," or catalog of unresolved mysteries, including: why Nancy is arrested, why she attempts suicide, who is the father of her unborn child, why and whence Jesus disappears, whether he actually returns, what happens to Nancy's pregnancy, and, above all, whether Nancy is still alive the morning after the story ends (295, 297). Critics have made the most of the story's inexhaustible ambiguities and have happily accepted the challenge of exercising their imaginations when seeking to make sense of "That Evening Sun" and to supply its missing pieces, often employing hypotheses and qualifiers as frequently as they make unequivocal claims.[37] As Skei puts it: "Faulkner may have sensed strongly that there was so much in the poetic language . . . and the narrative structure itself that the story should not reach closure but be open for new readers to contribute to the textual meaning of it by rewriting the experience it relays. . . . 'That Evening Sun' is . . . a text to be returned to over and over again, to find new layers of meaning, new combinations of images and fictional facts, new angles of approach" (190, 193).

Beyond the ongoing arguments about whether Nancy is doomed or just paranoid, some scholars hypothesize that the disappearance of references to her pregnancy in the latter stages of the tale implies that the character has suffered a miscarriage or has procured an abortion.[38] Louise Barnett postulates that Jesus is particularly enraged by Nancy's pregnancy because he is physically impotent (137). Although many readers are inclined to view Stovall—the white man who assaults Nancy—as the most likely father of the woman's unborn child, Noel Polk emphasizes that the story does nothing to confirm such a supposition, and he suggests that Nancy's employer, Mr. Compson, could just as easily be responsible for the woman's pregnancy, and thus "the author of her miseries." Polk even wonders if Nancy deliberately puts the Compson children "in harm's way to avenge herself on a white world, and a white man, that has wronged her" (*Children of the Dark House* 239). Finally, one of the most innovative readings of "That Evening Sun" explores Nancy's fears in relation to African American folk traditions. Dirk Kuyk, Betty Kuyk, and Andrew Miller theorize that Jesus may be "absent physically but present in spirit": they suggest he is a conjure man who has projected his spirit from his body in order to put a lethal curse on Nancy (40–41, 45), a dark echo of the out-of-body wanderings in "Last Kind Words Blues."

Although Kuyk and his colleagues emphasize that "That Evening Sun" is, at heart, Nancy's story (38),[39] much of the scholarship on the tale focuses upon its narrator. Critics continue to debate Quentin's motivation for telling Nancy's story and the extent to which he appreciates its ultimate implications. Since Quentin does not complete Nancy's tale, explain his reason for telling it, or make any explicit statement about his attitudes toward it, readers tend to draw very different conclusions about the white narrator. May Cameron Brown observes that, "[i]n contrast to the other members of his family, [Quentin] shows an unusual sensitivity to Nancy's situation" (355). In contrast, Joseph Garrison argues that Quentin "is both blinded and deceived by his cognitive and perceptual inclinations. . . . We know that the world of his childhood was not ideal, but he does not" (371, 372).[40]

That such disparate interpretations are possible indicates that Quentin is profoundly ambivalent about the story he tells. "That Evening Sun" is, in many respects, a companion piece to the later *Absalom, Absalom!*, in which Quentin struggles to balance his investment in his southern heritage with the horrifying facts of its racial past that gradually come to light as he researches and recreates the history of slaveholder Thomas Sutpen. The unresolved and enigmatic narrative of "That Evening Sun" reflects Quentin's inner conflict: he is caught between his ingrained racial attitudes and family loyalties, on one hand, and his sensitive recognition of Nancy's humanity on the other. Faulkner's story is not about either Quentin's triumphant enlightenment or his continuing ignorance, but his agonized and ongoing battle to come to terms with his heritage. The tale is necessarily incomplete because Quentin's struggle is incomplete—and remains forever incomplete because of the character's suicide in *The Sound and the Fury*.[41]

Quentin's pained efforts to make sense of southern history—and his complicity as a white man in that history—have an evident analogue in Faulkner's mercurial opinions about the continuing social repercussions of his region's past.[42] The author's writings on race—fiction and nonfiction alike—are characterized by such paradoxical qualities as revolutionary critique, stubborn conservatism, uncompromising commitment to social justice, wariness of social change, sensitive insight into African American experiences, and reiteration of one-dimensional racial stereotypes. Charles Peavy observes that the author "has been seen as a radical reactionary and a sentimental traditionalist . . . and he has been called a bigot and a 'nigger lover'" (13). Ralph Ellison, meanwhile, characterizes Faulkner as "a writer who has confronted Negroes with such mixed motives that he has presented them in terms of both the 'good nigger' and the 'bad nigger' stereotypes, and who yet has explored perhaps more successfully than anyone else, either white or black, certain forms of Negro humanity" (29–30).[43]

The fiction of the first two decades of Faulkner's career displays a clear evolution in racial sensitivity. As Irving Howe puts it, the author made "a quick and steep ascent: from benevolence to recognition of injustice, from amusement over idiosyncrasies to a principled concern with status, from cozy familiarity to a discovery of the estrangement of the races" (55). The familiar Negro stereotypes of the early fiction gradually gave way to more sophisticated characterizations of black people and more complex analyses of racial injustice, from the centrality of the noble Dilsey in *The Sound and the Fury* to the torturous tale of Joe Christmas and his lethal interactions with the Yoknapatawpha community in *Light in August*.[44] The unsparing dissection of the irrationality of race relations in *Absalom, Absalom!* represents for many the apex of Faulkner's interrogation of black experiences in the white South, although for some readers the true culmination of this process is the multifaceted presentation of African American lives in *Go Down, Moses*. Several critics, however, identify this latter work, for all its merits, as representing an impasse, a text in which the writer discovered that his portrayal of black people could go so far, but no further.[45] Michael Grimwood even speaks of "Faulkner's recognition [in *Go Down, Moses*] that writing truthfully about Negroes was for him an enterprise doomed to failure," and that this was the primary source of the author's subsequent "literary exhaustion" (*Heart in Conflict* 225).

After World War II and during the civil rights era, Faulkner often seemed to be in retreat from his most astute insights about black culture and from his most fully realized fictional portrayals of African American characters, even as he made public pronouncements about the racial crisis in the South and the nation at large. His outspoken support of school desegregation offended some reactionary neighbors, but the author soon became concerned that rapid change in the field of race relations—particularly if instituted by the federal government—would result in violent social rupture, and he began to call for moderation and patience rather than immediate justice.[46] As Faulkner's position on civil rights became more cautious and conservative, so did black lives become increasingly marginal in his fiction, playing only the smallest of roles in the Snopes trilogy. Appearances by African American characters in the later novels continue to be a source of debate: many readers dismiss them for nostalgic sentimentality in their treatments of race and for evasion of the harsh actualities of black life during segregation, while some revisionist scholars challenge such assumptions, and identify subversive racial subtexts in Faulkner's final works.[47]

Although some of his later portrayals of black characters are somewhat limited and his approach to the subject of race noticeably less daring after the 1940s, Faulkner's hard-earned realization that he never would get to the heart of African American experience in his fiction suggests more than just "literary exhaustion." Faulkner's first biographer notes that the author was often preoccupied with "the difficulty of understanding Negroes' thoughts and feelings" (Blotner, *Biography* 1038), and this difficulty was surely perplexing for a white novelist whose core subject was the South.[48] Yet, what was an impasse, even a retreat, was also an attempt by the author to come to terms with the inevitable partiality of the white southern purview: an acceptance that, in a truly multicultural society, the WASP male writer cannot presume that his experience is universal or his knowledge of humanity all-embracing. In a 1958 public address at the University of Virginia, the author flatly declared that "the white man can never really know the Negro, because the white man has forced the Negro to be always a Negro rather than another human being in their dealings, and therefore the Negro cannot afford, does not dare, to be open with the white man and let the white man know what he, the Negro, thinks" (*Faulkner in the University* 211). If Faulkner never ceased to wrestle with the tensions between his inherited ideologies and racial justice, he was at least able to acknowledge the limitations of his white southern male perspective in ways that Quentin never does.

However hard it was for Faulkner to accept his inability to fictionalize black experience authoritatively, he often made much of this drawback by writing powerfully about the questionable ways in which white people tend to view black experience.[49] Although Faulkner's sense of the yawning chasm between white and black cultures sometimes led him to depict people of color as being so unknowable that they are "disembodied from the reality of ordinary human life" (Thadious Davis, *Faulkner's "Negro"* 246), it also informs his most astute portrayals of American race relations. The quintessential example of a story about the tragic misunderstandings that habitually result from the efforts of whites to comprehend African American culture, communities, and individuals is "Pantaloon in Black," in which the white characters are incapable of appreciating that the cause of Rider's erratic and, ultimately, violent behavior is his grief for a recently deceased wife.[50]

"That Evening Sun" is, in some respects, an earlier version of the same story: it concerns the paradox between the imperative for white people to understand black humanity and the impossibility of their adequately doing so in a Jim Crow culture. Even as the story represents a concerted effort by a white writer to render black experience vividly and authentically, it incorporates the ultimate—perhaps even inevitable—frustration of such a project into its very fabric through its incomplete and unresolved narrative. It is, as Charles Peek says, a tale of "unbridgeable cultural differences" ("'Handy' Ways" 55), or, as Doreen Fowler puts it, an examination of "how white people *read* people of color" ("Tracing Racial Assumptions" 47). Kuyk and his colleagues theorize that the story conveys

> an experience that Faulkner had had or heard of but did not entirely comprehend. Further, his narrative strategy itself implies that he knew he did not comprehend it all. Like his narrator Quentin, Faulkner lived in a white culture that bordered a black one; and he knew that the two cultures continually touched on one another and often interpenetrated. His strategy therefore warns us to look more deeply into the story than Quentin ever looks. . . . Faulkner seems to have seen that the actions of "That Evening Sun" are fatal and their meanings are profound and to have known that no white man, not the child Quentin, not the adult Quentin, not even Faulkner himself could have read them. In "That Evening Sun" he therefore leaves them to speak for themselves. (47, 48)

Similarly, Craig Werner argues that the Mississippi author's work consistently emphasizes "the need for multiple voicing, especially in regard to racial concerns. Faulkner clearly realizes that no individual voice can express anything other than a partial racial truth" (718). The ambiguity and incompleteness of "That Evening Sun" maximize the potential for multi-voiced responses, regardless of the necessarily limited perspectives of any single white narrator, white author, or white reader.

If white misunderstanding of black lives is a recurring theme in Faulkner's fiction, it is also significant to African American music. In 1939, folklorist Lawrence Gellert published these unambiguous lyrics from "Me and My Captain," a song he had heard performed by an unnamed African American musician:

> Got one mind for white folks to see,
> 'Nother for what I know is me;
> He don't know, he don't know my mind. (5)[51]

At least one African American writer of Faulkner's era voiced a parallel philosophy. In *Mules and Men* (1935), Zora Neale Hurston observes that the "white man is always trying to know into somebody else's business. All right, I'll set something outside the door of my mind for him to play with and handle. He can read my writing but he sho' can't read my mind" (3). Ten years later, Richard Wright put it more bluntly still when he recalled how "the safety of my life in the South depended upon how well I concealed from all whites what I felt" (*Black Boy* 204).

The historical gulf between black and white lives continues to be a thorny issue in contemporary blues studies precisely because it is a field in which predominantly white, cosmopolitan, middle-class scholars in the present strive to understand pre–World War II recordings by lower-class, rural black people. There is no better illustration of this problem than the persistent myths surrounding Robert Johnson. Too often, overly imaginative fans have been inclined to characterize Johnson as a mysterious and tortured genius, or even to attribute his musical accomplishments to a pact made with Satan at the crossroads at midnight. Such portrayals of Johnson as an inexplicable—even supernatural—miracle of musical greatness wrench him out of his context, neglecting his place within African American culture and the historical development of the blues, while projecting the romantic obsessions of Euro-Americans onto black music. As Pearson and McCulloch conclude, "the best-known images of Johnson were the product of ignorance and economics: white ignorance about African American traditions and culture and the desire to find ways to market Johnson's music to new generations of mostly white blues fans long after Johnson's death" (3).[52]

Just as Gellert and other folklorists collected and recorded blues lyrics, "That Evening Sun" is rooted in Faulkner's close observation of—and even involvement with—southern black people, but it also suggests that white understanding of African American culture is necessarily circumscribed by the very assumptions, hierarchies, and barriers erected by white society. In terms of the blues tradition, Nancy has "one mind for white folks to see" and "'[n]other for what I know is me." Although Quentin appears to view Nancy as a tragic victim, he may only be seeing what she intends "white folks to see." In fact, even though Nancy has many reasons to despair, she may also be secretly triumphant.

If the sudden discontinuation of Quentin's narrative seems to establish Nancy's fate as the primary mystery in "That Evening Sun," the story's greatest obscurities actually concern Jesus. Quentin obviously knows whether Nancy survived the night, and it is precisely his withholding of this information that turns what is not a mystery for him into a mystery for the reader. The question of Nancy's life and death is, in other words, a red herring, serving to divert attention from other gaps in the narrative. Although Quentin must be aware of what happened to Nancy, it is unlikely that he knows why Jesus abruptly left his partner and Jefferson, where he went, and whether he has actually returned. The tale's abrupt termination allows Quentin to retain control over his narrative and authority over black lives by emphasizing the mystery that he could explain if he chose (Nancy's fate) and eclipsing the one that he cannot (Jesus's fate). Quentin, then, sets up his tale so that it focuses upon a terrified, despairing, and pathetic black female victim, while correspondingly de-emphasizing the story of an outspoken African American "badman." In Quentin's narrative, Jesus is merely an aggressor against black women, whereas Faulkner's tale implies that he is a militant rebel against white supremacy.

Since Quentin's narrative teasingly raises, but then diverts from—and even represses—the mysteries surrounding Jesus, the single, brief scene in which that character appears directly is of great significance:

> When Dilsey [the regular Compson cook] was sick in her cabin and Nancy was cooking for us, we could see her apron swelling out; that was before father told Jesus to stay away from the house. Jesus was in the kitchen, sitting behind the stove, with his razor scar on his black face like a piece of dirty string. He said it was a watermelon that Nancy had under her dress.
>
> "It never come off of your vine, though," Nancy said.
>
> "Off of what vine?" Caddy said.
>
> "I can cut down the vine it did come off of," Jesus said.
>
> "What makes you want to talk like that before these chillen?" Nancy said. "Whyn't you go on to work? You done et. You want Mr Jason to catch you hanging around his kitchen, talking that way before these chillen?"
>
> "Talking what way?" Caddy said. "What vine?"
>
> "I cant hang around white man's kitchen," Jesus said. "But white man can hang around mine. White man can come in my house, but I cant stop him. When white man want to come in my house, I aint got no house. I cant stop him, but he cant kick me outten it. He cant do that."
>
> Dilsey was still sick in her cabin. Father told Jesus to stay off our place. (292)

Although Quentin lacks the knowledge necessary to answer other questions about Jesus, the one thing he should be able to explain is why "Father told Jesus to stay off our place," but his narration only hints at the likelihood that the Compson children are the cause of his disappearance. The sudden and provocative jump from Jesus's speech to the bald description of his expulsion implies that Mr. Compson exiles Jesus specifically because of the suggestive nature of the black man's talk in the kitchen before the young white children. Since Mr. Compson is evidently not present during the exchange between Nancy and her partner, somebody must have reported Jesus's words to him. It is hardly feasible that Nancy would betray her lover to her white employer, and the only other people in the scene seem to be the children, any or all of whom could be responsible. The outspoken inquisitiveness of Caddy—the only child who speaks in the scene—is provocative, as is Quentin's studied silence. Although there is no specific confirmation that Jason is present, it is likely that he is among "these chillen," and the story consistently identifies him as being both particularly ugly in his attitudes toward black people as well as a notorious "tattletale" (309). This passage, then, raises crucial questions that critics have hitherto overlooked: which of the children told on Jesus—and what exactly did he, she, or they say to Mr. Compson?

Jesus's words in the kitchen potentially suggest—particularly if garbled by child informants—threats of violence against white men and rape of white women. Caddy may not understand the implications of his outburst, but Jesus clearly states his willingness to kill the unknown father of Nancy's unborn child—and all the available evidence suggests that, whoever he is, this man is probably white. Furthermore, Jesus's complaint that he is not able to "hang around white man's kitchen," even though the white man gets to enter his with impunity, is evidently an angry reference to white male sexual possession of the black female body. As Ken Bennett observes, there is a long tradition in the blues of employing kitchen imagery for the purposes of erotic entendre. He notes, for example, that the kitchen is often used as "a metaphor for a woman's body, as in Robert Johnson's well-known 'sexual blues' song, 'Come on in my kitchen'" (342). Similar examples include Bessie Smith's 1929 "Kitchen Man" ("No one else can touch my ham, I can't do without my kitchen man") and Leroy Carr's 1934 "Bread Baker" ("Because in your kitchen, baby, It's where the good stuff can be found").[53] If Mr. Compson heard a second-hand report of Jesus's words, he might well think that the black man intends to retaliate against invasions of his "kitchen" by violating the "kitchens" of white men.

The statements Jesus makes during his single appearance in the story thus invoke the two deeds most commonly used—or, more accurately, fabricated—by whites as rationales for murdering African American men in the Jim Crow era: violence against white men and sexual violation of white women. Jesus's threat about "cut[ting] down the vine it did come off of," and his complaint about being excluded from the white man's "kitchen" when the white man has full access to his, are precisely the kind of comments that could lead to a brutal lynching in Mississippi in this period. As Neil McMillen notes, "the 'rape complex' brought out the worst in any mob, but black Mississippians charged with violence against white men also met indescribable cruelties" (234). Faulkner's "Dry September" vividly dramatizes a situation in which nothing more than vague hearsay about Will Mayes committing some unspecified but inappropriate act against a white woman stimulates a mob to kill him.[54]

As McMillen notes, furthermore, even a trumped-up charge of attempted rape or murder was not required to rationalize the slaughter of black men in Mississippi: "[T]he record abounds in lynchings for lesser affronts: 'insubordination,' 'talking disrespectfully,' striking a white man, slapping a white boy, writing an 'insulting letter,' a personal debt of fifty cents, an unpaid funeral bill of ten dollars, a $5.50 payroll dispute, organizing sharecroppers, being 'too prosperous,' 'suspected lawlessness,' horse killing, conjuring, and, of course mistaken identity" (236). McMillen emphasizes that the perpetrators of such minor "affronts" were really murdered for perceived "transgressions of caste, the one cause common to nearly all Mississippi lynchings" (236). David Oshinsky similarly notes that the victims of lynching tended to be "young black men who appeared to challenge the racial boundaries that had seemed virtually impregnable only a generation before" (100). As one white citizen of the Magnolia State unashamedly put it in 1908, "When there is a row, we feel like killing a nigger whether he has done anything or not" (qtd. in Williamson, *William Faulkner* 392). In "Dry September," these words resonate in the response of the leader of the lynching to questions about Mayes's guilt: "What the hell difference does it make? Are you going to let the black sons get away with it until one really does it?" (171–72). Just like the male protagonist of "Last Kind Words Blues," Jesus's militant attitude in "That Evening Sun" makes him a walking target in this time and place, but, as the fate of Mayes reminds, the color of his skin alone is danger enough.

It is unsettlingly typical of Faulkner's painfully conflicted racial attitudes that, in between the incisive analysis of racist mob hysteria in "Dry September," published in *Scribner's* in January 1931, and the appearance of "That Evening Sun" in the *American Mercury* in March,[55] the author submitted a corrosive letter to the Memphis *Commercial Appeal* in response to another correspondent's praise of the Association of Southern Women for the Prevention of Lynching. In Polk's pithy summation, the author's letter is "pointless except for its meanspiritedness and mired in racial mythology," with Faulkner asserting "that though he himself holds no brief for lynching, it is nevertheless true that lynching is mostly caused by black lawlessness, usually for raping white women, and that the dispensers of home-made white justice are about as discriminating as the courts, and rather more expeditious" (*Children of the Dark House* 234–35). Just as Quentin knows that Nancy's tale exposes something fundamentally wrong with his society, but represses the implications of the story he tells about her, so could Faulkner imagine and vividly portray Nancy's misery and fear, Jesus's bitter anger, and Mayes's horrifying fate while publicly parroting the most reactionary, irrational, and inhumane racist clichés.[56]

Although racial violence was clearly on Faulkner's mind at the time that he published "That Evening Sun," there is no real evidence that the story's hidden secret and key to its mysteries is that the white people of Jefferson have secretly lynched—or crucified—Jesus. After all, the primary purpose of lynching was to terrorize black people, and, for this reason, many such murders, especially prior to World War II, were ghastly public spectacles.[57] At the very least, racially motivated killings tended to be open secrets since, in order for them to have the desired effect, the black community had to know that they had taken place. In "Dry September," the lynching of Mayes occurs under cover of night at an abandoned brick kiln outside town. Within hours, however, one white man observes the deserted streets of Jefferson with satisfaction: "There's not a Negro on the square. Not one" (181). McMillen cites a similar observation from a local newspaper report concerning the "noticeable absence of negroes on the streets" in the aftermath of a lynching in Vicksburg in 1919 (227).

It would be very unusual in this period for a lynching to be so covert that black and white communities were not aware of it, but there is no indication in "That Evening Sun" that even a rumor about Jesus's violent demise is making its way around Jefferson. To be sure, the lynching of the common-law husband of a family servant is precisely the kind of information from which white adults would likely shield their young children, which could explain Quentin's failure to suspect—or to explicitly acknowledge the possibility of—such an eventuality. In the absence of more compelling textual evidence, however, it would surely stretch the boundaries of even so open-ended a story as "That Evening Sun" to suggest that its dark secret is a literal lynching.

Nonetheless—as "Dry September" and the violent climax of the following year's *Light in August* demonstrate—the murder of black men by white mobs is a recurring theme in Faulkner's fiction of the early 1930s, and several scholars identify an oblique relationship between "That Evening Sun" and lynching. Some of the critics who assume that Jesus kills Nancy even speak of her murder as this very kind of crime. Most explicit is Charles Nilon, who asserts that, like Rider and Mayes, Nancy "may also be considered a lynch victim. Her husband murders her but he is merely the agent of the community" (44). Keith Cartwright operates from a similar assumption about Nancy's fate when he claims that, in "That Evening Sun," "Yoknapatawpha is clearly at a sacrificial crisis of faithlessness calling for a carrier's blood. For now it is Nancy. But it *will* claim Quentin" (89).[58] Finally, Hans Skei notes in his reading of the story how "numerous black characters in Faulkner's fiction share an irrational fear of nature, believing that some hidden force may strike and hurt. . . . [a fear] of something inexplicable and unmentionable which may come out of darkness and night and catch up with one"—a belief which "has a basis in traditional superstition and in general gossip and factual knowledge about members of the black race disappearing and vanishing without a trace" (190, 191). As Dollard's interviews in *Caste and Class in a Southern Town* make clear, what Skei constructs as a superstitious fear of nature is more likely a reasonable terror of white people's willingness to wipe out black humanity.

"That Evening Sun" may not involve a literal lynching, but its situations, language, and imagery continually conjure the specter of white-on-black violence. Faulkner's story, in other words, is about lynching in the same ways that the blues tradition is about lynching: it is not an overt subject, but, as Gussow says of the lyrics of African American musicians, is coded, figurative—even unconscious—subtext (*Seems Like Murder Here* 22).

Lynching haunts "That Evening Sun" from its very first paragraph, when Quentin complains about the local shade trees giving way to "iron poles bearing clusters of bloated and ghostly and bloodless grapes" (289). The narrator's nostalgia for a time when actual trees boasted juicy, blood-red fruit seems innocent enough on the face of it, but his florid language also suggests supernatural phantoms, distended husks, and gory viscera.

Quentin's unsettling imagery thus evokes the bloody body of Nelse Patton hanging from an Oxford telephone pole, as well as the lyrics of Billie Holiday's later song in which

> Southern trees bear a strange fruit
> Blood on the leaves and blood at the root
> Black bodies swinging in the southern breeze
> Strange fruit hanging from the poplar trees.[59]

What is more, if Jesus's language in the kitchen scene reiterates the traditional pretexts for lynching, then the imagery surrounding Nancy throughout the story evokes the means most commonly used to murder African Americans throughout the Jim Crow era: hanging and burning. As McMillen notes, after 1890, the customary "noose increasingly gave way to the faggot. . . . Between 1900 and 1940 at least fifteen blacks died in public burnings, a method described by one newspaper as 'NEGRO BARBEQUES'" (233, 234). In 1929, renowned civil rights campaigner Walter White even gave his study of lynching the stark title, *Rope and Faggot.*

In "That Evening Sun," Nancy performs parodies of conventional white-on-black violence, emulating and undermining the conventional methods of lynching by playing the roles of aggressor and victim simultaneously. At the beginning of the story, she both enacts and thwarts the traditional hanging, saving herself by clinging to the bars of her cell with the same hands that tied her dress into a noose (291–92). As the story progresses, Nancy becomes increasingly associated with heat and fire, culminating in the final sequence in her cabin at night, which is a feverish catalogue of imagery identifying her with burning and combustion. As the children enter the black woman's dwelling, Quentin observes that the "smell of the house was like the lamp and the smell of Nancy was like the wick, like they were waiting for one another to begin to smell." Even though it is "already hot," Nancy builds "a good blaze" in the fireplace. A few moments later, she does not even notice that she has burnt her hand on the hot globe of the lamp until Caddy points it out. Then, Nancy builds the fire up still more, causing Caddy to exclaim, "Look at Nancy putting her hands in the fire." Soon, Nancy is "sitting close to the fire. The lamp was turned up so high it was beginning to smoke." Even her eyes are "filled with red lamplight" (301–6). Describing this relentless pattern of images, Barry Sanders observes, "It is as if Faulkner ignited her cabin or, more specifically, as if Nancy's small world were being totally, literally destroyed. . . . [F]rom her description

Nancy herself seems to be on fire" (71). Although critics tend to read these passages as conjuring hellfire rather than the specter of lynching,[60] the narrative's earlier association of Nancy with hanging suggests that these fiery images allude to racial violence. In the process of twice re-enacting lynching, Nancy symbolically triumphs over it: she hangs and burns herself symbolically, yet still survives, asserting that she, not a white mob, has power over her life and death.

Although critics tend to view Nancy as the potential victim of Jesus rather than of a white lynch mob, there is almost unanimous consent that she *is* victimized, either because she is doomed to a grim fate at the hands of her former lover or because she has entirely succumbed to paranoia. Even though scholars increasingly acknowledge that the point of Faulkner's story is its determinedly inconclusive nature, they still tend to reduce Nancy's alternatives to just two: murder or madness.[61] Nancy's perverse reenactments of lynching—in which she is both active killer and passive victim, doomed subject and subversive agent—suggest that her story is more complicated and open than either Quentin or conventional interpretations allow.

In the eyes of most critics, Nancy not only has no future, no hope, and no agency, but she is also quite incapable of mobilizing language, either as a weapon of resistance or as a means of self-actualization. Hardly anyone questions the idea that Nancy has bought into the dominant culture's assumption that—as she repeatedly puts it—she "ain't nothing but a nigger" (293, 297).[62] Hoping that the Compson children will be inclined to stay with her in her cabin, she seeks to entertain them with an improvised fairytale, but they quickly grow bored. As Skei bluntly puts it, "her storytelling is no good" (189).[63] Even Laurel Bollinger, who claims that Nancy initially is "a powerful figure who threatens to disrupt white male hegemony," concludes that the ending of the story depicts the silencing of this potentially rebellious character and her "loss of authority" (55, 65, 66).[64]

One of the few critics to have found much hope in Nancy's situation interprets her experiences directly in relation to the lyrics of "St. Louis Blues." Carol Gartner argues that, "after its plaintive beginning, the mood [of Handy's song], like that in many woman-based blues, becomes aggressively positive," when the speaker decides to pack her trunk, find her man, and win him back. When there "is nobody left to protect her, Nancy, like the blues singer, must take sole responsibility for herself and confront her fate." In Gartner's reading, "Nancy seems to be a victim. The blues say that she is a survivor." This interpretation is appealing for locating agency within an apparently oppressed and defeated black character, but in Gartner's analysis this potential remains only at the level of possibility. The critic's claim that, by the story's end, Nancy is poised to overcome her "pain and crisis" is closer to wishful thinking about the character's future than a decisive statement about her present.[65] Nonetheless, Gartner's analysis is invaluable for suggesting that Nancy has the capacity to be as strong and independent as the archetypal female blues singers of the era (56, 54, 57).

In fact, Nancy is exactly what Gussow calls a "blues subject," a persona partly formed by the pervasive threat of racial lynching, who has "found ways, more or less covert, of singing back to that ever-hovering threat" (*Seems Like Murder Here* 4). Nancy is not just singing her blues as a way of "bravely facing what she perceives as terrible danger" (Gartner 57), she is doing so in order to work through her grief and to secure the best possible outcome for herself in perilous circumstances. Readers have been so inclined to view Nancy as a victim—whether to psychological disease or domestic violence—that no one seems to have considered that she just might have *invented* her story about Jesus's return, and for entirely rational reasons. Struggling with the loss of her lover, uncertainty over his fate, and the possibility of danger to her own life from vengeful whites against whom the Compsons will evidently offer no real protection, Nancy makes the most of the incredibly limited resources available to her, performing her victimization, just as she subversively performs her own lynching. She ingeniously constructs a narrative that expresses her pain, provides some protection from violence, and even causes her disloyal white employers some measure of the distress they have permitted her to suffer. Her apparent fear and despair are, as Gussow says about the blues, "[f]ar from a helpless capitulation" to the fear of white violence, but instead, "a startlingly creative response to it" (*Seems Like Murder Here* 22). Unorthodox though this reading of Nancy may be, it has the benefit of providing a consistent and comprehensive explanation for the character's motivations and actions throughout "That Evening Sun."

Nancy's public exposure of Stovall's behavior early in the story is the central source of trouble for its black characters, and the remainder of the tale—whether Quentin realizes it or not—concerns the black woman's desperate and inventive efforts to mitigate the consequences of her reckless action. When Nancy's imprudently overt—and apparently impromptu—

rebellion against Jefferson's racial mores puts her life and her partner's safety in jeopardy, she comes to understand that she must develop more circumspect strategies in order to resolve the situation or, at the very least, to survive.

Nancy's mistake within the racially oppressive climate of Jim Crow–era Jefferson is to speak out, just once, about the bitterness she feels toward white people. Quentin's narrative does not clarify precisely why Nancy—who apparently is no stranger to Jefferson's jail—has been arrested on this particular occasion, although Faulkner's text implies several possibilities, including disorderly behavior, drunkenness, cocaine use, and prostitution.[66] It hardly matters which; what is important is that, as the arresting marshal leads her past Stovall, something inside Nancy snaps: she is being taken to jail yet again while a self-righteous and hypocritical "cashier in the bank and a deacon in the Baptist church" gets to freely exploit black women precisely because he is white and male (291). Nancy is sufficiently angry or high, or both, at this moment, to do "something no Southern Negro would dare do in Mississippi at the turn of the century" (Lee 49): rail openly against the double standards of the Jefferson community by boldly demanding of Stovall, "When you going to pay me, white man? It's been three times now since you paid me a cent" (291). It is no wonder that Nancy's response to Stovall's kicking her to the ground is to laugh; the banker has provided a vivid confirmation of the very point she is making: Stovall not only gets to use a black woman sexually with impunity; he also gets to violently assault her without punishment while she goes to jail.[67]

Nancy's intense anger soon gives way to regret and a painful realization of the potentially deadly consequences of her rash act, just as the female speaker of "Last Kind Words Blues" comes to feel remorse for her "wild" ways. After spending the night fiercely "singing and yelling" in her cell (291), Nancy lapses into silence when sunrise approaches. If, later in the story, she expresses a fear of the dark, the occasion for her despair in jail is the hard reality of dawn, which must bring Nancy to the sober realization that her reckless outburst at Stovall will almost certainly bring down merciless retribution from the white community.

The memoir of one of Faulkner's Oxford contemporaries suggests that Nancy is in grave danger precisely because of the potential consequences of her accusations for Stovall. In his account of old times in "Faulkner country," John Cullen—who, as a young man, was instrumental in the capture of Nelse Patton—tells of a hypocritical Oxford mayor who presented himself as "a great crusader for law and decency," but who was seen one night "going into the cabin of a high-brown Negro woman" (108, 109). Cullen and his friends "converged around the cabin, pushed the door open, and captured his honor in his long-johns as he leaped from the bed of the Negro woman. . . . He begged and pleaded to ears that ignored his pleas for mercy. . . . He was escorted to the outskirts of Oxford, given a few dabs of warm tar and chicken feathers, and told to keep going. He was a sight to remember, dressed in his long-johns with his big bloated body and small legs decorated with tar and chicken feathers" (109).[68] The humorous tone in which Cullen explains how sexual relations between a white man and African American woman earned the former a humiliating and painful punishment indicates just how casually repressive violence could be dispensed in this culture, even when the victim was a white male. As a deacon in the Baptist church, Stovall has as much of a reputation for moral rectitude as the hapless mayor of Oxford in Cullen's reminiscence, and thus has reason to fear harsh retribution following the public exposure of his regular use of a black prostitute. There is a pressing need, then, for this "iconic figure of white male authority" to divert the disciplinary impulses of the local populace away from himself and onto someone else (Bollinger 58), whether Nancy herself, or her razor-scarred and razor-toting lover, who has a sinister reputation even before his veiled threats against whites in the Compson kitchen.

Fearing that she may become the victim of a lynching—or that Jesus or someone else could be lynched in her stead—Nancy bravely tries to take control of the situation while still in jail. If a member of the black community must die because of her actions, she will choose who it will be and she will be the agent of that death, not a white mob. Although Nancy attempts to lynch herself by hanging, her suicide attempt is thwarted, partly by the vigilance of the jailer and partly by her own irrepressible desire to live.

After her release from jail, Nancy's fears appear to subside for a time, until she feels so secure that her anger at the white world begins to surface again. Initially, she seems to assume that her failed suicide attempt and the subsequent beating she received at the hands of the jailer should be sufficient to placate local white anger at her actions. When, as a result of Dilsey's sickness, Nancy temporarily becomes the Compson cook and finds refuge in the white family's kitchen, she feels even safer. When Jesus makes a pointed comment about her pregnancy, Nancy recklessly goads him with a reminder that the baby is not his, as if she blames him for his failure to protect her from white men or wants him to be angry at the progenitor of her unborn child.

Jesus's response to Nancy's bitterness—a barely veiled threat of murder against the presumably white father—instantly reminds the black woman of the dangers they both are in, and she quickly cautions her partner, but it is too late: one or all of the Compson children tell their father some version of what Jesus said. In danger of becoming known for permitting his black workers to engage in unruly conduct and transgressions of their ascribed station—precisely the kind of behavior that lynching was designed to repress—Mr. Compson quickly banishes Jesus.

After his exile, Jesus must understand that he is in danger of becoming the community scapegoat. He is, after all, not only Nancy's husband, but probably her pimp as well, and it is likely that white patriarchal society will hold him accountable for Nancy's behavior as well as his own. Furthermore, he no longer has the protection that even a nominal connection to a white family might provide. Like Pontius Pilate, Mr. Compson has washed his hands of Jesus. In this light, Jesus's sudden departure from Jefferson is a shrewd act of self-preservation. "He quit me," Nancy tells the Compsons. "Done gone to Memphis, I reckon. Dodging them city *po*-lice for a while, I reckon" (293)—which is presumably less hazardous than dodging the agents of Judge Lynch in Yoknapatawpha County.

Nancy is left to carry the burden in Jesus's absence, and all the fears that she endured in prison now return with a vengeance. Like the speaker of "Last Kind Words Blues," she does not know for certain where her partner has gone, and, given the prevalence of white-on-black violence in her culture, she cannot help but dwell upon the possibility of her man meeting—or already having met—a violent end, whether at the hands of urban police or small-town mobs. What is more, Nancy must be aware that she remains in danger of becoming a victim of racial violence herself. Jesus's expulsion from the Compson place and his disappearance from town may not be sufficient to nullify the anger felt by the white men of the community after Nancy's exposure of Stovall's behavior, especially if Jesus's threats in the kitchen should become common knowledge. The town may still demand blood, and—although it was statistically much rarer for women to fall victim to lynching than men—after Jesus's disappearance, Nancy is the most viable target.

In these circumstances, Nancy has desperate need for protection, and Mr. Compson is the obvious candidate for a patron whose social prominence might provide a buffer between her and white mob violence. Oshinsky cites a real-life black Mississippian's acknowledgment that "every Negro got to have his white man, his boss, to look after him when he got in trouble with the white world" (127). Nancy's problem is that she cannot very well directly ask Mr. Compson to protect her from vengeful whites: African Americans could not safely broach the subject of racist violence with Caucasian men. Faulkner, in fact, later summarized "That Evening Sun" as the story of a "Negro woman who had given devotion to the white family" but who "knew that when the crisis of her need came, the white family wouldn't be there" (*Faulkner in the University* 21). Nancy's ingenious solution to her complicated problem is to encode her fear of white violence in an imaginative recreation of Jesus as an implacable and unstoppable murderer. She tells Mr. Compson of a rumor that "Jesus is back" and of her conviction that he aims to kill her (293), so that the white patriarch will be inclined to assuage her fears by walking her home at night. In the process, she turns the racist discourse of the dominant culture to her advantage, securing Mr. Compson's protection by invoking white stereotypes of the black male as razor-murderer and rapist.

Mr. Compson responds to Nancy's narrative with a story of his own that is equally dependent upon stereotypical representations of black life. When he speculates that Jesus is "probably in St. Louis now," and has "[p]robably got another wife by now" (295), he is doing nothing less than constructing Nancy's life in terms of the lyrics of Handy's song, in which a "Saint Louis woman wid her diamon' rings / Pulls dat man [of mine] roun' by her apron strings" (Handy 143). Kuyk and his collaborators rightly note that Nancy's situation is "much more complex" than that of the protagonist of "St. Louis Blues" (37). In fact, the Compson employee is living a scenario rather more like that in "Last Kind Words Blues."

Like Wiley's protagonist, Nancy must cope with her partner being, if not literally dead, then at the very least dead to her. It must begin to dawn on her that Jesus cannot ever safely return to Jefferson. Nancy's response to this situation is twofold: like the speaker of "Last Kind Words Blues," she resigns herself to death as a way of imagining reconciliation with her lover. Simultaneously, she invents a fantastic scenario in which Jesus can and does return to Jefferson—not just as a potential murderer, but as a supernatural force of retributive violence more than equal to any white mob.

Critics have always puzzled over the unlikely name of Nancy's partner, often characterizing it as a blunt, even heavy-handed, irony. In such readings, the author's eccentric choice of nomenclature is little more than an occasion for such determinedly provocative moments as Jason's notorious exclamation, "Jesus is a nigger" (297), or a strategy for emphasizing the profoundly unchristian attitudes of the Compsons and the white community of Jefferson.[69] For the version of the story published in the *American Mercury,* editor H. L. Mencken vetoed the use of the name "Jesus" for the character precisely because he considered that it "would make most readers believe we were trying to be naughty in a somewhat strained manner" (qtd. in Manglaviti 651). Faulkner assented to change the name to "Jubah" for Mencken's readers, but stubbornly restored "Jesus" for the story's appearance in *These Thirteen,* an indication of how important the author considered the religious implications of the character's name.

The founder of Christianity, of course, was a scapegoat, the victim of a corrupt community, before he rose from the dead to console his followers. If Faulkner's Jesus has not been lynched, he has passed from Jefferson, and it is Nancy who uses the power of narrative to bring him back: she is the evangelist who conflates the resurrection of Jesus and the Second Coming into a single event in which her man returns from the dead as a scourge to the white sinners of Jefferson. As Coburn puts it, Nancy's "Jesus is an avenging Christ as one imbued with a distorted Calvinism might see Him" (208). In this respect, "That Evening Sun" is no less an ironic story about resurrection than Faulkner's primary book about the Compsons, *The Sound and the Fury,* which—despite its Easter weekend setting—suggests that the dissolution of the family is permanent and irreversible.

Nancy uses her tale about Jesus to encourage the Compsons to provide her with at least a little protection, and to exact a small measure of revenge by making the white family share in her terror. She spreads the Good News and some very bad news simultaneously, constructing a horror story in which her former lover is both avenging Christ and sadistic Devil. Within southern African American oral tradition, after all, these are not such contradictory labels. In a chapter on "Bad Man Ballads" in their 1926 study of black folklore, Howard W. Odum and Guy B. Johnson note that musical paeans to such legendary rogues as Railroad Bill and Stagolee are curiously similar to oral tales celebrating the founder of Christianity: "One preacher even described Christ as a man who would 'stand no foolin' wid. . . . Lord, he could pop lion's head off jes' lak he wus fryin'-size chicken an' could take piece o' mountain top and throw it across the world'" (47–48).

Although he does not decapitate lions or relocate mountains, Nancy's

Jesus is a frightening supernatural being who not only can conceal himself and leave sinister symbols in cabins before spiriting them away, but is also able to penetrate a white household without detection. If, earlier in the story, the real Jesus complains that white men habitually violate his kitchen when he cannot enter theirs, Nancy constructs a scenario in which a ghostly Jesus haunts the Compson kitchen by night. The resulting consternation engulfs the household, so that Mr. Compson must prowl the house with his gun while Mrs. Compson demands that her husband call the police—as Nancy gets to sleep, for one night at least, in the children's room. "Wont no nigger stop him," Nancy tells the family ominously, and Mr. Compson suggests that whites are equally powerless when he asks helplessly, "What could the [police] officers do?" and "If Nancy hasn't seen him, how could the officers find him?" The black woman's triumph is that, by the end of the narrative, it is not just Jason who is a "Scairy cat" or "scairder than a nigger" (296–97, 298, 299, 293, 309).

The limp fairytale that Nancy improvises in her cabin for the children about a queen crossing a ditch may be a bust, but it is little more than a front for the more important story that she tells: an all-too-believable ghost story that disrupts the Compson household and has a profound effect upon the whole family, especially the impressionable young children. As May Brown observes, "That Evening Sun" is "the story of the child's initiation into the fear, injustice, and death which characterize the adult world" (347)[70]—and it is specifically Nancy who is the source of that painful initiation. Toward the end of the story, Jason complains to Nancy, "You hurt me. You put smoke in my eyes" (306). In fact, Nancy has brought psychological distress to all of the children and she has clouded the vision of the whole family with her nightmarish tale of the avenging Jesus. Listening to Nancy prompts the seven-year-old Caddy to begin asking inconvenient and penetrating questions about adult sexuality and violence, such as her inquiries about Nancy's pregnancy as well as about the black woman's jealous threats against any other person with whom Jesus might sleep. Caddy is even inspired to begin questioning inequities of social power, asking, "Why is Nancy afraid of Jesus?" and "Are you afraid of father, mother?" (292, 295, 299).[71] Furthermore, although young Quentin says little throughout the story, the very existence of his mature memoir about Nancy's experience suggests that it affected him deeply.

It is not just Jesus who has something of the Devil about him; critics conventionally read Nancy's declaration that she is "hellborn" as an indication of her helpless despair (298),[72] but in light of the terror and disruption that she brings to the Compson household, this self-description also has the air of a slyly vengeful boast. Significantly, Nancy makes this claim directly in response to Jason's insulting question, "Are you a nigger, Nancy?" (298). She answers this affront both by rejecting a white child's authority to defame her and by asserting her command of devilish powers as a form of resistance. Such disparaging racial epithets as Jason habitually dispenses were, of course, the first step toward the dehumanization of black individuals that was necessary for white mobs to torture and murder them without mercy or remorse. In response to a culture that demonizes black people and frequently burns them alive, Nancy chooses to characterize herself as an actual demon who has brought a little hellfire of her own to the Compsons' lives. In a community in which a hypocritical Baptist deacon uses and abuses a black prostitute and in which a man named Jesus is banished, Nancy invokes the powers of Hell as a way of asserting her agency. This strategy aligns Nancy with several blues singers who identified themselves with dark magic and Satanic might in order to advertise their potency, most notably the strutting Peetie Wheatstraw, who claimed to be both "the Devil's Son-in-Law" and "the High Sheriff of Hell."[73]

This is not to say that Nancy's despair is not real, but rather that it is only one part of her story. There is no question that she feels profoundly isolated and deeply depressed after suffering physical assault, incarceration, and abandonment, as well as surviving a suicide attempt, and having to fear continuously for her life. Simultaneously, however, Nancy proves herself a woman of great courage and cunning. She exposes Stovall for his abuse and hypocrisy, is willing to try to destroy herself rather than fall victim to others, and weaves an elaborate story about her own victimization in an attempt to manipulate the Compsons into protecting her—while also punishing them by making her problems their problems too.

The two sides of Nancy in the story—mournful victim and vengeful badwoman—are like the contrasting personae on either side of Geeshie Wiley's most enduring record.[74] On "Last Kind Words Blues," the lonely speaker is so desolate as to welcome the prospect of death, just as Nancy finally tells the Compsons, "When yawl go home, I gone" (308). On the record's flipside, however, in "Skinny Leg Blues," Wiley takes on the voice of a very different character who declares, "I'm gonna cut your throat, babe, gon' look down in your face. . . . I'm gonna let some lonesome graveyard be your restin' place." This "quintessential jook joint woman, a violent, dangerous black widow" (Cordeiro 31), resembles Nancy's darker side. Indeed, the threat that Wiley's speaker utters is reminiscent of Nancy's promise of what she would do if she ever were to find Jesus with another woman: "I'd stand there right over them, and every time he wropped her, I'd cut that arm off. I'd cut his head off and I'd slit her belly" (295).

The white people in "That Evening Sun" are willing to allow Nancy to suffer because they view her only in terms of crude stereotypes—such as cocaine-addicted "nigger" prostitute—but Nancy is able to exploit such stereotypes to achieve a sly, partial victory. Quentin and Mr. Compson may sympathize with Nancy's plight, but the status to which they reduce her in their thoughts and speech is no less one-dimensional than the status to which Stovall and the jailer reduce her through violence. Neither the white characters nor the story's white narrator can see the complex human behind the stereotypes, even if Quentin tries much harder than Stovall and even his father to do so.

Nor can any of the white people in the story begin to imagine that Nancy has the capacity to outwit them—that she has "one mind for white folks to see, / 'Nother for what I know is me." When Mr. Compson attempts to dismiss Nancy's fear of impending death by telling her, "You'll be the first thing I'll see in the kitchen tomorrow morning," Nancy's response to this platitude is to satirize the white man's failure to look past his assumptions about a black woman's character: "You'll see what you'll see, I reckon. . . . But it will take the Lord to say what that will be" (308). These words echo Clara Smith's 1925 blues song "It Takes the Lawd (To Tell What's On My Mind)": God knows who Nancy is behind her mask, but Mr. Compson evidently does not.

The abrupt termination of the narrative suggests that Quentin is less troubled by Nancy's plight than by his inability to make sense of it. He tells Nancy's story because he knows it is important, but he cannot quite bring himself to acknowledge why it is important, as his withholding of any resolution demonstrates. He is reluctant to complete the tale—reluctant to provide a conclusion in which Nancy does not fall prey to the razor of her "bad nigger" lover and thus does not prove to be an inevitable victim, which would complicate, rather than fulfill, his stereotypical expectations of black women being victims and black men being aggressors. Just as Quentin's narrative obscures how little he knows about the black badman, so does it divert from the possibility that Nancy could be a potent badwoman. The young Quentin's final statement in "That Evening Sun"—"Who will do our washing now, Father?" (309)—voices an assumption on the part of the character who is also the story's narrator that Nancy—defined solely by her function as paid caretaker to whites—will not survive the night, when so many details in the story suggest that both Jesus's return to Jefferson and his desire to kill Nancy are unlikely scenarios. Quentin is simply unable to accept that Nancy could be a victor of sorts, and he is even unwilling to tell a story about her as a survivor. Just as the tall convict in "Old Man" is unable to comprehend or emulate the guitarist's subversive agency, and just as his imitation of blackness operates in terms of incarceration and passivity, so is Quentin so concerned to project racial stereotypes upon Nancy that he cannot appreciate her ingenuity or learn from her ability to talk her way out of a tight place.

Quentin prefers the black woman to be a victim because that is what he feels himself to be. Where Nancy attempts suicide in a desperate last-ditch attempt to take control of a hopeless situation, Quentin successfully kills himself in *The Sound and the Fury* because he is unable to reconcile his unattainable ideals with the real world. Quentin chooses to die for a myth about the South focused upon his sister's lost innocence, whereas Nancy employs all the resources at her disposal in order to go on living, despite the loss of her man and despite her sexual exploitation at the hands of white men. Where Quentin cannot restore his beloved Caddy's innocence, even in his imagination, Nancy, like the speaker of "Last Kind Words Blues," imagines reconciliation with her lover so vividly that his presence seems real. Despite its eerie elements, Quentin's narrative does not fulfill the most basic requirements of the ghost story, while Nancy's tale of terror is so effective that it unsettles the lives of all the Compsons. Quentin's narrative about Nancy is uncomprehending and incomplete, but Nancy's storytelling—like that of Wiley—is a small triumph in the face of immense adversity. As Werner says, "the Afro-American tradition has been shaped by the demand for realistic survival techniques while Quentin's southern heritage has frequently encouraged romantic mythmaking which pays little attention to the facts" (726).

If Quentin's narrative in "That Evening Sun" is a confused and blinkered expression of a bankrupt heritage, Faulkner's story gets surprisingly close to the African American tradition for a white writer of his time and place, regardless of his inherited ideologies. Where the rebelliousness of the guitarist in 1939's "Old Man" is implicit rather than overt, Nancy's resistance in 1931's "That Evening Sun" is sufficiently ambiguous to be as much a matter of speculation or potential as fact. The enigmatic nature of both characters suggests, however, Faulkner's gradually evolving understanding throughout the 1930s that any black person might possess "one mind for white folks to see / 'Nother for what I know is me."

4

ALL MY SHRIMPS WAS DEAD AND GONE

MALE SEXUAL DYSFUNCTION IN *SANCTUARY* AND "DEAD SHRIMP BLUES"

The country blues and Faulkner's fiction were often notorious for indelicate subject matter, such as their unsparing portraits of visceral violence, and, in particular, their earthy—even coarse—depictions of sexuality. Folklorist Howard W. Odum—who researched African American music in and around Oxford, Mississippi[1]—declared that the "repulsive themes" and absence of "pure love emotions" in many blues songs made it quite impossible for their lyrics to appear in a reputable forum ("Folk-Song and Folk-Poetry" 276, 284).[2] Equally, Phil "Moon" Mullen—the editor of the Oxford *Eagle*—concluded from the works of the town's resident novelist that being "a successful author of the modern school" merely required "a good memory of all the dirty stories told in your teens," adding that some writers make sex "humorous and interesting; Faulkner makes it disgusting" (qtd. in Blotner, *Biography* 798).[3]

Rather than being merely vulgar and salacious, Faulkner's fiction and many blues songs demonstrate a serious concern with the conflict between natural and liberating erotic self-expression, on one hand, and the social repression of human sexuality—and thus individuality—on the other. Angela Davis argues that the "historical African-American vision of individual sexual love" in the blues "linked it inextricably with possibilities of social freedom in the economic and political realms" (10), just as Harry and Charlotte's passionate affair in "The Wild Palms" asserts their liberation from social strictures. If Faulkner's fiction and the blues elevate the self-fulfillment of healthy eroticism as an ideal, they more commonly depict harsh realities in which sexual disharmony and romantic failure symbolize submission and conformity to social orthodoxies. As Paul Garon points out, blues songs are often less about unfettered sexuality than about how an oppressive and puritanical society frustrates "the promise of sensuous human joy and sublime love" (67).[4] Similarly, in Faulkner's novels and stories, erotic dysfunction and sexual repression embody larger cultural disorders, social restraints, and historical traumas. In *The Sound and the Fury,* Quentin has inherited such diseased ideologies about white female purity that he obsesses over his sister's sexuality to the point that he claims to have had incestuous relations with her. Ike McCaslin's compulsive guilt over his ancestor's sexual exploitation of black people in *Go Down, Moses* fuels the failure of his marriage and his retreat into isolation. Joe Christmas's fanatical brooding about his ambiguous racial identity and Joanna Burden's mania about racial injustice in *Light in August* lead the two into a sordid carnal affair that ends in murder. Finally, in the Snopes trilogy, the grasping Flem dominates Jefferson economically and politically, but is an impotent cuckold.[5]

Although sexual dysfunction is a recurrent issue in Faulkner's fiction and the blues, it is particularly prominent in *Sanctuary* (1931) and Robert Johnson's "Dead Shrimp Blues" (1937). Horace Benbow in Faulkner's novel and Johnson's protagonist similarly attempt to cope with sexual failure by telling stories in which lifeless shrimp embody male impotence. These coded and circumlocutory confessions withhold and suppress as much as they divulge and expose, for, even as Horace and Johnson's speaker seek to relinquish the pose of taciturn invulnerability that traditionally defines masculinity, each reflexively camouflages his sexual vulnerabilities. Both attempt to transcend the limiting gender ideologies, erotic discourses, and even racial codes of their era, while—paradoxically—concealing their efforts to develop more functional forms of masculine carnal expression.

Johnson's speaker uses his story as a way of coming to terms with—and even overcoming—a temporary sexual crisis, whereas Horace's obscure reverie rationalizes impotence as an inevitable response to inherent human and social corruption. Attempting to function in a culture that constructs the black male as an aggressive sexual predator, Horace and other white male characters in *Sanctuary* can only perform caricatures of virile black sexuality or lapse into passive impotence. Equally, in a society that defines white women as either pure, virginal chalices or insatiable erotic monsters, the men of Yoknapatawpha are caught between imposing rigid codes of sexual morality on women or demeaning them as promiscuous prostitutes. Paralleling the tall convict's clueless imitation of the African American guitarist in the later "Old Man," Horace's initial response to the threat of impotence is to indulge in stereotypical fantasies about the freedom and potency of black men. Even Horace's later attempt to fashion his erotic dysfunction into a confessional narrative is no more functional or liberating than the convict's rationalization of his incarceration. The speaker of "Dead Shrimp Blues," in contrast, abandons the customary male role of virile lady-killer for a very different kind of voice and persona. His narrative reconfigures masculinity in terms of vulnerability and interdependence, and provides a basis for the song's protagonist to reclaim his sexual functionality and capacity for erotic pleasure. Where "Dead Shrimp Blues" presents a world in which sexual failure is little more than a short-term mishap, and eroticism an inexhaustible source of joyous and comic affirmation, Horace's monologue constructs sex as the unavoidable source of man's tragic ruin and thwarted self-fulfillment.

Although he was barely known outside the Delta in his day, no prewar Mississippi blues artist is more famous—or is ever likely to be more famous—than Robert Johnson. Critics, novelists, illustrators, and filmmakers continue to recount, embellish, and reimagine his legend to the point that even those who have little or no familiarity with Johnson's music know of the brooding and solitary guitarist who allegedly entered into a satanic pact at the crossroads at midnight.[6] That the "King of the Delta Blues Singers" died young by poisoning—apparently after he made the fatal mistake of seducing the wrong woman—only adds to his dark myth. For those inclined to hear the blues as the soundtrack of existential dread, Johnson's songs—including "Me and the Devil Blues" and "Hellhound on My Trail"—are the quintessence of the form.

The truth about Johnson has little to do with any Faustian drama down on the Delta. The fundamental problem with the fanciful, hyperbolic, and stubbornly enduring legends about the tormented and doomed artist who channeled his emotional agony into timeless songs of heartbreaking intensity is that they eclipse what really matters about Johnson: his musical craft, the dazzling breadth of his work, and his specific contribution to a vibrant musical culture and tradition. William Barlow's characterization of Johnson as a "key transitional figure," a bridge "between the music's rural beginnings and its modern urban manifestations," gets much closer to the bluesman's significance than any Mephistophelean fable (45).[7]

If, in some of his songs, Johnson is very much an avatar of blues despair, Elijah Wald emphasizes that he also enjoyed performing a range of music including cowboy ballads, Bing Crosby pop hits, and even polkas. Allegedly, one of the most beloved songs of the man who wrote the eerie "Hellhound on My Trail" was the Tin Pan Alley standard, "Yes, Sir, That's My Baby" (Wald, *Escaping the Delta* 118). In this respect, the country blues musician shared something in common with Faulkner, who identified it as "his favorite song" as well (Blotner, *Biography* 536).

Throughout his two recording sessions, Johnson constantly leapt between brilliance and bathos, desolation and delight, high seriousness and low comedy. He began the second day of his November 1936 recording date with the strutting hokum of "They're Red Hot," but soon was keening the haunting "Cross Road Blues," in which the speaker seems isolated and paralyzed as the world turns to darkness around him. Similarly, the second day of Johnson's June 1937 session saw the performer segue from passive submission to evil in "Me and the Devil Blues" to the immodest and energetic self-assertion of "Stop Breakin' Down Blues." To define Johnson as an implacable merchant of misery is to ignore a great deal of his recorded output. As Wald notes, Johnson could "communicate zest for life and searing misery with equal ease and power" (*Escaping the Delta* 275).

The significant tonal and thematic distinctions between—and even within—Johnson's songs on the single subject of sexual dysfunction provide an instructive demonstration of the variety of the bluesman's work. Given that the blues is a genre commonly associated with extravagant braggadocio, the existence of no fewer than three numbers about male impotence in Johnson's small repertoire of twenty-nine recorded songs—more than 10 percent of his studio output—is revealing in itself. The singer's treatment of the topic, furthermore, ranges from morose solemnity to outright ribaldry, sometimes within a single verse. Greil Marcus describes "Stones in My Passway" (1937)—the most abstract and despondent of these songs—as "a two-minute image of doom that has the power to make doom a fact" (*Mystery Train* 38). Stephen Calt, however, undermines the gravity of this reading in his study of blues slang when he suggests that "passway," in this particular instance, is a "figurative route to *pussy*" (179). From Marcus's perspective, "Phonograph Blues" (recorded in 1936)[8]—a song in which sexual failure is likened to a broken record player—is a harrowed confession by the speaker that carnal sins have made him impotent (*Mystery Train* 26). Plaintive though Johnson's performance is, the song also includes extravagantly racy lines about a couple no longer being able to play "it" on the sofa because of the man's rusty needle. Similarly, "Dead Shrimp Blues" is a pained lament about its speaker's wretched condition that also brazenly traffics in such outrageous innuendo as "someone [is] fishin' in my pond / Catchin' my goggle-eyed perches and they barbecuin' the bone."[9] In Johnson's diverse oeuvre, crude comic entendres coexist with haunting tragedies, whether about sexual failure, existential misery, or vengeful hellhounds.

Faulkner aficionados are fortunate that they do not have to devote their time to dismantling groundless rumors about the author selling his soul to Satan in return for the ability to write *The Sound and the Fury*; nonetheless, the popular image of Faulkner is sometimes almost as one-dimensional and reductive as that of Johnson. For the general reader, Faulkner's reputation as an icon of forbiddingly difficult, grotesque, tragic, and avant-garde modernism often overshadows the actual contents of his books. When Oprah Winfrey boldly devoted her TV book club to a whole "Summer of Faulkner" in 2005, the responses of some participants were all too predictable. "I didn't care about these characters even after having read the same page three times to try to figure out what was happening," one reader complained about *As I Lay Dying,* adding, "The title of the book suited my mood because most of the time I spent reading it did feel like I was dying." Another reader curtly dismissed Faulkner's fiction as merely "disturbing and just plain weird" (qtd. in Hamblin, "Oprah's 'Summer of Faulkner'" n.p.).

Although Faulkner is indisputably one of the great modernist tragedians and a classic exponent of gloomy and often obscure southern gothic, his canon—like Johnson's—is also distinguished by its breadth and diversity. In addition to his complex, experimental, and portentous novels about the South, Faulkner also produced dozens of accessible, entertaining, and often comic short stories for such popular periodicals as the *Saturday Evening Post* and *Harper's*. As the author's *Collected Stories* amply demonstrates, these tales concern a dazzling variety of topics, locations, themes, and moods, including the troubles of Hollywood screenwriters, the antics of stunt pilots, romantic tiffs between sailors, mythic Native American history, the outrageous manipulations of horse traders, the rigors of World War I, and the slapstick perils of fixing church roofs.[10] Just as clichés about

Faustian terror and morbid tragedy cannot adequately encompass the content of Johnson's songs, Faulkner's fiction involves a great deal more than impenetrable gothic-modernist nihilism.

More than any other work, *Sanctuary* encapsulates the author's complex diversity of moods and styles. On one hand, it *is* an unmistakably labyrinthine and non-linear Faulknerian tragedy, but, on the other, is an unashamedly—even gleefully—lurid tale of crime and punishment involving gangsters, bootlegging, sexual violence, murder, comic episodes in a whorehouse, political corruption, and a melodramatic courtroom denouement. *Sanctuary,* in short, is Faulkner's self-conscious engagement with populist genre fiction, an unpredictable mash-up of elitist literary experimentation and pulp sensationalism.[11] The author even claimed that the book sprang from his notion of "what a person in Mississippi would believe to be current trends," observing that the magazine store in his hometown carried "nothing that has not either a woman in her underclothes or someone shooting someone else with a pistol on the cover" (qtd. in Blotner, *Biography* 605, 610). Such images would have made—and, in later paperback editions, sometimes did make—appropriate cover illustrations for the salacious novel that Leslie Fiedler describes as "a potpourri of almost *all* the popular genres of the late 1920s" ("Pop Goes the Faulkner" 88).[12]

In addition to its flirtations with the themes and conventions of genre fiction, *Sanctuary*—as Erich Nunn's invaluable analysis of the book highlights—includes numerous references to popular music. Joseph Blotner claims that Faulkner wore out three copies of Gershwin's "Rhapsody in Blue" while writing the novel, which the author supposedly played repeatedly to "set the rhythm and jazzy tone" of the narrative (*Biography* 754).[13] *Sanctuary* also invokes the blues for a little gallows humor: in one scene, an orchestra leader proposes playing Strauss's *Blue Danube* at a deceased gangster's memorial service, a suggestion that both confuses and offends the proprietor of the venue, who remonstrates, "No, no; dont play no blues, I tell you. . . . There's a dead man in that bier" (244). No critic, however, has ever explored, or even acknowledged, the uncanny parallels between Horace's drunken monologue about dripping, lifeless shrimp and "Dead Shrimp Blues."

Johnson's song is vexingly paradoxical: it is a confession that is candid to the point of crudity while also being evasive to the point of incoherence; it is tragically despairing, yet uproariously comic. Bhesham Sharma praises the song for Johnson's "fearlessness in speaking frankly about his weaknesses and failures as a lover," but he is rare among critics for acknowledging that the titular "dead shrimp" suggests the "lifelessness and limpness" of a non-functioning phallus (n.p.). Despite the apparently overt nature of its imagery, Johnson's recording is a slippery and elusive text, as much an eel as a shrimp.

Although common usage of "shrimp" as a derisive slang term for the penis is primarily a late twentieth-century phenomenon,[14] Johnson was not the only prewar country blues performer to utilize the marine crustacean's potential for phallic innuendo. The speaker of "Shrimp Man" (1928)—a lewd hokum song by "Red Hot Ol' Mose" (Moses Mason)—tells a potential female customer, "Shrimp is the thing you love best," and promises to deliver his wares at any hour of the day or night: "If you['re] going to bed, you can call / I'll poke them through the window, that is all." Even this virile character, however, eventually falls victim to sexual exhaustion and failure, confessing that "[m]y shrimp [is] sick: it don't make no alarm."[15] When the protagonist of Johnson's "Dead Shrimp Blues" observes that he has "served my best bait" and complains that his lover has rejected him after the demise of his shrimp, what he is actually talking about should be evident even to the most innocent listener. As the 1930s edition of *Webster's Dictionary* notes, the shrimp derives its name from "its shriveled appearance" via the Anglo-Saxon "*scrimman,*" which means "to dry up, [to] wither. . . . [t]o contract" (2325).[16]

Despite the apparently transparent meaning of "dead shrimp," critics continue to puzzle over the precise implications of Johnson's song. Wald, for example, dismisses "Dead Shrimp Blues" as a minor piece of work, and suggests that "the most interesting thing" about it is not its explicitness, but, to the contrary, "the obscurity of its lyric." He seems to sidestep the most obvious implication of the song's central image when he observes that "it is hard to see how exactly the dead shrimps he [the speaker] invokes relate to the woman who has left him for another man," and concludes—somewhat abstractly—that "shrimp were used as bait, and symbolize what he had that his girlfriend wanted, but now she has had her fill and gone her way, so his bait is dead" (*Escaping the Delta* 154, 155).[17]

It is not that Wald's reading squeamishly evades the evident fact that the speaker's erectile dysfunction is the primary cause of his lover's desertion, for the song continually obfuscates and elides the manifest meaning of "dead shrimp," even as it shamelessly exploits the possibilities of this graphic symbol. In fact, Johnson complicates the central image in the very first line of the song: "I woke up this mornin' and all my shrimps was dead and gone." The use of the ungrammatical plural rather than the singular makes no sense since the speaker presumably has only one penis. Even as the lyric thus flirts with the obvious idea that "dead shrimp" refers to a flaccid and non-functioning phallus, it disavows that very possibility. It is little wonder that Wald ultimately dismisses Johnson's lyric as essentially incoherent, concluding, "Whatever the meaning, it is not one of his greatest pieces" (*Escaping the Delta* 155).

The obscurity and incoherence of "Dead Shrimp Blues" are, in fact, crucial to its basic theme. The entire song is rooted in opposing impulses: it is a boldly public declaration of the mortifying and emasculating condition of male sexual dysfunction, but the speaker also resists exposing himself to ridicule by undermining and denying the self-evident implications of his complaint. The protagonist's desire to safeguard and control his painful secret even as he yearns to confess it has an analogue in the songwriter's melding of comedy and tragedy, as well as his attempts to exploit sexually explicit material while cannily avoiding censorship.

Although "Dead Shrimp Blues" is a plaintive and somber song, its innuendo and wordplay are consistently comic and as playful as the whimsically ribald "Shrimp Man." Even though the protagonist is heartbroken by his partner's rejection, his summation of this state of affairs is undeniably funny: "At the hole where I used to fish, baby, you've got me posted out."[18] The song's characterization of sexual activity as "Catchin' my goggle-eyed perches" is even reminiscent of the clown's infamous description of "Groping for trouts in a peculiar river" in Shakespeare's *Measure for Measure* (I.ii.65).[19] In fact, in his study of erotic language in Early Modern English literature, Gordon Williams identifies several Renaissance works that use fishing and seafood imagery for sexual comedy. Prominent among them is George Rogers's 1661 treatise on cuckoldry, *The Horn Exalted,* which speaks of adultery as "*angling* in other *mens ponds*" (qtd. 495), a phrase that is almost exactly replicated in Johnson's complaint that "someone is fishin' in my pond."

If "Dead Shrimp Blues" indulges in a tradition of bawdily comic seafood imagery that dates back at least as far as Shakespeare, the song's beleaguered speaker also resembles the emasculated male protagonists of modernist American fiction—not just the shrimp-haunted Horace in Faulkner's novel, but also the impotent Jake Barnes in Ernest Hemingway's *The Sun*

Also Rises (1926). Like Johnson's narrator, the hero of Hemingway's novel suffers intense emotional agony because of his sexual incapacity—the cruel consequence of a war wound—and he attempts to cope with his situation by characterizing it as bitter comedy. Early in the narrative, Jake tells his would-be lover, Brett Ashley, that his condition "is supposed to be funny." He later repeats this thought to himself as he privately surveys his battle-ravaged body in a mirror, remembering the ridiculously overblown speech given by an Italian colonel in tribute to the debilitating injury he suffered on "a joke front" in World War I: "You, a foreigner . . . have given more than your life." Jake's sardonic reverie ends in tears of despair, however, as he acknowledges the harsh reality that he can never be with Brett sexually (34, 38, 39).

If Jake cannot adequately deal with his impotence through silent reflection, he comes closest to achieving control over it when engaged in fast-paced, eclectic, and esoteric repartee with his friend, Bill Gorton—who may also be impotent—during the pair's idyllic fishing trip at Burguete (117–30). "That's the sort of thing that can't be spoken of," Bill says jocularly of Jake's wound in this safe context. "That's what you ought to work up into a mystery. Like Henry [James]'s bicycle."[20] Bill then tells Jake with uncharacteristic openness, "[Y]ou're a hell of a good guy and I'm fonder of you than anybody on earth." Within a few pages, the two men are suggestively comparing the sizes of the trout that each has caught (120, 121, 125). Comic badinage thus provides a way for these usually stoic and reserved men to discuss male sexual frailty and to express camaraderie.[21] As Jackson Benson suggests, Hemingway's novel illustrates Martin Grotjahn's notion that "laughter is based on previously mastered anxiety" (57). It is strangely appropriate, then, that Ralph Ellison once identified Hemingway's work as being "imbued with a spirit . . . very close to the feeling of the blues" (140).

Just as Jake masters anxiety by constructing his condition as both comedy and mystery, the speaker of "Dead Shrimp Blues" frankly expresses his anguish while asserting control over his condition by coding it as an ironic and enigmatic joke. He talks around his impotence, mobilizing sly innuendo, addressing it elusively and allusively, reveling in the power of language to simultaneously acknowledge and neutralize his disability. The thinly veiled predicament of the song's speaker is, in its way, no less serious than those of "poor Charley" in "High Water Everywhere," the bereft speaker of Wiley's "Last Kind Words Blues," or the terrified Nancy in "That Evening Sun." Like all of these characters, the narrator of "Dead

Shrimp Blues" seeks to wrest victory from the jaws of defeat by affirming his discursive potency in the face of threatening or paralyzing forces.

Having guardedly confessed his condition, the protagonist of Johnson's song is able to take steps to overcome it. The lyrics emphasize that the speaker's impotence is a recent and, in all likelihood, temporary condition: "I woke up this mornin' and all my shrimps was dead and gone. . . . I got dead shrimps here." Instead of consigning his relationship to the past tense, the speaker continues to plead with his lover about her response to his situation, even complaining of her impatience when he observes, "Everything I do, you got your mouth stuck out."[22] He is evidently dismayed that the woman's response to his appeals for forbearance and assistance is dismissive rather than cooperative. His candid acknowledgment of his vulnerabilities, and his implied efforts to satisfy his partner sexually other than through intercourse ("Everything I do"), brings only her contempt ("you got your mouth stuck out").

The shift to the past tense in the song's final line ultimately suggests that, even if the protagonist may not win back this particular woman, he has successfully resolved his physical problem: "Babe, I couldn't do nothin' until I got myself unwound." In this context, "unwound" has multiple connotations. In relation to the imagery that dominates the song, it is evidently another form of phallic symbolism, describing the man's need to unwind a tangled fishing line before he is able to resume catching "goggle-eyed perches." The term also implies that the speaker was too anxious—or "wound-up"—to perform sexually, and has had to calm himself to regain his potency. He has achieved this equilibrium by constructing a story about his impotence—by unfolding or unwinding a narrative about his situation. That these multiple meanings are couched in punning wordplay further emphasizes the triumph of ingenious comedy over disabling tragedy in the song. His partner may not take him back, but the speaker has regained both the capacity and the inclination to become a lover again.

This reading suggests significant parallels between "Dead Shrimp Blues" and Johnson's other songs about impotence. Wald's analysis of "Stones in My Passway" concedes that the first three verses create a mood of "loneliness and frustration," but then the speaker "recalls that at one time he had a good relationship, and reaches out for a lifeline—if his girlfriend will just take him in again, everything could be all right. He shakes off his despondency, and the final verse fits the quicker pace of the guitar. He is on the road again, and hope springs eternal" (*Escaping the Delta* 169–70). In the final verse of this song, Johnson's protagonist seems to have regained both his virility and his sense of humor, observing that he now has "three legs" to carry him home. "Dead Shrimp Blues" similarly involves a protagonist who divulges and narrates his failings in order to help restore and reassert his potency.

The singer-songwriter displays the same mastery over discourse as his embattled character, confidently mobilizing a series of ingeniously salty entendres that are sufficiently obscure for him to circumvent record-company censorship while addressing intimate sexual problems with unusual frankness. Several of Johnson's recordings languished in the vaults for decades, possibly because—at least in some instances—of salacious content. Paul Oliver suggests that, if Johnson's language "was obscure in *Stones in My Passway,* [it] was more obvious in *Phonograph Blues*; the Vocalion company chose to censor it and it was unissued" (*Screening the Blues* 188). Equally, one of Johnson's most vibrant songs, "Traveling Riverside Blues," may have failed to make it onto a phonograph disc because of the protagonist's bawdy suggestion that his lover squeeze his "lemon" until juice spurts all over his leg—a line that later enjoyed a new lease of life courtesy of the rock band Led Zeppelin.[23] Johnson organized "Dead Shrimp Blues" around one of the most graphic images of his career, while evading expurgation through obfuscatory treatment of it, much like the strategies employed by Hemingway. Just as blues critics often overlook the phallic imagery of Johnson's song, anyone who regularly teaches *The Sun Also Rises* knows that the book's references to Jake's condition are sufficiently coded that today's undergraduate readers sometimes do not understand the nature of the character's wound or realize that Jake is impotent. As Kenneth Lynn says of one suggestive scene in *The Sun Also Rises,* "There is no way to be utterly positive, of course, about Hemingway's meaning, for in order to keep [editor] Max Perkins's blue pencil still, an artful vagueness was essential" (324).

Johnson proudly displays his potency as an artist while dramatizing the mortifying impotence of the song's narrator in "Dead Shrimp Blues." He boldly takes on the persona of an impotent individual—a problem that most men would be reluctant to acknowledge publicly—while distancing himself from such a condition through his lyrical and musical mastery. He also makes mortifying sexual failure an occasion for comedy and triumph. Johnson thus invokes sympathy, ridicule, and admiration all at once, performing a masculine identity that is simultaneously openly vulnerable and frankly erotic. He thoroughly fulfills the oft-repeated—and sung—advice of Bill in *The Sun Also Rises* to "Give them Irony and Give them Pity" (118–19).

In between the publication of Hemingway's novel and Johnson's recording of his blues about erotic dysfunction,[24] Faulkner employed shrimp as an ambiguous symbol for male sexual insecurity in *Sanctuary*. Like Johnson, furthermore, Faulkner sought to dramatize lurid topics without altogether transgressing the boundaries of what was publicly permissible—even if he was not always successful in this endeavor. According to the author, editor Harrison Smith rejected the first version of *Sanctuary* because he was convinced that "[w]e'd both be in jail" if it were published (*Sanctuary* 323). The author radically revised and altered the manuscript before its eventual appearance in February 1931. Nowadays, critical studies of *Sanctuary* tend to consider both versions, for, as Noel Polk puts it, the two together "form a single text that is far more significant than either of the versions taken singly" (*Children of the Dark House* 43).[25]

Sanctuary concerns Horace's attempts to discover the truth about mysterious events at the decaying Old Frenchman place, ten miles outside Jefferson, which culminated in the murder of the childlike Tommy. The authorities arrest local moonshiner Lee Goodwin for the killing, but Horace—in his capacity as Goodwin's lawyer—is convinced that a blank-eyed Memphis gangster named Popeye is responsible for the crime. Horace's investigation leads to Temple Drake—the vulnerable young daughter of an eminent judge—who was also on the property at the time of the murder, having been abandoned there by her drunken escort. Temple privately confesses to Horace that Popeye not only killed Tommy but also viciously raped her before installing her in a Memphis brothel. Horace's naïve hopes that Temple's public testimony will result in Goodwin's acquittal are dashed when—following a series of Byzantine political machinations—a Memphis lawyer and the district attorney arrange for the traumatized debutante to incriminate the moonshiner instead. A vicious mob subsequently lynches Goodwin for acts that he did not commit.

Even in its revised form—which is barely less outrageous than the original—the fervid subject matter of *Sanctuary* proved sufficiently appealing to readers that it outsold Faulkner's two preceding books in just three weeks (Blotner, *Biography* 685). Alexander Woollcott's sensationalist radio review may have been instrumental to the novel's commercial success: the master of the Algonquin Round Table described Faulkner's work as an "extraordinary" work of "grandeur," while also warning that "[t]here are plenty of intelligent and sensible people whom the book would make really ill. For compared with 'Sanctuary,' the later Emile Zola's most earnest quests into the squalor of life seem like merry sunlit pages out of 'Little Women'" (qtd. in Blotner, *Biography* 686, 99n).

Woollcott's florid hyperbole obscures the fact that *Sanctuary* is incredibly vague in its treatment of the graphic act of sexual violence around which the plot turns. Just like "Dead Shrimp Blues," Faulkner's most notorious novel continually obfuscates its sensationalist subject matter even while reveling in it. As Florence Dore notes, *Sanctuary* "is vexing in its structural duality: its hyperbolic indecency, on the one hand, and its unspoken quality on the other" (70). The narrative ultimately reveals that the supposedly virile Popeye is congenitally incapable of performing sexually, and used a corncob to perpetrate his sadistic rape of Temple. Although this episode made Faulkner infamous as "the corncob man," the book evades Popeye's horrific act even as it exploits it. As Robert Dale Parker says, even though "it is the key event of the novel, it is simply skipped over, present only as an absence, a gap" (59).[26]

Faulkner's novel is no less ambiguous in its treatment of male sexual dysfunction than in its depiction of rape. Parker describes *Sanctuary* as "a novel about impotent men" (71–72), but there is only one demonstrably impotent character in the story, and the narrative is indirect even about that. In one of the more explicit passages concerning Popeye's condition, the friends of Miss Reba—the madam of the Memphis brothel at which Temple is imprisoned—discuss the gangster's private behavior. "I heard two years ago he wasn't no good that way," one observes blandly (255), while another speculates that Popeye "went off and got fixed up with one of these glands, these monkey glands, and it quit on him" (257). Even the account of Popeye's childhood in the book's final chapter only hints at the inherited syphilis that is the reason why the character could "never be a man, properly speaking," as a doctor puts it (308). Ultimately, Popeye's impotence is quite evident, but the narrative reveals his disability very gradually and in euphemistic language.

If the novel is indirect in its depiction of Popeye's condition, it is yet more ambiguous about the sexual inadequacy of its other male characters. Even though the words "impotent" and "impotence" do not appear anywhere in the published version of *Sanctuary,*[27] male anxiety, paralysis, and failure are, as Parker suggests, central to the book. It is clear that many of the men of Yoknapatawpha County are painfully ineffectual and spiritually emasculated, but recurrent patterns of suggestive imagery imply—without ever stating—their erotic, as well as social and psychological, incapacity. Amy Glaves's analysis of the novel, for example, highlights numerous passages that identify men with gelded horses, thus suggesting their "inability to sustain and beget life" (n.p.).

Numerous critics have used the word "impotent" to describe Horace in *Sanctuary,* but, true to the ambiguities of Faulkner's novel, such characterizations tend to be figurative, vague, speculative, or rooted in assumption instead of specific or concrete textual evidence. Danna Voth describes Horace as "intellectually impotent" (114), and John Irwin similarly speaks of the character's "spiritual impotence" (206),[28] both implying that Horace is effete and enervated rather than sexually incapable. In fact, the most popular word that scholars employ to categorize the lawyer is "Prufrockian," a reference to T. S. Eliot's famous character. This term suggests an inability to speak in social settings, alienation from the modern world, paralyzing inaction, and sexual anxiety—all forms of "impotence" in a broad sense—but not specifically erectile dysfunction.[29] Equally, when Philip Cohen asserts that Horace is "a perverse but impotent voyeur" (75), it is unclear whether he means that Horace is literally incapable of sexual performance or is referring to the lawyer's general discomfort with female sexuality. Those critics who are most convinced of, and most explicit about, Horace's physical incapacity tend to couch their claims in highly speculative terms. Dore explains the lawyer's torturous account of his reasons for fleeing his family in a striking, but doubly qualified manner: "The failure of Horace's narrative *appears* to *imply* a failure of his phallus" (80, my emphasis). As Parker astutely sums up the character and the uncertainty surrounding him, "[t]he sense of Horace's impotence, be it literal or figurative, is admittedly general and impressionistic but for all that seems no less apparent" (155n).[30]

None of the passages in *Sanctuary* that vaguely imply Horace's sexual impotence is conclusive in and of itself, but multiple insinuations throughout the narrative create a cumulative impression of a man who is suffering from erectile dysfunction. The novel begins with Horace—"a man given to much talk and not much else"—stumbling upon the Old Frenchman place and into an immediate standoff with the hostile Popeye. When the latter produces a phallic gun from his pocket, the former can conjure only a book from his. Later, the lawyer confesses of himself—ostensibly describing his lack of courage—"The machinery is all here but it wont run," an observation that echoes the speaker's complaint in "Phonograph Blues" about the failure of his rusty needles (13, 4–5, 17).

In fact, two particular passages in *Sanctuary* are reminiscent of songs by Johnson that relate travel to the sexual act. The bluesman's first record release was the salacious "Terraplane Blues," which slyly—but relentlessly—likens driving an automobile to intercourse.[31] At one point, the speaker begs the song's addressee not to block the road, a plea repeated in the later "Stones in My Passway," which utilizes the same tune as its predecessor, but for a story in which formidable obstacles impede the path to physical love.[32] In Faulkner's novel, meanwhile, the impotent Popeye has deliberately blocked the driveway to the Old Frenchman place with a felled tree (6, 20), which Glaves reads as a symbol of phallic dysfunction (n.p.). Such connotations also pervade the passage in the 1929 *Sanctuary* in which Horace thinks of the "treeless lawn" at the house he has built for his wife, Belle—who has a previous marriage behind her—and muses, "Perhaps it's trees that affect her so. . . . Perhaps she lived among too many trees before" (64). The published version of *Sanctuary,* furthermore, includes a vague echo of "Terraplane Blues," when Horace broods about his inability "to drive a motor car" at the same moment that he mopes about his "lost hammer" (120). Like numerous blues songs, the pages of Faulkner's novel are rife with descriptors of male ineffectuality that are—simultaneously—sexually suggestive and blandly amorphous, much like the "artful vagueness" that Lynn finds in Hemingway's fiction (324).

The blues tradition, then, provides a way of cutting through the ambiguity surrounding Horace's condition. In light of such songs as "Shrimp Man" and "Dead Shrimp Blues," Horace's repeated references to shrimp in his convoluted explanations of how he came to leave his wife and stepdaughter suggest that his problems are specifically phallic, as well as emotional and psychological. Allusions to multiple connotations of "shrimp" in Faulkner's novel specifically imply that Horace was once a philanderer—whose sexual virility enabled him to lure his wife away from her previous husband—but who now struggles with erectile dysfunction. Horace shares the insecurity, desperation, and physical incapacity of the protagonist of "Dead Shrimp Blues," and, like the speaker of Johnson's song, seeks to unburden himself of his painful secret, even as he feels impelled to conceal it, in an obscure story about defunct and inanimate seafood.

At the beginning of the novel, Horace, having fled his wife, rambles aimlessly around the Mississippi Delta before happening upon the Old Frenchman place, where he becomes equally rambling in his speech as he seeks to rationalize his behavior while under the influence of the local moonshine. He first describes to Popeye, Goodwin, and Tommy an argument he had with Little Belle, his stepdaughter, regarding her frequent assignations with young men, which ended with her dismissing him as a "shrimp." Horace then tells Ruby Lamar, Goodwin's lover, about his hatred for the weekly task of carrying home boxes of shrimp for his wife's dinner. Having hit upon a symbol that apparently encapsulates the fundamental nature of his situation without being overly explicit, Horace compulsively reiterates his shrimp tale throughout the novel, telling it to his sister, Narcissa, and her imperious mother-in-law, Miss Jenny (14, 108, 119).

Horace's monologue to Ruby—the most extensive passage about shrimp in the novel—has its basis in a passage Faulkner originally wrote for *Flags in the Dust* in 1927, but which did not make it into *Sartoris,* the published abridgment of that novel. The fact that Faulkner recycled the material several years later suggests its importance to the author and his conception of Horace. In *Sanctuary,* the lawyer confesses to Ruby that that he left his wife specifically "[b]ecause she ate shrimp," and then elaborates upon this incoherent explanation by describing his regular errand of ferrying packages of dripping shrimp for his family: "You see, it was Friday, and I thought how at noon I'd go to the station and get the box of shrimp off the train and walk home with it. . . . I have done it for ten years, since we were married. And I dont like to smell shrimp. . . . All the way home it drips and drips, until after a while I follow myself to the station and stand aside and watch Horace Benbow take that box off the train and start home with it, changing hands every hundred steps, and I following him, thinking Here lies Horace Benbow in a fading series of small stinking spots on a Mississippi sidewalk" (17).

While acknowledging the evident suggestiveness of Horace's strange confession, critics have struggled to explain its precise meanings, just as blues scholars wrestle with the cryptic "Dead Shrimp Blues." Michel Gresset, for example, notes only that the lawyer's confession is "full of non sequiturs and confusion," and that it is "a stream-of-consciousness monologue in which the lucid voice of intelligence is upset by the most irrational components of the character's (one is tempted to say the patient's) psychic life" (158).[33]

At most, scholars tend to read the passage as an expression of Horace's general revulsion toward women and sex. Kevin Railey suggests that the lawyer's "odd overreaction to the dripping of the shrimp seems to indicate an aversion to getting his hands wet, here associated with Belle and indirectly to the foulness of her [Delta] homeland and her sexuality" (82). Edwin Arnold and Dawn Trouard similarly observe that "Horace's disgust with shrimp is a metaphor for his disgust with his wife Belle and female sexuality," and that the passage alludes to "the misogynist joke comparing the smell of fish and female genitalia" (28).[34] Such crude sexist humor is certainly reminiscent of the lyrics of blues songs, including Peetie Wheatstraw's "I Want Some Seafood" (1936) and Blind Boy Fuller's "What's That Smells Like Fish?" (1938).

As the blues tradition demonstrates, however, shrimp can refer to male, as well as female, genitalia,[35] and Horace's tale comes across not only as an expression of his discomfort with women's bodies, but also—like "Dead Shrimp Blues"—as a veiled confession of physical sexual dysfunction. *Flags in the Dust* situates Horace's weekly shrimp errand on a Tuesday (851, 852), but *Sanctuary* changes the day to Friday, thus making the passage part of the novel's system of allusions to Pagan and Christian mythologies.[36] Although critical readings frequently cite the Catholic tradition of eating fish on Friday,[37] folklore also commonly associates that day with sexual relations—particularly within marriage—after Freya, the Norse goddess of love, for whom it may be named, and Venus, the source of the Roman designation of Friday as *Dies Veneris* (Couzens 133).[38] Some sources, in fact, suggest that ancient Romans ate fish on Fridays in honor of Venus (W. Cobb 419). For Horace, the day of Venus, Freya, and marital love is a day of dread, as he heads home toward his wife's loving arms and the carnal demands that he apparently cannot fulfill. The dripping shrimp is a pathetic parody of penile ejaculation, a symbolically weak and premature climax that occurs before Horace reaches his wife's bed, where he will be unable to perform. The lawyer is not merely repelled by female sexuality, but also disgusted at his inability to satisfy the erotic needs of a woman who likes to eat shrimp—or consume the phallus—voraciously.[39]

In addition to their echoes of the phallic innuendo of Johnson's song, Horace's obscure complaints have other sexual connotations, "shrimp" having served as a colloquial term for "prostitute" since at least the seventeenth century.[40] The speaker of Nathaniel Whiting's 1637 poem *The Pleasing History of Albino and Bellama* claims that he avoids the company of pimps and refuses to waste his money on "light-teale shrimpes" (475). Although dictionaries of American slang do not provide any conclusive evidence that this meaning of "shrimp" was common in Mississippi during the 1920s and 1930s, Wald notes of "Dead Shrimp Blues" that the "usual blues scholar gloss is to explain that 'shrimp' was slang for prostitute" (*Escaping the Delta* 154).[41] Given his literary interests, Faulkner is likely to have been familiar with the connotation.

The notion that "shrimp" can signify both a shriveled phallus and a prostitute certainly illuminates Miss Jenny's pointed comment later in the narrative regarding Horace's flirtatious interactions with Ruby. The southern grand dame describes Goodwin's partner to the lawyer as "one woman you know that dont know anything about that shrimp" (119). If Ruby does not understand the significance of Horace's shrimp tale—if she is the one woman who does not comprehend that the lawyer is impotent—then she might be the only woman sufficiently misguided to be interested in him sexually. Miss Jenny's sharp words also suggest that, if Ruby may not understand anything about Horace's shrimp, she knows everything about *being* a shrimp, or prostitute. Horace evidently has had no qualms about sharing his intuitions concerning Ruby's past with the women of his family, since Narcissa bluntly characterizes Ruby as "a woman you said yourself was a street-walker" (117).[42]

Horace's report to the denizens of the Old Frenchman place of the argument he had with his stepdaughter also invokes several sexual connotations of "shrimp" simultaneously. The lawyer tells of how Little Belle, in response to her stepfather's insinuations about her promiscuity—specifically regarding the men she habitually meets when traveling on the railroad—declared, "You're a fine one to talk about finding things on the train! You're a fine one! . . . Shrimp! Shrimp!" (14). Critics typically gloss this description of Horace in terms of the conventional slang for a diminutive or puny person.[43] As Arnold and Trouard acknowledge, Horace is not physically small or weak, but Little Belle's language "challenges his vaunted courage, drawing attention instead to his weakness of character and, by implication, his questionable masculinity since he is fetcher for her mother's whims" (25). For all its accuracy, such a gloss does not adequately explain why Horace is "a fine one" to be lecturing anyone about sexual morality. If, however, "shrimp" in this context implies both phallic dysfunction and prostitution, then Little Belle's outburst makes much more sense, even if the girl may not be conscious of these implications herself.

Horace has no right to question his stepdaughter's relations with men, since he is a "shrimp," in the sense of "prostitute," not because he is a literal sex worker, but because of his former promiscuity and sexual incontinence. In *Flags in the Dust,* set a decade earlier, Horace has an affair with Little Belle's mother when she is married to another man, as well as a brief fling with the girl's aunt around the same time.[44] The lawyer's first name, furthermore, is a virtual homophone for "whores," and his sister's nickname for him in *Flags in the Dust,* "Horry," equally suggests "whore-y" (664, 675, 680, 798–801). It is in keeping with Faulkner's treatment of gender and sexual anxiety that Horace, even at his most sexually active, is not a masculine "stud," but a "whore" or "shrimp," pejorative terms traditionally applied to women.

Furthermore, while Little Belle's reference to "finding things on the train" obviously alludes in her case to the young men that she has met on public transportation, when she turns it around as an accusation against Horace, it becomes part of an ongoing pattern of language in the novel likening train travel to sexual intercourse. Later in the narrative, Miss Reba berates Senator Clarence Snopes for making himself at home in her brothel without paying for custom: "Look here, mister, folks what uses this waiting-room has got to get on the train now and then" (209). In many blues lyrics, of course, "to flag a train" similarly means to "accost another sexually" (Calt 92–93).[45] In another scene, Horace overhears two young men on a train speaking crudely of the sexual availability of a female acquaintance, observing that she has "traveled a thousand miles without a ticket" (170). In other words, the youths suggest that the woman has freely ridden a train-like phallus many times.[46] Regardless of what Little Belle knows or understands about Horace's history with her mother or any other women, her statement about her stepfather's being "a fine one to talk about finding things on the train" echoes this innuendo, suggesting that Horace acquired his wife through purely sexual activities: he "found" a married woman with his "train," or he stepped out of the waiting room and onto her "train," and was then obliged to elope with her.

If Little Belle's accusations emphasize Horace's history as a philanderer, then the girl's evident contempt for her stepfather simultaneously signals his increasing sexual irrelevance. The ultimate implication of the exchange between the two is that Horace no longer possesses the virility that once enabled him to steal the elder Belle from her former husband. Horace was a shrimp—a promiscuous playboy or "prostitute"—but he is now a shrimp, a weak and effete man, who is, furthermore, troubled by his shrimp, his limp and non-functioning penis.

The multiple meanings of "shrimp" construct Horace as a paradoxical figure: a sexually dysfunctional would-be lothario or impotent Don Juan. Every woman in the novel awakens something in him: not only has he stolen another man's wife, but he also flirts with Ruby as soon as he meets her, is fixated upon his sister, and seems as aroused as he is troubled by his stepdaughter's burgeoning sexuality. He desperately seeks an object of desire that is sufficiently novel, exotic, or even dangerous to arouse him and make him sexually functional again—a moonshiner's moll, his sister, his stepdaughter. Yet, Horace's obsession with essentially unavailable women reveals his profound reluctance to become sexually involved. Although Ruby assumes that Horace expects to sleep with her, she remains fiercely loyal to Goodwin; Little Belle sees her aging stepfather as "just Horace," an individual who is irrelevant to her sexual world; and Narcissa is cold and remote, barely available to eligible men, never mind her own brother (275–76, 13). Horace is obsessed with the idea of female sexuality, even as he recoils from the reality of it, and constantly seeks company with women to whom he will never actually have to prove himself sexually.[47] Caught between simultaneous attraction and revulsion, Horace is reminiscent of Gordon, the sculptor in Faulkner's second novel, *Mosquitoes* (1927), who describes his statue of a woman's torso as "my feminine ideal: a virgin with no legs to leave me, no arms to hold me, no head to talk to me" (275).

Sanctuary is a scathing portrait of a world in which Horace's assumptions about women and his attitudes toward sex are pervasive, from the aggressive innuendo of the male youths on the train to Popeye's brutal sexual assault of Temple. As Linda Dunleavy points out, the novel's "horror lies less in its depiction of a brutal rape and more in its representation of a social system that casts women as sexual objects, thereby inviting violence against them" (180). It is not a misogynistic novel—as some early commentators took it to be[48]—but a novel *about* misogyny and its contexts and consequences. Faulkner's narrative interrogates the diseased and dysfunctional ways in which patriarchal societies condition men to construct and respond to female sexuality.[49]

Specifically, *Sanctuary* is about male fear of the mythic female: erotically insatiable, habitually unfaithful, and inherently uncontrollable. After he rapes Temple with the corncob and imprisons her in Miss Reba's brothel,

Popeye arranges for a fellow gangster to have sex with his captive while he watches. Despite Popeye's tight psychological grip over Temple, the degraded girl's irrational desire for the potent Red soon consumes her, making her "wild as a young mare," ultimately emboldening her to reject her rapist and to disdain his supposed power. She exclaims to Popeye that Red is "a better man than you are! . . . You're not even a man! . . . You, a man, a bold bad man, when you cant even—When you had to bring a real man in to—" (258, 231). In retribution, Popeye kills Red, penetrating his head with a phallic bullet, but his authority over Temple is permanently broken.

Although Miss Reba claims that a "woman that wants to fool with more than one man at a time is a fool" (254), the men of Faulkner's narrative are convinced—like Popeye—that no woman can be satisfied with just one lover. Explaining his abandonment of Belle, Horace observes that, "[w]hen you marry your own wife, you start off from scratch. . . . . . . maybe scratching. When you marry somebody else's wife, you start off maybe ten years behind, from somebody else's scratch and scratching." Exhausted and dejected from trying to catch up after ten years of "scratching," Horace just wants "a hill to lie on for a while," safe from the endless flow of femininity (16, ellipses in original).[50] In the original 1929 *Sanctuary,* Horace even goes so far as to ask Belle bluntly, "Isn't one man at a time enough for you?" (17). Equally, Gowan Stevens jealously accuses Temple of thinking that she "can play around all week with any badger-trimmed hick that owns a ford, and fool me on Saturday" (38). Even the minor male characters in the novel obsess about female licentiousness and infidelity. Early in the narrative, a truck driver is impatient to get going because "I got a woman waiting for me." His associate's automatic response is that she must be "[w]aiting on her back" (21), implying that the woman is enjoying relations with another lover while her partner is absent.

The male sense of self in Faulkner's novel is predicated upon the bachelor's freedom to pursue multiple women—as is the case with Gowan, who dates Temple and Narcissa simultaneously—whereas the reality of marriage or a long-term relationship brings to the surface a man's sense of erotic inadequacy and his fear of sexual rivals. In *Sanctuary,* men desire women, attempt to seduce them, and seek to legitimize their possession of them—sexual and otherwise—within the institution of marriage, or, at least, an approximation of it. Marriage, however, requires a man to embrace monogamy and cease the cycle of seduction and promiscuity. No longer free to chase women indiscriminately, while feeling incapable of satisfying what they view as the insatiability of a single female partner, the male characters—exemplified by Horace—are rendered impotent, or, rather, render themselves impotent. In the 1929 *Sanctuary,* Horace complains that "any woman makes a better mistress than she does a wife" (66), while the published version encapsulates the issue in pithy wordplay concerning the dilapidation of the Old Frenchman place: "nowhere was any sign of husbandry" (41). In such a culture, eroticism is not an avenue to freedom or self-fulfillment but a joyless aspect of repressive gender politics. *Sanctuary* thus invokes the patriarchal world described eloquently by Shakespeare more than three hundred years earlier in *Othello,* in which Emilia observes: "'Tis not a year or two shows us a man: / They are all but stomachs, and we are all but food: They eat us hungerly, and when they are full / They belch us" (III.4, 109–12).

Sanctuary is not only about how men construct women in patriarchal culture, but also about how men are conditioned to construct themselves. As Paula Pinto Elyseu Mesquita observes, *Sanctuary* depicts a world in which "white males too are oppressed, in the sense that a model of identity (hegemonic masculinity) is also forced upon them, leaving little or no space for individual development" (159). In such a culture, males are caught between two available sexual identities: the potent and rapacious seducer or the weak and impotent husband. Faulkner's men see themselves as one stereotype or the other—as Popeye's rigid and ruthless corncob or Horace's pathetic and flaccid shrimp—and are unable to imagine viable alternatives. They respond to female sexuality by fleeing it in terror, like Horace, or aggressively seeking to dominate it, like Popeye or the preening salesman who observes of Temple toward the end of the story, "She was some baby. Jeez. I wouldn't have used no cob" (294).

Regardless of their differing responses to women, the haplessly impotent Horace is no less misogynist than the impotently violent Popeye, and no less complicit in the horrors that consume Yoknapatawpha County. Critics habitually observe that the gangster's graphic assault of Temple is an overt expression of the same lustful objectification of, and antipathy toward, women that the repressed lawyer awkwardly articulates.[51] Rebecca Keane-Temple speaks for many when she describes Popeye as "a mirror, reflecting and acting out [Horace's] own desires" (447).

It is not simply that Popeye mirrors Horace; in fact, the lawyer's view of women anticipates, informs, and potentially even inspires the gangster's most monstrous and misogynist acts. Polk theorizes that Horace's "darkest fantasies" are "projected outward into the grotesque shapes of those characters from the Memphis underworld" (*Children of the Dark House* 43–44), an invaluable psychological reading that draws attention to a literal facet of the text: the terrible things that Popeye does in *Sanctuary* are manifestations and parodies of—even responses to and reactions against—Horace's drunken account of his physical impotence, fear of female sexuality, and frustration with marriage. In one of the very first pieces of scholarship on *Sanctuary*—published just three years after the novel—Lawrence S. Kubie observes that a man can "handle his sense of powerlessness in one of several ways. In the first place, he can people the whole world with other impotent figures, spreading his own sense of infirmity to include everyone, and thus reducing his feeling of painful humiliation. . . . Or he can turn with his rage against the sources of his humiliation and imagine them overwhelmed with disaster" (30).[52] Popeye may or may not understand the nature of Horace's ramblings about his family life or overhear the lawyer's shrimp story, but the narrative evidently projects both Horace's impotence and rage against women into the world in the grotesque form of the Memphis gangster. Although Horace plays detective in his quest for the truth, the real solution to the mystery—like the story of Oedipus—is that the investigator himself is the guilty party, since Popeye is merely the monster that the lawyer's attitudes toward women and female sexuality have created.

Popeye's behavior when Temple arrives at the Old Frenchman place is nothing less than a grim pastiche of Horace's acquisition of Belle from her husband in *Flags in the Dust*. Whether or not Popeye recognizes Horace as a fellow sufferer of sexual incapacity, the Prufrockian lawyer's ability to seduce a married woman and then lust after her daughter seemingly inspires the impotent gangster to prove that he is at least equally capable of playing Don Juan, and can take Temple from the complacent and drunken Gowan. If Horace seeks to repress his erotic feelings toward his nubile stepdaughter, Popeye has no qualms about making an adolescent girl his sexual prey. Where Horace feels henpecked by his spouse and unsettled by his stepdaughter's sexuality, Popeye symbolically takes revenge upon both—on Horace's behalf—by violently raping Temple.

Popeye's ghastly caricature of Horace's marriage is also a vicious parody of traditional courtship customs and conjugal rituals.[53] At heart, Faulkner's narrative is a hideous distortion of the familiar tale in which a lowly boy from the wrong side of the tracks wins the hand of the beautiful rich girl—

or fairytale princess—in marriage. Although Temple is beset by numerous suitors at the Old Frenchman place—Gowan, the adoring Tommy, the ruthless Goodwin, and the predatory Van—it is the unlikely Popeye who takes her for his own. Terrell Tebbetts characterizes the relationship between Temple and Popeye as the "liaison furthest from marriage" in the novel (48), but it is, in fact, an acid caricature of patriarchal wedding rites. The chaotic, drunken atmosphere in the criminals' country lair on the Saturday evening that Temple arrives there is a perverse combination of stag party and *charivari*. The men get noisily and aggressively drunk before depositing the comatose Gowan—a poor excuse for a groom—in a bedroom with Temple. Ruby's horrifying description to Temple of what "real" men do to women is a grotesque version of a mother giving sexual advice to a daughter on her wedding night.[54] When Temple later describes her rape, she even imagines herself wearing "a veil like a bride." The Memphis lawyer's prominent display of Popeye's stained corncob in the courtroom, furthermore, invokes the custom in some cultures of exhibiting the bloodied bedsheets from the wedding night as evidence of both the bride's prior virginity and the fact of consummation (57–61, 219, 283, 288). Finally, the gangster's abduction of Temple and imprisonment of her in a Memphis brothel is a cruel pastiche of a honeymoon in an exotic location.

The couple's living situation soon degenerates into a violent cartoon of conventional marital strife. Temple dramatically rejects the lavish gifts that her "husband" procures in a vain effort to appease her, smashing bottles of expensive perfume and tossing elegant clothes into the corner of her room. Miss Reba later explains that, in response to Temple's rebellion, Popeye "shut her up and wouldn't let her leave the house"—a disturbing echo of those clichéd cultural representations of the bored wife who complains that her husband never takes her anywhere anymore. Miss Reba's descriptions of the quarreling couple—with Temple demanding "to get out and he wouldn't let her," until "she'd get mad and lock the door and wouldn't even let him in"—characterize Popeye as both a domineering domestic abuser and a frustrated husband who is unable to satisfy his partner (225–26, 256, 257), one who might even observe, like the protagonist of "Dead Shrimp Blues," "Everything I do, you got your mouth stuck out." Although the exact process by which Temple is freed from her quasi-marital misery in the Memphis brothel and restored to her family in Jefferson remains a mystery, it is unlikely that Popeye objected to being liberated from this travesty of a marriage either.

The grim joke at the heart of *Sanctuary* is that, although Popeye's actions initially recreate Horace's repressed and frustrated relationships with women in terms of violent domination and patriarchal mastery, the gangster ultimately reproduces and reenacts the lawyer's passive and sexless marital existence. Popeye, finally, is no more able than Horace to catch up with the "scratchings" of his sexual rivals. Even the gangster's assassination of the potent Red is insufficient to resolve the situation, for the impotent Popeye simply cannot fulfill the sexual needs of a "wife" who—like Belle—desires regular erotic satisfaction. If the gangster initially defines himself in relation to the rigid and bloody corncob with which he rapes Temple, his experiment in conjugal living ultimately proves him to be no less a dead shrimp than Horace.

Just as Popeye replicates and re-enacts Horace's life in nightmare form, numerous characters in Faulkner's novel echo, emulate, or perform the actions or experiences of other people. Much like the situations and conventions of pulp fiction determine the criminal actions of the tall convict in "Old Man," the characters of *Sanctuary* are constructed and colonized by preexisting roles and discourses. Arnold and Trouard observe several such instances, including Temple acting out with Popeye and Red a version of Ruby's memory of her possessive father shooting and killing one of her lovers; the perverse echoes between Temple's disorienting existence in the brothel and the mundane routine of her college life; and the parallels between the absurd escapades of the naive Snopes boys in the whorehouse and Temple's traumatic sojourn there (66, 129, 163). John T. Matthews, meanwhile, notes that the Old Frenchman place provides a recognizable parody of Temple's family and home life, while the scene in which Horace vomits in response to a nightmare fantasy inspired by Temple's description of her rape echoes the earlier story of a girl in Temple's dorm who threw up in response to hearing graphic stories about sexual realities ("The Elliptical Nature of *Sanctuary*" 113, 118).[55] *Sanctuary*, then, presents a circular world of compulsive repetition and unconscious impersonation.

Horace is unique in this novel because he not only re-enacts the experiences of other white people but also emulates two African American archetypes, one from within the narrative and one from outside it. The forms and representations of black masculinity that are available to Horace, however, do not provide him with viable models for redefining himself or resolving his sexual obsessions and failings. If Faulkner's later works often include

African American vernacular eloquence as an alternative to the corrupt and limiting discourses of the dominant mainstream, black oral culture in *Sanctuary* is no more functional or empowering than the diseased misogyny and repressive patriarchy that already pervade Horace's world.

In his journey from the Delta to the Old Frenchman place at the beginning of the book, Horace recreates the travels of "Black Ulysses," the itinerant, blues-singing archetype who came to prominence in a trilogy of novels by Howard Odum. The first of these, *Rainbow Round My Shoulder: The Blue Trail of Black Ulysses,* appeared in 1928, the year before Faulkner produced the original version of *Sanctuary.* Accounting for his travels, Horace explains to the men at the Old Frenchman place that he has "been walking and bumming rides ever since [leaving his wife and stepdaughter]. I slept one night in a sawdust pile at a mill, one night at a negro cabin, one night in a freight car on a siding." As the bigoted Narcissa later puts it, Horace deserted his wife "just like a nigger" (16, 108, 117). Certainly, as Cheryl Lester notes, the lawyer's journey "deploys racially coded tropes that became commonplace in the discourse on black vagrancy and migration" ("Same as a Nigger on an Excursion" 49). More precisely, the details of Horace's flight from marriage echo the "blue trail" of Odum's "*natural bo'n ram'ler*"—based upon the life of John Wesley "Left Wing" Gordon"[56]—who works in sawmills, rides the rails, sleeps in broken-down shacks or outdoors, and never stays with one woman for long (105, 10, 70–74, 102, 149, 221–22, 226–31, 240–41). When he first appears out of the November twilight in *Rainbow Round My Shoulder,* Black Ulysses even performs a song that Horace might equally sing as a summation of his circumstances: "I'M PO' BOY 'LONG WAY FROM HOME / OUT IN THE WIDE WORLD ALONE. / I'M GOOD MAN, JUST AIN'T TREATED RIGHT. / BAD LUCK IN THE FAMILY SHO' GOD FELL ON ME" (2).

Faulkner likely knew Odum's novels, for, as Toby Veeder argues, the characterization of Joe Christmas in 1932's *Light in August* also seems indebted to Black Ulysses (151).[57] Even if Faulkner never read *Rainbow Round My Shoulder,* the image of the blues-singing itinerant laborer was manifestly part of the American cultural scene at the time of *Sanctuary*'s composition. Playwright Paul Green characterized Odum's Black Ulysses as "[t]his roustabout, who for so many years has wandered around in our land as well as in our consciousness" (qtd. in Lynn Sanders 136).

Echoing Green's division of Black Ulysses into two—historical African American figure and white imaginary projection—Horace's wanderings in *Sanctuary* are not so much a performance of blackness as they are a performance of a white construction of blackness. Black Ulysses—"*a travelin' man de luxe*" and "*veteran two-timer moving on to new places*" (222, 153)—exemplifies white fantasies about virile, vagrant African American men being free from responsibility and attachments. Daniel Singal suggests that Odum placed "himself inside Black Ulysses' skin to explore the exotic but forbidden world of black culture" (*The War Within* 144), while Gerald Johnson exclaimed in response to the novel and its real-life model, "What sedentary white man can fail to feel a twinge of envy of the magnificent vitality of Left-Wing Gordon. In spite of his sufferings and his wallowings, how the fellow has lived!" (qtd. in Lynn Sanders 53).

If, as Angela Davis suggests, the blues tradition often presents sexual freedom as a marker of individual self-expression and social liberation, Odum's novels depict black culture and sexuality as merely promiscuous and pathological. The protagonist of *Rainbow Round My Shoulder* unashamedly confesses that "nothin' satisfy us but gittin' in meanness," and he describes initiating fights out of sheer mischief, enjoying "hundreds an' hundreds" of sexual conquests, and habitually exploiting, abusing, and then abandoning any woman with whom he is briefly involved: "I jes' beat hell out o' her," and "after I gits her money an' ruint her I'm gone from there" (81, 144, 146, 148). Where Faulkner's later white protagonists often misunderstand black culture, Horace falls under the spell of a highly selective white caricature of black folkways, one that merely echoes and amplifies the dysfunction of mainstream society just as Popeye's actions actualize and exaggerate Horace's repressed misogyny.

By the time he arrives at the Old Frenchman place, Horace is poised to abandon his performance of quasi-black masculinity—apparently having gained nothing from impersonating Black Ulysses—but he first gives a drunken performance of his own dead shrimp blues. Unlike the lawyer, Black Ulysses finds both consolation and agency in his skills as a musician and songster: "Seems like when I gits to goin' good, pickin' out my tunes an' singin,' make me forgit ever'thing, ain't no time, ain't no troubles, ain't nothin' but myself an' my feelin's" (3). Caught up in his stereotypical projections, Horace cannot fashion a blues tale that enables him to express his feelings or forget his troubles, and he cannot begin to imagine the kind of liberating impotence blues that Johnson recorded only five years after the publication of *Sanctuary*. Just as the tall convict in "Old Man" emulates the superficial elements of the guitarist's discourse while remaining deaf to the implications of his understated musical discourse, Horace impersonates the lifestyle of the wandering rural bluesman—as imagined by a white folklorist and novelist—without beginning to approximate the power of his music.

The novel's nightmare projection of Horace's obsessions and frustrations—the vicious Popeye—also carries faint echoes of the lawyer's compensatory fantasies about the African American *picaro*. Faulkner's narrative consistently—if abstractly—identifies the gangster with blackness, including Horace's observation that Popeye "smells black," Temple's identification of him as "that black man"—which Horace later repeats—and the description of the gangster's "black presence lying upon the house" (7, 42, 49, 109, 121).[58] A pseudo-black projection of a white man's performance of a white novelist's fantasy about African American culture, Popeye is no less violent and misogynist than Black Ulysses, embodying empty and sensationalist mass culture, rather than approximating the vibrant and subversive blues tradition: he is a "manufactured, commercial product" that is merely "[m]achine-like, synthetic, and brittle" (Lurie 27, 33). Just like the tall convict in "Old Man," Horace and Popeye are coded as black, but neither is able to turn his figurative association with African American culture into a productive transcendence of reductive racial or gender ideologies.

Where other Faulkner fictions present genuinely functional and liberating black alternatives to white repression and oppression, African American characters in *Sanctuary*—even the musical ones—are marginal, dysfunctional, and thwarted. The narrative's most prominent black figure is a convicted murderer who sings from his cell: "Aint no place fer you in heavum! Aint no place fer you in hell! Aint no place fer you in whitefolks' jail!" (127). Despite his fluency in black vernacular tradition, the Negro prisoner is a passive, static, and doomed figure. On one hand, Nunn observes, this character's songs are subtle "remonstrances against the racial violence undergirding the system of Jim Crow" that are "transparent to the other negroes, who seamlessly join in singing them, while they appear obscure in both form and meaning to the whites who gather to listen."; on the other hand, Nunn acknowledges, the man's lyrics are palpably "anti-consolatory and non-redemptive" (89, 86, 90). Lester similarly characterizes the Negro murderer as a "figure of black immobility, fatality, and resignation" ("Same as a Nigger on an Excursion" 40). Like Horace's shrimp tale, the black prisoner's songs express only a sense of tragic victimization and, furthermore, provide no coherent explanation or expiation for the man's crime—the brutal slaughter of his wife. Just as Horace's tale elides the lawyer's complicity in patriarchal misogyny, the African American murderer evidently blames female sexuality for male woes. He may be the "bes ba'ytone singer in nawth Mississippi" (115), but he is also a cold-blooded killer who performs only from a jail cell, and soon disappears from the narrative, the silenced victim of a state execution.

Although the published *Sanctuary* does not introduce the singing prisoner until chapter 16, Faulkner's original version begins with a gruesome account of his crime. In the first paragraph of the 1929 manuscript, Horace thinks about how the man "killed his wife; slashed her throat with a razor so that, her whole head tossing further and further backward from the bloody regurgitation of her bubbling throat, she ran out the cabin door and for six or seven steps up the quiet moonlit lane" (3). This passage literalizes the scenario that Nancy ostensibly fears in "That Evening Sun."[59] It is even conceivable that Faulkner placed this scene later in the narrative in the final version of the novel because, in between the original 1929 *Sanctuary* and its 1931 revision, he completed "That Evening Sun," and decided that he did not want his new book to begin with what appears to be a direct continuation of the short story, since this would work against the determinedly open-ended and ambiguous nature of the tale.

Regardless of the author's specific process, the 1929 *Sanctuary* has as its primal scene a black man's slaughter of a woman, even if it is not the first event in the narrative chronology. As the dramatic opening of the novel, this killing anticipates what is to come, informing Horace's horror of female sexuality, Popeye's rape of Temple, and the mob killing of Goodwin. Polk notes that Horace "is fascinated with the Negro's simple solution to his marital troubles. Doubtless he wishes he were passionate enough, *masculine* enough, to solve his own problems so easily" (*Children of the Dark House* 48–49). Although Horace will not act upon such misogynist fantasies, Popeye is no less capable than the African American killer of repressing women or asserting his masculinity through violence. In the 1929 text, then, Popeye is ultimately a projection, not of Horace, but of the Negro murderer.

The organization of the 1931 *Sanctuary*—in which Horace's arrival at the Old Frenchman place replaces the Negro prisoner's crime as the opening event—thus changes the meanings of the book fundamentally. Instead of the stereotypical black razor-murder prefiguring the subsequent violent actions by white men, the published revision begins with Horace, a book in his pocket, poised to narrate his tale of demanding women and dead shrimps. He expresses his impotent misogyny, to which Popeye's rape of Temple and killing of Tommy are seemingly a response, before the black killer—a convenient racial scapegoat for the lawyer's dark impulses—even appears. In the 1931 version, in other words, the lawyer is the "author" not just of Popeye, but of all that follows. In this respect, Horace resembles the female protagonist of a later novel concerned with the projection of imagination into reality: in Thomas Pynchon's *The Crying of Lot 49* (1965), Oedipa Maas recalls a painting that depicts female prisoners in a tower "embroidering a kind of tapestry which spilled out the slit windows and into a void, seeking hopelessly to fill the void: for all the other buildings and creatures, all the waves, ships and forests of the earth were contained in this tapestry, and the tapestry was the world" (11).[60] Where Oedipa anxiously asks, "*Shall I project a world?*" (64), Horace, for all his timidity, unwittingly projects a universe in which he is a helpless tragic victim and everyone else is equally subject to tragedy and victimization—a world in which misogyny, rape, and murder are inevitable, even natural. The 1931 *Sanctuary* is thus organized around the idea of Horace not just as a failed storyteller (Watson 75), but as a dysfunctional narrator of his world.[61]

Horace's discursive failings are fully evident in the book's opening scene, in which the lawyer and Popeye engage in a tense stand-off, staring at each other across a mirror-like spring for two hours (3–6). Where *The Sun Also Rises* depicts two impotent men using witty repartee to acknowledge and resolve their problems while fishing the Irati River, the 1931 *Sanctuary* begins with two sexually dysfunctional men regarding each other across a body of water in impassive silence, neither capable of expressing his vulnerabilities openly. Horace hides behind the persona of the bookish "professor" no less than Popeye hides behind the mask of the tough, gun-toting gangster (8, 9). There is evidently no way in this patriarchal culture for either the taciturn criminal or the verbose lawyer to discuss male sexual weakness candidly or productively.

The blues is a sufficiently flexible form of discourse to allow open expression of the state of impotence, a freedom denied Horace and Popeye and the other men in *Sanctuary,* who cannot imagine a viable male persona that could acknowledge, confess, construct a healing narrative about, or overcome impotence. Johnson's songs concerning erotic incapacity assert that—despite being unmanned by sexual failure, and despite the despair caused by this unmanning—the protagonists are still subjects with agency. Where the speaker of "Dead Shrimp Blues" sings about his impotence in an attempt to resolve it, Horace can only clumsily articulate his pain. Johnson's protagonist acknowledges the fault within himself that he must overcome—"Babe, I couldn't do nothin' until I got myself unwound"—whereas Horace defines female sexuality and the demands that women make upon men as inherently adversarial. Where Johnson's speaker confesses his limitations to his partner and hopes for her assistance, Horace apparently tells everyone except his wife about his dripping shrimp. Johnson's song defines ongoing sexual relations as a desirable and attainable goal, whereas Horace's bitter tale implies the impossibility of a fulfilling long-term sexual relationship between a man and a woman. "Dead Shrimp Blues" presents male sexual failing as a comic situation, but Horace insists upon viewing himself as a tragic figure. Despite his Delta odyssey, the hapless lawyer simply cannot create a tale or song of himself that is simultaneously plaintive in its vulnerability and cocky in its bawdiness—a narrative that is tragic, comic, sneering, and therapeutic all at once.

Like a blues song, Faulkner's novel is not limited to Horace's narrowly tragic vision of the world or his blinkered and sour view of sexuality. If *Sanctuary* is often bitter or ironic in its burlesque touches—such as the tale of the two clueless Snopes boys lodging, without realizing it, in a brothel while they guiltily visit prostitutes elsewhere—the book is not without its glimpses of the comic and liberating possibilities of sexual expression. At the end of the story, Horace glumly returns home and, rather than face his wife, telephones his stepdaughter. Little Belle is supposedly at a "house party," but it is quite apparent that she is actually engaged in passionate activity with a young man while she is trying to get her stepfather off the phone (299–300). If, for Horace, this is just one more occasion for despair, Little Belle and her lover are clearly having a fine time. As Jessica Smith characterizes the scene, Little Belle is evidently "in complete control" and her erotic activity is "healthy" and "playful" (n.p.), regardless of her stepfather's interruption and unwitting telephonic voyeurism.[62]

If Horace cannot harness the power of black discourse or blues rhetoric, it is because there is no reliable model of African American culture available to him, beyond his one-dimensional projection of Black Ulysses as an enviably virile rover or the stereotypically doomed and incarcerated Negro razor-murderer. *Sanctuary* provides no fully realized equivalent of the tall guitarist of "Old Man," or Nancy from "That Evening Sun," or even Job in *The Sound and the Fury*. Yet, while Horace "dont play no blues" in *Sanctuary* (244), the narrative—with its confident blending of horror and comedy, vulgarity and seriousness, somber despair and gleeful self-assertion, modernist complexity and vernacular simplicity—echoes the diverse moods and styles of Robert Johnson's canon.

5

LOST LIGHTNING

SELF-REFLEXIVITY AND SOUTHERN NOSTALGIA IN *THE BACK DOOR WOLF* AND *THE REIVERS*

Where Faulkner's fiction revels in loquacity, the blues is a genre rooted in minimalism. Almost every one of Faulkner's nineteen novels exceeds 250 pages, whereas few blues songs get close to 250 words. Even a single Faulkner short story—such as "That Evening Sun"—is likely to contain a greater number of words than all of Robert Johnson's twenty-nine recorded songs combined. There is nothing remotely surprising about such statistics: for Faulkner, words were "my meat and bread and drink" (qtd. in Blotner, *Biography* 413), whereas southern blues musicians took their sustenance from rhythm and melody and tempo. Lyrical economy is not a shortcoming, but one of the most essential attributes of the blues. As Ernest J. Gaines observes, "William Faulkner writes over one hundred pages describing the Great Flood of '27 in his story 'Old Man.' Bessie Smith gives us as true a picture in twelve lines" (27–28).[1] If, furthermore, many blues performers recorded only a few thousand words during their careers, they sang their repertoires to audiences for years, each of them disseminating their minimalist poetic corpus to listeners new and old, night after night.

Nonetheless, the fundamental distinction between the volubility of the novelist and the laconic nature of the blues has an inevitable consequence for any comparative study of Faulkner's fiction and the songs of rural black southerners. Faulkner's work has been the subject of approximately twice as many pages in this study as the blues—for the simple reason that it requires more pages to elucidate the meanings of a three-hundred-page novel than to analyze a six-stanza song. Consequently, even as this book affirms that the blues of Patton, his peers, and his successors, are no less significant than the works of Faulkner, the white author's voice is still in danger of overwhelming those of black musicians.

This chapter turns the tables: where interpretations of "High Water Everywhere," "Last Kind Words Blues," and "Dead Shrimp Blues" have served as springboards for comprehensive analyses of, respectively, "Old Man," "That Evening Sun," and *Sanctuary,* in this instance the existing critical discourse about Faulkner's last novel provides an interpretive framework for songs from Howlin' Wolf's final record. *The Reivers* (1962) and *The Back Door Wolf* LP (1973) are similarly self-referential works in which two Mississippi artists rewrite their past creations, resituate old materials in illuminating new contexts, and address human experience as an unending process of becoming—in which pain flowers into joy, the energy of youth becomes the exhaustion of old age, rigid certainties blur into complex ambiguities, and disjunction and continuity are in perpetual tension with one another. Both works, furthermore, concern black elders who pass on the diversity and complexity of their life experiences to young white auditors in the form of narratives about paradox, multiplicity, and mobility.

Chester Arthur Burnett was born in 1910 and became a professional blues performer in his twenties, but did not make his first record—under the *nom de plume* "Howlin' Wolf"—until 1951, when he was forty years old and had left his native Mississippi. In Sun Studios in Memphis, and later at Chess Records in Chicago, Wolf proceeded to make up for lost time, his aggressive band and cavernous voice delivering the blues with remarkable energy and authority. If almost all of his Mississippi predecessors and peers were as renowned for their musicianship as their singing, Wolf—although he played a fair harmonica and some guitar—was primarily a vocalist, achieving fame for a voice that resembled "a raucous echo from Africa" or "a hurricane filtered through a letterbox" ("100 Greatest Singers" 60; Murray 240).[2] As Sam Phillips, the sultan of Sun Records, famously declared of Burnett's extraordinary vocal prowess, "When I heard Howlin' Wolf, I said 'This is for me. This is where the soul of man never dies'" (qtd. in Segrest and Hoffman 87). A singer who had once taken guitar lessons from Patton on the plantation[3] became one of the key innovators of urban blues in the nuclear age.

Wolf's "Smokestack Lightnin'" (1956)[4] is one of the most vital expressions of the blues, a compelling blend of electrified urban modernism and country tradition. It dazzled British poet Philip Larkin, who gushed about the singer's "amazing performance, a piece of pure jazz Gothic," in which Wolf created "with no more properties than an echo chamber and his own remarkable voice an impression of Coleridge's demon love wailing for his woman" (qtd. in Segrest and Hoffman 131). This recording has inspired covers by artists and groups as diverse as The Who, Soundgarden, Lynyrd Skynyrd, and Bob Dylan, and it has been used to advertise products as varied as Budweiser and Viagra.[5]

Although "Smokestack Lightnin'" is one of the most iconic works of the postwar electric blues, there is little about it that is original. James Segrest and Mark Hoffman—Wolf's biographers—acknowledge that the bluesman's "single greatest recording" is little more than "a pastiche of ancient blues lines and train references" (131). "Smokestack Lightnin'" certainly owes a great deal to earlier country blues recordings, such as Patton's "Moon Going Down" and the Mississippi Sheiks' "Stop and Listen Blues" (both 1930). Wolf, furthermore, had already recorded a version of the song in 1951, then called "Crying at Daybreak." It is the 1956 revision, however, on which the elements coalesce perfectly, resulting in a magnificent new monument constructed out of old materials.

Improvising blues singer-songwriters—from Patton and Wiley through Johnson to Wolf and his contemporaries—customarily created radically new texts out of traditional tunes and standard lyric formulae. Calt and Wardlow note that "Patton even made a song from scraps of his own songs. Booker Miller said: 'He had one piece he used to play a stanza out of every song he played, each song; put it together, and make a song out of that'" (55).[6] Such self-referential *bricolage* always has been central to the blues: Pete Welding argues that it is, at heart, "a music of re-composition," and he suggests that "the creative bluesman is the one who . . . by his realignment of commonplace elements, shocks us with the familiar" and "makes the old newly meaningful" (qtd. in Taft, *Blues Lyric Formula* 306).

In this respect, Wolf and other blues artists are very similar to Faulkner, who, as biographer Jay Parini notes, was "at heart, a revisionist, concerned with retelling stories more than telling them" (244). Robert Penn Warren similarly defined Faulkner's creative process as "remaking what was made, turning a story over in your mind, finding new angles, embellishing, exaggerating, making transformations and substitutions, deepening character and motive'" (qtd. in Parini 244).[7] In his later years, Faulkner told a student at the University of Virginia that, when a single story is "repeated time after time with different people motivated by it or trying to cope with it, you can learn about people that way" (*Faulkner in the University* 117). If Wolf and Faulkner always had a predilection for cannibalization and self-reference, these tendencies became central in their twilight years. The author's novels after the 1940s and the bluesman's final recordings consistently engage in self-conscious dialogue with their creators' respective artistic traditions and existing bodies of work.

The books of Faulkner's final decade constantly revisit and re-imagine the Yoknapatawpha mythology established in the classic novels and stories from the late twenties to World War II. Karl Zender characterizes the self-reflexivity of Faulkner's later fiction as the author's attempt to cope with waning artistic powers and the threat of obsolescence in an era of emergent postmodernism and revolutionary social change. The aging novelist defied "the loss of self and subject matter" by "making fiction out of his own earlier works" (144). Zender echoes Philip Roth's 1961 article, "Writing American Fiction"—published when Faulkner was at work on *The Reivers*—which argues that, in an age of incomprehensible historical rupture and bewildering media saturation, an American novelist might resolve "the loss of a subject" by turning to "a celebration of the self, which may, in a variety of ways become his subject" (33, 42). For Zender, Faulkner's use of "his own past artistic achievement [as] the subject of his art" was nothing less than the defining "strategy of the final phase of his career" (108).[8]

In his last years, Wolf similarly struggled to adapt to the effects of old age and the disorienting cultural changes that threatened his potency and relevance as a musician. In the late 1960s, record company chieftains pressured Wolf into dubious endeavors to remain contemporary in a musical culture increasingly shaped by the tastes of white teenagers. At the very moment that the traditional African American audience for the blues was shifting its allegiance to more fashionable black musical forms, white youths began to display an interest in the prewar musical roots of contemporary rock, particularly the blues. Muddy Waters could not help but brood about the fact that white Britons and Americans were enjoying "the blues that my black kids was bypassing" (qtd. in Wald, *Escaping the Delta* 247). Under the supervision of Marshall Chess—the callow executive and son of the founder of Chess Records—Wolf went in pursuit of the white rock audience, prioritizing long-playing albums over three-minute jukebox-friendly singles, a shift that such rock outfits as the Beatles and the Rolling Stones had made several years earlier (Segrest and Hoffman 242).

Traditionally, blues purists have had little regard for the music that Wolf created for young white listeners, often characterizing his late 1960s albums as regrettable concessions to prevailing market forces. The bluesman's first LP of previously unreleased recordings, *The Howlin' Wolf Album* of 1968, is a collection of grinding "psychedelic" remakes of some of the singer's earlier hits. The record's cover tries to make the best of a bad situation, eschewing art for a stark, semi-apologetic statement in large, bold letters: "This is Howlin' Wolf's new album. He doesn't like it. He didn't like his electric guitar at first either." The bluesman was not alone in his evaluation of the music; Segrest and Hoffman deride the record as "comically bombastic" and "a mishmash of sound and fury signifying . . . Well, Wolf said it best in a profile in *Rolling Stone* that drove the Chess PR team to despair. 'Man . . . that stuff's dogshit'" (249, ellipses in original). The singer's biographers are equally disparaging about the follow-up LP—another blatant attempt to pander to the teenage market entitled *Message to the Young* (1971)—which they encapsulate as "a tie-dyed, hippie-headed plea for peace, love, and understanding," and "the nadir of Wolf's recording career" (276).

What is significant about this latter album, however, is the notion implied by its title: that an elderly black man from rural Mississippi has something to teach suburban, white, middle-class youths in the present. The same concept of black mentorship of a new generation of whites is evident on *The London Howlin' Wolf Sessions* (1971), in which the bluesman covers some of his signature songs accompanied by a band of admiring British rockers, including Eric Clapton, Ringo Starr, and several members of the Stones. The album's highlight comes when an exasperated Wolf tries to teach the reverential English rock stars how to play "The Red Rooster" with a little dynamism. "Oh, man, come on!" he chides the young pretenders. "You ain't got nothin' to do but count it off." This LP put Wolf on the *Billboard* album charts for the only time in his career, even if its versions of the bluesman's classic songs palpably lack the verve of the originals.

Wolf ultimately resolved his "loss of self and subject matter," not by pandering to white consumers or by indulging in collaborations with the British rock aristocracy, but—like Faulkner—by making songs "out of his own earlier works" (Zender 144). While enduring the indignity of producing his psychedelic "dogshit" album, the bluesman took time out in the studio to record a few spoken reveries about his past and some solo acoustic blues, including a gently crooned and haunting "Ain't Goin' Down That Dirt Road." These casual, quasi-field recordings—which went unreleased for many years—possess a resonance and richness notably absent from the stilted and artificial LP projects that Chess foisted upon the singer.[9]

Wolf's final album, *The Back Door Wolf,* continues in this retrospective vein, with the singer revisiting and rewriting the blues of his lifetime, from the earliest recordings of Patton, his onetime mentor, to his own electrically amplified hits of the 1950s and early 1960s. The result is a "musical mélange" in which "past and present coexisted naturally," a record on which Wolf "looked as far back as he did forward" (Humphrey 3; Rishell qtd. in Segrest and Hoffman 296). On this final LP, in fact, Wolf develops a persona and a form of discourse that enables him to communicate with contemporary white youngsters while celebrating African American culture, asserting the value of tradition, and acknowledging the limits of old age.

The playful invocation of past works and the emphasis upon comic resolution in Faulkner's last novel—in contrast to the author's customary literary innovation and tragic irresolution—initially led some critics to underestimate the book's accomplishments. Several early commentators derided *The Reivers* as a trite, sentimental, and didactic fairytale, with Leslie Fiedler going so far as to dismiss it as "a surrender to sententious banality" (Review 6).[10] Despite its Pulitzer Prize and the efforts of revisionist scholars, the book has never enjoyed the reputation of Faulkner's classic prewar works, but if it necessarily pales beside such achievements as *The Sound and the Fury* and *Absalom, Absalom!, The Reivers* is, nonetheless, a complex engagement with "the open-ended quality of life and literature" (Samway 257).

In acknowledgment of the author's promise that "My last book will be the Doomsday Book, the Golden Book, of Yoknapatawpha County" (*Lion in the Garden* 255), critics tend to characterize *The Reivers* as a grand literary farewell, or even—as William Rossky notes—"Faulkner's *Tempest,*" the work of a "mellowed Prospero" (82).[11] The narrative concerns young Lucius Priest, who accompanies his family's roguish retainers—the white Boon Hogganbeck and the black Ned McCaslin—on a clandestine journey to Memphis in a Winton Flyer "borrowed" from Lucius's father. Ned recklessly swaps the car for a racehorse named Forked (rather than "Smokestack") Lightning, and the trio spends the remainder of the novel trying to win back the vehicle in wagers on a series of horse races. Although the novelist had no idea that this breezily comic tale—which he had been planning to write since the 1930s[12]—would be his swansong, the book's endlessly self-referential nature makes for an apt summation of the Yoknapatawpha chronicle. As Michael Millgate says, "In *The Reivers* . . . Faulkner returns again and again to incidents, settings, and characters first created in earlier novels and stories, often elaborating, reworking, and even revaluing his previous treatment of such material" (*Achievement of William Faulkner* 253).[13]

It is not just that *The Reivers* evokes, alludes to, or even revises other novels in the Yoknapatawpha saga, but that it fundamentally reinvents them. Faulkner's last book takes the tragic characters, materials, and themes of such serious predecessors as *Go Down, Moses,* and unexpectedly forges comic affirmation out of them. In Judith Wittenberg's summation, "Many of the figures and elements from Faulkner's previous works appear in the novel, but they are now viewed with warmth and sentiment rather than with bitterness or despair" (*Faulkner* 241).[14]

The duality of the book's narrative voice is crucial to this project. Kevin Eyster observes that *The Reivers*—in which Lucius Priest, an elderly man in the early 1960s, tells the story of his youthful exploits of 1905 to his grandchildren—has "a double perspective: that of the young Lucius participating in the experience and that of the mature Lucius exploring the experience many years later, recounting and explaining it for himself and his audience" (12). The fears and dangers that are so real to young Lucius in 1905 are a source of wistful comedy for the elder Lucius of 1961. It is through this dual viewpoint that Faulkner's novel, in Millgate's formulation, "manages to achieve both nostalgic retrospect and narrative immediacy" (*Achievement of William Faulkner* 256).[15]

The Reivers is not just distinguished by the doubleness of its narrative voice; the whole work is characterized by paradox and multiplicity. To a great extent, the novel is indeed a gloriously affirmative resolution to the often-tragic Yoknapatawpha chronicle, as the older, serene Faulkner rewrites the younger, cynical Faulkner.[16] The bleak tale of the McCaslins in *Go Down, Moses* miraculously becomes the heartwarming story of the self-proclaimed "cadet branch" of that clan, the Priests (18). Miss Reba's brothel, the site of Temple's abuse and enslavement in *Sanctuary,* now becomes an arena for comic hijinks and the blossoming of love. Elizabeth Kerr says of Faulkner's final portrait of his "little postage stamp of native soil" (*Lion in the Garden* 255), "The sun breaks through the clouds at the end of the long day of the author and of his creation" (113). Yet, the ceaseless invocation of Faulkner's other works in *The Reivers* emphasizes that it is not only a conclusion but also a prelude; its 1905 setting predates many of the horrors imagined by the younger Faulkner. *The Reivers* resolves the crisis of young Lucius Priest while setting the stage for the unresolved crises of Quentin Compson, Temple Drake, Horace Benbow, and many others. The optimism of *The Reivers* does not negate the pessimism of Faulkner's other work, but provides a larger context for it. In short, the author's final novel foregrounds the often-underappreciated tonal variety of the Faulknerian cosmos. As Olga Vickery puts it, *The Reivers* reveals Yoknapatawpha as a place that "encompasses elemental good and elemental evil, but above all it is a world of infinite freedom and therefore of infinite possibility" (228).

The complex mixture of allusion, self-reflexivity, and plurality in *The Reivers* is manifest even in such apparently minor and whimsical elements as its depiction of the mule. As William Stafford notes, the scene in which the black Uncle Parsham Hood explains this animal's contradictory nature to Lucius is clearly indebted to a passage in 1929's *Sartoris,* which itself alludes to Josh Billings's 1860 classic of southern vernacular comedy, "Essa on the Muel" (190–96).[17] As well as evoking Faulkner's earlier work and the broader southern cultural tradition, this passage slyly incorporates an additional literary allusion that highlights the novel's emphasis upon paradox and multiplicity. As Stafford notes, Uncle Parsham's conviction that a mule "can hold two notions at the same time" suggests F. Scott Fitzgerald's "famous modern definition of 'a first-rate intelligence' as 'the ability to hold two opposed ideas in the mind at the same time and still retain the ability to function'" (196).[18]

Through Uncle Parsham's astute understanding of the mule, *The Reivers* implicitly associates mastery of paradox with its African American characters. Stafford notes that the mule and Uncle Parsham are alike in "their stubborn patience and no less than their sagacity their solid unpretentiousness *and* their ties to land and region" (196). If the equation of a beast of burden with a man of color is at the very least problematic, if not downright offensive,[19] it is nonetheless true that Faulkner's black characters, like the mule in this passage, commonly possess the ability to mediate between conflicting ideas, a type of "first-rate intelligence" that the author's Anglo protagonists often lack.

African American mastery of paradox is a recurring theme in Faulkner's fiction, but only in the novels and stories after 1940 are elder black characters able to bequeath this mastery to white students. During his verbal conflicts with Jason Compson in *The Sound and the Fury,* Job skillfully mobilizes an African American worldview rooted in contradiction to which his white adversary remains oblivious; Quentin is deaf to the multiple implications of Nancy's story in "That Evening Sun"; Horace—despite his Delta wanderings—is unable to harness the potential of blues discourse to transform his tragedy of sexual dysfunction into constructive erotic comedy; and the convict in "Old Man" misunderstands the potential of blues music to subvert the status quo. In contrast, the relationships between Sam Fathers and Ike McCaslin in *Go Down, Moses,* Lucas Beauchamp and Chick Mallison in *Intruder in the Dust,* and Uncle Parsham and Lucius in *The Reivers*—just like Wolf's *Message to the Young* and the old bluesman's interactions with white rockers—emphasize the value of black tutelage of young whites. As Frank Fury notes of the Mississippi author's swansong, "Whatever lessons Lucius learns from either his father or grandfather in the novel's conclusion, Faulkner quite ingeniously renders superfluous, for Lucius has already received the same 'wisdom' from his [black and lower-class] accomplices" earlier in the narrative (445). Equally, Theresa Towner suggests that white characters in Faulkner's later fiction consistently gain from their association with "key 'black' speakers" who embody "the demands and rewards of orality—the ability to speak oneself, to define and express aloud one's inner life, in such a way as to influence a specific audience" (30).

Although Lucius clearly benefits from his African American teachers, the depiction of race relations in *The Reivers* is—like everything else in the novel—complex and paradoxical, as the profoundly differing critical responses to the book indicate. Daniel Singal dismisses Faulkner's final work as a regressive fantasy that presents "Yoknapatawpha County at the turn of the century as a mellow land free of all social division and tension" (*William Faulkner* 292), whereas Towner lauds the novel as "a thorough criticism of the ideology of whiteness," in which "Faulkner asserts the integrity of the black subject" (39, 47). It is not simply that Singal is misguided and Towner correct, for the book's dual perspective permits both characterizations to be simultaneously valid. *The Reivers* is a nostalgic reminiscence that consistently undermines its own nostalgia, a reactionary celebration of a rose-tinted past that includes subversive social critique. As Wittenberg sums it up, "despite the ostensible conservatism of *The Reivers* . . . it proves, like Faulkner's great works, a novel persistently engaged in an ongoing debate with itself" ("*The Reivers*" 224).

The Reivers embodies its conception of the world as complex and multivalent in Lucius's definition of "participating in life, being alive," as simply "Motion" (155). This was not Faulkner's first expression of this idea; in the foreword to *The Mansion,* published three years before *The Reivers,* the novelist sought to explain the inconsistencies between the individual volumes in his Snopes trilogy in terms of artistic evolution: "Since the author likes to believe, hopes that his entire life's work is a part of a living literature, and since 'living' is motion, and 'motion' is change and alteration and therefore the only alternative to motion is un-motion, stasis, death, there will be found discrepancies and contradictions in the thirty-four-year progress of this particular chronicle" (331). Like the author, characters and situations in Faulkner's fiction are, as Olga Vickery says, "not only what they have been but what they are capable of becoming" (238).[20] *The Reivers,* in other words, is fundamentally concerned with progression, fluidity, and engagement with change, even as it lionizes traditional values, the wisdom of the elders, and the beauty of the past. At its heart, Faulkner's last book addresses the necessity of an ongoing dialectic between such polar opposites as past and present, young and old, conservatism and radicalism, black and white.

Like *The Reivers, The Back Door Wolf* tends to be dismissed by critics as a mediocre work by a declining talent. Wolf recorded his last LP at the age of sixty-three, when he was recovering from a serious motor accident and had little more than two years of life awaiting him. For most blues aficionados, *The Back Door Wolf* does not hold a significant place in the singer's pantheon, despite the revisionist efforts of Wolf's biographers to characterize it as a "neglected gem" (Segrest and Hoffman 294). If this album transcends the empty commercialism of *The Howlin' Wolf Album* and *Message to the Young* in its return to the classic electric blues of yore, much of *The Back Door Wolf* is tamely formulaic. The elderly Wolf struggles to approximate the power of his previous work, audibly stumbling over lines on several songs. "Trying to Forget You," meanwhile, reworks the tune of "Smokestack Lightnin'" with more smoke than fire. What is more, blues purists commonly balk at the gimmicky and awkward presence of an electric harpsichord on some of the album's tracks.

For all the record's limitations, the opening and closing songs on *The Back Door Wolf*—"Moving" and "Can't Stay Here"—provide an analogue to Faulkner's accomplishments in *The Reivers,* and reveal Wolf's final album to be an appropriate "last testament . . . of one of the titans of the blues" (Humphrey 3). The self-reflexive and allusive lyrics of these two songs involve Wolf—like the elder Faulkner—revisiting and rewriting earlier works: his own and those of his Delta predecessors. "Moving" and "Can't Stay Here" also establish the same kind of dual narrative perspective and the same degree of complex paradox that characterize *The Reivers,* and they establish the same dialectic between past and present, youth and age, progress and retreat, black and white. Framed by these two songs, *The Back Door Wolf* is Howlin' Wolf's *Tempest,* and, like Faulkner's final work, a record "engaged in an ongoing debate with itself" (Wittenberg, "*The Reivers*" 224).

"Moving" and "Can't Stay Here" are fundamentally concerned with how the blues might engage with the contemporary world while remaining connected to its prewar roots. More specifically, the lyrics of these two songs resolve the very problem that Wolf's previous albums struggled to address: how an aging artist can make meaningful contact with a new generation without compromising his integrity—a project that Wolf shares with both the author and narrator of *The Reivers.* As their titles clearly indicate, furthermore, the opening and closing songs on *The Back Door Wolf* construct the world in terms of fluidity rather than stasis, equating motion to participation in life, just like Lucius in Faulkner's novel. In the first song, an aging African American in the modern North dreams of returning to Dixie, whereas, in the other, a hounded young black male in what appears to be the Jim Crow South aspires to escape the region. What matters in each case is not the destination so much as the dynamic tension between the two viewpoints. The underlying theme of *The Back Door Wolf* is an old urban bluesman of the 1970s interrogating the relevance of his southern past and African American heritage to his present and the nation's future.

"Moving" highlights the ongoing affection that members of African American communities in the North have retained for the region below the Mason-Dixon Line. Sung from the perspective of an elderly black man who fantasizes about recreating his youth in Mississippi, the first number on *The Back Door Wolf* begins with the resolute declaration, "I'm gonna leave this town and I'm goin' back down South." Although blues songs—especially before World War II—often construct the urban North as a site of opportunities that traditionally were lacking for men and women of color in the South, the notion that something significant was lost in the Great Migration also permeates the blues tradition.[21] If southern states had often proven to be hostile and forbidding places for black Americans, the lure of down-home roots nonetheless remained considerable, and nostalgic paeans to country life were common in urban black song. As Jeff Todd Titon sums up the paradox, for black emigrants the "land of Jim Crow and lynch law was also the land of fish fries and barbecues, good music and getting religion, long talks and deep loves, the feel and the smell of soil and farm" (*Early Downhome Blues* 3).[22] Faulkner's portrayals of his native soil involve a similar duality. As Thadious Davis notes, the author "shows a deep affection for his native land. He has provided numerous descriptions of the virginal beauty of that land. . . . Yet his land is Mississippi, a land of violence, brutality, and oppression" (*Faulkner's "Negro"* 162).

Wolf's boldly contemporary electric blues had always relied upon the nostalgic charge provided by rural southern content, such as the farmhouse tale of "The Red Rooster" (1961), the story of a 1940 Mississippi dancehall fire, "The Natchez Burning" (1956), and the tongue-twisting litany of names attending the Delta fish fry in "Wang Dang Doodle" (1960). So anachronistic is this last song, in fact, that even Wolf was moved to complain to lyricist Willie Dixon that it was "too old-timey," and resembled "some old levee camp number" (qtd. in Segrest and Hoffman 174). Francis Davis argues that such qualities are standard in the electric blues of the postwar era, and that "you'll listen in vain for references to Chicago's stockyards and elevated trains in Muddy [Waters]'s songs of the forties and fifties, or in the songs of those who followed in his path." Instead, the lyrics of the postwar electric blues emphasize such phenomena as "black cat bones and mules kicking in their stalls. Even the singers' accents sound Southern, as though they and their listeners were still living there" (181). Despite his eager embrace of electric amplification, Wolf was still doggedly singing songs from and about old-time Mississippi into the 1970s. On both *The London Howlin' Wolf Sessions* and 1972's *Live and Cookin' at Alice's Revisited,* he performs versions of the Mississippi Sheiks' country chestnut from 1930, "Sittin' on Top of the World," a song he had first recorded in 1957.

The first line of "Moving" is one of the most adamant rejections of the urban North in favor of the down-home South in all of Wolf's canon, and—as the opening assertion of the record's first song—sets the stage for the whole album. It is a statement not only about geography, but also about music: implicit in Wolf's declaration about returning to the South is his intention to abandon his recent misguided efforts to produce psychedelic, hippie blues-rock for white kids; he is going back to his Mississippi roots musically too.

"Moving" and *The Back Door Wolf* as a whole are thus concerned with the tensions in African American culture between what Robert Stepto calls the impulses toward "ascent" and "immersion." In his famous analysis of the two archetypal narrative patterns in black literature, Stepto describes the recurring tale of ascent as one in which an individual rises to a more comfortable social position, usually through literacy, migration to the North, and/or achieving mainstream success. In the process of ascending, however, a protagonist often must abandon his or her family, community, or tradition. The immersion narrative is a common reaction to the alienation or dislocation brought about by ascent, and involves a black protagonist (re-)embracing his or her ethnic traditions and roots. Such stories commonly feature a literal or symbolic journey to the South and a protagonist's acceptance of some of the restrictions from which he or she had escaped through ascent (167–68).

"Moving" is about both the necessity and the complications of reconnecting with the southern past—which is to say, immersion. Burnett was a Mississippi tenant farmer who, as Howlin' Wolf, had become a wealthy and respected musical celebrity in Chicago, where he enrolled in adult education classes for self-improvement well into his fifties.[23] The speaker of "Moving," however, dismisses the northern city in which he has achieved both status and prosperity in the very first line of the song—referring to it only as the anonymous "this town"—and never mentioning it again. Throughout the lyrics, the speaker's single-minded focus is upon the life he dreams of building for himself back in the home of his youth.

With as much rose-tinted romanticism as the elderly narrator of *The Reivers,* the protagonist of Wolf's song imagines a region rooted in his affectionate memories of the past, where the celebrity he has earned in the urban North will make him a social lion. His name, he says, is "ringin' in Miss'ippi, and Alabama and Georgia too," and the women of the South will "treat me like a king." He will return a conquering hero, drinking wine every night, fishing every day, and eating chicken at every house. In his fantasy version of the rural South, the speaker imagines that he will continue to enjoy the status and success that migration to the North enabled him to secure, without enduring any of the oppression, inequality, or lack of opportunity that presumably motivated his migration in the first place.

The ending of the song acknowledges that such an easy reconciliation between ascent and immersion is little more than a dream. As "Moving" reaches its conclusion, the narrator is still merely thinking about returning to his roots. Following the final line—in which the protagonist reasserts his plan to go back down South—Wolf gives one of his trademark howls, but, unlike the proud lupine keening of the bluesman's younger years, this particular wail sounds like a pained and disheartened groan, as if the speaker recognizes that his idealized odyssey will never take place. He is too old and too integrated into urban life to make such a fundamental shift, and the actual South cannot begin to compete with the nostalgic image of the region that exists in his imagination.[24]

Equally, while "Moving" seems to promise that *The Back Door Wolf* will exhibit a return to the musical traditions of rural Mississippi, it is plainly apparent that, like Thomas Wolfe, Howlin' Wolf can't go home again, physically or musically. Subsequent numbers on the album address such determinedly modern topics as black astronauts and the Watergate break-in—a far cry from the red roosters and wang dang doodles of old. By the third song, furthermore, the incongruous electric harpsichord has joined the proceedings. Although the record eschews the awkward funk-rock efforts of its immediate predecessors and approximates the sound of Wolf's classic recordings, the singer can no more reinvent himself as a traditional country bluesman than he can restore his lost southern youth.

If "Moving" ultimately implies the impossibility of resurrecting history, it also asserts the continuing relevance of the past to the present by incorporating the titles of several of Wolf's earlier songs into its lyrics. Much of the meaning of "Moving"—like that of *The Reivers*—is dependent upon an audience's ability to recognize and understand its self-reflexive allusions. Taken by itself, for example, the opening line of the song's third verse does not mean very much: "I'm still a back door man, but I ain't gonna tote my Forty-Four no more." Blues fans, however, know that "Back Door Man" is the title of Wolf's 1960 song about a compulsive philanderer,[25] while "Forty-Four" is a 1954 number (based upon Roosevelt Sykes's seminal 1929 recording) about a man who wears his large-caliber pistol so compulsively that it gives him a sore shoulder. The joke here is that the narrator of "Moving" uses the titles of two previous Wolf songs to assert that he will continue to enjoy clandestine sexual liaisons, but will no longer carry a firearm: that he will "make love, not war," as the fashionable catchphrase of the 1960s put it. "Moving" thus simultaneously invokes and parodies the efforts of Wolf's two preceding LPs to pander to the white youth market. Just as Wolf had repeatedly counseled, on "If I Were a Bird"—the first track on *Message to the Young*—"We need more love," he again articulates trendy sentiments, but this time recasts them in the language of his own song titles, demanding that the listener remember his past glories.[26] No longer compromising his work for the sake of a young white audience, Wolf now requires that auditors be familiar with his oeuvre.

On *The Back Door Wolf,* then, the bluesman continues his tutelage of white youth, but in a more astringent manner than on previous releases. If *Message to the Young* is "full of transparent appeals to the youth market" (Segrest and Hoffman 276), Wolf's final album includes such provocative material as the satirically titled "Coon on the Moon." In this song—which succeeds "Moving" in the album's running order—Wolf employs direct address as he cites the achievements of notable African Americans, resulting in a lyric that operates as a pop quiz on black history. "Tell me who was the first man to go to the North Pole?" he asks in the second stanza, and, in the third, "Tell me who was the first man, [to] make oil out of a peanut?" Where, on the previous record, Wolf pandered to hippie culture by endorsing long hair and mini-skirts, on *The Back Door Wolf,* he now challenges white listeners to identify Matthew Henson and George Washington Carver. In a world in which whites are prone to project such demeaning labels as "coon" upon people of color, Wolf demands instead that they speak the names of the race's most distinguished individuals.

Although *The Back Door Wolf* directly addresses white rock fans, the vocal performance on its opening song underlines the distance between the aging bluesman and his increasingly young audience. If a very casual listen might suggest that "Moving" is an encouragingly perky return to form, attentive auditors habitually complain that a promising number is ruined by the audible presence of a sideman—presumably saxophonist and songwriter Eddie Shaw, one of the guiding forces behind the record—prompting Wolf with each and every line of the song. Even with the benefit of such a crutch, the elderly singer still fluffs the first line of the second verse. The reliance upon an audible prompter and the bungling of lines are a drastic departure from the supreme confidence of Wolf's classic performances.

What is particularly striking about "Moving" is that the record's producers do not seem to be trying very hard to hide the singer's frailties, even though they conceal them reasonably well elsewhere on the album. Although the elderly bluesman had difficulty remembering lines and reading lyric sheets, there were alternatives to having a prompter shout every line of "Moving" into Wolf's—and the listener's—ears. Even in the 1920s, associates whispered lyrics to Blind Lemon Jefferson while he was recording, and Buddy Boy Hawkins wore headphones so that he could receive instructions from the engineer during his performances. Wolf himself relied upon prompts via earphones when making *Message to the Young.*[27] Alternatively, and although Chess Records maintained fairly traditional recording practices in the 1970s, a more competent performance easily could have been pieced together from several takes. To be sure, the album was recorded very rapidly in a mere two days, and Wolf—who could be capricious and intractable in the studio—may have rejected such options as headphones and multiple takes on this occasion. Nonetheless, it is striking how awkwardly the old bluesman struggles with the relatively simple lyrics of "Moving" while displaying considerably less difficulty with equally complicated songs elsewhere on the album. In addition, Shaw's prompting on "Moving" is considerably more audible than on other numbers on the record.[28]

Regardless of whether the record's producers intended to make Wolf's waning powers of performance a prominent element of "Moving" or simply failed to disguise the singer's condition, the result is a song that, for all its infectious instrumental pep, is also defined by the ravages of old age. This sort of "warts-and-all" portrait of the artist as an old man is familiar to twenty-first century listeners of Johnny Cash's final albums, such as *The Man Comes Around* (2002). In collaboration with producer Rick Rubin, the elderly country singer made a virtue out of his declining abilities by constructing his last recordings around the theme of old age and mortality. This strategy is at its most evident and affecting in the unblinkingly stark presentation of the wizened singer in the 2003 video promo for "Hurt," in which Cash, surrounded by the relics collected over a lifetime, croakily intones Trent Reznor's bitter lyrics about "my empire of dirt."[29] In light of Cash's last works, what makes "Moving" compelling—as opposed to merely inept—is the juxtaposition between youth and age: between the dynamism of the band (particularly Hubert Sumlin's assured and fluid guitar playing) and the invocation of Wolf's earlier triumphs, on one hand, and the elderly bluesman's flawed—if intrepid—vocal performance, on the other.

That Wolf's moan at the end of the song sounds nothing like the proudly voluminous nonverbal exclamations of his classic recordings is as central to the song's effect as the eerie howling that pervades "Smokestack Lightnin'." Wolf's pained wail on "Moving" not only sounds like an expression of the speaker's inability to believe in his fantasies about moving to a utopian South, but also as if the performer is moaning in frustration—at the proceedings in general, or specifically at his failure to vocalize as strongly as he once could. Yet, even at his frailest, Wolf remains a consummate showman. If he can no longer provide the potent and capacious cry of his younger self, his weary exclamation at the end of "Moving" emphasizes that, even as an old man in poor health and with diminished powers, he is still fronting his band, still singing his blues, still trying to howl like a wolf. He is sufficiently self-aware to be vexed at his limitations, but, if he lacks the virile authority of old, he possesses a different kind of authority: that of age and experience, as similarly displayed by Cash on "Hurt" and the elderly Lucius in *The Reivers*. Segrest and Hoffman are not wrong when they characterize Wolf's performance of "Moving"—for all its flubs and audible prompts—as "vehement singing that really was moving," or when they suggest that the album as a whole contains "[s]ome of Wolf's most passionate singing" (294). The point of "Moving" is embodied in its simple title: the Wolf may be old, but he is still in motion, still participating in life, still projecting new journeys, however unlikely it is that he will undertake them.

Another paradox of "Moving" is that it is both a nostalgic paean for an idealized Dixie of the past and a prescient vision of the significance of the real South for black Americans in the present and future. Just one year after the release of *The Back Door Wolf,* the *New York Times* reported on a "Reverse Migration" by which "significant numbers of blacks are returning to the South, coming 'back down home' to a region that seems, at last, to offer as many economic opportunities and as much brotherhood as any other section of the United States" (Ayres n.p.). A decade later, Thadious Davis observed of this social shift that, "[w]hile anthropologists and sociologists may see the increasingly frequent pattern of black return migration as flight from the hardships of urban life, I would suggest that it is also a laying of claim to a culture and to a region that, though fraught with pain and difficulty, provides a major grounding for identity. At times, I like to think too that this return to the South is a new form of subversion—a preconscious political activity or a subconscious counteraction to the racially and culturally homogenous 'Sunbelt'" ("Expanding the Limits" 6). The blues is, of course, a foundational expression of a black southern culture "fraught with pain and difficulty" that nonetheless "provides a major grounding for identity." The presentation of the South in "Moving," where a black man can be "a king" is, furthermore, a subversive reclamation of the region, emphasizing its potential to serve as the site for the establishment of new black identities in the future, rather than just embodying an impossibly romantic dream about the Jim Crow South of the rural past. In its way, the album's opening song is as much of a social statement as the more overt celebrations of black uplift elsewhere on *The Back Door Wolf.*

The juxtaposition between "Moving" and the lyrics of the following "Coon on the Moon" emphasizes that Wolf's lifetime has witnessed unprecedented progress for black Americans, and that, while the individual must decline into old age, the larger group will continue to thrive. Throughout *The Back Door Wolf,* the bluesman acknowledges the growing divergence between his waning powers as an individual and the ever-increasing agency of the African American community as a whole. Where the speaker of "Moving" yearns to return to the South of his youth, the narrator of "Coon in the Moon" instead emphasizes the advances that people of color have made since mass migration to the North. The song's refrains highlight the breakdown of educational segregation and the emergence of black astronauts: "They wouldn't let us play together, now we can go to most any school. . . . We're on the moon now." Wolf emphasizes, furthermore, that such dramatic strides forward will continue in the future, asserting provocatively: "You know they call us coons, say we didn't have no sense / You gonna wake up one mornin' and the old coon will be the President." The profound disjunction between the offensive epithet "coon" and the singer's uncompromising expectation of a black chief executive vividly dramatizes the historical failure of racist rhetoric to limit either the aspirations or the achievements of African American citizens. Indeed, barely more than a decade after Wolf passed away in his longtime home of Chicago, a young man of color moved to the city to take a job as a community organizer, beginning a path that would take him to the White House and into the pages of history.

The Back Door Wolf is a neatly symmetrical record: it opens with a song about an elderly black man's dream of returning to his southern roots and youth, and ends with "Can't Stay Here," which appears to be sung from the perspective of an African American in the South many years earlier, who fantasizes about fleeing the region for better opportunities elsewhere. It is typical of the album's complexities that it begins with a dreamy present-day view of old times and concludes with a pragmatic vision from that past about the possibilities of the future.

Where "Moving" invokes songs made by Wolf in the 1950s, "Can't Stay Here" goes back to the very roots of the recorded Mississippi blues by recycling the lyrics of Patton. Specifically, the first and second verses of "Can't Stay Here" borrow the A lines of their AAB structures from the second and fifth stanzas of Patton's 1929 recording "Down the Dirt Road Blues": "Feel like choppin,' chips flyin' everywhere," and "Every day seem like murder here." The use of traditional formula lines from Patton's old-time Mississippi blues implies that the unbearable "Here" in this last song is not the modern North, but the Jim Crow South of the 1920s, the world of Wolf's youth. Where "Moving" is about the reverse migration beginning in the 1970s, "Can't Stay Here" seems to concern the Great Migration of the first half of the century.

In "Can't Stay Here," Wolf distinguishes his history from that of his predecessor by recasting the endings of each of Patton's verses. "Down the Dirt Road Blues" only hints at the impediments that plagued black people in Mississippi—Patton's home throughout his career—whereas Wolf boldly overcame such obstructions by leaving the region behind. Patton completes one of the verses quoted by Wolf with the line, "I been to the Nation, Lord, but I couldn't stay there," and the other with, "I'm gonna leave tomorrow, I know you don't 'bide my care." Such phrases elide the specific obstacles faced by African Americans in the Delta, suggesting that romantic disappointment is the decisive reason for the speaker's desire to leave Mississippi, and that life in the Indian Nation—Oklahoma—is no better. In contrast, Wolf's adaptation explicitly defines the fundamental issue as one of economics and suggests that permanent relocation is the only realistic solution: both of Wolf's stanzas end with the complaint that the speaker "can't make a dollar, no, and I can't stay here." The only way for this character to prosper is to migrate, and Wolf's own such journey took him first to Memphis and then to Chicago.

The bookends of *The Back Door Wolf* thus construct a double perspective—like that of *The Reivers*—in which the elderly Howlin' Wolf of "Moving" only fantasizes about going back home, just as the youthful Chester Burnett of "Can't Stay Here" only dreams about leaving it. In terms of Stepto's categories, "Moving" is an unfinished immersion narrative and "Can't Stay Here" an incomplete ascent narrative. The protagonist of *The Back Door Wolf* is thus suspended between his youthful intent to move north and his elderly fantasy of returning south. Wolf's last album is about the journey, not the destination, about the value of the dream and the process, rather than the result—which is why the end of his story appears at the record's beginning, and the beginning at its end. As in Vickery's reading of *The Reivers,* the speaker of "Moving" and "Can't Stay Here" is not only what he has been but also what he is capable of becoming (238).

While establishing a clear-cut symmetry between its opening and closing songs, *The Back Door Wolf* also undermines it through the ultimate ambiguity of the setting and perspective of "Can't Stay Here." The use of traditional formula lines from Patton's rural blues in the album's final song certainly suggests that the unbearable "Here" is the South of the 1920s. The absence of any historical or geographical specificity in the lyrics, however, makes it equally conceivable that the speaker is located in the urban North in the present day. After all, by the time Wolf recorded "Can't Stay Here," some African Americans *were* beginning to define northern cities as places in which every day was like murder and where they could not make a living. In the 1974 *New York Times* article on reverse migration, Freddie Lee Reese of Alabama explains that he abandoned Chicago for the region of his birth because "I didn't see any reason to stay up there in that madhouse when all I found was just as much discrimination and poverty, and even more crime, than there is down here." In the same article, Mary Lee Jones similarly complains about her time in the North that she "couldn't save any money and people were rude" (Ayres n.p.): In the language of Wolf's song, Jones could not make a dollar and she could not stay there.

The lyrics throughout *The Back Door Wolf* emphasize how far the black community has come during the singer's lifetime, but the ambiguity of the setting of "Can't Stay Here" simultaneously suggests how little has changed since Patton's day in some respects. On one hand, the songs on Wolf's last album proudly celebrate that people of color now attend the same schools as whites, participate in the space program, and—in the case of the intrepid janitor cited in "Watergate Blues"—can even play a crucial role in bringing to light the criminal activities of some of the most powerful people in the land. On the other hand, the album's final song implies that the poverty, fear, and frustration associated with the Deep South in Patton's songs before World War II persist into the nuclear age and potentially into any part of the nation. "Can't Stay Here" thus blurs the distinctions between the regional and the national, the past and the present, by suggesting that the history of racial oppression commonly associated with the South in the Jim Crow era has evident analogues in the North of the 1970s.

Rather than providing a trite or simple resolution to the complex conflicts and contradictions addressed by the record, the ending of "Can't Stay Here" resists any certainty or totalization in its final, provocative use of blues sources. The third and last verse of the song recycles the A-line from the concluding stanza of another Patton number, "Pony Blues": "Something to tell you, baby, when I get a chance." Patton's bawdy punch line to this formula in 1929 was "I don't wanna marry, just wanna be your man," which Wolf had repeated in his recording of the song in 1952.[30] In "Can't Stay Here," however, this famous payoff never materializes; in fact, there is no B-line at all. The recording begins to fade out as Wolf is first singing the A-line, and has slipped entirely into silence before he can articulate the B-line. It is apparent that Wolf sings *something,* but the fade-out renders it inaudible, just out of reach. The blues aficionado who has identified Patton's recording as the source of the song's lyrics is led to anticipate a traditional punch line that the record tantalizingly withholds.

As with Wolf's flawed vocals on the record's opening track, this curiously incomplete ending is consonant with the central themes of *The Back Door Wolf.* It clearly is not the case that such sentiments as "Don't want to marry, just want to be your man," do not suit Wolf, for he has already told us on "Moving" that he is still a "back door man." It is not like this album, furthermore, to fade out prematurely simply because the singer may have botched a line. The unexpected and untimely fadeout means that the song—and thus the record as a whole—does not achieve a firm conclusion. On Howlin' Wolf's final LP—one of the last works of the great Mississippi blues singers—the very first record release by Charley Patton, the Founder of the Delta Blues, is left in permanent suspension, perpetually unfinished, eternally open-ended, suggesting that, although individual blues singers may die, the blues itself never ends, remaining always in process.

Wolf's final album flaunts the paradoxes of personal, regional, national, and racial history, rather than evading them. *The Back Door Wolf* presents the South as a pastoral utopia, where one drinks wine and eats chicken all day, and as a living hell, where every day is like murder. It suggests that the lost land of youth is a desirable destination while acknowledging that, for a person of color, an escape into the past means turning the clock back on whatever racial progress has been achieved in America. The album salutes the generation that emerged out of the era of Jim Crow while also celebrating the rise of a generation born into the civil rights age. The record reaches out to a white audience while emphasizing African American uplift and black education of whites. Finally, *The Back Door Wolf* asserts a profound distinction between the South of the singer's youth and the North of his dotage, only to imply that the roles of the regions may now be reversed and that, the more things change, the more they stay the same. Like *The Reivers,* then, *The Back Door Wolf* achieves complex meaning through dual perspective and paradox. Wolf's last record and Faulkner's final novel exploit the potential of narrative to create worlds in which even the loss of lightning—whether "Smokestack Lightnin'" or a racehorse named Forked Lightning—can be a source of unexpected triumph.

CONCLUSION

A LONG LOOP DOWN INTO THE DELTA

Today, the blues—especially the Mississippi country blues—enjoys a reputation as one of the foundations of modern American culture, but few of the music's progenitors and pioneers received adequate recognition during their lifetimes. Even the president of the United States can now be coaxed into singing "Sweet Home Chicago" at a White House event,[1] but its composer, Robert Johnson, died ignobly of poisoning without so much as an obituary in a local newspaper to mark his passing. Such American novelists as Sinclair Lewis, Pearl Buck, Ernest Hemingway, and John Steinbeck—like Faulkner—enjoyed the recognition of the Nobel Prize committee, but Howlin' Wolf could only hope that "[w]hen I'm dead, I'll get all the greatness I was supposed to get when I was alive" (qtd. in Segrest and Hoffman 316). Historian C. Vann Woodward nominated 1929—the year of *The Sound and the Fury* and *Look Homeward, Angel*—as the beginning of the Southern Renaissance (222), but it did not occur to him to note that 1929 also witnessed the release of such canonical records as Charley Patton's "Pony Blues," Mississippi John Hurt's "Stack O' Lee," Garfield Akers's "Cottonfield Blues," and "When the Levee Breaks" by Kansas Joe McCoy and Memphis Minnie. Finally, Keith Dockery—whose husband owned Dockery Plantation when it was a center of blues activity during the heydays of such luminaries as Patton, Son House, and Tommy Johnson—could only confess in later years that she had "never heard these people sing. . . . I wish we had realized that these people were so important" (qtd. in Palmer 55).

Blues musicians from rural Mississippi—neighbors and contemporaries of Faulkner—were, for many decades, among the most neglected of great twentieth-century American artists.

The complicated, overlapping journeys of the blues—from popular orchestral and sheet-music phenomenon to respected bedrock of American music, from local folk tradition to national commerce, from rural plantation to urban nightclub, from African American performers and listeners to global stages and multicultural audiences—appear in Faulkner's fiction only in diffuse, sporadic, and partial form. Even so, the Yoknapatawpha chronicle obliquely addresses the processes by which mainstream American culture embraced, dismissed, romanticized, adapted, and came to respect the blues and other forms of folk and popular music. From the scenes of white people dancing to an African American band in *Soldiers' Pay,* through the country blues guitarist emerging out of the flood in "Old Man," to Mink Snopes's symbolic engagement with a broad multicultural tradition of vernacular song in *The Mansion,* Faulkner's fiction reflects shifting social attitudes to southern roots music.

Readers today commonly imagine, assume, or wish that Faulkner was one of those rare white people who treasured the blues—especially the country blues—long before the world at large belatedly caught on to the music's greatness. It is tempting to think that Faulkner belongs in the company of such individuals as John and Alan Lomax, the famous father-and-son team who made field recordings of southern folk music; H. C. Speir, the Jackson-based purveyor of blues records who was also a talent broker for the musicians of the Delta; or Howard Odum, who collected and published blues lyrics as well as novels about Black Ulysses.[2]

It is undeniable that Faulkner had broad exposure to African American vernacular music. His black caretaker, "Mammy Callie" Barr, may have taken him to a local jook joint when he was a child, and, as a young man, he likely heard Lucius Pegues's string band at the home of his future wife, certainly danced to W. C. Handy's orchestra at local functions, and regularly visited a honky-tonk roadhouse during excursions into the Delta with his lawyer friend, Phil Stone. Joseph Blotner's biography even includes a photograph of the young Faulkner brandishing a guitar (151), and the budding author submitted a sketch of a seven-piece black jazz band to the 1921 Ole Miss annual.[3] Later in life, he listened to the singing of black farmhands on his Greenfield Farm and played Bessie Smith records on an old wind-up Victrola at Rowan Oak.[4] David Krause goes so far as to claim that Faulkner "listened compulsively to the music of Afro-American experience" (80), while Judith Sensibar asserts that blues and jazz were "the only music Faulkner *chose* to listen to" (*Faulkner and Love* 61).

Nonetheless, there were evident limits to the author's appreciation of popular, roots, and African American music. Alan Lomax complains that Faulkner's fiction marginalizes the black communities that produced the blues and gives no clear indication that the author ever listened closely to the music (327–28). Karl Zender's characterization of Faulkner having a "profound antipathy toward American popular culture" may also stretch a point (22), but the writer's dislike of amplified or recorded music was sufficiently well known to the proprietors of Oxford stores and restaurants that they needed no prompting to turn off radios or unplug jukeboxes whenever Faulkner entered their premises.[5] The author would not permit a radio in his home, and, when his spouse ignored this injunction and bought one anyway, he unceremoniously ejected it from Rowan Oak.[6] Beginning in the 1930s, Faulkner's fiction regularly featured diatribes against phonographs, radios, and amplified sound in general, such as the vivid descriptions of the cacophony of recorded music in Jefferson town square in both *Intruder in the Dust* and *Requiem for a Nun*.[7] Stephen Ross even suggests that, in Faulkner's later works, "the natural community of speakers within earshot of each other and of nature's sounds is silenced by the 'hollow inverted air' that encloses individuals in a sterile collection of isolated listeners to 'static or needle'" (64). This older Faulkner sounds very much like the modernist intellectuals who habitually decried the prevalence and baneful effects of what they considered "low" mass culture.[8]

In conversation, Faulkner's descriptions of African American music—even when based on memories of his youth—tended to emphasize his distance and separation from black folkways rather than intimate knowledge of them. Toward the end of his life, the author told a friend how "the Negroes used to have these parties where you could hear the drumming all night long in the distance. They called them 'picnics.' But no white person ever went near them and we didn't know what went on. The younger Negroes now are ashamed of all that. It's the same in the churches. They used to have trombones and banjos at the services. From outside you could hear the music, and it was fine" (qtd. in Blotner, *Biography* 1776). Such an account displays Faulkner's familiarity with African American music, while also clearly emphasizing that he was not in a position to hear it closely or as black people heard it.

Although conflicting characterizations of the author's attitudes to popular music and the contradictory details about his knowledge of vernacular songs may appear to be irreconcilable, those critics who laud Faulkner's appreciation of the blues and celebrate its significance to his fiction are no less correct than those who question his knowledge of black music and wonder why there is so little of the blues in the Yoknapatawpha novels and stories. As T. Austin Graham notes in his study of popular songs and modernist literature, "[m]usically inclined writers tended to be idiosyncratic and contradictory on the subject of cultural value, with the same author who admired his era's popular arts at one moment being quite likely to deride them the next" (26).

The truth is that Faulkner understood both much more and much less about the blues than we do. As much as any white person who came of age in the early twentieth century, Faulkner was acutely aware of the blues as a popular phenomenon—as sheet music, orchestral dance numbers, and recordings by white and vaudeville singers. Furthermore, as an inquisitive soul and a Mississippian, the writer was also familiar with the blues as a regional African American folk form. If, however, Faulkner was attentive to local black musicians and relished mainstream pop adaptations of the blues, it is highly unlikely that he ever heard—or even heard of—the particular Mississippi musicians and blues records that fans and scholars consider canonical today.

Just as the published versions of such works as "A Rose for Emily" and *As I Lay Dying* are Faulkner's cultural legacy, our only access to the author's imaginary world, the records of such songs as "High Water Everywhere" and "Last Kind Words Blues" are the permanent and available texts of the prewar country blues. The development of recording technology in the late nineteenth century was one of the great cultural revolutions of the modern age, as fundamental an innovation in human history as the invention of movable type a few hundred years previously. Without the printing press, Faulkner could not have been anything more than a local storyteller, whose oral narratives would have been unknown outside of his home region and would have eventually disappeared into the same historical fog that permanently enshrouds Homer's predecessors and contemporaries. Equally, Patton, Johnson, Wiley, and Wolf would be entirely forgotten today, save perhaps in the dim memories of a few elderly members of black communities, had it not been for the development of the phonograph. After all, virtually no information survives about the generation of blues pioneers who lived immediately prior to the age of recording, except a few scattered and mysterious names—such as Henry Sloan and Ben Maree[9]—even though they died only a century ago. If live performance was and is central to the blues, the history of the music nonetheless goes hand-in-hand with the evolution of phonograph technology.[10]

Although Faulkner famously claimed to have worn out several copies of Gershwin's "Rhapsody in Blue" while writing *Sanctuary* and listened to Bessie Smith's urban blues, he never gave any indication that he purchased so much as a single record of the Mississippi blues. In fact, while Smith's records—like Handy's music—were broadly popular, the consumers of country blues records were primarily African American. Few white people were aware of Patton, Wiley, Johnson, or their works until well after World War II. Even middle-class black people tended to know relatively little about those country blues artists that history has subsequently enshrined as the avatars of twentieth-century vernacular music. Langston Hughes may have made the blues central to his poetry and fiction in the 1920s and 1930s, but his frequent litanies of blues greats habitually emphasized such stars of the vaudeville blues as Smith and Ma Rainey. As Steven C. Tracy acknowledges, "Hughes never noted any blues figure associated with Mississippi Delta blues in any of his essays," even as he openly relished—like Faulkner—the popular blues compositions of Handy (119–20, 10, 172). If Hughes—an avowed champion of black vernacular culture and author of such poems as "The Weary Blues"—gave no sign of ever having listened to such records as "High Water Everywhere," "Hellhound on My Trail," or "Last Kind Words Blues," it is yet more doubtful that the white novelist of Oxford would have been familiar with them.

Like folklorists of his time, Faulkner largely seems to have valued the blues he heard locally as what he took to be a reassuringly pure and enduring African American oral tradition, not for what many critics now consider it to be: black America's primary contribution to the modernist arts and popular culture. If the blues fan of today cannot but envy the opportunities Faulkner had to hear prewar Mississippi musicians in person, the notion that commercial recordings of the rural blues constitute some of the greatest American art of the century would have been alien to the author. Krause may be correct that the Oxford novelist sometimes listened intently to the music of the African American experience, but Faulkner was probably no more aware than Keith Dockery of the historical importance of particular artists on local plantations.

If a twenty-first-century blues enthusiast were able to talk with Faulkner about roots music, he or she would likely find very few shared points of reference with the Mississippi author. Many of the records that fans and critics today laud as the most important works of the prewar country blues are precisely the ones that were marginal—if not obscure—in their time, whereas the local blues singers with whom Faulkner may have been familiar are lost to history, and many of the popular adaptations of the blues that he enjoyed are considered by aficionados to be minor works. For Faulkner to have heard rural African American singers locally but not to have known the crucial records of the country blues is rather like somebody having been present at some of Faulkner's public addresses without ever having read any of his fiction.

It is no less true of novelists than musicians that those feted in their heyday often do not endure the test of time. If asked to identify the most important contemporary American writers, an avid reader in the 1930s reasonably might have nominated such Pulitzer Prize–winning novelists as Harold L. Davis, Margaret Ayer Barnes, and Josephine Winslow Johnson, and well may have overlooked such now-canonical figures as Zora Neale Hurston and Faulkner. Today, only specialists tend to remember the works of Davis, Barnes, and Johnson, whereas nobody denies the centrality of the Yoknapatawpha fiction to American modernist writing. Similarly, those aficionados today who lionize the once-obscure works of Patton, Wiley, and Johnson commonly consider such musical stars of the prewar blues as Leroy Carr and Lonnie Johnson to be relatively marginal. Faulkner was evidently familiar with the blues equivalents of such authors as Davis, Barnes, and Johnson and with local amateur performers, but he almost certainly did not know those records which, from a twenty-first-century perspective, stand in relation to the blues in the same ways that *The Sound and the Fury, Sanctuary,* and *Absalom, Absalom!* stand in relation to American literature. Canons are, of course, retroactive and artificial constructions, but the processes that gradually established Faulkner's novels and stories as major literary works of the twentieth century are the same kind of processes that belatedly elevated such once-little-known songs as "Last Kind Words Blues" and "High Water Everywhere" into the musical pantheon.

* * *

Lovers of modernist southern culture must reconcile a disappointing absence of hard evidence for Faulkner's appreciation of the canonical country blues with their understandable desire for there to have been a tangible and meaningful connection between the legendary southern author and the major bluesmen and blueswomen of Mississippi. Any fan of the Yoknapatawpha fiction and roots music will, at one time or another, have entertained a fantasy about Faulkner strolling through Oxford town square on a warm Friday night in the early thirties, perhaps already buzzing from one too many of his beloved mint juleps, as scenes and situations from his current project—say, *Light in August*—play through his mind. His creative reverie is interrupted by the insistent sound of a guitarist on a street corner. The author snaps back to reality, pausing to watch as a lean, young black man in an unusually sharp suit sings with feverish intensity—to an audience consisting of an inattentive passing couple and a single curious child—about his experience of paralysis and terror at the darkening crossroads. For a moment, William Faulkner locks eyes with Robert Johnson—the white novelist and the black musician poised in brief, silent communion. The ghost of a smile plays across the bluesman's face, and the author cannot help but respond in kind, before abruptly turning away and striding off into the Mississippi twilight. That night, the author dreams of his haunted protagonist, Joe Christmas, sinking to his knees at the crossroads as the demons of his past swirl around him and the baying of pursuing hounds echoes in the darkness. This is the same kind of wildly romantic mythologizing of the Depression-era South that informs *O Brother, Where Art Thou?*, and its undeniable appeal indicates that our appreciation of Johnson and Faulkner is so profound, and the fact of their historical and geographical proximity so provocative, that we cannot bear to think that they were entirely unaware of each other.

Fortunately, we do not need to invent mystical encounters between Faulkner and Mississippi blues artists on the streets of Oxford in the 1930s for the simple reason that the author and the musicians are in regular and meaningful contact with one another whenever we think about their creative works in tandem—as Jake Adam York does in "Before Knowing Remembers," a poem that invokes both Johnson and Faulkner. If it were not for "High Water Everywhere," what would illuminate the significance of the cameo appearance of the black guitarist in "Old Man"? What else but the emphasis upon counterpoint in *If I Forget Thee, Jerusalem* might suggest that Patton's two-part song operates in a similar fashion? How can Horace's fixation with shrimp make any clear sense isolated from the tangled imagery of "Dead Shrimp Blues"? Moreover, is anyone likely to have imagined that either "Last Kind Words Blues" or "That Evening Sun" had anything to do with lynching without considering them in tandem? Finally, without the insights provided by scholarly discussions of *The Reivers,* who would be inclined to think of the opening and closing songs of *The Back Door Wolf* as a framework for the record's complex dual perspective?

These few comparative readings of Faulkner's fiction and the blues do not begin to exhaust the possibilities. Scholars would do well, for example, to attend to the many parallels between the blues tradition and Faulkner's examination of black culture and southern race relations in *Go Down, Moses*: from the similarities between "The Fire and the Hearth" and Patton's dramatization of tensions between black moonshiners and white authorities in "Tom Rushen Blues" to the echoes between the treatment of capital punishment and burial rites in the title story and Blind Lemon Jefferson's two-sided record on those subjects, "Lectric Chair Blues" / "See That My Grave Is Kept Clean" (1928). Future studies might also address such issues as modes of transportation—from horses through trains to cars—in works including *Flags in the Dust,* Patton's "Pony Blues," and Johnson's "Terraplane Blues," or hybrid racial identity in Patton's "Down the Dirt Road Blues" and *Light in August.* Traces of numerous blues texts in "That Evening Sun" could provide sufficient material for a book in itself. Indeed, the chapter on that tale in this study began life as an analysis of Nancy's alleged cocaine use in relation to the lyrics of Patton's "A Spoonful Blues," and initially included extensive discussion of the provocative parallels between Faulkner's story and the 1929 short film of *St. Louis Blues* starring Bessie Smith.[11]

If anything has the potential to provide scholars with a fuller sense of the relevance of the blues to Faulkner's work, it is such comparative analysis, rather than any quest for concrete biographical or historical interconnections, which have largely eluded researchers for decades and seem unlikely to come to light now. To be sure, echoes of country blues songs in the Yoknapatawpha fiction provide tantalizing hints of a greater familiarity with the blues on the author's part than the few explicit references to the music in his books or the details of his biography suggest. Is the discussion of the boll weevil in *The Sound and the Fury* a direct reference to Handy's "Yellow Dog Blues"? Was the author inspired to include the black guitarist in "Old Man" because he had heard an African American musician sing a song about the 1927 flood? Did Faulkner know a blues song that used shrimp as a symbol for male impotence—like "Shrimp Man" or "Dead Shrimp Blues"—and did he incorporate the image into *Sanctuary* for that very reason? Such questions are necessarily speculative, however, and there is a good chance of them tempting scholars into mere fantasies—rather than more informed hypotheses—about the author's understanding of African American musical traditions.

"Old Man" is a useful case in point, for it not only illuminates and is illuminated by blues lyrics about the Mississippi flood, but it also operates as an enlightening counterpoint to songs about imprisonment in general, and Parchman Farm in particular, by such artists as Bukka White and Lead Belly. The tall convict's notion of prison as a peaceful haven from the chaos of the larger world in Faulkner's story contrasts sharply with the depictions of incarceration in such songs as White's "Parchman Farm Blues" and Lead Belly's "The Midnight Special," both of which show how deceptively simple and formulaic discourses might enable psychological self-liberation and even literal freedom. If Lead Belly's and White's songs clearly share significant elements with Faulkner's fiction, evidence suggests that, while the author may well have been familiar with one of these artist's lyrics, he could not possibly have known those of the other at the time he wrote "Old Man." What is most valuable, then, is not what the songs suggest about the author's knowledge of the blues—or lack of it—but what they reveal about the meanings of his fictional works.

Legend suggests that Lead Belly, the most famous convict of the blues tradition, sang his way to freedom. In 1925, Huddie William Ledbetter of Louisiana had served the bare minimum of a seven-to-thirty-five-year sentence for murder at Sugarland prison in Texas when he was pardoned and released by Governor Pat Neff, who had run for office on a pledge never to issue such pardons. According to some accounts, the enterprising prisoner won his liberty by charming the governor with his musical talents and composing a song that directly enlisted Neff's aid. By 1930, however, the singer was incarcerated again—this time at Angola in Louisiana—for an alleged attempt on a white man's life. On this occasion, two white musicologists—the ubiquitous Lomaxes—petitioned another governor for the singer's release. Again, Ledbetter gained his freedom after having served the minimum possible time for his crime (Wolfe and Lornell 85–87, 97–99, 117–21).

The singer made the most of his liberty on this second occasion, becoming a professional recording artist as "Lead Belly."[12] As Charles Wolfe and Kip Lornell—Ledbetter's biographers note—the press feted him as the "singing convict," and he starred in a brief fictionalization of his checkered career on the *March of Time* radio show and a companion movie newsreel (Wolfe and Lornell 134–45, 156–58, 163–67). Lead Belly was as much a repository of a broad folk-music tradition as a blues singer.[13] The songs that he wrote—or, at least, that he popularized—include such enduring numbers as "In the Pines," "Cotton Fields," "Goodnight Irene," "On a Monday," "Rock Island Line," and "The House of the Rising Sun," as well as a version of the "Boll Weevil" song. Such diverse artists as the Beach Boys, Nirvana, ABBA, Harry Belafonte, the Rolling Stones, and Tom Waits have performed Lead Belly's songs.

Faulkner is more likely to have heard of Lead Belly than any country blues recording artist from Mississippi. Even if the author missed the *March of Time* newsreel in which the singer and John Lomax awkwardly reenact their first encounter in prison, he had plenty of opportunities to learn about the singer in the pages of the nation's leading newspapers and periodicals. Walter Lippmann wrote about Lead Belly in the *Herald Tribune* in early 1935, and, just a couple of weeks later, William Rose Benet published a poetic profile of the singer in the *New Yorker* (Wolfe and Lornell 138–39, 167). At roughly the same time as Faulkner was avowedly taking "sadistic pleasure" in "ejecting from the house . . . Cab Calloways and so forth" after his wife's unsanctioned purchases (Wilde and Borsten 103), a tipsy Lead Belly was taking similar delight in telling Lippmann, "I can beat Cab Calloway singin' every time. . . . He don' know nothin' 'bout singin'." Further profiles of the musical ex-convict appeared in national periodicals over the next two years, including one in *Life* in April of 1937 and another by Richard Wright in the *Daily Worker* in August of that year (Wolfe and Lornell 140, 197, 200).

Lead Belly was also one of very few blues artists of the era to move—briefly, at least—in similar literary circles to Faulkner. In December 1934, the singer even participated in two sessions at the annual meeting of the Modern Language Association, the nation's foremost conference in English studies. The first of these was a Friday evening program of vernacular music that ran the gamut from "Elizabethan Ayres" to "Negro Folksongs" ("Proceedings" 1324). Henry Seidel Canby—who, as editor of the *Saturday*

Review of Literature, had reviled Faulkner's *Sanctuary* for its "sadism" and lauded *Light in August* for its "extraordinary force and insight" (qtd. in Blotner, *Biography* 685, 789)—introduced the singer at this event. Lead Belly also performed at the following morning's session on "Popular Literature," but presumably did not attend the Thursday afternoon session on "Contemporary Literature," at which Donald Davidson—who had penned a series of perceptive and glowing reviews of Faulkner's early novels that contributed significantly to the author's burgeoning literary reputation[14]—spoke on "Regionalism in Modern American Literature" ("Proceedings 1325, 1300). Davidson's was likely the only session that year to mention Faulkner, however, and thus the 1934 conference stands as perhaps the one occasion that a blues singer enjoyed greater prominence at the MLA than the creator of *The Sound and the Fury*. In the weeks immediately following this academic conference, Lead Belly continued to socialize with the nation's literary elite, enjoying Sunday tea at the Bryn Mawr deanery with novelist Owen Wister, giving a concert for a select audience of Columbia and New York University professors, and speaking with the president of Macmillan regarding a book project (Wolfe and Lornell 136–38).

Faulkner was busy completing *Pylon* in Oxford during Lead Belly's brief season as a social lion in New York,[15] but the tale of the musical convict was so prominent in various media in the mid-to-late 1930s, and so prevalent among the nation's literary establishment, that it is unlikely the author could have avoided hearing about it. Just a couple of years after Lead Belly's sojourn with the literati, Faulkner began work on what would become *If I Forget Thee, Jerusalem*. The "Old Man" section of that novel is the exact reverse of the musician's experience: where Lead Belly, a convicted black murderer, apparently sang his way to liberty and fame, Faulkner's tall convict—who is technically free after having been erroneously proclaimed dead—talks himself back into the obscurity of prison.

A particularly illuminating contrast to the tall convict's situation in "Old Man" is Lead Belly's famous prison anthem, "The Midnight Special." The Lomaxes captured Lead Belly performing this song at Angola in July 1934, although this version was not released for many years. Lead Belly's first commercial recording of this number appeared on *The Midnight Special and Other Prison Songs* album in early 1941,[16] postdating the 1939 publication of *If I Forget Thee, Jerusalem*. Nonetheless, by the time Faulkner began writing "Old Man," the song had appeared in *Negro Folk Songs as Sung by*

Lead Belly, a book edited by the Lomaxes, published in November 1936, and reviewed by such prominent literary figures as Constance Rourke and James Weldon Johnson (Wolfe and Lornell 196).

Faulkner need not have heard of Lead Belly to be familiar with "Midnight Special" anyway. Odum first published some of the lyrics of the song in the *Journal of American Folklore* in 1911, and Carl Sandburg included two different texts of "Midnight Special" in his *American Songbag* anthology of 1927. In addition, several country and blues artists recorded versions of the song some years before Lomax discovered Lead Belly in Angola.[17] If it was hardly as pervasive or popular as "St. Louis Blues," "Midnight Special" was in relatively wide circulation in a variety of forms by the time Faulkner began to write about Parchman Farm.

Unlike Faulkner's tall convict in "Old Man," who uses the same terse, minimalist discourse in all situations, the central speaker in "Midnight Special" is highly attentive to issues of context: to what one can and cannot say or do in particular circumstances. In the second verse, the song's narrator complains about the monotony and drudgery of the daily routine in prison, and, having captured the dreary tedium of yet another morning of incarceration in a mere three lines, cautions that, "if you say anything about it, [you're] havin' trouble with the man." What convicts may tell each other in the bunkhouse—or in coded form in work songs—cannot be uttered explicitly within the hearing of the prison authorities.

Both "Midnight Special" and "Old Man" operate as dialogues between convicts, and both are characterized by laconic humor, but one is about a prisoner obsessed with the prospect of freedom while the protagonist of the other passively accepts incarceration. The interjection in the song's opening verse—"How in the world do you know?"—clearly indicates a conversation between two or more convicts. Equally, frequent interjections by other inmates in Faulkner's tale emphasize that the tall convict is telling his story to an audience.[18] In "Midnight Special," the inmates cover a variety of topics in their confidential conversations, including romantic disappointment in Mexico, the pain of bereavement, and the disagreeable nature of Houston lawmen. Their dialogue, furthermore, involves the same understated and cynical deadpan humor as the convict's narrative in Faulkner's story. In reference to the paltry rations they receive in prison, one character observes, "Knife and fork are on the table, [but] there['s] nothin' in my pan." In contrast to the tall convict, however, the utterances of the prisoners in "Midnight Special" consistently express their frustration at prison life and their fervent desire for liberty, whether they are imagining "Miss Rosie" petitioning the governor for her man's freedom or simply thinking about the lights from the eponymous "Midnight Special" train shining into the cells and reminding them of a world beyond the penitentiary walls.[19]

If it is quite possible that "Old Man" ironically reverses the emphases of a song with which its author was familiar, then several blues lyrics that postdate the publication of Faulkner's story shed no less light on the tall convict than the headlamps of the "Midnight Special." The parallels between "Old Man" and the 1940 songs of Bukka White are, in fact, just as striking as those between Faulkner's story and Lead Belly's prison lyric.

White was sentenced to a term at Parchman Farm for murder in 1937, one year before Faulkner's Harry Wilbourne in "The Wild Palms." Between his arrest and his incarceration, the singer somehow found an opportunity to travel to New York and record the energetic "Shake 'Em on Down," which became a hit, thus making the bluesman a celebrity during his time in prison. Ted Gioia reports that the "inmates and guards pooled their money to buy him a guitar, and he was exempted from much of the heavy labor that oppressed his fellow convicts" (92). When John Lomax visited the penitentiary in the summer of 1939 to make further field recordings of prison songs, the authorities "proudly produced" their star, but Lomax was not inclined on this occasion to petition for a blues singer's freedom. For his part, White—who had earned top-dollar for his commercial recordings—was reluctant to surrender his songs to a musicologist free of charge, and he provided Lomax with only two pieces for his archive (Gioia 89–90).

Although White did not sing his way to freedom like Lead Belly, he converted his experiences at Parchman into powerful musical narratives during a March 1940 recording session in Chicago soon after his release.[20] At a time when commercial blues music was increasingly dominated by the easygoing formula of the cosmopolitan "Bluebird" sound—"a popular mixture of dance tunes, hokum, and suggestive double entendre" (Gioia 93)—and when recordings of the country blues were of more interest to musicologists than record companies, White produced a dozen songs, several of which rank alongside the most significant Mississippi blues. Gioia goes as far as to claim that White's 1940 recordings come "as close to art song as traditional blues has ever dared to go, but without losing any of the essential qualities of the Delta heritage. This was Delta blues at its best: a personal statement of deep emotional intensity but with larger, inescapable social overtones" (94). The recurrent subject of these songs is imprisonment, and they present vivid descriptions and blistering critiques of life as a black prisoner at Parchman.

White's songs about the penitentiary possess numerous superficial similarities to the tall convict's story in "Old Man," but their worldviews are quite distinct. In "District Attorney Blues," the singer castigates the justice system for separating loving couples, declaring that the law has "taken me from my woman, cause[d] her to love some other man." Similarly, the final pages of "Old Man" reveal that much of the tall convict's bitterness and misogyny are a response to his sweetheart rejecting him in favor of marriage to one of the prison guards (286). Equally, just as a central issue at stake in Faulkner's story is the convict's ability to convert his experiences into narrative, so does the protagonist of White's "Parchman Farm Blues" emphasize the importance of communicating his jailhouse trials to an audience. At the end of the second verse, the speaker expresses his hope that "some day you will hear my lonesome song," emphasizing that the audience for which the singer yearns—whether a lover or record listener—is located outside the prison walls. Faulkner's convict, in contrast, is quite content to narrate his adventures only to his fellow Parchman inmates.

White's speaker and Faulkner's protagonist most clearly demonstrate their profound differences through their attitudes toward clothing. During his adventures in the flood, the convict in "Old Man" cares obsessively for his prison uniform, initially refusing to remove it, and, later, when working as a trapper in the swamps, carefully wrapping it, and, finally, having it cleaned so that it is in excellent condition when he puts it back on just prior to surrendering himself (212, 232). He fetishizes the uniform that reduces him to an interchangeable cog in the Parchman machine. In contrast, White's "When Can I Change My Clothes?" constructs the humiliation, privations, and suppression of individuality that incarceration entails specifically in terms of dress. In this song, the speaker defines the moment of his future freedom simply by wondering plaintively again and again, "how long before I can change my clothes."

"Old Man" may seem to be no less indebted to White's work than to "Midnight Special," but the Mississippi bluesman composed and recorded his Parchman songs immediately before his recording session,[21] more than a year after the publication of *If I Forget Thee, Jerusalem.* Furthermore, the resulting records—released throughout 1940—disappeared into obscurity. As Gioia notes, "With the exception of a brief notice in the *Amsterdam News* in July 1940—which dismissed them in a single sentence, not even calling them blues but rather folk music—the songs were virtually ignored in the black press, and their subject matter made them distinctly unsuitable for crossover appeal to white record buyers" (94). White's songs about Parchman thus stand as instructive reminders to fans of Faulkner and the blues to beware assuming that even provocative or seemingly substantial parallels between fiction and song lyrics provide a reliable basis for conclusions about the author's knowledge of black music.

The general impression given by Faulkner's fiction and biography are that the author possessed an evident interest in blues, pop, and jazz—as well as traditional art music—as a young man, but that his attitudes to popular songs and symphonies alike became more reactionary and resistant by the mid-1930s, when he developed an outspoken antipathy toward music of any kind. The young man who danced enthusiastically to Handy's band and raved about Beethoven evolved into the middle-aged author who refused to attend concerts and told an interviewer, "I prefer silence to sound" (*Lion in the Garden* 248).[22]

What critics have not noted, however, is that the elder Faulkner of the 1950s and early 1960s lived in an era in which prewar vernacular music was becoming increasingly prominent. By the time the author published his penultimate novel, *The Mansion,* in 1959, a "blues revival" was bringing the rural forms of the music squarely into the American mainstream for the first time. That year witnessed the publication of Samuel Charters's groundbreaking study, *The Country Blues,* and an accompanying LP of long-unavailable recordings by such figures as Robert Johnson, Blind Lemon Jefferson, Sleepy John Estes, Bukka White, and Blind Willie McTell.[23] The growing national interest in prewar roots music was not limited to the blues, either: the folk music revival began even earlier, in the era of World War II.[24]

If Faulkner hardly became a diehard blues or folk aficionado in his later years, he was nonetheless part of this culture of revivalism. At the time of his death in 1962, his library included a copy of Frederic Ramsey's richly illustrated—if rather romanticized—book about rural black folkways and African American music, *Been Here and Gone* (1960).[25] In 1956, furthermore, Moneta Sleet—*Ebony*'s star photographer—captured a memorable shot of the author's encounter with legendary 1930s jazz chanteuse Billie

Holiday, a vocalist who was—and still is—frequently misidentified as a blues singer. One of Holiday's biographers even suggests that this meeting came about specifically at the author's request (Clarke 456–57).[26]

The revival of prewar vernacular music performed a significant function for those—like Faulkner—who were skeptical about, or disillusioned by, the contemporary age. In an era of social upheaval and atomic anxiety, the musical traditions of the rural South suggested the durability and integrity of an older America. Blues and folk revivalists tended to embrace prewar popular music not as a determinedly modern commercial product of the twentieth century, but as an embodiment of eternal folk values.[27] For many in the first half of the century, in fact, traditional southern culture provided a vital antidote to the blight and corruption of the modern world. As early as 1930 in *I'll Take My Stand,* twelve southern writers—commonly known as "the Fugitives" or "the Agrarians"—offered the customs of the rural South as a viable alternative to an America increasingly dominated by unchecked industrialization and rampant consumerism. They endorsed "the genuine humanism" of an "imaginatively balanced life lived out in a definite social tradition," as exemplified by "the agrarian life of the older South" (xvi). In the wake of World War II and during the Cold War, increasing numbers of Americans—like the protagonist of Howlin' Wolf's "Moving" and the creators of *I'll Take My Stand*—similarly looked back to an imaginary rural golden age for comfort and solidity.

Faulkner and several major blues musicians—or, in some instances, their record companies—habitually emphasized their down-home authenticity and association with the traditional occupations of the rural South, even when such claims often had limited basis in reality. When declining an invitation to an awards ceremony at the American Academy of Arts and Letters in 1950, the professional author—who only occasionally visited the agricultural estate that he owned—explained disingenuously, "I am a farmer this time of year; up until he sells his crops, no Mississippi farmer has the time or money either to travel anywhere" (qtd. in Blotner, *Biography* 1317).[28] Despite Patton's renowned aversion to field labor, the bluesman's death certificate lists him as a farmer, which encouraged Calt and Wardlow to speculate that "Patton liked to promote this impression of himself as a farmer turned recording artist" (110). In the same year as *The Mansion* appeared, the liner notes of Howlin' Wolf's compilation album, *Moanin' in the Moonlight,* shamelessly claimed that the professional Chicago-based musician from Mississippi "was born in West Memphis, Arkansas, and in that country, where he lives with his wife, he works a cotton patch of over twenty acres. He has several mules and jackasses to help him with his plowing and other farm chores" (qtd. in Segrest and Hoffman 168).

Despite its conservative preference for the past over the present, postwar revivalism lionized a prewar rural musical culture that was decidedly multicultural. The overlap between such supposedly distinct genres as country, blues, folk, Cajun, cowboy songs, and gospel is evident in one of the central artifacts of the renaissance of traditional roots music: Harry Smith's *Anthology of American Folk Music* (1952). By placing such disparate artists as the Carter Family, Charley Patton, Columbus Fruge, the Reverend J. M. Gates, Dock Boggs, Ken Maynard, and the Alabama Sacred Heart Singers alongside each other, this collection of commercial recordings from the late 1920s to early 1930s suggests that, whatever their differences, these musicians were part of a coherent American cultural movement.

The Mansion is a fitting novel for an era in which the nation was beginning to appreciate the golden age of prewar music by black and white artists alike, as well as the broader southern culture from which so much of it sprang. Mink Snopes—one of the book's white protagonists—is a living embodiment of what the blues and folk revivals of the late 1950s and early 1960s sought: a figure who maintains the values associated with prewar rural culture in a rapidly changing postwar world. As Eileen Gregory puts it, Mink's vision of the world is "archaic, pre-modern" (419). Like the lean-hipped guitarist in "Old Man," and Nancy in "That Evening Sun"—and unlike the tall convict, Quentin Compson, and Horace Benbow—Mink is part of a vital and liberating vernacular tradition: one that found its fullest and most enduring expressions in blues, folk, and country songs.

Mink serves a sentence of thirty-eight years at Parchman for murdering Jack Houston over ownership of a cow in 1908, a crime first dramatized in *The Hamlet* (1940),[29] the initial volume in Faulkner's trilogy about the rise of the grasping Snopes family. *The Mansion*—the final installment of the series—reprises Mink's history as he prepares for his long-awaited freedom just after World War II and plans to avenge himself upon the man he has always blamed for his long incarceration: his powerful relative Flem Snopes. Mink is a marginal figure in the earlier fiction, but in *The Mansion* he becomes central, his long imprisonment and eventual release framing the novel's retrospective survey of Yoknapatawpha throughout the first half of the century.

Like the convict in "Old Man," Mink is an inmate at Parchman, but he is the reverse of his unresisting predecessor and—despite his whiteness—spiritual kin to the protagonists of Lead Belly's and White's prison songs. Where the tall convict is subject to the fantasies of mass-produced contemporary pulp fiction, Mink seems to have stepped directly out of the lyrics and scenarios of southern "old-timey" music. Concerned about Mink's intentions, the Parchman warden offers him a full pardon and regular cash payments in return for staying away from Flem, as long as the prisoner acknowledges that "once he teched the money he had done give his sworn word and promise and bible oath to strike for the quickest place outside the State of Missippi" (675). Although he is no more educated or eloquent than the tall convict, Mink rejects this brazen manipulation, boldly taking his freedom and leaving the money behind. Nothing will prevent him from writing his own story—and that story is a revenge tragedy. If the Snopes trilogy begins with *The Hamlet,* it ends more like Shakespeare's *Hamlet,* but Mink suffers none of the indecision that plagues the melancholy Dane.

Having been isolated in Parchman Farm for nearly four decades, the newly freed Mink is like a time traveler—a "twentieth-century Rip Van Winkle" as Judith Bryant Wittenberg calls him (*Faulkner* 234)—struggling to understand the world of the mid- to late 1940s in terms of 1908. In one scene, a truck driver gives Mink a ride and points out a local POW camp, the presence of which mystifies the ex-convict, who explains: "I been away. . . . I mind one war they fit with the Spaniards when I was a boy, and there was another with the Germans after that one. Who did they fight this time?" (427). Mink's exaggerated dislocation from history is reminiscent of an account of a real-life blues singer from Parchman. Paul Oliver reports that, in June 1936, a Mississippi convict, accompanied by prison guards, entered the Decca studios, where, by special arrangement, he recorded some songs under the archaic alias "Jesse James." The lyrics of these numbers reveal that their creator "had been so long severed from the outside world that Oklahoma was to him still the 'Territory' of the Indian nations" (*Blues Fell This Morning* 213).

It is largely because he readily embraces the role of cultural anachronism that Mink is able to do what the most admirable citizens of Yoknapatawpha have failed to achieve for decades: get rid of the corrupt Flem. Throughout the Snopes trilogy, lawyer Gavin Stevens and his loyal confederate, the itinerant salesman V. K. Ratliff, vainly seek to arrest the inexorable rise of the Snopes clan. It takes Mink's direct, violent action in this final novel in the series to detach the head from this hydra of corruption, an act that is reminiscent of the traditional revenge and murder ballads collected by Harry Smith.[30]

The Mansion implicitly associates Mink with vernacular American music of both the past and present. In one scene, Mink remembers how he used to think of the trains that regularly passed Parchman as symbols of impossible freedom, and he recalls how, even before his incarceration, he used to watch locomotives with a similar sense of alienation from the luxury and liberation they represented (693–94). If this passage initially seems to evoke the traditional lyrics of "Midnight Special," its specific language suggests a modern country song: Mink's envious glimpse of "the lighted cars . . . in which people were eating supper while more niggers waited on them," echoes the verse in Johnny Cash's hit, "Folsom Prison Blues," in which a jealous convict observes of a passing train, "I bet there's rich folks eating in a fancy dining car / They're probably drinkin' coffee and smoking big cigars." Mink's description of the train as "a long airtight chunk of another world dragged along the dark earth for the poor folks in overalls like him to gape at" also parallels the ending of Cash's song (694), in which "those people keep a-movin' and that's what tortures me." "Folsom Prison Blues" was a big hit on the country chart in early 1956, at the very time that Faulkner was working on the second installment of the Snopes trilogy, *The Town*.[31] If the author had been anywhere near a radio that winter, he would have heard the song.

Whereas *The Mansion* invokes contemporary country music in this specific moment, it later associates Mink with the vernacular tradition that Faulkner had drawn upon in his earliest works: the prewar blues. Although Mink's lengthy prison term means that he essentially misses the emergence and evolution of this African American musical genre—from Handy's "St. Louis Blues" in 1914 to Bukka White's 1940 recordings—the journey Mink takes upon his release from Parchman to his destiny in Yoknapatawpha is instantly recognizable as a blues odyssey: "It had taken thirty-eight years and he had made a long loop down into the Delta and out again" (691–92). The generation that created and disseminated the Mississippi blues had taken a similar route, flocking to the Delta for its economic opportunities and then taking the blues they created there into the wider world. The markers of Mink's journey echo the place names that recur throughout the history and lyrics of the classic country blues. His travels take him from Parchman (subject of White's songs),[32] to Tutwiler (where Handy first heard the blues), to Clarksdale (which appears in Patton's "Moon Going Down"), to Lake Cormorant (home of bluesman Willie Brown, immortalized in the lyrics of Robert Johnson), to a crossroads where Mink hopes to "catch a ride" (just like the protagonist of Johnson's "Cross Road Blues"), and then onto Memphis, a city celebrated in dozens of blues songs, before he returns to Jefferson (563, 565, 566, 668).[33] Mink thus completes the "blue trail" of Black Ulysses that Horace could not fulfill in *Sanctuary,* as well as performing a more purposeful odyssey than that of Charlotte and Harry in "The Wild Palms."

The new world that Mink discovers after almost four decades of imprisonment involves—or, at least, appears to Mink to involve—profoundly altered racial mores. Although the South into which the character emerges is still a region defined by racial segregation and oppression, Mink encounters instances of relative interracial cooperation, notably his brief involvement with the Reverend Goodyhay and his harmoniously multiracial flock who worship in what was once "*a nigger schoolhouse*" (579).

Critics differ on the nature of Mink's response to this new world. Theresa Towner argues that "Mink's belief in white superiority in *The Hamlet* redoubles in the last novel of the trilogy, even as throughout the book he relies on black people he meets for food, information, shelter, and transportation. . . . He has learned to hold in his racial views when he needs something; such restraint stems from his more general knowledge that the world outside Parchman is not as he left it" (114, 115). In contrast, Gregory suggests that Mink evolves from seeing people of color as threats to his identity at the outset of the novel to viewing black men and women as allies and confreres by its conclusion (416).

Mink's initial affinity for white country music and his later symbolic connection to the blues suggest that the latter reading is closer to the mark—that the character's shift from association with an essentially white form of popular music to membership in a multiracial vernacular culture signals the evolution of his racial attitudes.[34] At the outset of the novel, Mink can only resent a fellow member of the tenant-farming class on racial grounds. He recalls the time before his imprisonment when he cursed Houston's servant "for his black skin inside the warmer garments than his"—garments that are, in fact, "warmer clothing than any he [Mink] and his family possessed." Toward the end of his journey, however, Mink helps a black family pick cotton and enjoys the hospitality of their household. In this latter episode, Mink's language consistently emphasizes racial cooperation: "Looks like you could use another hand in here. . . . I'll help you a spell" (341, 688).

Mink thus develops an identity that has the potential to transcend racial boundaries. By performing experiences that are commonly associated with the black southern population, Mink is able to find a way of negotiating white and black worlds comfortably, transcending the barriers between them. His imprisonment in Parchman, his journey through the Delta, his collaboration with African American sharecroppers, and his embodiment of southern vernacular traditions suggest how much he has in common with all members of the rural laboring class, regardless of race. In Gregory's words, "Mink represents those who are dispossessed of a truly human existence . . . and deprived of hope, but who nevertheless triumph out of their spiritual poverty" (413): a statement that would serve equally well as a valediction for many of the prewar Mississippi blues singers.

As the closest thing to a black blues musician in Faulkner's fiction after "Old Man," Mink is a symptom of—and even a partial resolution to—the author's evolving sense of the difficulty of writing about African American characters. After World War II, as Faulkner became ever more convinced of the inaccessibility and unknowability of black subjectivities, people of color became less and less central to his fiction. Mink, however, serves as a surrogate for—or even as a bridge to—the southern black population that Faulkner apparently no longer dared write about extensively or frequently. In fact, Mink performs many of the characteristics common to black people in earlier Faulkner novels. Thadious Davis suggests that the African American Gibson family in *The Sound and the Fury* represents "opposition to the sterility and decay evidenced by the white [Compson] family" and that its members "project a vital creativity, an inventiveness in looking at life and a spiritedness in confronting it all" (*Faulkner's "Negro"* 70). Mink equally embodies an alternative to the sterility and decay of Snopesism.

That one of Faulkner's last major blues figures is white, rather than black, reflects the fact that, in the period in which the author was writing and publishing *The Mansion,* many young Caucasians were eagerly embracing African American culture via roots music—and often, along with it, a vision of a truly multicultural society. In the late 1950s, teenage Robert Zimmerman—who lived along Minnesota's exclusively white Iron Range—so much enjoyed the blues-drenched broadcasts of "Jim Dandy" on WHLB that he sought out the DJ in person, and was "startled, but pleased" to discover that Dandy was a man of color. They "spent hours playing old blues and R&B disks" together, and the adolescent Minnesotan "discovered a new Iron Range that his family scarcely knew" (Shelton 40–41). When Zimmerman—rechristened "Bob Dylan"—released his debut album in 1962, just a few months before Faulkner's death, it included two blues covers: Jefferson's "See That My Grave Is Kept Clean" and White's "Fixin' to Die." Dylan's second LP, the following year, featured "Oxford Town," a sardonic indictment of the white response to James Meredith's attempts to become the first black student enrolled at the University of Mississippi in Faulkner's hometown. Meanwhile, over in England, the teenaged Keith Richards and Mick Jagger were bonding over folk, jazz, and, especially, blues records. As the former remembers of first hearing Muddy Waters, "it all fell into place for me. . . . I realized the connection between all the music I'd heard. He made it all explainable. He was like a codebook" (qtd. in Bockris 38).

From the 1950s to the present, white youths—from Paul Butterfield and Eric Clapton to Stevie Ray Vaughan and Adam Gussow[35]—have found resonance and release in vernacular American music and black cultural traditions, particularly the blues. Although Faulkner could not have known of either the Rolling Stones or Bob Dylan in 1959, Mink's performance of a multiracial southern self parallels the postwar discovery of the blues by a white audience, the increasing influence of prewar rural culture—especially African American culture—upon the mainstream, and evolving white investment in multiculturalism and civil rights.

What might seem like a throwaway passage during Mink's brief sojourn in Memphis gestures to the diverse and multicultural genres of southern vernacular music associated with the character throughout *The Mansion*. In the city, Mink expects to see the levee on the Mississippi River lined with steamboats from his youth, "bearing names like Stacker Lee and Ozark Belle and Crescent Queen" (587).[36] These three steamboats invoke the central forms of twentieth-century southern music. *Crescent Queen* suggests New Orleans, the "Crescent City," the birthplace of jazz: a genre of music that made its way north via Mississippi riverboats, including one on which the young Louis Armstrong played early in his career.[37] *Ozark Belle,* meanwhile, gestures to the white southern mountain culture that produced fiddle and country music. At the time that Faulkner wrote *The Mansion,* in fact, America identified country music with the Ozarks even more than with the Appalachian region that had produced such prewar legends as Jimmie Rodgers and the Carter Family: between 1955 and 1960, the weekly live TV show *Ozark Jubilee* was instrumental in popularizing country music nationally.[38] Finally, *Stacker Lee* is the name of the legendary villain of one of the most renowned blues songs.

The presence of *Stacker Lee* in *The Mansion* further emphasizes the cross-pollination, interrelationship, and continuing relevance of southern musical forms. Stacker Lee (or Stagger Lee, or Stagolee, or Stag O'Lee) is the legendary "badman" of the African American oral tradition, based upon the historical Stagger Lee Shelton who shot Billy Lyons in St. Louis in 1895, allegedly in an argument over a Stetson hat. Although Stagger Lee has been most prominent in the blues—including songs by Ma Rainey (1926), Furry Lewis (1927), and Mississippi John Hurt (1928)—his tale has also been the subject of music in a variety of genres, including jazz (Duke Ellington in 1928, Cab Calloway in 1931, and Sidney Bechet in 1946), folk and country (Frank Hutchison in 1927, Carson Robison in 1932, and Woody Guthrie in 1944), and even a Hawaiian guitar version (by Sam Ku West in 1928).[39] Faulkner must have encountered the legendary character in some form or other, for, as Jane Isbell Haynes demonstrates, a passage in *The Hamlet* alludes to the Stagger Lee story (439–41). When Faulkner was still working on *The Mansion,* furthermore, the "Stagger Lee" song took on a new lease of life in a pop version by Lloyd Price that entered the charts early in December 1958 and spent four weeks at the top of the hit parade early in 1959 (Whitburn, *Joel Whitburn's Top Pop Singles* 515).

Mink is disoriented by the disappearance of the *Stacker Lee, Ozark Belle,* and *Crescent Queen* from the banks of the Mississippi, but the musical traditions those names embody had left the Ole Man far behind long before Faulkner's protagonist got out of prison. Blues, jazz, country, and folk had become national rather than regional or ethnic forms by the time the Snopes trilogy reached its conclusion. Faulkner once observed that African American "music and poetry have passed to the white man, and what the white man has done with them is not Negro any more but something else" (*Lion in the Garden* 264).[40] He might equally have made the broader statement that multiracial southern music and song have passed to the United States and to the world as a whole, and what people have done with them ever since is not southern or even necessarily American anymore, but something else—and that something else was one of the major artistic movements of the twentieth century.

If historical evidence concerning Faulkner's knowledge of the blues—particularly the now-canonical Mississippi country blues—remains sketchy, comparative analysis of the author's fiction and the songs of the region puts novels, stories, and lyrics alike in a revealing new light. Although the novelist often disdained recorded music, while his interest in local black performers may have been cursory, and if he depicted African American singers only rarely in his fiction, there is a great deal of the blues in Faulkner's work—as well as country, folk, gospel, and jazz. The melodies, lyrics, sensibilities, and attitudes of southern music seeped into his tales, "immersing the reader in a polyphonic discourse" (Ross 4), just as, throughout the twentieth century, they seeped into the larger American culture until they had become inextricable from the very fabric of the nation. Equally, there is no evidence that the guitarists, pianists, songwriters, and singers of the rural South ever read any of Faulkner's fiction, but as "Mississippi Boweavil Blues," "High Water Everywhere," "Last Kind Words Blues," "Dead Shrimp Blues," "Moving," "Can't Stay Here," "Parchman Farm Blues," and "Stack O'Lee" eloquently demonstrate, there was no need for them to have done so. The best of the bluesmakers were as attuned as Faulkner to the drama of the world in which they lived, and they created artistic monuments every bit as immortal as those of the Oxford novelist.

APPENDIX

BLUES LYRIC TRANSCRIPTIONS

The purpose of the following transcriptions is to demonstrate the value of using the same scholarly strategies for editing blues verses that editors customarily employ for canonical literary texts. My renderings of blues lyrics differ from conventional transcriptions in that they list variant readings by other scholars in footnotes, just as editors of Shakespeare often list textual variants. Since distinctions in transcription necessarily result in different—sometimes even substantially different—interpretations, it is crucial that variants be clearly in view.

Since most prewar country blues songs exist only as recordings, one of the biggest challenges faced by the pioneers of modern blues scholarship was the establishment of reliable transcriptions of lyrics. Neither the creators of the classic country blues nor the phonograph companies that recruited them tended to publish their songs. Rural blues artists in that era were not composers or authors in the traditional senses of those terms: they usually did not read music or even keep handwritten copies of their lyrics (Taft, *Blues Lyric Formula* 22). Any written versions of Wiley's "Last Kind Words Blues"—an oral performance preserved only on record—are constructions by subsequent editors.

Many country blues musicians before World War II did not consider their records definitive performances of songs—or even as particularly significant other than as evidence of their prominence or as publicity for their live appearances. Blues songs were fluid texts that could—and usually did—alter on each occasion that an artist sang them, sometimes drastically. Most blues singers in this era habitually performed partly from memory and partly through improvisation. Every time Charley Patton played "Mississippi Boweavil Blues," it is likely that he amended, revised, reimagined, expanded, or compressed it depending on such variables as audience, context, and mood. It is evident from the existing alternate takes recorded by Robert Johnson—a musician who was more conscious of himself as a recording artist than many of his predecessors—that, while a number such as "Come On in My Kitchen" had a general framework, its lyrics could vary significantly from performance to performance.

For listeners today, the records that singers improvised in often-makeshift studios are *the* texts of the prewar country blues. Our only access to Patton's "High Water Everywhere" is the version of it that the bluesman happened to perform before a microphone, either in late 1929 or early 1930—and we only have access to it at all because a few fragile commercial phonograph discs endured sufficiently that postwar enthusiasts had an opportunity to preserve the music that they contained for posterity.

Much other great American vernacular music on record has been lost forever. Paramount—the company for which Patton made most of his recordings—went out of business in the early 1930s and sold its masters for scrap (Calt and Wardlow 224). Scuffed, scratched, and sometimes warped 78s are the only ultimate source of any of Patton's music, and some of his work simply has not survived at all. At his final recording session for another label, the American Record Company, in 1934, Patton sang pieces with such intriguing titles as "Charley Bradley's Ten Sixty Six Blues," "The Delta Murder," and "Whisky Distillery." Since the company did not deign to release any of these numbers on phonograph discs at the time, nobody outside the studio ever heard them—and nobody ever will (Calt and Wardlow 241–46).

Coupled with the poor sound quality of the many extant prewar country blues recordings that derive from battered and aged 78s, Patton's notoriously incomprehensible diction is a serious obstacle to any attempt to reproduce his lyrics on the printed page. Even some of Patton's colleagues complained about the incoherence of his vocal style. As Son House once observed, "You could sit at Charley's feet and not understand a word he sang" (qtd. in Titon, *Early Downhome Blues* 52). More recently, the British rock band Gomez sang, "I spend a lifetime trying to decipher Charley Patton songs / I don't know why I bother: even if I think it's right, it always comes out wrong." A classic illustration of Patton's customary impenetrability is the opening line of "Down the Dirt Road Blues" (1929), which, as Elijah Wald notes, could be the prosaic statement, "I'm going away to Illinois," or the rather more abstract declaration, "I'm going away to a world unknown" ("Charlie Patton" n.p.). Although few singers are quite as challenging in this regard as Patton, many prewar blues records contain problematic passages, such as the issue of what the male protagonist of "Last Kind Words Blues" promises to bring the speaker.

Like Shakespeare's plays or even Faulkner's fiction, blues lyrics do not just exist as texts but require construction. The late Noel Polk devoted much of his career to scrutiny of typescripts, manuscripts, and published editions to ensure that the current versions of Faulkner's novels are as reliable as possible. Equally, scholars, editors, and directors alike must continue to choose, for example, whether Othello says of Desdemona in Shakespeare's play, "She gave me for my pains a world of kisses" (as in the Folio I.3.173), or "She gave me for my pains a world of sighs" (as in the Quarto 540). This is a significant variant in that it obviously has considerable implications regarding the nature of Othello's relationship with his wife, just as the difference between "Illinois" or "a world unknown" has a substantial effect upon how listeners might interpret Patton's song.

As successive generations of scholars have built upon the work of their predecessors, the lyrics of prewar blues records have become significantly clearer and increasingly fixed. Peter Guralnick acknowledges that the difficulty he had deciphering Robert Johnson's words as a young man is barely imaginable after several decades of rigorous study by tireless auditors and editors. "The lyrics over which we agonized," he observes, "have long since been thoroughly deciphered, annotated, and analyzed, and seem almost laughably accessible today when one thinks of the hours spent in fruitless speculation" (*Searching for Robert Johnson* 6).

Even so, the act of transferring a blues lyric with any degree of accuracy from the medium of recording to the printed page remains necessarily complicated and can never be definitive, just as there is no such thing as a definitive or final text of *Othello.* Scholars and fans continue to debate the precise wording of several crucial passages in such songs as "High Water Everywhere."

Rather than provide transcriptions of all the blues lyrics discussed in this study, I have chosen to present as examples of blues textual editing the three songs that have never been copyrighted and which include passages that are still sources of debate: Patton's "Mississippi Boweavil Blues" and "High Water Everywhere," and Wiley's "Last Kind Words Blues." In each case, I have used the recording as the copy text, while noting diverse renderings by previous transcribers.

CHARLEY PATTON, "MISSISSIPPI BOWEAVIL BLUES"

Recorded: 14 June 1929, Richmond, Indiana
Released: September 1929 on Paramount 12805, b/w "Screamin' and Hollerin' the Blues," both credited to "The Masked Marvel"

This text of Patton's recording[1] makes reference to several other transcriptions, giving priority to the most recent and reliable. Dick Spottswood's renderings of Patton's verses for the *Screamin' and Hollerin' the Blues* box set (2001) are the most definitive texts of the artist's work currently available, but I have also consulted readings by David Evans ("Charley Patton" [1991]) and Stephen Calt and Gayle Dean Wardlow (1988). These three works supersede the necessarily provisional efforts of earlier scholars, but my footnotes cite other transcriptions—such as those provided by John Fahey (*Charley Patton* [1971])—when they are particularly illuminating, interesting, or provocative. It would be both redundant and unjust, however, to enumerate every error or dubious notation in groundbreaking—but now outdated—transcriptions by the pioneers of blues studies.

N.B. In this and other transcriptions, italics denote spoken interjections.

1. It's a little boll weevil,[2] see it movin' in a empty . . . ,[3] Lordy
   You can plant your cotton and you won't get a half a cent,[4] Lordy

1. "Mississippi Boweavil Blues" features one of Patton's more coherent vocal performances. There are relatively few significant variants between the most recent transcriptions, except for minor issues of pronunciation. For example, Spottswood includes such contractions as "I's," "yo'," and "an'" (60), whereas Evans prefers "I was," "your," and "and" respectively (179). My transcription presents words in their full form unless the contraction is so substantial or audible as to demand acknowledgment.

2. Spottswood employs the "boll weavil" spelling (60), whereas Calt and Wardlow often transcribe the name of the titular insect as "Bo weevil" (328). Like Evans (179), I have elected to use the standard spelling.

3. Spottswood inserts "[square]" for the elided word here (60), thus connecting the song's opening line to similar lines in the fifth and ninth stanzas concerning an "empty square." Evans notes that the boll weevil "bores into the cotton bud (known as a 'square'), preventing it from blossoming" (178). Patton's opening line carries a trace of the "Ballet of de Boll Weevil," collected by John Lomax, which begins, "De farmer say to de weevil: 'What you doin' on de square?'" (Sandburg 253).

4. Calt and Wardlow's transcription of this word as "bale" is unorthodox (328). Most transcriptions read "cent" (Fahey 72, and Spottswood 60).

2. "Boll weevil, boll weevil, where's your native home, Lordy?"[5]
   "A-Louisiana an' Texas is a-where I[6] bred and born,[7] Lordy"

3. Well, I saw the boll weevil, Lord, a-circle, Lordy, in the air, Lordy
   The next time I seed him, Lord, he had his family there, Lordy

4. Boll weevil left Texas, Lord, he bid[8] me fare ye[9] well, Lordy
   "Where you goin' now?"
   "I'm going down to Mississippi,[10] gonna give Louisiana hell, Lordy"

5. Boll weevil said, "Farmer, think I treat you fair, Lordy"[11]
   "How is that, boy?"
   "Suck all the blossom and leave you a empty square,[12] Lordy"
   And next time[13] I see you, know you had your family there, Lordy

6. Boll weevil and[14] his wife: "We [can] sit down on the hill, Lordy"
   Boll weevil told his wife: "Let's take this forty here,[15] Lordy"

5. Scholars customarily use quotation marks to indicate passages of dialogue in the song, but Calt and Wardlow make a point of leaving Patton's frequent exclamation "Lordy" outside of quotation marks, attributing it to the narrator of the song, rather than its characters (328).

6. Fahey and Spottswood transcribe this as "I's" (Fahey 72, and Spottswood 60), and Evans as "I was" (179).

7. Calt and Wardlow's "A-Louisiana raised in Texas, least is where I was," is an anomalous reading (328).

8. Most transcriptions read "bid" (Calt and Wardlow 328; Evans 179; and Fahey 72), but Spottswood suggests the present-tense "biddin'" instead (60).

9. Evans renders this as "you" (179), and Spottswood as "thee" (60), but I prefer the "ye" of earlier transcriptions (Calt and Wardlow 328, and Fahey 72).

10. Only Calt and Wardlow suggest "goin' down the Mississippi," changing the referent from state to river.

11. Spottswood renders this line as "Boll weevil said [to] the farmer, 'Think I treat you fair, Lordy'" (60). Calt and Wardlow suggest the unorthodox "Bo weevil said to the farmer, ''Tain't got ticket fare,' Lordie" (328).

12. Calt and Wardlow suggest "your hedges square" (328), a reading that subsequent transcriptions have superseded.

13. Spottswood presents this as "A-next time" (60), Calt and Wardlow "The next time" (328), and Fahey just "Next time" (72).

14. Most transcriptions render this word as "told" (Evans 179, and Fahey 72), but, as Spottswood's placing it in parentheses signals, the word is obscure (60). Calt and Wardlow suggest "meet" (328).

15. Calt and Wardlow suggest "Let's trade this forty in" instead of the now-customary "Let's take this forty here," and note that this is a reference to "forty acres of land" (328).

7. Boll weevil told his wife, said, "I believe I may go north, Lordy"
   Lord, I won't tell nobody[16]
   "Let's leave Louisiana and go[17] to Arkansas, Lordy"

8. Well, I saw the boll weevil, Lord, a-circle, Lordy, in the air, Lordy
   Next time I seed him, Lord, he had his family there, Lordy

9. Boll weevil told the farmer that "I think I[18] treat you fair,[19] Lordy
   Sucks[20] all the blossom and leave you a empty[21] square,[22] Lordy"

10. "Boll weevil, boll weevil, where your native home, Lordy?"
   "Most anywhere they raise[23] cotton and corn, Lordy"

11. Boll weevil, boll weevil, oughta treat me fair,[24] Lordy
   Next time I did you had your family there, Lordy.

16. Evans gives this spoken interjection as "Boy, I'm gonna tell all about it" (179), and Calt and Wardlow provide the similar "Hold on, I'm gonna tell all about that" (328). Spottswood's "Lord, I won' tell nobody" is more persuasive (60).

17. Calt and Wardlow render this as "we can go" (328), but most transcriptions suggest "and go" (Evans 179; Fahey 72; and Spottswood 60).

18. Evans transcribes this as "I'll" (179). I follow Spottswood's "I" (60). Fahey renders the line as "Ain't going to treat you fair" (72).

19. As in the fifth stanza, Calt and Wardlow transcribe this as "I 'tain't got ticket fare" (328).

20. Evans gives this as "sucked" (179), while Fahey suggests "took" (72). A slim majority—myself included—hear "sucks" (Calt and Wardlow 328, and Spottswood 60).

21. Spottswood indicates the lack of certainty regarding this word by placing it in parentheses (60). Most transcriptions assume it is "empty" (Evans 179, and Fahey 72).

22. As in the fifth stanza, Calt and Wardlow suggest "your hedges square" (328).

23. Evans and Spottswood render this as "they're raising" or "they're raisin'" (Evans 179, and Spottswood 60). I prefer Calt and Wardlow's "they raise" (328).

24. Calt and Wardlow take the unusual step of placing only "Oughta treat me fair" in quotations in this line (328), probably because of Patton's audible pause before he sings that part of the line.

NOTE ON "THE BALLAD OF THE BOLL WEEVIL"

Songs by African American musicians about the boll weevil date at least as far back as the 1890s. Gates Thomas first transcribed vernacular verses about the infamous pest in 1897, and John Lomax recorded the lyrics of what was to become the most familiar version of the ballad from a black farmer in 1909. Carl Sandburg observes that the song existed in multiple versions across the South by the early twentieth century, and he included two renditions of it in his 1927 *American Songbag* collection (Sandburg 8–10, 252–53; Lawson, "First Century" 49).

Numerous songs about the boll weevil—some of them related both musically and lyrically to the ballads collected by southern folklorists and some not resembling them at all—appeared on records in the early-to-mid 1920s, largely by jazz orchestras, pop singers, or country performers. These included numbers by Al Bernard (ca. 1921), Ernest Hare (ca. 1921), Noble Sissle (1921), Tim Brymm's Black Devil Orchestra (1921), Vernon Dalhart (1924), Gid Tanner's Skillet Lickers (1924), the Miami Lucky Seven (1924), Fiddlin' John Carson (1924), the International Novelty Orchestra (1924), and Charlie Oaks (1925). Even Sandburg recorded the piece for Victor in 1926. A song most likely created by rural black southerners thus first achieved national fame primarily through versions by white artists.

The first blues records about the boll weevil were those by Ma Rainey (1923) and Bessie Smith (1924), although these vaudeville numbers bear little resemblance to either the folk lyrics or melody of the traditional song. The first country blues recording of the boll weevil song was by Coleman Bird (a.k.a. Jaybird Coleman) for the short-lived Black Patti company in 1927. By the time that Patton recorded "Mississippi Boweavil Blues," the number had been a common part of the repertoire of southern songsters for thirty years, and a variety of artists had recorded it throughout much of the preceding decade. Nonetheless, Patton's record may well have been, as James C. Giesen suggests, "the first widely disseminated commercial" country blues version of the song (96).

It is ironic that, although Patton's version was one of the first rural blues about the boll weevil committed to wax, the musician's radical revision contains only faint echoes of the traditional ballad, such as the catchy melody and the dialogue between farmer and weevil. Lead Belly's numerous recordings of the song are much closer to the versions collected by such folklorists as Lomax and Sandburg, and became the template for subsequent artists. Lead Belly did not record his take on the boll weevil number until 1934, however, and did not make a commercially available version until 1939—a whole decade after Patton's record—even though the text of the song appears in 1936's *Negro Folk Songs as Sung by Lead Belly*, edited by the Lomaxes (184–87). The boll weevil ballad enjoyed a new lease of life during the 1950s, largely because of the booming folk revival. Burl Ives, the Weavers, and

Fats Domino were among numerous artists who recorded it in this period. Brook Benton's 1961 version even peaked at number two on the pop charts (Whitburn, *Joel Whitburn Presents Top R&B Singles* 28, and *Joel Whitburn's Top Pop Singles* 48).

CHARLEY PATTON, "HIGH WATER EVERYWHERE"

Recorded: October 1929 or early 1930, Grafton, Wisconsin[25]
Released: Mid-1930 on either side of Paramount 12909

As with "Mississippi Boweavil Blues," I have cross-referenced my rendering of this song with transcriptions by other scholars. "High Water Everywhere" contains many obscure passages and lines, so, in addition to consulting the standard transcriptions by Spottswood (2001), Evans ("High Water Everywhere" [2006]), and Calt and Wardlow (1988), I cite earlier efforts by John Fahey (*Charley Patton* [1971]), Don Kent (in Samuel Charters, *The Blues Makers* [originally 1967]), Paul Oliver (*Blues Fell This Morning* [1960]), Robert Palmer (1982), Eric Sackheim (1969), and Michael Taft (*Talkin' to Myself* [2005]).

Part I

1. The backwater done rose around Sumner[26] now,[27] drove me down the line
   Backwater done rose at Sumner, drove poor Charley down the line
   And I'll tell the world the water done struck Drew'ses town[28]

2. Lord, the whole round country, Lord, river[29] has overflowed
   Lord, the whole round country, man, is[30] overblowed[31]

25. For many years, scholars assumed that Patton recorded this song in October 1929, but unpublished research now suggests that it may date from early in 1930 instead, and that the second part of the song concerns not the Great Mississippi Flood of 1927 but a similar, if smaller, disaster in Alabama in January 1930 (Evans, "e-mail").

26. Spottswood is unusual for rendering the A line as "The backwater done rolled and tumbled" (62). I follow the majority's "done rose around Sumner" (Calt and Wardlow 200; Oliver 219; and Sackheim 193). Evans inserts an extra word to make it "done rose all around Sumner" (60).

27. Most readings suggest "now" (Calt and Wardlow 200; Oliver 219; Sackheim 193; and Spottswood 62), whereas Evans reads this as "Lord" (60).

28. It is indicative of the challenges presented by Patton's performance of the song that Calt and Wardlow tentatively heard the B line as "An' no tellin' what the water, done to (Joe Lee's?) town" (200).

29. Evans, Spottswood, and Taft suggest "creek water" instead of "river" (Evans 60; Spottswood 62; and Taft 474), but, like Calt and Wardlow and many earlier listeners, I hear "river" (Calt and Wardlow 200; Fahey 91; Palmer 75; and Sackheim 193).

30. Evans suggest "it's" instead of "is" (60).

31. Virtually all extant transcriptions prefer the sense and repetition of "overflowed" in the second A line, but I hear "overblowed."

You know I can't stay here, I'm—I'll go[32] *where it's high, boy*
I would go to the hill country, but they got me barred[33]

3. Now looky here, now,[34] Leland,[35] river was risin' high
Looky here, boys around Leland tell me, river is ragin' high
Boy, it's risin' over there, yeah[36]
I'm gonna move over to Greenville 'fore I bid you goodbye[37]

4. Looky here, the water done, Lordy, *done broke,*[38] rose most everywhere
The water at Greenville *and Leland,* mowin' down rows[39] everywhere
Boy, you can't never stay here
I would go down to Rosedale, but they tell me it's water there

32. Patton apparently stumbles over this spoken interjection. Spottswood renders it as "I'm boun' go" (62), whereas Evans's transcription, "I'm . . . I'll go," is more persuasive (60).

33. Many transcriptions—including the most recent and reliable—concur on this reading (Evans 60, and Spottswood 62). Calt and Wardlow render the line as "I was goin' to the hilly country, 'fore they got me barred" (200).

34. Spottswood draws attention to an elided "[at]" here (62), whereas Evans incorporates the "at" firmly into his transcription (60), but, although the inclusion allows the line to make more sense, Patton does not seem to sing it.

35. Evans inserts "Lordy" here (60), and Spottswood "Lord" (62), but, like earlier scholars, I hear no additional word (Oliver 219, and Palmer 75).

36. Calt and Wardlow are in a minority for hearing this "yeah" as "y'hear?" (201).

37. Most transcriptions agree on "'fore I tell you," "bid you," or "say" goodbye" for this line (Calt and Wardlow 201; Fahey 91; Palmer 75; Sackheim 193; and Spottswood 62). Evans's unorthodox—but intriguing—reading is "Bought our tickets. Good-bye" (61), which makes more immediate literal sense, but is less convincing aurally.

38. This is one of the song's most challenging lines. Evans and Spottswood essentially agree upon "Looky here, [the] water dug out, levee broke" (Evans 61, and Spottswood 62). Fahey provides the similar "the water dug out, something broke" (91). I think, however, that Sackheim's "water done, now lordy, done broke" is closest to Patton's delivery (193). As in other instances, I think Patton is stumbling over the lines here, and, while "levee broke" makes sense in a song about the Mississippi flood, I hear no clear evidence for it.

39. Evans and Spottswood—like many before them—transcribe this as "it done rose" (Evans 61; Spottswood 62; Calt and Wardlow 201; Fahey 91; Sackheim 193). I find Palmer's unorthodox "mowin' down rows" highly convincing, however (76), and I like the homonymic echoes of "rose," "rows," and "Rosedale" in this stanza. At the time of the flood, it was too early in the season for the water to mow down rows of cotton, but the implied idea of the rampaging river usurping the harvest is appealing. The line could equally refer to rows of houses or cabins.

5. Now, the water now, mama, done struck[40] Shaw'ses[41] town[42]
   Well, they tell me the water done struck Shaw'ses town
   Boy, I'm goin' to Vicksburg
   Well, I'm goin' to Vicksburg for a high of mine[43]

6. I am goin' out high[44] water, where lands[45] don't never flow
   Well, I'm goin' over the hill where water, oh it don't never blow[46]
   Boy, Sharkey County and Issaquena's drowned and inched[47] over
   Bolivar County was inchin'[48] over that Tallahatchie shore[49]
   Boy, went to[50] Tallahatchie, they got it over there

40. Although "struck" is a common reading (Evans 61; Fahey 92; Oliver 219; Sackheim 193; and Spottswood 63),"shook" is also a possibility. A few auditors suggest "took" (Calt and Wardlow 202, and Palmer 76).

41. Although transcriptions now tend to agree upon "Shaw'ses town" (Evans 61, and Spottswood 63), many earlier transcriptions suggested "Charley's town" (Fahey 92; Palmer 76; and Sackheim 193). Calt and Wardlow heard it as "short little town" (202).

42. In between the first and second A line in this stanza, there is a spoken interjection. The words are inaudible, and the voice does not seem to be close enough to the microphone to be Patton's.

43. A majority of critics prefer a variant of "on a higher mound" (Calt and Wardlow 202; Evans 61; Oliver 219; and Spottswood 62). Nonetheless, at least three auditors suggest "on that high of mine" or "for that high of mine" (Kent in Charters 41; Palmer 76; and Sackheim 193). I consider this the most persuasive reading, and I suspect that the "higher mound" rendering is an example of critics seeking a construction that makes the most immediate literal sense—in this instance, the quest for safety on a raised Indian mound, just like the convict and pregnant woman in Faulkner's "Old Man" (148). See chapter 2 for an explanation of why "for that high of mine" conceivably makes sense.

44. Evans suggests "going out on high water" (61), and Spottswood "going on high water" (63). The meaning of the line seems to be "I'm going out [of] high water."

45. Evans and Spottswood render this as the singular "land" (Evans 61, and Spottswood 63).

46. Evans suggests "flow" (61), whereas Spottswood provides "blow" (63). I hear the latter—and note the echo of the "overflowed"/"overblowed" A lines from the second stanza.

47. I follow Evans's persuasive reading of this difficult line. Spottswood's transcription is similar, but suggests "beached" rather than "inched" (63). Instead of "Issaquena's drowned and inched over," Calt and Wardlow suggest "an' everything was down in Stover" (202), approximating readings by previous auditors (Fahey 92; Kent in Charters 41; and Sackheim 193).

48. Spottswood suggests "leakin'" instead of "inchin'" (63).

49. Patton swallows the end of this line so that it is not clearly audible. It is both customary and logical to transcribe it as "Tallahatchie shore" or "Tallahatchie's shore" (Evans 61; Fahey 92; Kent in Charters 41; Oliver 219; Palmer 76; and Spottswood 63). Sackheim suggests "sure" rather than "shore" (193). Calt and Wardlow postulate "'Tallahatchie skid" (202).

50. Evans suggests "in" instead of "to" (61). Calt and Wardlow render the line as "Boy went in Tallahatchie to find it over there!" (202).

7. Lord, the water done rushed all up[51] that old Jackson road
   Lord, the water done raise-ed[52] over the Jackson road
   Boy, it starched my clothes[53]
   I'm goin' back to the hilly[54] country, won't be worried no more

Part II

1. Backwater at Blytheville, backed up all around[55]
   Backwater at Blytheville, done took[56] Joiner town
   It was fifty families and children suffer to sink and drown[57]

2. The water was risin' up in my friend's door
   The water was risin' up in my friend's door
   The[58] man said to his womenfolk, "Lord, we'd better go"

3. The water was risin', got up in my bed
   Lord, the water[59] rollin', got up to my bed
   I thought I would take a trip, Lord, out on the big ice sled[60]

51. Evans's transcription is "all over that" (61), and Spottswood's "all up that" (63). Calt and Wardlow suggest "rushed over, down" (202).

52. Evans's rendering is unusual for inserting "up" here (61).

53. The majority of transcriptions prefer a variant of "Boy, it got [in] my clothes!" (Evans 61; Fahey 92; and Spottswood 62), but I stand with Calt and Wardlow and Palmer on the humorous "Boy, it starched my clothes" (Calt and Wardlow 202, and Palmer 76). Kent and Sackheim even suggest, "Boy, it got my car" (Charters 41, and Sackheim 194).

54. Evans renders this as "hill" (61), but most transcriptions suggest "hilly" (Fahey 92; Kent in Charters 41; Palmer 76; Sackheim 194; and Spottswood 63).

55. Virtually all transcriptions agree upon the opening line of the song's second part, with the exception of Palmer, whose intriguing alternative is "doctor weren't around" (76).

56. Both Evans and Spottswood render this as "struck," echoing similar constructions in the first and fifth stanzas of Part I of the song (Evans 63, and Spottswood 63). I agree with the earlier scholars who transcribe it as "took" (Calt and Wardlow 205; Fahey 92; Kent in Charters 41; Oliver 219; and Palmer 76).

57. Spottswood notes that the line is obscure, but suggests "some a them sink and drown" (63). Evans postulates that, after the narrator's observation of the fate of the families and children, Patton impersonates a cruel and racist onlooker who says, "Tough luck; they can drown" (63). Of all the existing readings, I am most swayed by Palmer's "suffer to sink and drown" (76). See the note on a similar line in the fifth stanza.

58. Evans's "The" and Spottswood's "Some" are equally credible (Evans 63, and Spottswood 63).

59. Evans inserts "was" here (63), whereas Spottswood inserts "is" (63), but it is questionable if Patton sings a verb at all.

60. Ice sleds may have been used as rescue vehicles during the flood. See the fourth stanza. Cora Lee Campbell's historical memories of her rescue from the levee at Greenville are similar

4. Oh, I [61] hear the horn blow, blowin' upon my door[62]
Blowin'? . . . Couldn't hear it[63]
I hear the ice boat, Lord, was[64] sinkin' down
I couldn't get no boat there, levee and city gone down[65]

5. Oh, high[66] the water risin,' our men sinkin' down[67]
Sayin' the water was risin,' airplanes is[68] all around
Boy, they's all around
It were fifty men and children: "Tough luck, they can drown"[69]

---

to Patton's narrative in this song. She recalls, "the water just come up on me. . . . Then, in three days a boat come . . . and the boat it like to sunk" (qtd. in Daniel, *Deep'n* 16).

61. Spottswood inserts "can" here (63), but Evans does not (63).

62. This line—its last half especially—has puzzled scholars for years. Evans and Spottswood suggest that the horn is blowing upon "my shore" (Evans 63, and Spottswood 63). Kent suggests waters that "roll above my door" (Charters 42), whereas Fahey, Palmer, and Sackheim have "water upon my door" (Fahey 92; Palmer 76; and Sackheim 195). I am persuaded by Evans's and Spottswood's readings of much of the line, but I believe earlier auditors are correct that the final word is "door."

63. Patton's spoken interjection here is particularly muffled. Evans suggests "You know, I couldn't hear it" (63), whereas Spottswood has "Blowin' [sighs] . . . look here!" (63). My version combines elements of both transcriptions.

64. Spottswood postulates "when [she]" (63), while Palmer suggests "went" (76). I follow Evans's reading (63).

65. The final half of this line presents another substantial challenge for transcribers. Evans suggests "so I let 'em sink on down" (63), and Kent has "left me sink on down" (Charters 42). Fahey, Palmer, and Sackheim even suggest the unlikely "Marion City gone down" (Fahey 92; Palmer 76; and Sackheim 195). I think that Spottswood comes closest to Patton's delivery with "the levee [an' city] gone down" (63).

66. Spottswood and Palmer suggest "So high" (Palmer 76, and Spottswood 63), whereas Evans follows other critics by constructing this as a wordless moan, "Oh-ah" (Evans 63; Fahey 92; Kent in Charters 42; Oliver 220; and Sackheim 195). My transcription combines both readings.

67. There is no critical consensus regarding what is "sinkin' down" here. It could be "islands" (Evans 63); "I been" (Calt and Wardlow 205; Palmer 76; and Spottswood 63); "and we're" (Fahey 92); or "families" (Kent in Charters 42; Oliver 220; and Sackheim 195). The benefit of my "our men"—which is no less credible than any other reading—is that it establishes a connection to the subsequent "women [and] children sinkin' down" in the fifth stanza.

68. The majority of transcriptions read this as "was" (Evans 63; Oliver 220; and Spottswood 63), but I agree with Kent's "is" (Charters 42). Several earlier critics tended not to hear "airplanes," but "at places" instead (Fahey 92; Palmer 76; and Sackheim 195).

69. Critics often transcribe this line as they transcribe the last line of the first stanza. See the note above. Although I am not convinced by Evans's reading in the earlier instance, I can very clearly hear it on this occasion (63). I think the song is more effective for retaining this

6. Oh-oooh, Lordy, women and grown men down[70]
   Ahh-oh, women,[71] children sinkin' down
   Lord, have mercy!
   I couldn't see nobody home[72] and was no one to be found.

---

devastating statement for a later verse rather than unveiling it in the first stanza. In this transcription, the early verses describe a natural tragedy, but the penultimate verse then offers a shock revelation of the social attitudes that exacerbate the human impact of such a disaster.

70. Evans reads this line as "women is groanin' down" (63), which is credible. There is, however, a clear consensus for "women and grown men down" (Calt and Wardlow 205; Fahey 92; Kent in Charters 42; Palmer 77; Sackheim 195; and Spottswood 63).

71. Virtually all scholars insert "and" here (Calt and Wardlow 205; Evans 63; Kent in Charters 42; Oliver 220; and Sackheim 195), but I agree with Spottswood that Patton does not sing it (62).

72. Spottswood does not include this word in his transcription (63), but virtually all other scholars do (Evans 63; Fahey 92; Kent in Charters 42; Oliver 220; Palmer 77; and Sackheim 195).

GEESHIE WILEY, "LAST KIND WORDS BLUES"

Recorded: ca. March 1930, Grafton, Wisconsin
Released: Mid-1930 on Paramount 12951 b/w "Skinny Leg Blues"

Wiley's diction is notably clearer than Patton's, but, as another Paramount recording artist, her surviving recordings are inevitably a little rough in sound quality. I compared my transcription of "Last Kind Words Blues" with those by John J. Sullivan ("Unknown Bards" [2008]), AnneMarie Cordeiro in her unpublished MA thesis on Wiley (2011), Greil Marcus (*Invisible Republic* [1997]), and a partial transcription by Ted Gioia (2008). I also consulted a variety of transcriptions available online (including a fascinating discussion at the Weenie Campbell website, weeniecampbell.com/yabbse/index.php? topic=377.45).

1. The last kind[73] words[74] I heard my daddy say
   Lord, the last kind words I heard my daddy say:[75]

2. "If I die, if I die in the German War
   I want you to send my body,[76] send it to my mother-in-law"[77]

73. Sullivan suggests that "kind" in this context carries the traditional connotation of "natural," the reverse of "supernatural," as opposed to the modern meaning of "nice" (87).

74. Although Paramount released the song as "Last Kind Words Blues," both Cordeiro and Gioia suggest that Wiley sings the singular "word" (Cordeiro 59, and Gioia 126), whereas Sullivan insists upon "words" (86).

75. The biggest challenge for any transcription—and thus any interpretation—of Wiley's lyric is the question of who is speaking and when. Transcriptions differ as to precisely how many verses of the song constitute the eponymous last words uttered by the speaker's "daddy." Cordeiro's otherwise impeccable rendering does not indicate where the male character's speech ends (59). Sullivan's transcription implies that the man's speech ends with the second line of the third stanza (86), and, while this is the most persuasive rendering, I should acknowledge that there are other possibilities—such as the eighth stanza returning to the "last kind words" of the male protagonist.

76. Both Cordeiro and Sullivan render this as "money" (Cordeiro 59, and Sullivan 86), a reading that makes more immediate sense than "body," since, otherwise, the two sets of instructions for disposal of after death—burial and non-burial—are contradictory. Although it complicates the lyrics, Wiley's delivery suggests "body" to me. See the analysis in chapter 3.

77. Gioia suggests "mother, lord" (126), but Cordeiro's and Sullivan's "mother-in-law" is at least equally credible (Cordeiro 59, and Sullivan 86).

3. "If I get killed, if I get killed, please don't bury my soul[78]
I cry,[79] just[80] leave me out, let the buzzards eat me whole"

4. "When you see me comin' look 'cross the rich man's field
If I don't bring you flour, I'll bring you bolted meal."[81]

5. I went to the depot, I looked up at the sun[82]
Cried, "Some train don't come, gon' be some walkin' done"

6. My mama told me[83], just before she died
"Lord, precious[84] daughter, don't you be so wild"[85]

7. The Mississippi River, you know it's deep and wide
I can stand right here, see my baby[86] from the other side

8. What you do to me, baby, it never gets out of me
I may not see you[87] after I cross the deep blue sea.

78. One online transcription suggests "don't tell a soul."

79. Some transcriptions suggest "prefer" instead of "cry." Marcus imaginatively constructs this as two lines: "Iiiiiiiiiiiiiii / Cried . . ." (203).

80. Cordeiro omits "just" from her transcription (59).

81. This line has proven the most challenging to transcribers. Sullivan initially heard it as "If I don't bring you flowers, I'll bring you a boutonniere" (86). One online transcription even suggests "Beaujolais." With John Fahey's help, Sullivan came to the realization that the line refers instead to "bolted meal": "finely sifted meal"—"the rich man's flour" (88).

82. Some online transcriptions suggest "stars" or "sign" instead of "sun."

83. As with the "last kind words" of the male character, it is unclear when the speech of the speaker's mother (beginning in the sixth stanza) ends. Most transcriptions that make the distinction suggest only that the second line of the sixth stanza belongs in quotation marks, but there are other possibilities. For example, if the seventh stanza is also spoken by the mother—making it the mother who is looking at her "baby" (daughter) from the other side—this would affect the meanings of the song profoundly.

84. Sullivan (after Fahey) suggests "blessed" instead of "precious" (88).

85. Cordeiro suggests the unusual "Lord, since the dawn, I thought you'd be so wise" (59). One online transcription posits "don't you weep and whine."

86. Marcus suggests "face" instead of "baby" (203).

87. Both Cordeiro and Sullivan both read this as "I believe I'll see ya" instead of "I may not see you" (Cordeiro 60, and Sullivan 87).

NOTES

INTRODUCTION

1. An offshoot of the Wisconsin Chair Company, this Paramount—which went out of business in 1932—has no relation to the famous film company of the same name. See van der Tuuk.

2. For an account of the blues scene around Dockery Plantation and Drew, see Evans, *Big Road Blues*. The standard biographies of Patton are Calt and Wardlow, *King of the Delta Blues,* and Evans, "Charley Patton: The Conscience of the Delta."

3. For further details about the nature of early recording studios and Patton's June 1929 session, see Gioia (66–71), and Taft, *Blues Lyric Formula* (290–92).

4. There are no extant sales figures for "Pony Blues," but Calt and Wardlow estimate that it may have sold as many as 50,000 copies (186). Recently, blues scholars have suggested that Patton may have recorded some of the songs traditionally attributed to the October 1929 session in early 1930 (Evans, e-mail).

5. Walter Rhodes from Ruleville was "the first Sunflower County bluesman to appear on records" (Calt and Wardlow 174). Other Mississippi blues artists who preceded Patton into recording studios were William Harris in 1927, Tommy Johnson in 1928, and Mississippi John Hurt, also in 1928.

6. Many of the prewar records of Booker T. Washington White—including his 1937 hit and his 1940 songs about Parchman Farm—spell his name "Bukka" White. In this study, I refer to him by the name under which his records were originally released, despite it being a misnomer.

7. See the picture at www.livebluesworld.com/profiles/blogs/1598513:BlogPost:471.

8. This is the title of Yazoo's compilation of Patton's songs, the standard edition of the bluesman's work until the appearance of Revenant's definitive seven-CD set, *Screamin' and Hollerin' the Blues,* in 2001.

9. See the appendix for discussion of the song's history and other recordings of it, as well as a full transcription of the lyrics of Patton's version.

10. On *Screamin' and Hollerin' the Blues,* "Mississippi Boweavil Blues" appears as the twelfth track on the first disc, preceded by virtually every other song that Patton recorded on 14 June 1929. Meanwhile, the earlier anthology, *Founder of the Delta Blues,* reserves "Mississippi Boweavil Blues" for its second track. Before the gradual rediscovery of Patton began in the late 1950s, however, the only widely available recording of any of his songs was "Mississippi Boweavil Blues," tucked away—anonymously—on the *Anthology of American Folk Music* (1952).

11. For accounts and analyses of Handy's story, see Evans, *Big Road Blues* (34–35); Gussow, *Seems Like Murder Here* (94, 100); and Wagner (25–29).

12. Handy quotes the lyrics of a rural boll weevil song in his autobiography only a page after mentioning the Tutwiler episode (74, 75).

13. For discussion of the boll weevil in southern history and culture, see Giesen, and Helms.

14. For further analysis of the song's pointed parallels between the boll weevil and African Americans in the South, see Evans, "Charley Patton" (178–79); Garon (116–17); Giesen (95–98); Jahn (29); Oliver, *Blues Fell This Morning* (16, 275); Spottswood (60); and Wald, "Charlie Patton" (n.p.).

15. Regarding the anonymous release of "Mississippi Boweavil Blues," see "Appendix 5: Collecting Patton 78s" in the liner notes for *Screamin' and Hollerin' the Blues* (122).

16. For discussion of this novelistic genre, from the early nineteenth century to the 1980s, see Stephens.

17. Regarding Faulkner's friendship with Hudson and the novelist's likely familiarity with *Specimens of Mississippi Folk-Lore,* see Ryan, "A Little Music Aint About the Nicest Thing a Fellow Can Have."

18. My reading of the boll weevil passage is indebted both to Thadious Davis's analysis of Jason's view of people of color (*Faulkner's "Negro,"* 84–92), and Peters's observations about Job (190–92).

CHAPTER ONE

1. See Middleton for analysis of the film's treatment of the blues. An earlier Coen Brothers film, *Barton Fink* (1991), features John Mahoney as W. P. "Bill" Mayhew, a mustachioed, alcoholic southern author—"the finest novelist of our time"—working in Hollywood, who is quite evidently a caricature of Faulkner.

2. See Thadious Davis, "From Jazz Syncopation to Blues Elegy"; Gussow, "Plaintive Reiterations and Meaningless Strains"; *Soldiers' Pay* (156–59); and *Flags in the Dust* (638–39). For one of the first critical discussions of the blues in relation to Faulkner's early fiction, see Bluestein (120–24).

3. Son House was a contemporary, associate, and rival of Patton who recorded "Dry Spell Blues" in the summer of 1930, while "Dry September" (1931) is Faulkner's powerful tale of a racial lynching. The Holston House—the primary hotel in the town of Jefferson—makes frequent appearances in Faulkner's fiction.

4. Houston A. Baker's *Blues, Ideology, and Afro-American Literature.*

5. Graham notes that scholarship on the presence of popular music in the works of another modernist author, F. Scott Fitzgerald, suffers from a similar limitation (81).

6. For an instructive survey of the history of blues scholarship and its critical trends, see Lawson, "The First Century of the Blues." Studies of blues lyrics as social documents or critiques include Angela Davis; Garon; Gussow, *Seems Like Murder Here;* Lawson, *Jim Crow's Counterculture;* Oliver, *Blues Fell This Morning;* several of the essays in Springer, ed., *Nobody Knows Where the Blues Come From*; and van Rijn, *Roosevelt's Blues.* Studies of the blues as vernacular poetry—often focused upon the evolution and dissemination of lyric formulae—include Charters, *The Poetry of the Blues*; Evans, *Big Road Blues,* and "Formulaic Composition"; Springer, "On the Electronic Trail of Blues Formulas"; and Taft, *Blues Lyric Formula.*

7. If Faulkner is renowned as a modernist literary writer, many of his works emphasize oral storytelling and voice. See Grimwood, *Heart in Conflict,* and Ross.

8. As one blues scholar counseled me in response to my analysis of Patton's lyrics, "I wouldn't read too much into these expressions" (Anon., e-mail).

9. See Barry Lee Pearson for a critique of the tendency in blues writing to construct "biography from repertoire" (223). See also the debate in Gruver, "The Blues as Dramatic Monologues"; Titon, "Autobiography and Blues Texts"; and Gruver, "The Autobiographical Theory Re-Examined."

10. Thirty years later, Fahey explained that he had made such sweepingly dismissive comments precisely because one of his primary goals at the time had been to discourage scholarly efforts to read blues songs merely as instances of didactic social protest. His view had evolved to the point that he now characterized the bluesman as an "intelligent, complex, interesting and first-class artist," even as he confessed that he still considered "some of Patton's lyrics preposterous, incoherent, disjunctive" ("Charley Reconsidered" 47).

11. See also van Rijn, "Imagery in the Lyrics." One possible reason for the relative dearth of close textual analysis in blues studies is that, while fair-use conventions enable literary scholars to quote extensively from novels, poems, and plays, copyright policies for songs are much more rigid. Estates that own—and, rather more commonly, faceless corporations that have acquired the rights to—the works of African American musicians sometimes levy stiff licensing fees for any critics wishing to quote lyrics in their studies, making it impractical for scholars to analyze such texts in depth and detail.

12. Regarding the modernism of African American vernacular music, see also Wagner (35).

13. Recent critical studies dismantle the traditional assumption—exemplified in the works of Andreas Huyssen and Theodro Adorno—of a binary opposition between modernist art/literature and popular culture. See also conclusion, note 8, below.

14. Although the earliest documented references to the blues date from the very beginning of the twentieth century, several researchers estimate the earliest rural beginnings of the music in the late 1880s or early 1890s (Barlow 3).

15. Although Patton's birth certificate is dated 1891, some suggest that he might have been born as early as 1887. See Calt and Wardlow (48, 85); Evans, "Charley Patton" (111); and Wardlow (30). Other major blues artists born within a decade of Faulkner include Huddie Ledbetter, or "Lead Belly," and Frank Stokes in 1888; Mississippi John Hurt in 1892 or 1893; Blind Lemon Jefferson, Blind Blake, and Furry Lewis in 1893; Bessie Smith in 1894; Tommy Johnson in 1896; Memphis Minnie and Sam Chatmon in 1897; Blind Willie McTell in 1898; and Sleepy John Estes in 1899. Very few members of the first generation of blues recording artists were born more than a decade before Faulkner, two notable exceptions being "Ragtime" Henry Thomas (1874) and Ma Rainey (1886).

16. Regarding the youthful Faulkner's encounters with blues and blues-based music, particularly Handy's compositions, see conclusion, note 4, below.

17. The first blues sheet-music composition was published in 1908 (Wald, *Escaping the Delta* 15–16). The first blues instrumental appeared on record in 1914 and the first vocal blues in 1915—both by white artists (Evans, *Big Road Blues* 62; Wald, *Escaping the Delta* 17–18).

18. For discussions of the music variously termed "classic," "urban," or "vaudeville" blues, see Barlow (113–52); Francis Davis (80–86); Dixon and Godrich (250–70); Oliver, *Story of the Blues* (66–80); and Wald, *Escaping the Delta* (21–26).

19. Fahey observes that the first black singer to record with only a stringed instrument as accompaniment was Bessie Brown on "Hoodoo Blues" in 1924 (*Charley Patton* 10–11). Wald notes that both Ma Rainey and Sara Martin also made records with acoustic guitar accompaniment that year (*Escaping the Delta* 26, 27), while Dixon and Godrich point out that Ed Andrews recorded two self-accompanied guitar tunes in 1924 (270).

20. Traditional rural country music made a similar breakthrough almost simultaneously, with the first historic recordings by the Carter Family and Jimmie Rodgers taking place in 1927. See Malone (62–63, 86–87).

21. For estimates of sales and statistics relating to the peak years of blues recording, see Dixon and Godrich (277), and Odum and Johnson (25).

22. My thanks to Ann J. Abadie for reminding me of the importance of the North Mississippi blues. Hemphill (born 1876) made no commercial recordings during his lifetime—although Alan Lomax captured him on tape for the Library of Congress in 1942—and McDowell (born 1904) did not make any records until 1959. See Alan Lomax, *The Land Where the Blues Began* (314–57).

23. Skip James produced eighteen sides at his only pre-1960s recording session in February 1931, including such masterpieces as "Hard Time Killin' Floor Blues" and "Devil Got My Woman." Tommy Johnson is renowned for such classic songs as "Big Road Blues" and "Maggie Campbell Blues" (both recorded in 1928). Mississippi John Hurt was one of very few Mississippi blues artists to record in New York City in this period. His highly accessible recordings include "Frankie" and "Stack O'Lee" (both recorded in 1928). Among Son House's most notable songs are "Dry Spell Blues" and "My Black Mama Blues" (both 1930).

24. Patton's recording of the ballad—which did not achieve a release until 1932—was preceded by versions by such artists as Charlie Poole (under the title "Leaving Home" in 1926), Mississippi John Hurt (as "Frankie" in 1928), and Jimmie Rodgers (in 1929). For further details about the song and its history, see Huston.

25. For discussion of the decline of record sales and the disintegration of the race labels in the early years of the Depression, see Barlow (115); Dixon and Godrich (295, 305–6); and van Rijn, *Roosevelt's Blues* (26).

26. *These Thirteen* appeared in 1931 and *Dr. Martino* in 1934. Faulkner's short fiction is available today in *Collected Stories* and *Uncollected Stories.*

27. For further discussion of Johnson and "Spirituals to Swing," see Charters, *Blues Makers* (211–12), and Wald, *Escaping the Delta* (205, 226–29).

28. For a comprehensive historical survey of the journey of the blues from the country to the city, see Barlow. Regarding the shift from country blues to urban novelties, see Dixon and Godrich (245, 309, 319–20). For a more celebratory evaluation of the blues scene between the mid-thirties and late-forties, see Francis Davis (164). John Lee Williamson was the first of

two blues musicians to adopt the moniker "Sonny Boy," the second being postwar harmonica player Rice Miller.

29. Regarding the American Federation of Musicians strike from 1942 to 1944 and wartime rationing of shellac, see Dixon and Godrich (323).

30. The original stories that Faulkner cannibalized for *The Unvanquished, The Hamlet, Go Down, Moses,* and other later novels are available in their original form in *Uncollected Stories.*

31. Although Wolf's first 78 in 1951—"Moanin' at Midnight" backed with "How Many More Years"—was a revolutionary record, Wolf was not the first bluesman to use the electric guitar or a full band. Texas bluesman T-Bone Walker began working with an electric guitar as early as the mid-1930s. Helena radio station KFFA presented "the first electric blues band heard on the airways anywhere in the country" in its famous "King Biscuit Time" blues show in late 1941. Mississippian Arthur "Big Boy" Crudup's "Mean Old Frisco Blues" (1942) was "the first Chicago blues recording that featured an electric guitar" (Barlow 233, 330, 308). Son House claims that Wolf was playing an electric guitar by the late 1930s (Segrest and Hoffman 45, 65).

32. Regarding chart placings for Wolf and Waters, see Whitburn, *Joel Whitburn Presents Top R&B Singles* (197, 471).

33. The song—also known as "That's Alright, Mama"—was originally recorded by blues artist Arthur "Big Boy" Crudup in 1946.

34. Ironically, Elvis's early singles and another pioneering rock 'n' roll song, "Rocket 88" (1951), emerged from the same studio that produced Howlin' Wolf's first records: Sam Phillips's Sun Records. See Escott and Hawkins.

35. Similarly, after eight hit records between 1953 and 1956, Waters would appear on the Rhythm and Blues chart just one more time, with 1958's "Close to You" (Whitburn, *Joel Whitburn Presents Top R&B Singles* 471).

36. For further discussion of the black audience's abandonment of blues in this era, see Wald, *Escaping the Delta* (207–12).

37. Grimwood discusses the aging Faulkner's artistic decline in *Heart in Conflict* (260–61).

38. See Singal's evaluation of *The Mansion* (*William Faulkner,* 256, 286).

39. Patton's birth certificate lists him as "Charlie," whereas his early Paramount records identify him as "Charley Patton." Some blues fans (such as Calt and Wardlow, Patton's biographers) prefer to employ "Charlie," whereas a majority—myself included—elect to use the name under which Patton's records first appeared.

40. Following "Red Rooster," the Stones recorded such blues standards as Robert Johnson's "Stop Breakin' Down" and "Love in Vain," while Eric Clapton's group, Cream, put out covers of Wolf's "Spoonful" and Johnson's "Crossroads."

41. See Gioia for discussion of the rediscovery of Hurt and other prewar Mississippi blues musicians in the 1950s and 1960s (353–56).

42. For many years, the only confirmed photograph of Patton was a publicity headshot discovered by Max Tarpley, until John Tefteller unearthed the original full-length photograph from which the Tarpley picture had been cropped. The question of ownership of the surviving photographs of Johnson—of which several more have surfaced in recent years—has long been the subject of animosity and threats of litigation. See DiGiacomo, and Graves (87–96).

43. Prewar studies of the blues tended to dismiss the significance of commercial recordings in favor of a view of the music as an earthy folk form. See, for example, Odum and Johnson, *Negro Workaday Songs.*

44. Here, Faulkner echoes Walter Pater's oft-cited dictum, "All art constantly aspires towards the condition of music." See Graham for discussion of the varied responses by modernist authors to this idea (1–2).

CHAPTER TWO

1. Sources on the flood include Barry; Daniel, *Deep'n as It Come*; Saxon; and the PBS *American Experience* documentary, *Fatal Flood.*

2. See the appendix for a full transcription of the lyrics of "High Water Everywhere," including discussion of variant readings. For discussion of Patton's song and other flood blues, see Evans, "High Water Everywhere."

3. Regarding Wright's tales, see Hoefer, and Howard.

4. See McHaney, *William Faulkner's* The Wild Palms, for discussion of the text's complex web of literary and cultural allusions. For further analysis of the novel's exploration of the philosophies of Nietzsche and Schopenhauer, see McHugh, "The Birth of Tragedy." For the text's Hollywood allusions, see Grimwood, *Heart in Conflict* (118–34), and Lurie; and for its relation to popular romance fiction, see Anne Jones.

5. See Hoefer for a survey of literary and cultural representations of Katrina and its aftermath (537–38).

6. See the appendix for discussion of alternative transcriptions of this line.

7. Regarding these recurring themes in Faulkner, see, for example, Broughton, and Vickery. Atkinson suggests that Faulkner's novels and stories often address political realities in terms of abstract concepts, and that "socioeconomic themes pervade Faulkner's fiction of the Depression" in the guise of such issues as "the inherent tension between independence and interdependence," rather than in the form of direct social realism (50).

8. This is the title of Clifton Fadiman's review of the book in *The New Yorker* in January 1939.

9. Regarding the publishing history of "Old Man" and "The Wild Palms," see McHaney, *William Faulkner's* The Wild Palms (xiv–xv).

10. See McHaney, *William Faulkner's* The Wild Palms, for a discussion of the title's source and an account of the book's change in title (xiii). The 1995 Vintage International edition still bears the main title, *The Wild Palms,* but includes *If I Forget Thee, Jerusalem* as an alternative title or subtitle in parentheses on the cover.

11. Son House also famously released several two-part songs, all derived from a single 1930 recording session, including "Dry Spell Blues," "My Black Mama," and "Preachin' the Blues."

12. Patton's second release was a two-part gospel number, "Prayer of Death," issued under the pseudonym, "Elder J. J. Hadley." He also recorded two parts of the song "Jim Lee" immediately prior to recording "High Water Everywhere," but they appeared on different discs, the first with "Some Summer Day" in the summer of 1931, and the second backed with "Joe Kirby Blues" in the spring of 1932 as Patton's final release for Paramount.

13. Similarly, Wald calls "High Water Everywhere" "a six-minute description of a Mississippi River flood, telling of the suffering caused throughout the Delta" ("Charley Patton" n.p.). See also Barlow (39), and Lawson, *Jim Crow's Counterculture* (140–42).

14. See also Calt and Wardlow's valuable description of the song's dynamics (198–99, 203).

15. For discussion of Johnson's song, see Evans, "High Water Everywhere" (50–52).

16. For explanation of the non-narrative structures of blues verses, see Angela Davis (78), and Evans, *Big Road Blues* (27).

17. Evans argues that "High Water Everywhere" is "exceptional" among blues songs for its focused treatment of a single theme (*Big Road Blues* 200).

18. Taft's *Blues Lyric Poetry: A Concordance* lists eighteen songs that include a "won't be worried" construction (2849). Patton also uses such a construction in the sixth stanza of "Green River Blues": "I'm worried now, but I won't be worried long."

19. See the appendix for discussion of different readings of this line.

20. See the appendix regarding alternative transcriptions of this line.

21. See the appendix for variant readings of this ambiguous line.

22. Regarding mobility and dislocation as a recurrent issue in Patton's songs, see also Comentale (46).

23. Regarding the relationship between the flood and the Great Migration, as well as vain efforts by whites to arrest the black exodus, see Barry (149, 304–15, 416–17), and Lester, "*If I Forget Thee, Jerusalem*" (202–10).

24. Lurie even argues that Wilbourne's and Charlotte's behavior ultimately "serve[s] the interests of the mine's owning company" against the workers (154).

25. See the appendix for consideration of alternative renderings of this line.

26. For discussion of this characteristic of the fugitive slave narratives, see Ryan, *Calls and Responses* (85).

27. Regarding the longer versions of songs that prewar blues artists performed live, see Ferris (70); Palmer (67); Titon, *Early Downhome Blues* (32); and Wald, *Escaping the Delta* (132, 159).

28. For discussion of Patton's engagement with white audiences, see Calt and Wardlow (79), and Evans, "Charley Patton" (152, 157).

29. "High Water Everywhere" was one of Patton's biggest commercial successes. Calt and Wardlow note that this song "quickly rivaled *Pony Blues* as his signature song and gave his recording career a respite from an otherwise certain termination when Paramount issued it" (198).

30. Reviewing the novel for the *New Republic,* Malcolm Cowley described the tall convict as "the ideal soldier for a fascist army" (qtd. in Blotner, *Biography* 1015). See Anne Jones for a comparison of the convict and the members of Hitler's *Freikorps* (157).

31. Other views of the convict's failures as narrator include Gary Harrington, and King, "The Wages of Pulp."

32. Grimwood similarly observes that, "when the hero of 'Old Man' opens his mouth . . . he cannot speak quickly or articulately enough for the circumlocutory narrator, who impatiently breaks in to translate" (*Heart in Conflict* 108).

33. Regarding allusions to Hemingway in Faulkner's novel, see Fruscione (84–102); Godden (207), Moses; O'Connor, "Faulkner's One-Sided Dialogue"; and Richardson.

34. For a different reading of "Old Man" as a story of failed enlightenment, see Rhodes and Godden.

35. For discussion of the musical and the song, see Decker; Friedwald; and Kreuger.

36. My thanks to Donald Kartiganer for identifying these ideas as the key insights in my original paper about *If I Forget Thee, Jerusalem* at the Faulkner and Yoknapatawpha conference in 2008, and for encouraging me to develop them further.

37. Oshinsky reports a parallel instance in Hernando, Mississippi, in 1934 in which white onlookers sang "Bye Bye, Blackbird" at the funerals of three African American men who had been executed for allegedly raping a white girl (213).

38. For discussion of Faulkner's use of Saxon's work, see Grimwood, "Lyle Saxon's *Father Mississippi*," and Millgate, *Achievement of William Faulkner* (325n).

39. Oshinsky here cites David Cohn (102–4).

40. Regarding further parallels between slaves and the Parchman convicts in Faulkner's novel, see Lester, "*If I Forget Thee, Jerusalem*" (201–2).

41. Robbins notes that Charlotte's sculptures in "The Wild Palms" involve "a deft blending of high and low imagery," and he argues that "[h]er high-low fusions do not signal dumbing down but rather her mastery of a breadth of seemingly antagonistic influences" (n.p.).

42. Moreland identifies another work published in 1939—the story "Barn Burning"—as marking a "pivotal moment in Faulkner's career" (7), after which the author's work became more attentive to the voices of lower-class, female, and black characters (7–8).

43. There is some critical debate over Lucas Beauchamp: Margaret Walker Alexander describes him as "the only one of Faulkner's black characters who approaches or approximates a man" (115), whereas Thadious Davis sees him as "a polemical creation growing out of Faulkner's attempt to explain, or perhaps expiate, the South's irresponsible and peculiarly selective morality (*Faulkner's "Negro,"* 5).

CHAPTER THREE

1. Regarding the Patton lynching, see Blotner, *Biography* (113–14); Doyle (323–26); and Williamson, *William Faulkner* (157–61). For transcriptions of the original newspaper reports about the lynching, see Kinney (136–40). For a personal memoir of the event, see Cullen and Watkins (89–98). For discussion of the relationship between Patton's lynching and the contents of "Dry September" and *Light in August,* see Blotner, *Biography* (704); Thadious Davis, *Faulkner's "Negro"* (162–64); Pilkington (119, 136); and Wittenberg, *Faulkner* (121).

2. Numerous critical studies have considered the content and meanings of Faulkner's story in relation to Handy's song. See Coburn (211–12); Fisher (17); Gartner (55–57); Gerlach (140); Kuyk et al. (37); Nilon (45); Norman Pearson (61); Peek, "That Evening Sun[g]" (133–34, 141–42); Slabey "Faulkner's Nancy" (411); and Towner and Carothers (153–54). For analysis of other connotations of the story's title, see Gerlach (140–41), and Johnston (98–99).

3. Critics who characterize Jesus as such a "badman" include Bennett (340); Kuyk et al. (40); and Peek, "That Evening Sun(g)" (138–39). For broader discussion of the black "badman" tradition, see Brearley; Gussow, *Seems Like Murder Here* (168–75); and Odum and Johnson (47–70). See Perkins for discussion of Faulkner's "Black Razor Murderers."

4. Quentin also narrates "A Justice" (1931) and "Lion," which was first published in *Harper's* in December 1935, and which Faulkner incorporated in amended form (without Quentin) into "The Bear" in *Go Down, Moses* (1942). See Matthews, "Faulkner's Narrative Frames," for analysis of these interconnected texts.

5. For discussion of the childlike perspective of the tale, see May Brown (352–53); Carothers, *William Faulkner's Short Stories* (12); Gerlach (133); Evans Harrington (55); Skei (182); Sunderman (304); and Towner (20).

6. Although "Stovall" is a relatively common name in Mississippi, it is striking that this character in "That Evening Sun" bears the same name as a Coahoma County planter who hired the Chatmon family musicians—associates of Charley Patton—to serve as his "personal minstrels" (Calt and Wardlow 144). See also Gussow, "Plaintive Reiterations" (60–62).

7. For further discussion of the problems raised by reading "That Evening Sun" in relation to other Faulkner works, see Kuyk et al. (33–35), and Towner and Carothers (150–51).

8. See Diane Jones's survey of the criticism that misidentifies the Nancy of *The Sound and the Fury* with the character in "That Evening Sun" (278–79), and Calvin Brown's argument that Nancy in *The Sound and the Fury* is "obviously a horse, and doubtless one of a MATCHED TEAM with the horse Fancy" (136).

9. Among other similar statements Faulkner made about his flexible attitude toward his characters are "They're horses in my stable and I can run them whenever I want to" (qtd. in Blotner, *Biography* 1309), and "I can move these people around like God, not only in space but in time too" (*Lion in the Garden,* 255).

10. The date of the story's setting is ambiguous, but internal evidence suggests that the main action occurs in the mid-1910s and that Quentin's retrospective narration is roughly contemporaneous with the period in which tale was written and published. See Diane Jones (275); Johnston (94–95); Kuyk et al. (34); and Perrine (295n). In other words, the story is most likely set around the time that "St. Louis Blues" debuted and when World War I began in Europe.

11. In specific instructions to the editor, Faulkner added, "Don't worry . . . about chr[o]n[ology]. in EVENING SUN" (qtd. in Cowley 55).

12. Similarly, the single chapter of *As I Lay Dying* (1930) narrated by Addie Bundren appears midway through the book, about a hundred pages after the character's death, so that her tale seems to come from beyond the grave.

13. See also May Brown's analysis of the ghostly language in the story (350, 358).

14. For discussion of the meanings of "bloody bones" in African American folk culture, see Bennett (342), and Kuyk et al. (46).

15. Regarding Faulkner's telling of ghost stories to children, see Blotner, *Biography* (1087, 1336). The author's niece, Dean Faulkner Wells, even published a collection entitled *Ghosts of Rowan Oak: William Faulkner's Ghost Stories for Children.* For characterizations of "That Evening Sun" as a tale of terror or the supernatural, see Gerlach (143); Kuyk et al. (45); Snell (99); and Toker (436). My thanks to Justin Ness for a stimulating conversation about ghostly elements in Faulkner's story, a discussion that provided the germ of the idea from which this chapter developed.

16. Concerning the notion of Quentin as ghost-narrator, see Matthews, "Faulkner's Narrative Frames," and Parrish (50). In her discussion of *Absalom, Absalom!*—whose narrative takes place prior to Quentin's suicide—Thadious Davis also characterizes the tortured Compson as a ghost (*Faulkner's "Negro"* 234).

17. In addition to "Blues Is Only a Ghost" (1931), Johnson recorded "Lonesome Ghost Blues" (1927) and "Blue Ghost Blues" (1938).

18. Smith also recorded such eerie numbers as "Cemetery Blues" and a version of Ida Cox's "Graveyard Dream Blues" (both 1923).

19. The label of "Last Kind Words Blues" identifies the singer as "Geeshie," but L. V. Thomas called her partner "Geetchie," and some scholars spell the name "Geechie." See Cordeiro (6), and Sullivan, "Ballad of Geeshie and Elvie" (44).

20. Equally, several informants have suggested that Charley Patton was part-Mexican. See Calt and Wardlow (43), and Evans, "Charley Patton" (127).

21. Regarding the anomalous nature of this key, see Sullivan, "Unknown Bards" (86).

22. See the appendix for a complete transcription of the song's lyrics, including variant readings.

23. Skei similarly notes that Nancy "wants to die but clings to life" (185).

24. See the appendix for variant renderings of this line.

25. See the appendix for alternative transcriptions of this word.

26. Any Faulkner buff will recognize a profound contrast between this reading of Wiley's lyrics and the author's *As I Lay Dying,* in which Addie Bundren's last request is that she be buried, not with her husband's family, but with her own people.

27. Pearson and McCulloch cite as examples "When I die, don't bury daddy at all . . . Just pickle my bones in alcohol" and "When I die just throw me in the sea . . . So the tadpoles and minnows can make a fuss over me" (124n). Taft's *Blues Lyric Poetry: A Concordance* identifies fifteen recorded blues songs that contain burial instructions (402).

28. In both content and rhetoric, this statement resembles Muhammad Ali's famous 1966 refusal to serve in the military during the Vietnam War: "I ain't got no quarrel with them Viet Congs" (qtd. in Edmonds 68, 79).

29. In light of the relationship between World War I and lynching, it is significant that Hewlett's comments derive from his book, *Race Riots in America: Judge Lynch's Record, 1917–1924* (Barbeau and Henri 205n). For discussion of blues songs about World War I, see Lawson, *Jim Crow's Counterculture* (122–24), and van Rijn, *Roosevelt's Blues* (6–9). Regarding African American memoirs of the war, see Lynn Sanders (106–7); and Chad Williams (310–14).

30. Barbeau and Henri suggest that, of the two African American divisions serving in World War I, the Ninety-third Division lost 584 lives and had 2,582 of its members wounded (136), and that the Ninety-second had 1,700 casualties (163). Although this latter figure makes no distinction between dead and wounded, if the proportion of dead to wounded was similar to that in the Ninety-third Division, around 350 of the 1,700 casualties may have been fatalities, suggesting an approximate total of 950 black soldiers killed in the conflict. Even if all 1,700 casualties were mortal, the total number of African American fatalities in the war would be around 2,290, still substantially lower than the total number of murders by lynching between 1880 and 1930.

31. For further description of the effects of lynching upon African American psyches, see Wright, *Black Boy* (65). Regarding the particular prevalence of lynching in Faulkner's Mississippi, see Doyle (322); Lawson, *Jim Crow's Counterculture* (49); McMillen (229); Shay (100–101); and Tolnay and Beck (273).

32. For discussion of white responses to black veterans after World War I and the "Red Summer" of 1919, see Barbeau and Henri (178–87); Lawson, *Jim Crow's Counterculture* (125); McWhirter; Chad Williams (224–60); and Wright, *Black Boy* (69).

33. Regarding the black struggle for citizenship rights after the war, see Chad Williams (206–13, 261–98).

34. Military authorities preferred to relegate black soldiers to menial labor rather than mobilize them in combat. See Lawson, *Jim Crow's Counterculture* (119), and Chad Williams (107–12).

35. See evaluations of Caspey by Blotner, *Biography* (1247); Grimwood, "Faulkner and the Vocational Liabilities of Black Characterization" (257–58); Howe (51–52); Nilon (71); Peters

(43–45); and Lynn Sanders (108). Thadious Davis provides a judicious and nuanced reading of Caspey's rebellion in *Faulkner's "Negro"* (67).

36. See Lemann for further details about the *Chicago Defender*'s "Great Northern Drive" (16).

37. Polk's invaluable discussion is a classic instance of the speculative nature of criticism on "That Evening Sun" (*Children of the Dark House,* 237–39).

38. Regarding theories about the fate of Nancy's pregnancy, see Perrine (302–3), and Pitcher (134–35).

39. Other critics who characterize "That Evening Sun" as being essentially Nancy's story include Bollinger (55), and Fowler, "Tracing Racial Assumptions" (47).

40. Those who argue that Quentin develops an empathetic understanding of Nancy include Carothers, *William Faulkner's Short Stories* (12); Hamblin, "Before the Fall" (86); and Volpe, *Reader's Guide: Short Stories* (76). Critics who suggest that Quentin remains essentially blind to the nature of Nancy's suffering and its causes include Gerlach (139).

41. Equally, Thadious Davis notes that, in *Absalom, Absalom!,* Quentin is marked "for an irreparable, nightmare stasis. He is impotent and unable to resolve the moral dilemma posed by the legend and the southern past" (*Faulkner's "Negro"* 234).

42. For comparison of Quentin and Faulkner, see Werner (730).

43. For further discussion of Faulkner's complex and changeable racial attitudes, see Thadious Davis, *Faulkner's "Negro"* (14); Fowler and Abadie, ed., *Faulkner and Race*; Jenkins; Nilon; Peavy; Peters; Polk, *Children of the Dark House* (224–32); Sensibar, *Faulkner and Love* (100–103, 111–19); Singal, *William Faulkner* (291); Sundquist (ix); and Towner.

44. For discussion of Faulkner's evolving treatment of race in this period, see Grimwood, "Faulkner and the Vocational Liabilities of Black Characterization" (258), and Taylor (57).

45. Critics who characterize *Go Down, Moses* as the work in which Faulkner's depiction of black characters reached an impasse include Thadious Davis, *Faulkner's "Negro"* (239–47), and Grimwood, *Heart in Conflict* (223–98).

46. See Peavy regarding Faulkner's public pronouncements on race during the 1950s (50–93).

47. Critiques of Faulkner's treatment of race in his later works include Thadious Davis, *Faulkner's "Negro"* (5), and Peavy (84). For a reconsideration of depictions of race in Faulkner's later works, see Towner.

48. Faulkner also discussed the difficulty of writing female characters from a male perspective, but he tended to construct this challenge as a pleasure rather than as a threat to his literary authority. He once claimed, "It's much more fun to try to write about women because I think women are marvelous, they're wonderful, and I know very little about them, and so I just—it's much more fun to try to write about women than about men—more difficult, yes" (*Faulkner in the University* 45).

49. See Werner for analysis of Faulkner's explorations of the limitations of the white racial purview (718).

50. See, for example, discussions of "Pantaloon in Black" by Blotner, *Biography* (1038–39); Grimwood, "Faulkner and the Vocational Liabilities of Black Characterization" (265); and Peavy (44). Faulkner revised the tale for inclusion in *Go Down, Moses* (1942).

51. Kuyk et al. cite a folklorist's interview of one Braziel Robinson of Georgia at the turn of the century, who claimed, "I have two spirits, one that prowls around, and one that stays in my body" (qtd. 43). Ames acknowledges that "the lack of published parallels to many of

Gellert's [collected] protest songs . . . has made some folksong scholars suspicious of Gellert's materials," but he concludes that "Gellert's song texts . . . do seem to be authentic" (489). See also van Rijn, *Roosevelt's Blues* (xvi). As Odum and Johnson note, informant "Left Wing" Gordon—later the model for Odum's "Black Ulysses"—identified one of his favorite blues lyrics as "You don't know my mind, / You don't know my mind; / When you see my laughin,' / I'm laughin' to keep from cryin'" (27). The folklorists observe that Gordon freely adapted the words from "*You Don't Know My Mind Blues,* a popular sheet music and phonograph piece" (27), recorded by numerous artists, including Virginia Liston in 1923. Evidently, Gellert's unidentified performer was also exploiting the refrain from this song, if in a radically different context and for profoundly different purposes.

52. See chapter 4, note 7, below, regarding critiques of the myths about Johnson.

53. Taft's *Blues Lyric Poetry: A Concordance* identifies thirty-six blues songs that mention the "kitchen," many of them involving sexual innuendo (944–45). Peek, meanwhile, notes that the use of repetition in Jesus's observations about the white man in his kitchen resembles the AAB of blues verse ("That Evening Sun[g]" 134).

54. The story of Will Mayes and Minnie Cooper in "Dry September" is reminiscent of the 1905 case involving Charlie Bennett and Josie Hudson, although Bennett escaped lynching and was pardoned after serving thirty years in Parchman (Oshinsky 198–201).

55. The two stories later appeared alongside each other in Faulkner's collection *These Thirteen,* published in September 1931. See Manglaviti for details on the differences between the two versions of "That Evening Sun." An early manuscript draft of the story, entitled "Never Done No Weeping When You Wanted to Laugh," appeared in 1983.

56. For the text of Faulkner's letter, see McMillen and Polk. Critical discussions of the letter include Lightweis-Goff (87–93), and Towner (121–23, 127–29).

57. For discussions of lynching as public spectacle, see Gussow, *Seems Like Murder Here* (184–85); Hale, *Making Whiteness* (199–239); Williamson, *The Crucible of Race* (183–89); and Wood, *Lynching and Spectacle.*

58. Other critics who suggest that Jesus violently projects his anger at white society upon Nancy include Fowler, "Tracing Racial Assumptions" (50); Gerlach (142); Johnston (99); Nilon (46); Perrine (302); Polk, *Children of the Dark House* (238); and Volpe, *Reader's Guide: Short Stories* (78).

59. Although Cartwright does not suggest "That Evening Sun" is about lynching, and while he makes no connection between Holiday's song and Faulkner's story, the title of his essay derives from the lyrics of "Strange Fruit": "Blood on the Leaves, Blood at the Root."

60. Critics who relate the fire imagery surrounding Nancy to hell include Coburn (210–11), and Barry Sanders (69, 71).

61. In his 1985 survey, Perrine estimates that "critics who believe that Nancy will be murdered outnumber their opponents by almost three to one" (296).

62. Critics who suggest that Nancy accepts the designation of "nigger" and all it implies include Bethea (89); Peters (108); and Taylor (56).

63. Other critics who characterize Nancy as a failed storyteller include Bollinger (64–65); and Flora (39).

64. Regarding Nancy's potential for liberation, see also Young-Minor (173–74).

65. Peek's otherwise invaluable analysis—drawing upon Samuel Floyd's work on the blues—is similarly vague about the extent to which, and precisely how, Nancy is able to transcend

the pain of her circumstances through the "cathartic, affirming, and restorative powers" of the blues ("That Evening Sun[g]" 143).

66. For hypotheses about the reasons for Nancy's arrest, see Perrine (299), and Polk, *Children of the Dark House* (238). Years later, when writing *Requiem for a Nun,* Faulkner described Nancy as "a known drunkard and dope user, a whore with a jail record in the little town, always in trouble" (qtd. in Blotner, *Biography* 1309).

67. For an interpretation that characterizes Nancy's behavior during her arrest as a form of rebellion, see Bollinger (58–59).

68. Cullen and Watkins suggest that this episode may have inspired the affair between Major De Spain and Eula Varner (and the former's sudden disappearance) in *The Town* (108). Both De Spain and Eula are white, however, and De Spain evades punishment, so there is little commonality between fact and fiction in this case. Cullen's story about Mayor Adams has a much clearer relationship to the experience of Gail Hightower in *Light in August,* who is taken by the Klan into the woods, beaten, and told to leave town, merely on suspicion of his having had sexual relations with his black cook (71–72).

69. For analysis of the connotations of Jesus's name, see Barnett (137); Coburn (207–8); Gerlach (141); Johnston (96–97); Kuyk et al. (42–43); Barry Sanders (70); Slabey, "Faulkner's Nancy" (411), and "Quentin Compson's Lost Childhood" (179); Taylor (56); Volpe, *Reader's Guide: Short Stories* (78); and Young-Minor (174). Faulkner later acknowledged that the choice of name "was probably a deliberate intent to shock" (*Faulkner in the University,* 21). Kuyk et al. dispute Faulkner's disingenuous assertion that "Jesus" is "a valid name among Negroes in Mississippi . . . it's nothing unusual" (*Faulkner in the University* 21; Kuyk et al., 42).

70. Other readings of the story as an initiation into the adult world include Edel (254, 255), and Hamblin, "Before the Fall" (86).

71. See Barnett's discussion of how Caddy asks "questions that probe fundamental issues of human relationships" (134–35), and Hermann's analysis of Caddy (320–23).

72. See Bollinger's reading of Nancy's being "hellborn" (62–63). Slabey suggests it may be a reference to her mixed racial heritage ("Faulkner's Nancy" 409).

73. All but two of Wheatstraw's records billed him as either "The Devil's Son-in-Law" or "the High Sheriff of Hell." On his 1937 recording, "Peetie Wheatstraw Stomp," he vocally identifies himself as the latter.

74. "Last Kind Words Blues" and "Skinny Leg Blues" appeared on either side of Paramount 12951, likely recorded in March or April of 1930 and released a month or two later.

CHAPTER FOUR

1. For details about Odum's folklore work in Faulkner's hometown, see Lynn Sanders (10, 22–23, 29).

2. Regarding the centrality of sexuality to the blues, see Charters, *Poetry of the Blues* (122–26); Guy Johnson, "Double Meaning in the Popular Negro Blues"; and Oliver, *Blues Fell This Morning* (97–98), and *Screening the Blues* (23–24, 185–86).

3. For further examples of early reviewers identifying excessive emphasis upon sexual crudity in Faulkner's novels, see Inge, ed. *William Faulkner: The Contemporary Reviews* (15, 122, 152, 181, 221).

4. For further discussion of the relationship between the sexual and the social in the blues, see Angela Davis (xvii, 3–4, 8); Garon (67, 71); and Ryan, "The Matter with Your Line."

5. My thanks to Scott Romine for suggesting that I acknowledge instances of white male sexual dysfunction in Faulkner's canon beyond *Sanctuary*.

6. Mythic reimaginings of Johnson in criticism, fiction, and film include Marcus, *Mystery Train*; *Crossroads*; Ellis; and Hiramoto.

7. Wald simultaneously confirms, extends, and complicates Barlow's characterization of Johnson in *Escaping the Delta*. Other revisionist studies of Johnson include Graves; Lipsitz; Pearson and McCulloch; Rothenbuhler; and Schroeder.

8. This recording did not receive a public release until 1970 on the second volume of the *King of the Delta Blues Singers* LP.

9. Big Bill Broonzy liked these lines sufficiently to borrow them on "Louise, Louise Blues," recorded in June 1937.

10. See, for example, such stories as "Golden Land" (1935) about Hollywood; "Honor" (1930) and "Death Drag" (1932), concerning barnstorming stunt pilots; "Divorce in Naples" (1931), which focuses upon a relationship between gay sailors; "Red Leaves" (1930), "A Justice" (1931), "Lo!" (1934), and "A Courtship" (1948), all of which concern Chickasaw and Choctaw Indians in the nineteenth century; "Spotted Horses" (1931) and "Fool About a Horse" (1936), tales of rural wheeler-dealers; "Ad Astra" (1931), "All the Dead Pilots" (1931), "Victory" (1931), "Crevasse" (1931), and "Turnabout" (1932), about World War I; and "Shingles for the Lord" (1943), a comedy about the building of a church roof. Some of these stories—specifically ones that Faulkner later cannibalized for episodes in novels—are not included in *Collected Stories,* but appear in *Uncollected Stories*.

11. For characterizations of *Sanctuary* as a combination of modernist literature and pop culture, see Atkinson (118–48); Fiedler, "Pop Goes the Faulkner"; King, "Faulkner's Brazen Yoke" (308–15); Lurie (8, 25–67); Singal, *William Faulkner* (154); and Wenska.

12. See Madden for discussion of the sensationalist cover illustration on a later paperback edition of *Sanctuary* (94–95).

13. Regarding Faulkner and "Rhapsody in Blue," see Blotner, *Biography* (754, 1054); and Nunn (77n). Although some now question the veracity of the claims about Faulkner's debt to Gershwin's music, Paul Whiteman and His Orchestra re-recorded "Rhapsody in Blue" in 1927 for Victor as a replacement for their pre-electric recording of 1924, and this new version would have been widely available at the time Faulkner composed *Sanctuary*.

14. *Green's Dictionary of Slang* identifies the use of "shrimp" to refer to a "small penis" as originating in American gay culture, citing as a primary source the 1972 *Queens' Vernacular* (931). See also Dalzell and Victor (1743), and Richter (135).

15. The Ginger Snaps recorded a rather more innocuous pop novelty entitled "The Shrimp Man" in 1945.

16. For further discussion of the Anglo-Saxon roots of the word "shrimp," see Rawson (355).

17. Here, Wald seems to read "shrimp" in terms of the African American slang term "shrimps and rice," which Green defines as being a "metaphor for whatever it is one wants" (931).

18. For discussion of the reluctance of some contemporary blues scholars and listeners to address bawdy sexual comedy in prewar blues lyrics, see Hamilton, "Authenticity and the Making of the Blues Tradition" (133–35, 139); Ryan, "The Matter with Your Line"; and, specifically regarding Johnson's "Terraplane Blues," Wald, *Escaping the Delta* (xvii–xviii, 145–47).

19. Coincidentally, yet appropriately, Millgate refers to *Sanctuary* as "Faulkner's *Measure for Measure*" (*Achievement of William Faulkner* 119). Calt suggests only that "goggle-eyed perches" refers to "girlfriends" (107), but, within the suggestive context of "Dead Shrimp Blues," the word evidently has more specifically carnal connotations as well.

20. This is a sly reference to the long-lived rumor that a cycling accident rendered James impotent. For further details, see Hemingway's 1926 letter to Maxwell Perkins in Carlos Baker, ed. (208–9).

21. For analysis of the treatment of impotence in the exchanges between Bill and Jake during the Burguete episode, see Rudat (173–86), and Stallman (173–75).

22. Hall's *Dictionary of American Regional English* notes that the word "shrimp" is sometimes pronounced with "the letter *h* being entirely suppressed. This is the affected pronunciation of over-refined school girls, who cannot bring themselves to utter the homely English sound of *sh* when combined with an *r,* for fear apparently of distorting their faces" (937). The woman in Johnson's song apparently has no such qualms for she does not mind if her "mouth [is] stuck out" when she likens her partner's condition to a dead shrimp.

23. Wald questions the conventional assumption that the sexual content of "Traveling Riverside Blues" was an obstacle to its release (*Escaping the Delta* 181–82).

24. Johnson recorded "Dead Shrimp Blues" at his first session on 27 November 1936, and it appeared on his third 78 release the following spring.

25. For discussions of the distinctions between the two versions of *Sanctuary,* see Canfield (4); Philip Cohen (70); Matthews, "The Elliptical Nature of *Sanctuary*" (104, 110–11); Lurie (28); Millgate, "Faulkner's First Trilogy" (92); and Polk, *Children of the Dark House* (42–43). Critics commonly emphasize the extent to which Faulkner's revisions downplay Horace's psychological states and highlight Temple's experiences instead.

26. Other discussions of the text's implicit and veiled treatment of its central event include Dore (72), and Matthews, "The Elliptical Nature of *Sanctuary*" (103).

27. The word "impotent" does appear in the 1929 version of *Sanctuary,* in reference to Horace's rage when Popeye detains him at gunpoint (23).

28. Other discussions of Horace's spiritual or figurative impotence include Atkinson (135); Creighton (266); Mesquita (162); Sundquist (55); Tebbetts (47); and David Williams (98).

29. For discussions of Horace as a Prufrockian character, see Blotner, *Biography* (617); Philip Cohen (67); Hodgin (652); Polk, "Afterword" (299); and Singal, *William Faulkner* (159).

30. Other critics who tentatively suggest, or at least seem to imply, that Horace is physically impotent include Arnold and Trouard (152); Parker (155–56n); and Kubie (28, 30–31).

31. See Ownby for analysis of the sexual content of "Terraplane Blues" (119–20).

32. See Wald's analysis of "Stones in My Passway" as a grim sequel to "Terraplane Blues" (*Escaping the Delta* 167–70).

33. Similarly, Maurer lists "*box of shrimp*" among conventionally taboo sexual terms that appear in *Sanctuary,* but without explaining what it connotes (17).

34. The earlier version of Horace's shrimp tale places considerably more emphasis upon odor than the revision in *Sanctuary* (*Flags in the Dust* 851).

35. My thanks to Patricia Schroeder for reminding me of similarly ambiguous sexual terms in the blues—such as "jelly-roll"—which can refer to either male or female genitalia (Calt 135).

36. Regarding the pattern of Christian and Pagan allusions in the novel, see McHaney, "*Sanctuary.*"

37. Critics who read Horace's shrimp errand in relation to Catholicism include Arnold and Trouard (28), and McHaney, "*Sanctuary*" (90n).

38. For further discussion of the origins of the word "Friday" and the association of the day with eroticism and marital sex through Freya (or "Freyja"), see Grundy (64, 60), and Näsström (71, 73).

39. Bassett even characterizes Horace's weekly shrimp errand as "a reminder of his figurative castration" ("*Sanctuary*" 75).

40. For references to "shrimp" as "prostitute," see Farmer and Henley (200); Green (931); Partridge (765); Richter (135); and Spears (353).

41. Wald provides no source for this claim, and I can locate no evidence that this meaning would have been common in African American or southern culture of the period. Calt, for example, does not include the term "shrimp" in his blues dialect dictionary, *Barrelhouse Words.* Berrey and Van Den Bark's *American Thesaurus of Slang,* Hall's *Dictionary of American Regional English,* and Weseen's *Dictionary of American Slang* make no mention of "shrimp" as a term for prostitute. As Wald acknowledges, furthermore, the idea that "shrimp" means "prostitute" "does not in any way fit the way the word appears in Johnson's lyric. (If the shrimp are prostitutes, what does he mean by telling his lost girlfriend, 'You take my shrimp, baby, you know you turned me down'?)" (*Escaping the Delta* 154).

42. Ruby later tells Temple that she once sold herself to a lawyer in hopes of freeing Goodwin from Leavenworth penitentiary (58–61).

43. Green cites such a use of "shrimp" from Shakespeare's *Henry VI,* Part 1 (II.iii): "This is a child, a silly dwarf: It cannot be this weak and writhled shrimp Should strike such terror to his enemies" (930). See also Marquardt (118). As Rawson notes, "Geoffrey Chaucer employed the term in the sense of 'weakling' in *The Monk's Prologue*" (355).

44. Philip Cohen points out that much of the material relating to Horace's affairs with Belle and Joan Heppleton was excised from *Sartoris,* the version of the novel published during Faulkner's lifetime (72–73).

45. As Arnold and Trouard explain Miss Reba's comment, "To 'pull a train' means to take on a series of sexual partners" (172). Sexual references to "flagging" a train appear in such blues songs as Blind Lemon Jefferson's "Match Box Blues" (1927), Julius Daniels's "My Mama Was a Sailor" (1927), and Peetie Wheatstraw's "Don't Take a Chance" (1936). Odum's novel, *Rainbow Round My Shoulder,* also includes an African American woman exclaiming, "If he flag my train sho' gonna let him ride" (157).

46. As Bassett notes, Horace associates carnality with trains throughout the novel ("*Sanctuary*" 77, 80). In the blues tradition, "train"—like "shrimp" and "jelly roll"—is often a gender-neutral euphemism rather than a specifically phallic symbol.

47. For analysis of Horace's simultaneous attraction to and fear of women, see Bassett, "*Sanctuary*" (76); Matthews, "The Elliptical Nature of *Sanctuary*" (106); and Railey (87).

48. Singal surveys the tendency of earlier critics to read the novel as misogynist (*William Faulkner* 157). Fiedler's argument in *Love and Death in the American Novel* about the author's inherent misogyny is a classic example of such scholarship (320–25).

49. See Philip Cohen for discussion of Faulkner's literary exploration of "a deep ambivalence and anxiety about masculine roles, about what it means to be a man in the modern period" (67).

50. For analysis of the relation between femininity and fluidity in Faulkner's fiction, see Gwin, particularly the chapter on *If I Forget Thee, Jerusalem.*

51. For further discussion of the parallels between Horace and Popeye, see Arnold and Trouard (7, 9, 30, 107, 182, 187, 245); Bassett, "*Sanctuary*" (81); Canfield (6, 8); Philip Cohen (75); Eddy (30); Irwin (205–6, 222); King, "Faulkner's Brazen Yoke" (311–14); Lurie (30); Madden (102); Matthews, "The Elliptical Nature of *Sanctuary*" (119–20); Mesquita (165); Parker (75); Polchin (152); Polk, *Children of the Dark House* (51); Railey (85–89); Vickery (110); and Voth (114).

52. Kubie also suggests as an option, "which never works too successfully, but which is always tried—that is, an effort to ridicule and make fun of his own yearnings, and thus to make his own frustrations more bearable" (30–31). Recorded two years after Kubie's analysis, "Dead Shrimp Blues" suggests that controlled self-ridicule may be more productive than the critic assumes.

53. Parker observes that Faulkner "identified this grimmest of his books with his own marriage," which took place the year that the author produced the first version of *Sanctuary* (77). See also Bassett, "*Sanctuary*" (74).

54. For discussion of Ruby's influence on Temple, see Muhlenfeld (154–55).

55. Regarding Horace's nightmare vision, see Arnold and Trouard (183); Irwin (224–25); Matthews, "The Elliptical Nature of *Sanctuary*" (121); and Polk, *Children of the Dark House* (45–46).

56. See Lynn Sanders for discussion of Gordon (52–54, 96).

57. For his part, as Singal notes, Odum detected in Faulkner's fiction "the same studied ambivalence, the same concern for the irrational forces lurking beneath the apparent calm of southern life portrayed in his own work" (*The War Within* 153).

58. Regarding the racial implications of Popeye's "blackness," see Guttmann (25–29); and Lester, "Same as a Nigger on an Excursion" (39–40).

59. Both works, in fact, seem to have been partly inspired by the same real-life event, in which a local black man named Dave Bowdry slit his wife's throat (Cullen and Watkins 72–73).

60. This painting—the second panel of Remedios Varo's triptych, *Bordando el Manto Terrestre* (1961)—is available at www.notbored.org/crying.html.

61. Appropriately, Lurie characterizes Horace as "an allegorical figure for the modernist artist" (50), while Polk suggests that "all the characters in *Sanctuary* are the nightmare formulations of Horace's repressed sexual life" and "projections of his unconscious" (*Children of the Dark House* 47, 46).

62. My thanks to Patricia Schroeder for encouraging me to develop this aspect of the chapter.

CHAPTER FIVE

1. My thanks to John Wharton Lowe for drawing my attention to Gaines's statement.

2. *Mojo* magazine's 1998 feature on the "100 Greatest Singers of All Time" places Wolf in its top fifty and offers a pithy summation of the bluesman's uniquely powerful voice (60).

3. For discussion of Wolf's apprenticeship with Patton, see Guralnick, *Feel Like Going Home* (153), and Segrest and Hoffman (19–20).

4. On its initial release, the song was titled "Smoke Stack Lightning," but subsequent releases have standardized it as "Smokestack Lightnin'."

5. One of the few highlights of *Cadillac Records* (2008), an inept Hollywood dramatization of the postwar Chicago blues scene, is Eamonn Walker's remarkable portrayal of Wolf, particularly his performance of "Smokestack Lightnin'." Appearances by Wolf in literature include Stanley Crouch's poem "Howling Wolf: A Blues Lesson Book" (1972) and Nathan Singer's novel, *Chasing the Wolf* (2006).

6. Blues musician James Thomas told William Ferris that he got his verses "out of records. You can git a verse out of each record and make you a recording of your own" (51).

7. For further discussion of revision of previous works as a recurring characteristic in Faulkner's later fiction, see Moreland (239–41).

8. Towner argues that one particular character in the Yoknapatawpha chronicle embodies this authorial impulse: "In the evolving portrait of the citizen-storyteller Ratliff . . . we can locate Faulkner's own astonishing capacity to make even his old fictions 'new' again by 'telling them slant'" (143).

9. Excerpts from the bluesman's spoken reveries and the acoustic recordings of "Ain't Goin' Down That Dirt Road" and "I'm the Wolf" are available on *The Chess Box*.

10. Another dismissive early evaluation of *The Reivers* appears in Volpe, *Reader's Guide: Novels* (344, 347). See Towner's useful survey of traditional critical attitudes toward the novel (38).

11. For other discussions of *The Reivers* as a self-consciously final statement—including some that liken the novel to Shakespeare's play and Faulkner to Propero—see Bassett, "*The Reivers*" (53, 54); Kerr (95, 96, 113); Mellard; and Rossky. For a critique of the notion of *The Reivers* as such a valedictory summation, see Meriwether.

12. Regarding Faulkner's plan to write his "Huck Finn"–like novel in the 1930s, see Carothers, "The Road to *The Reivers*" (97–100).

13. Carothers similarly notes that "the other thirteen Yoknapatawpha novels and perhaps two dozen of the short stories are evoked by specific allusions to identifiable characters in *The Reivers*" ("The Road to *The Reivers*" 116).

14. For analysis of how the novel revises *Go Down, Moses,* see Bassett, "*The Reivers*" (54–59); Carothers, "The Road to *The Reivers*" (103–5); Kerr; Millgate, *Achievement of William Faulkner* (255); Taylor (186); and Wittenberg, *Faulkner* (238). For discussion of the novel's rewriting of *Sanctuary,* see Kerr (99, 106); and Millgate, *Achievement of William Faulkner* (253).

15. Other discussions of the book's double perspective include Carothers, "The Road to *The Reivers*" (113); Koyama (237, 240); Vickery (228, 238); Vorpahl (5, 10, 12); and Wittenberg, *Faulkner* (241).

16. For discussion of the emphasis upon tranquility, resolution, and acceptance in the novel's rewriting of earlier works, see Bassett, "*The Reivers*" (56); Carothers, "The Road to *The Reivers*" (123–24); Mellard (31); Moreland (239–41); Parini (415); and Volpe, *Reader's Guide: Novels* (343–44).

17. The mule passage appears in both *Sartoris* (226–27), and the unabridged, posthumously published version of that novel, *Flags in the Dust* (779–80).

18. See *The Reivers* (245–46). The source of Fitzgerald's observation is his 1936 essay "The Crack-Up" (69). For further discussion of the treatment of paradox in *The Reivers,* see Devlin (337); Eyster (19); and Tanner (51, 55).

19. See Thadious Davis, *Faulkner's "Negro,"* for analysis of the racial ideologies implicit in the comparison between people of color and mules in the author's fiction (49–51, 156, 246).

20. For further discussion of motion and fluidity in *The Reivers,* see Carothers, "Road to *The Reivers*" (118); Devlin; and Yoshida. Lucius's statement also recalls Alexis De Tocqueville's

famous observation that "America is a land of wonders in which everything is in constant motion" (471).

21. For discussion of the treatment of the Great Migration in Faulkner's fiction, see Lester's articles on *The Sound and the Fury, Sanctuary,* and *If I Forget Thee, Jerusalem.*

22. See Garon for a Freudian interpretation of the theme of returning to the South in the blues (88).

23. Regarding Wolf's pursuit of adult education, see Segrest and Hoffman (195).

24. Bonnie Miller has suggested to me that Wolf's moan at the end of the song may be more orgasmic than despairing. Even if this is the case, it is not so much a coital orgasm as an emptily masturbatory one. The speaker's notion of the South where "the women know just what to do" is an erotic fantasy, not actual sexual engagement with women of the South.

25. For a provocative reading of this song, see Lott, "Back Door Man."

26. Some listeners might prefer to read this line in terms of phallic imagery: the song's narrator will continue to visit women, but he will not be wielding his "gun" anymore, since old age has robbed him of his potency. The apparent tension between the sexually vibrant "back door man" and the impotent man who is unable to shoot his gun anymore certainly speaks to the issues at the heart of *The Back Door Wolf* regarding an aging artist seeking to reassert his creative powers.

27. Regarding these studio practices, see Gioia (66); Segrest and Hoffman (276); and Taft, *Blues Lyric Formula* (291).

28. In this instance, furthermore, the singer apparently has difficulties with his own lyrics, for "Moving" is one of only two songs on the album attributed to Wolf. Segrest and Hoffman imply that, regardless of his composer credit, they doubt Wolf's authorship of "Moving" (294).

29. "Hurt" is available at www.youtube.com/watch?v=3aF9AJm0RFc.

30. Wolf's cover of "Pony Blues" bore the title "Saddle My Pony."

CONCLUSION

1. President Obama performed a verse of Johnson's song at a Black History Month celebration of the blues at the White House on 21 February 2012, accompanied by such luminaries as Buddy Guy, B. B. King, and Mick Jagger. See a film clip of the event at www.youtube.com/watch?v=Z7x4ZS7ZZWc.

2. John and Alan Lomax describe their work in, respectively, *Adventures of a Ballad Hunter* and *The Land Where the Blues Began.* See also Szwed. For discussion of Speir's involvement with the Delta blues, see Calt and Wardlow (11–17, 176, 185, 189, 218–19); Gioia (51–59); and Wardlow (125–49). See Lynn Sanders for details about Odum's career.

3. Regarding this illustration, see Thadious Davis, "From Jazz Syncopation" (75); Gussow, "Plaintive Reiterations" (59); Peters (29–30); and Wilhelm.

4. For details of Faulkner's direct encounters with African American music, see Blotner, *Biography* (155, 174, 175); Thadious Davis, "From Jazz Syncopation" (70–77); Gussow, "Plaintive Reiterations" (58–64); Haynes (441); Sensibar, *Faulkner and Love* (22, 57–61); and Williamson, *William Faulkner* (173, 201).

5. For discussion of Faulkner's dislike of music—particularly recorded music on phonograph or radio—see Blotner, *Biography* (1220, 1291, 1698, 1713, 1774–75); Lester, "Make Room for Elvis" (158–63); and Zender (20–23).

6. Regarding this incident, see Wilde and Borsten (103), and Williamson, *William Faulkner* (254).

7. See *Intruder in the Dust* (231–32), and *Requiem for a Nun* (637).

8. Regarding Theodor Adorno, Walter Benjamin, Clement Greenberg, and other writers and thinkers who were wary of, or defined modernism as being antagonistic to, mass culture—and how subsequent scholarship has complicated and transcended such viewpoints—see Graham (13–14, 24–32); King, "Faulkner's Brazen Yoke" (304–5); Lurie (2–8); Matthews, "Faulkner and the Culture Industry" (53–56); and Phil Smith (75–77, 87, 92). For a reading of the implications of the "graphophone" in *As I Lay Dying,* see Ryan, "A Little Music Aint About the Nicest Thing a Fellow Can Have."

9. For discussion of these and other blues pioneers, see Barlow (35); Calt and Wardlow (56–57, 104); Evans, *Big Road Blues* (175, 178); and Gioia (112).

10. Regarding the blues music that "the records missed," see Wald, *Escaping the Delta* (43–69).

11. For comparative analysis of "That Evening Sun" and "A Spoonful Blues," see Ryan, "Go to Jail About This Spoonful."

12. Although it is now more conventional to render this singer's stage name as "Leadbelly," his records of the 1930s and 1940s conventionally identified him as "Lead Belly," and I have followed this convention.

13. Purists sometimes marginalize Lead Belly by categorizing him as a populist folk singer rather than an authentic blues singer. See Lawson, *Jim Crow's Counterculture,* for reappraisal of the artist's work (28–44).

14. Regarding Davidson's reviews and support of Faulkner's career, see Atkinson (61–62); and Blotner, *Biography* (506, 549, 611, 1016).

15. For details of Faulkner's activities in late 1934 and early 1935, see Blotner, *Biography* (873–78).

16. Regarding the 1934 prison recording, see Wolfe and Lornell (290). The discography by these biographers identifies Lead Belly's commercial recording of "Midnight Special" with the Golden Gate Quartet as taking place on 16 June 1940 (298), but the *New York Times* did not review the album until February 1941. Furthermore, the serial numbers of the three individual 78s that make up the album come sequentially after the serial numbers of other discs that were recorded in early 1941. See the Victor 27000 series at the *Online Discographical Project.*

17. For further details of the song's history and its earliest recordings, see Norm Cohen, *Long Steel Rail* (478–84).

18. There are numerous interjections by other prisoners while the tall convict tells his story in "Old Man" (136, 144, 145, 201, 203, 213, 230, 281).

19. See Oshinsky for discussion of the historical "Midnight Special" train (179–80).

20. Dixon and Godrich suggest that Lester Melrose of the Vocalion record label secured White's release in 1940 (320).

21. Regarding the date of composition of White's Parchman songs, see Gioia (93–94).

22. For discussion of the youthful Faulkner's enthusiasm for Beethoven, popular phonograph records, and dancing, see Blotner, *Biography* (183, 260, 337, 345). Regarding Faulkner's later dislike of all music, see Sensibar, *Origins of Faulkner's Art* (206–7); and Wilde and Borsten (64, 65, 140).

23. See Hamilton, *In Search of the Blues,* regarding the beginnings of the blues revival and the response to Charters's work by the emerging "blues mafia" (224–35).

24. For an account of the folk revival, see Ronald Cohen, *Rainbow Quest*. Lead Belly's active involvement with this movement was subsequently responsible for his frequent categorization as a folk singer instead of as a blues singer.

25. See Blotner, *Library* (48). Regarding Ramsey's book, see Hamilton, *In Search of the Blues* (193–200).

26. None of Holiday's other biographers—nor any of Faulkner's—mentions the encounter between these two iconic figures. For discussion of the frequent mislabeling of Holiday as a blues singer, see Clarke (51, 66, 69, 137, 445).

27. For discussion of the blues revival's tendency to romanticize country blues as an embodiment of enduring pre-modern values, see Wald, *Escaping the Delta* (230–31).

28. Later that year, Faulkner used the same excuse in his initial attempt to avoid flying to Stockholm for the Nobel Prize ceremony: "It's too far away. I am a farmer down here and I can't get away" (qtd. in Blotner, *Biography* 1338). For further instances of Faulkner's habit of characterizing himself as a farmer, see Blotner, *Biography* (1395, 1415, 1428, 1429, 1646).

29. An early version of Mink's story, "The Hound"—in which the killer is named "Cotton"—appeared in *Harper's* in 1931 and is now available in *Uncollected Stories* (152–64).

30. Classic murder ballads include Dick Justice's "Henry Lee" (1929), G. B. Grayson's "Omie Wise" (1927), and "Fatal Flower Garden" (1929) by Nelstone's Hawaiians, all included on the *Anthology of American Folk Music*. See also Burt, *American Murder Ballads*.

31. Cash recorded "Folsom Prison Blues" in July 1955, released it on the Sun label at the end of the year, and watched it climb the country chart in early 1956, peaking at number four (Whitburn, *Joel Whitburn's Top Country Singles* 61).

32. Parchman also appears in two of Patton's songs, "A Spoonful Blues" and "Hammer Blues."

33. Taft's *Blues Lyric Poetry: A Concordance* lists more than fifty songs that refer to Memphis (1632).

34. Towner may overlook Mink's potential for evolution precisely because her analysis focuses upon the progression of Ratliff's racial attitudes instead (81).

35. Gussow's *Mister Satan's Apprentice* is an illuminating account of a contemporary white musician's engagement with the blues and black culture.

36. *Stacker Lee* and *Ozark Belle* were real steamboats of the late nineteenth and early twentieth centuries, but the only *Crescent Queen* I have been able to locate was a steamboat originally named *The Captain Weber* and renamed *Crescent Queen* specifically for its use in *Swanee River* (1939), a film about folk composer Stephen Foster.

37. Regarding Armstrong's riverboat phase, see Giddins (42–43).

38. In its later years, the show became *Country Music Jubilee* and then *Jubilee U.S.A.* For discussion of the show, see Malone (272).

39. For further information on the historical Stagger Lee Shelton, and the many versions of the song about him, see Cecil Brown, *Stagolee Shot Billy*.

40. Faulkner's statement echoes two significant observations by American cultural observers, one black and one white. In 1941, W. J. Cash claimed that "Negro entered into white man as profoundly as white man entered into Negro—subtly influencing every gesture, every word, every emotion and idea, every attitude" (70). Ten years earlier, James Weldon Johnson had asserted that the various genres of African American folk music have "permeated our national life" and are "no longer racial, they are wholly national" (260–61).

WORKS CITED

Alexander, Margaret Walker. "Faulkner & Race." *Maker and the Myth: Faulkner and Yoknapatawpha, 1977.* Ed. Evans Harrington and Ann J. Abadie. Jackson: UP of Mississippi, 1978. 105–21. Print.

American Experience: Fatal Flood. PBS, 2001. DVD.

Ames, Russell. "Protest and Irony in Negro Folksong." 1950. Dundes, ed. 487–500. Print.

Angoff, Charles, and H. L. Mencken. "The Worst American State: Part III." *American Mercury* 24.95 (November 1931): 355–71. Print.

Anonymous. "Comments to the Author." 3 January 2011. E-mail.

Anthology of American Folk Music. Comp. Harry Smith. 1952. Smithsonian Folkways, 1997. 6 CDs.

Arnold, Edwin T., and Dawn Trouard. *Reading Faulkner:* Sanctuary. Jackson: UP of Mississippi, 1996. Print.

Atkinson, Ted. *Faulkner and the Great Depression: Aesthetics, Ideology, and Cultural Politics.* Athens: U of Georgia P, 2006. Print.

Ayres, B. Drummond, Jr. "Blacks Return to South in a Reverse Migration." *New York Times,* 18 June 1974. partners.nytimes.com/library/national/race/061874race-ra.html. Accessed 16 September 2012. Web.

Baker, Carlos, ed. *Ernest Hemingway: Selected Letters, 1917–1961.* New York: Scribner's, 1981. Print.

Baker, Houston A. *Blues, Ideology, and Afro-American Literature: A Vernacular Theory.* Chicago: U of Chicago P, 1984. Print.

——. *Turning South Again: Re-thinking Modernism/Re-reading Booker T.* Durham, NC: Duke UP, 2001. Print.

Barbeau, Arthur E., and Florette Henri. *The Unknown Soldiers: Black American Troops in World War I.* Philadelphia: Temple UP, 1974. Print.

Barlow, William. *"Looking Up at Down": The Emergence of Blues Culture.* Philadelphia: Temple UP, 1989. Print.

Barnett, Louise K. "Caddy and Nancy: Race, Gender, and Personal Identity in 'That Evening Sun' and *The Sound and the Fury.*" *Approaches to Teaching Faulkner's* The Sound and the Fury. Ed. Stephen Hahn and Arthur F. Kinney. New York: Modern Language Association, 2006. 134–39. Print.

Barry, John M. *Rising Tide: The Great Mississippi Flood of 1927 and How It Changed America.* 1997. New York: Simon & Schuster, 1998. Print.

Barton Fink. Dir. Joel Coen and Ethan Coen. 1991. Twentieth Century Fox, 2003. DVD.

Bassett, John E. "*The Reivers:* Revision and Closure in Faulkner's Career." *Southern Literary Journal* 18.2 (Spring 1986): 53–61. Print.

———. "*Sanctuary*: Personal Fantasies and Social Fictions." *South Carolina Review* 13.1 (Fall 1981): 73–82. Print.

Bennett, Ken. "The Language of the Blues in Faulkner's 'That Evening Sun.'" *Mississippi Quarterly* 38.3 (Summer 1985): 339–42. Print.

Benson, Jackson J. *Hemingway: The Writer's Art of Self-Defense.* Minneapolis: U of Minnesota P, 1969. Print.

Berrey, Lester V., and Melvin Van Den Bark. *The American Thesaurus of Slang.* 2nd ed. New York: Thomas Y. Crowell Co., 1953. Print.

Bethea, Sally. "Further Thoughts on Racial Implications in Faulkner's 'That Evening Sun.'" *Notes on Mississippi Writers* 6 (1974): 87–92. Print.

The Bible: Authorized King James Version. Ed. Robert Carroll and Stephen Prickett. New York: Oxford UP, 2008. Print.

Billington, Sandra, and Miranda Green, eds. *The Concept of the Goddess.* London: Routledge, 1996. Print.

Bleikasten, André, and Nicole Moulinoux, ed. *Douze lectures de* Sanctuaire. Rennes, France: PU de Rennes/Fondation William Faulkner, 1995. Print.

Blotner, Joseph. *Faulkner: A Biography.* 2 vols. New York: Random House, 1974. Print.

———. *William Faulkner's Library: A Catalogue.* Charlottesville: UP of Virginia, 1964. Print.

Bluestein, Gene. *The Voice of the Folk: Folklore and American Literary Theory.* Amherst: U of Massachusetts P, 1972. Print.

Bockris, Victor. *Keith Richards: The Biography.* New York: Da Capo, 2003. Print.

Bollinger, Laurel. "Narrating Racial Identity and Transgression in Faulkner's 'That Evening Sun.'" *College Literature* 39.2 (Spring 2012): 53–72. Print.

"Booster Blues" by Blind Lemon Jefferson. Advertisement. *Chicago Defender* 3 April 1926. 7, col. 5. Print.

Brearley, H. C. "Ba-ad Nigger." 1939. Dundes, ed. 578–85. Print.

Broonzy, Big Bill. "Louise, Louise Blues." 1937. *Big Bill Blues: His 23 Greatest Recordings 1927–1942.* Wolf Records, n.d. CD.

———. "Mississippi River Blues." 1934. *Big Bill Blues: His 23 Greatest Recordings 1927–1942.* Wolf Records, n.d. CD.

Broughton, Panthea Reid. *William Faulkner: The Abstract and the Actual.* Baton Rouge: Louisiana State UP, 1974. Print.

Brown, Calvin. *A Glossary of Faulkner's South.* New Haven, CT: Yale UP, 1976. Print.

Brown, Cecil. *Stagolee Shot Billy.* Cambridge, MA: Harvard UP, 2004. Print.

Brown, May Cameron. "Voice in 'That Evening Sun': A Study of Quentin Compson." *Mississippi Quarterly* 29.3 (Summer 1976): 347–60. Print.

Brown, Sterling A. "The Blues as Folk Poetry." 1930. *The Book of Negro Folklore.* Ed. Langston Hughes and Arna Bontemps. New York: Dodd, Mead & Co., 1958. 371–86. Print.

———. "Cabaret." 1932. *The Collected Poems of Sterling A. Brown.* 111–13. Print.

———. "Children of the Mississippi." 1931. *The Collected Poems of Sterling A. Brown.* 66–67. Print.

———. *The Collected Poems of Sterling A. Brown.* Evanston, IL: Northwestern UP, 1996. Print.

Brumm, Ursula. "Theme and Narrative Voice in Faulkner's 'Old Man.'" *Faulkner's Discourse: An International Symposium.* Ed. Lothar Hónnighausen. Tübingen: Niemeyer, 1989. 242–47. Print.

Burt, Olive Wooley. *American Murder Ballads and Their Stories.* New York: Citadel, 1964. Print.

Cadillac Records. Dir. Darnell Martin. 2008. Perf. Jeffrey Wright, Eamonn Walker, Adrien Brody, and Beyoncé Knowles. Sony, 2009. DVD.

Calt, Stephen. *Barrelhouse Words: A Blues Dialect Dictionary.* Urbana: U of Illinois P, 2009. Print.

———, and Gayle Dean Wardlow. *King of the Delta Blues: The Life and Music of Charlie Patton.* Newton, NJ: Rock Chapel P, 1988. Print.

Canfield, J. Douglas. "Introduction." Canfield, ed. 1–13. Print.

———, ed. *Twentieth-Century Interpretations of* Sanctuary. Englewood Cliffs, NJ: Prentice Hall, 1982. Print.

Carothers, James B. "The Road to *The Reivers.*" *"A Cosmos of My Own": Faulkner and Yoknapatawpha, 1980.* Ed. Doreen Fowler and Ann J. Abadie. Jackson: UP of Mississippi, 1981. 95–124. Print.

———. *William Faulkner's Short Stories.* Ann Arbor, MI: UMI Research P, 1985. Print.

Carr, Leroy. "Bread Baker." 1934. *Complete Recorded Works in Chronological Order.* Vol. 6: *1934–1935.* Document, 2004. CD.

Cartwright, Keith. "Blood on the Leaves, Blood at the Root: Ritual Carriers and Sacrificial Crises of Transition in Yoknapatawpha and Oyo." *Global Faulkner: Faulkner and Yoknapatawpha 2006.* Ed. Annette Trefzer and Ann J. Abadic. Jackson: UP of Mississippi, 2009. 78–98. Print.

Cash, Johnny. "Folsom Prison Blues." *The Essential Johnny Cash 1955–1983*. Columbia, 1992. Disc 1. CD.

———. *The Man Comes Around*. American, 2002. CD.

Cash, W. J. *The Mind of the South*. 1941. London: Penguin, 1973. Print.

Charters. Samuel. *The Blues Makers*. New York: Da Capo P, 1991. Print.

———. *The Country Blues*. 1959. New York: Da Capo, 1975. Print.

———. *The Poetry of the Blues*. 1963. New York: Avon, 1970. Print.

Clarke, Donald. *Wishing on the Moon: The Life and Times of Billie Holiday*. London: Penguin, 1995. Print.

Cobb, James C. *The Most Southern Place on Earth: The Mississippi Delta and the Roots of Regional Identity*. New York: Oxford UP, 1992. Print.

Cobb, W. F. *Mysticism and the Creed*. London: Macmillan, 1914. Print.

Coburn, Mark D. "Nancy's Blues: Faulkner's 'That Evening Sun.'" *Perspective* 17.3 (1974): 207–16. Print.

Cohen, Norm. *Long Steel Rail: The Railroad in American Folksong*. Urbana: U of Illinois P, 1981. Print.

Cohen, Philip. "William Faulkner, the Crisis of Masculinity, and Textual Instability." *Textual Studies and the Common Reader: Essays on Editing Novels and Novelists*. Ed. Alexander Petit. Athens: U of Georgia P, 2000. 64–80.

Cohen, Ronald D. *Rainbow Quest: The Folk Music Revival and American Society, 1940–1970*. Amherst: U of Massachusetts P, 2002. Print.

Cohn, David. *Where I Was Born and Raised*. 1948. Notre Dame, IN: Notre Dame UP, 1967. Print.

Comentale, Edward P. *Sweet Air: Modernism, Regionalism, and American Popular Song*. Urbana: U of Illinois P, 2013. Print.

Cordeiro, AnneMarie. "Geechie Wiley: An Exploration of Enigmatic Virtuosity." MA thesis, Arizona State University, May 2011. repository.asu/edu/attachments/56662content/Cordeiro_asu_0010N_10725.pdf. Accessed 20 July 2012. Web.

Couzens, Reginald C. *The Stories of the Months and Days*. New York: Frederick A. Stokes Co., 1923. Print.

Cowley, Malcolm. *The Faulkner-Cowley File: Letters and Memories, 1944–1962*. New York: Viking, 1966. Print.

Creighton, Joanne V. "Self-Destructive Evil in *Sanctuary*." *Twentieth Century Literature* 18.4 (October 1972): 259–70. Print.

Crossroads. Dir. Walter Hill. 1986. Sony, 2004. DVD.

Crouch, Stanley. "Howling Wolf: A Blues Lesson Book." *Ain't No Ambulances for No Nigguhs Tonight*. New York: Richard W. Baron, 1972. 56–60.

Cullen, John B., and Floyd C. Watkins. *Old Times in the Faulkner Country*. 1961. Baton Rouge: Louisiana State UP, 1976. Print.

Cummings, E. E. "VIII: Buffalo Bill's." 1923. *Poems 1923–1954*. New York: Harcourt, Brace & Co., 1954. 50.

Dalzell, Tom, and Terry Victor, eds. *The New Partridge Dictionary of Slang and Unconventional English*. London: Routledge, 2006. Print.

Daniel, Pete. *Deep'n as It Come: The 1927 Mississippi River Flood*. New York: Oxford UP, 1977. Print.

———. *Standing at the Crossroads: Southern Life in the Twentieth Century*. New York: Hill & Wang, 1986. Print.

Daniels, Julius. "My Mama Was a Sailor." 1927. *Atlanta Blues*. Disc 1. JSP, 2005. CD.

Davis, Angela. *Blues Legacies and Black Feminism: Gertrude "Ma" Rainey, Bessie Smith, and Billie Holiday*. New York: Pantheon, 1998. Print.

Davis, Francis. *The History of the Blues*. New York: Hyperion, 1995. Print.

Davis, Thadious. "Expanding the Limits: The Intersection of Race and Region." *Southern Literary Journal* 20.2 (Spring 1988): 3–11. Print.

———. *Faulkner's "Negro": Art and the Southern Context*. Baton Rouge: Louisiana State UP, 1983. Print.

———. "From Jazz Syncopation to Blues Elegy: Faulkner's Development of Black Characterization." *Faulkner and Race*. Ed. Fowler and Abadie. 70–92. Print.

Davis, Walter. "Blue Ghost Blues." 1932. *First Recordings: 1930–1932*. JSP, 1994. CD.

De Tocqueville, Alexis. *Democracy in America*. Vol. 2. Trans. Henry Reeve. New York: D. Appleton & Co., 1904. Print.

Decker, Todd. Show Boat: *Performing Race in an American Musical*. New York: Oxford UP, 2012. Print.

Devlin, Albert J. "*The Reivers*: Readings in Social Psychology." *Mississippi Quarterly* 25.3 (Summer 1972): 327–37. Print.

DiGiacomo, Frank. "Portrait of a Phantom: Searching for Robert Johnson." *Vanity Fair* (November 2008). www.vanityfaor.com/culture/features/2008/11/johnson200811. Accessed 30 September 2013. Web.

Dixon, Robert M. W., and John Godrich. *Recording the Blues*. 1970. Rpt. in *Yonder Come the Blues: The Evolution of a Genre*. Cambridge, UK: Cambridge UP, 2001. 243–342. Print.

Dobbs, Cynthia. "Flooded: The Excesses of Geography, Gender, and Capitalism in Faulkner's *If I Forget Thee, Jerusalem*." *American Literature* 73.4 (December 2001): 811–35. Print.

Dollard, John. *Caste and Class in a Southern Town*. 1937. London: Routledge/Thoemmes P, 1998. Print.

Dore, Florence. "Counting as Decent: Obscenity and Masculinity in William Faulkner's *Sanctuary*." *The Novel and the Obscene: Sexual Subjects in American Modernism*. Palo Also, CA: Stanford UP, 2005.67–89. Print.

Doyle, Don. *Faulkner's County: The Historical Roots of Yoknapatawpha*. Chapel Hill: U of North Carolina P, 2001. Print.

Dundes, Alan, ed. *Mother Wit from the Laughing Barrel: Readings in the Interpretation of Afro-American Folklore*. Englewood Cliffs, NJ: Prentice-Hall, Inc., 1973. Print.

Dunleavy, Linda. "*Sanctuary*, Sexual Difference, and the Problem of Rape." *Studies in American Fiction* 24.2 (Autumn 1996): 171–91. Print.

Dylan, Bob. "Fixin' to Die." *Bob Dylan*. 1962. Sony, 2005. CD.

———. "High Water (For Charley Patton)" *Love and Theft*. Columbia, 2001. CD.

———. "Oxford Town." *The Freewheelin' Bob Dylan*. 1963. Columbia, 2004. CD.

———. "See That My Grave Is Kept Clean." *Bob Dylan*. 1962. Sony, 2005. CD.

Eddy, Charmaine. "The Policing and Proliferation of Desire: Gender and the Homosocial in Faulkner's *Sanctuary*." *Faulkner Journal* 14.2 (Spring 1999): 21–39. Print.

Edel, Leon. "How to Read *The Sound and the Fury*." *Varieties of Literary Experience: Eighteen Essays in World Literature*. Ed. Stanley Burnshaw. New York: New York UP, 1962. 241–57. Print.

Edmonds, Anthony O. *Muhammad Ali: A Biography*. Westport, CT: Greenwood P, 2006. Print.

Ellis, Walter. *Me and the Devil Blues*. Bloomington, IN: iUniverse, 2000. Print.

Ellison, Ralph. *Shadow and Act*. 1964. New York: Vintage, 1972. Print.

Escott, Colin, and Martin Hawkins. *Good Rockin' Tonight: Sun Records and the Birth of Rock 'n' Roll*. New York: St. Martin's P, 1991. Print.

Evans, David. *Big Road Blues: Tradition & Creativity in the Folk Blues*. 1982. New York: Da Capo P, 1987. Print.

———."Charley Patton: The Conscience of the Delta." *The Voice of the Delta: Charley Patton and the Mississippi Blues Traditions*. Ed. Robert Sacre. Liège, Belgium: Presses Universitaires Liège, 1987. 111–214. Print.

———. E-mail to author. 17 August 2009.

———. "Formulaic Composition: A View from the Field." *Journal of American Folklore* 120.478 (Fall 2007): 482–99. Print.

———. "High Water Everywhere: Blues and Gospel Commentary on the 1927 Mississippi Flood." Springer, ed. 3–75. Print.

Eyster, Kevin I. "The Personal Narrative in Fiction: Faulkner's *The Reivers*." *Western Folklore* 51.1 (January 1992): 11–21. Print.

Fadiman, Clifton. "Mississippi Frankenstein." *The New Yorker* 14.49 (21 January 1939): 60–63. Print.

Fahey, John. *Charley Patton*. London: Studio Vista, 1970. Print.

———. "Charley Reconsidered, Thirty-Five Years On." *Screamin' and Hollerin' the Blues: The Worlds of Charley Patton*. Revenant, 2001. Liner notes: 46–53. Print.

Farmer, John S., and W. E. Henley. *Slang and Its Analogues*. Vol. 6: *Rea to Stozzle*. 1902. New York: Kraus Reprint Corporation, 1965. Print.

Faulkner, William. *Absalom, Absalom!* 1936. New York: Vintage International, 1990. Print.

———. *As I Lay Dying*. 1930. New York: Vintage International, 1990. Print.

———. *Collected Stories of William Faulkner*. New York: Random House, 1950. Print.

———. "Dry September." *Collected Stories*. 169–83. Print.

———. *A Fable.* 1954. *William Faulkner: Novels 1942–1954.* New York: Library of America, 1994. 665–1072. Print.

———. *Faulkner in the University.* Ed. Frederick L Gwynn and Joseph L. Blotner. New York: Random House, 1965. Print.

———. *Flags in the Dust. William Faulkner: Novels 1926–1929.* New York: Library of America, 2006. 541–875. Print.

———. "Frankie and Johnny." 1925. *Uncollected Stories.* 338–47. Print.

———. *Go Down, Moses.* 1942. New York: Vintage International, 1990. Print.

———. *The Hamlet.* 1940. New York: Vintage International, 1991. Print.

———. *Intruder in the Dust.* 1948. New York: Vintage International, 1991. Print.

———. *Light in August.* 1932. New York, Vintage International, 1990. Print.

———. *Lion in the Garden: Interviews with William Faulkner 1926–1962.* Ed. James B. Meriwether and Michael Millgate. New York: Random House, 1968. Print.

———. *The Mansion.* 1959. *William Faulkner: Novels 1957–1962.* New York: Library of America, 1999. 327–721. Print.

———. *Mosquitoes.* 1927. *William Faulkner: Novels 1926–1929.* New York: Library of America, 2006. 257–540. Print.

———. "Never Done No Weeping When You Wanted to Laugh." Ed. Gail Moore Morrison. *Mississippi Quarterly* 36.3 (Summer 1983): 461–74. Print.

———. *Pylon.* 1935. *William Faulkner: Novels 1930–1935.* New York: Library of America,1985. Print.

———. *The Reivers.* 1962. New York: Vintage International, 1992. Print.

———. *Requiem for a Nun.* 1951. *William Faulkner: Novels 1942–1954.* New York: Library of America, 1994. 471–664. Print.

———. *Sanctuary.* 1931. New York: Vintage International, 1993. Print.

———. *Sanctuary: The Original Text.* 1929. Ed. Noel Polk. New York: Random House, 1981. Print.

———. *Sartoris.* 1929. New York: Signet, 1964. Print.

———. *Soldiers' Pay.* 1926. *William Faulkner: Novels 1926–1929.* New York: Library of America, 2006. 1–256. Print.

———. *The Sound and the Fury.* 1929. New York: Vintage International, 1990. Print.

———. "That Evening Sun." 1931. *Collected Stories.* 289–309. Print.

———. *The Town.* 1957. *William Faulkner: Novels 1957–1962.* New York: Library of America, 1999. 1–326. Print.

———. *Uncollected Stories.* 1979. New York: Vintage International, 1997. Print.

———. *The Unvanquished.* 1938. New York: Vintage International, 1991. Print.

———. *The Wild Palms* [*If I Forget Thee, Jerusalem*]. 1939. New York: Vintage International, 1995. Print.

Ferris, William. *Blues from the Delta.* Garden City, NY: Anchor/Doubleday, 1978. Print.

Fiedler, Leslie. *Love and Death in the American Novel.* Rev ed. London: Penguin, 1984. Print.

———. "Pop Goes the Faulkner: In Quest of *Sanctuary.*" *Faulkner and Popular Culture.* Ed. Fowler and Abadie. 75–92. Print.

———. Review of *The Reivers. Manchester Guardian.* 28 September 1962. 6. Print.

Fisher, Marvin. "The World of Faulkner's Children." *University of Kansas City Review* 27.1 (October 1960): 13–18. Print.

Fiske, John. *Understanding Popular Culture.* Boston: Unwin Hyman, 1989. Print.

Fitzgerald, F. Scott. "The Crack Up." 1936. *The Crack Up.* Ed. Edmund Wilson. New York: New Directions, 1993. Print.

Flora, Joseph M. "The Device of Conspicuous Silence in the Modern Short Story." *The Teller and the Tale: Aspects of the Short Story.* Ed. Wendell M. Aycock. Lubbock: Texas Tech P, 1982. 27–45. Print.

Fowler, Doreen A. "Measuring Faulkner's Tall Convict." *Studies in the Novel* 14.3 (Fall 1982): 280–84. Print.

———. "Tracing Racial Assumptions: Teaching 'That Evening Sun.'" *Teaching Faulkner: Approaches and Methods.* Ed. Stephen Hahn and Robert W. Hamblin. Westport, CT: Greenwood P, 2001. 47–52. Print.

———, and Ann J. Abadie, eds. *Faulkner and Popular Culture: Faulkner and Yoknapatawpha.* 1988. Jackson: UP of Mississippi, 1990. Print.

———. *Faulkner and Race: Faulkner and Yoknapatawpha, 1986.* Jackson: UP of Mississippi, 1987. Print.

Friedwald, Will. *Stardust Memories: The Biography of Twelve of America's Most Popular Songs.* New York: Pantheon Books, 2002. Print.

Frost, Robert. "The Flood." *West-Running Brook.* New York: Henry Holt & Co., 1928. Print.

Fruscione, Joseph. *Faulkner and Hemingway: Biography of a Literary Rivalry.* Columbus: Ohio State UP, 2012. Print.

Fuller, Blind Boy. "What's That Smells Like Fish?" 1938. *Complete Recorded Works in Chronological Order.* Vol. 4: *15 December 1937 to 29 October 1938.* Document, 2011. CD.

Fury, Frank. "Snaffles and Derbies: Horseracing and Southern Folk Culture in William Faulkner's *The Reivers.*" *Mississippi Quarterly* 59. 3–4 (Summer–Fall 2006): 435–54. Print.

Gaines, Ernest J. *Mozart and Leadbelly: Stories and Essays.* Ed. Marcia Gaudet and Reggie Young. New York: Alfred A. Knopf, 2005. Print.

Garon, Paul. *Blues and the Poetic Spirit.* 1975. New York: Da Capo, 1979. Print.

Garrison, Joseph M., Jr. "The Past and the Present in 'That Evening Sun.'" *Studies in Short Fiction* 13.3 (Summer 1976): 371–73. Print.

Gartner, Carol B. "Faulkner in Context: Seeing 'That Evening Sun' through the Blues." *Southern Quarterly* 34.2 (Winter 1996): 50–58. Print.

Gellert, Lawrence. *Negro Songs of Protest.* Vol. 2: *Me and My Captain—Chain Gang.* New York: Hours P, 1939. Print.

Gerlach, John. "Faulkner, 'That Evening Sun.'" *Toward the End: Closure and Structure in the American Short Story*. Tuscaloosa: U of Alabama P, 1985. 130–43. Print.

Giddins, Gary. *Satchmo: The Genius of Louis Armstrong*. 1988. New York: Da Capo P, 2001. Print.

Giesen, James C. *Boll Weevil Blues: Cotton, Myth, and Power in the American South*. Chicago: U of Chicago P, 2011. Print.

Ginger Snaps. "Shrimp Man." 1945. *The Chronological Jimmy Mundy and His Orchestra, 1937–1947*. Classics, 2001. CD.

Gioia, Ted. *Delta Blues: The Life and Times of the Mississippi Masters Who Revolutionized American Music*. New York: W. W. Norton & Co., 2008. Print.

Glaves, Amy. "'He Will Never Be a Man': Reading Males as Castrated Horses in William Faulkner's *Sanctuary*." Faulkner and Morrison Conference. Southeast Missouri University, Cape Girardeau, MO. 30 October 2010. Conference Presentation.

Glaze, Rube, with Blind Willie McTell. "Lonesome Day Blues." 1932. *Mr. McTell Got the Blues*. 2 CDs. Recall. 2004. Disc 1.

Godden, Richard. *Fictions of Labor: William Faulkner and the South's Long Revolution*. Cambridge, UK: Cambridge UP, 1997. Print.

Gomez. "Charley Patton Songs." *How We Operate*. ATO/Independiente, 2006. CD.

Graham, T. Austin. *The Great American Songbooks: Musical Texts, Modernism, and the Value of Popular Culture*. New York: Oxford UP, 2013. Print.

Graves, Tom. *Crossroads: The Life and Afterlife of Blues Legend Robert Johnson*. Spokane, WA: Demers Books, 2008. Print.

Green, Jonathon. *Green's Dictionary of Slang*. London: Chambers, 2010. Print.

Gregory, Eileen. "The Temerity to Revolt: Mink Snopes and the Dispossessed in *The Mansion*." *Mississippi Quarterly* 29.3 (Summer 1976): 401–21. Print.

Gresset, Michel. *Fascination: Faulkner's Fiction, 1919–1936*. Durham, NC: Duke UP, 1989. Print.

———, and Kenzaburo Ohashi, eds. *Faulkner: After the Nobel Prize*. Kyoto, Japan: Yamaguchi Publishing House, 1987. Print.

Grimwood, Michael. "Faulkner and the Vocational Liabilities of Black Characterization." *Faulkner and Race*. Ed. Fowler and Abadie. 255–71. Print.

———. *Heart in Conflict: Faulkner's Struggles with Vocation*. Athens: U of Georgia P, 1987. Print.

———. "Lyle Saxon's *Father Mississippi* as a Source for Faulkner's 'Old Man' and 'Mississippi.'" *Notes on Mississippi Writers* 17.2 (1985): 53–62. Print.

Grundy, Stephan. "Freyja and Frigg." Billington and Green, eds. 56–67. Print.

Gruver, Rod. "The Autobiographical Theory Re-Examined." *JEMF Quarterly* 6 (1970): 129–31. Print.

———. "The Blues as Dramatic Monologue" *JEMF Quarterly* 6 (1970): 28–31. Print.

Guralnick, Peter. *Feel Like Going Home: Portraits in Blues and Rock 'n' Roll*. 1971. Boston: Little, Brown & Co., 1999. Print.

——. *Searching for Robert Johnson.* New York: Plume, 1998. Print.

Gussow, Adam. *Mister Satan's Apprentice: A Blues Memoir.* 1998. Minneapolis: U of Minnesota P, 2009. Print.

——. "Plaintive Reiterations and Meaningless Strains: Faulkner's Blues Understandings." *Faulkner's Inheritance: Faulkner and Yoknapatawpha, 2005.* Ed. Joseph R. Urgo and Ann J. Abadie. Jackson: UP of Mississippi, 2007. 53–81. Print.

——. *Seems Like Murder Here: Southern Violence and the Blues Tradition.* Chicago: U of Chicago P, 2002. Print.

Guttman, Sondra. "Who's Afraid of the Corncob Man? Masculinity, Race, and Labor in the Preface to *Sanctuary.*" *Faulkner Journal* 15.1–2 (Fall 1999–2000): 15–34. Print.

Gwin, Minrose C. *The Feminine and Faulkner: Reading Beyond Sexual Difference.* Knoxville: U of Tennessee P, 1990. Print.

Hale, Grace Elizabeth. *Making Whiteness: The Culture of Segregation in the South, 1890–1940.* New York: Pantheon, 1998.

Hall, Jean Houston, ed. *Dictionary of American Regional English.* Vol. 6: *P–Sk.* Cambridge, MA: Belknap P, 2002. Print.

Hamblin, Robert W. "Before the Fall: The Theme of Innocence in Faulkner's 'That Evening Sun'" *Notes on Mississippi Writers* 11 (1979): 86–94. Print.

——. "Oprah's 'Summer of Faulkner.'" 2006. www.faulnerjapan.com/journal/N08/Hamblin2006.htm Accessed 30 September 2013. Web.

Hamilton, Marybeth. "Authenticity and the Making of the Blues Tradition." *Past and Present* 169 (November 2000): 132–60. Print.

——. *In Search of the Blues.* New York: Perseus, 2008. Print.

Handy, W. C. *Father of the Blues: An Autobiography.* New York: Macmillan, 1941. Print.

Harrington, Evans B. "Technical Aspects of William Faulkner's 'That Evening Sun.'" *Faulkner Studies* 1.3 (Fall 1952): 54–59. Print.

Harrington, Gary. "The Con-Artist in *The Wild Palms.*" *Dalhousie Review* 65.1 (Spring 1985): 80–88. Print.

Haynes, Janc Isbell. "A Note on Faulkner and the Stagolee/Faust Legends." *Mississippi Quarterly* 64.3–4 (Summer–Fall 2011): 439–42. Print.

Helms, Douglas. "Just Lookin' for a Home: The Cotton Boll Weevil and the South." PhD diss. Florida State University, 1977.

Hemingway, Ernest. *A Farewell to Arms.* 1929. New York: Charles Scribner's Sons, 1969. Print.

——. *The Sun Also Rises.* 1926. New York: Scribner, 2003. Print.

Hermann, John. "Faulkner's Heart's Darling in 'That Evening Sun.'" *Studies in Short Fiction* 7.2 (Spring 1970): 320–23. Print.

Hill, Patricia Liggins, et al., eds. *Call and Response: The Riverside Anthology of the African American Literary Tradition.* New York: Houghton Mifflin Co., 1997. Print.

Hiramoto, Akira. *Me and the Devil Blues: The Unreal Life of Robert Johnson.* Vol. 1. Trans. David Ury. New York: Ballantine, 2008. Print.

Hodgin, Katharine C. "Horace Benbow and Bayard Sartoris: Two Romantic Figures in Faulkner's *Flags in the Dust.*" *American Literature* 50.4 (January 1979): 647–52. Print.

Hoefer, Anthony Dyer. "'They're Trying to Wash Us Away': Revisiting Faulkner's *If I Forget Thee, Jerusalem* [*The Wild Palms*] and Wright's 'Down By the Riverside' After the Flood." *Mississippi Quarterly* 63.3–4 (Summer–Fall 2010): 537–54. Print.

Holiday, Billie. "Strange Fruit." 1939. *The Commodore Master Takes.* GRP, 2000. CD.

House, Son. "Dry Spell Blues." 1930. Patton, *Screamin' and Hollerin' the Blues.* Disc 4.

———. "My Black Mama Blues." 1930. Patton, *Screamin' and Hollerin' the Blues.* Disc 4.

———. "Preachin' the Blues." 1930. Patton, *Screamin' and Hollerin' the Blues.* Disc 4.

Howard, William. "Richard Wright's Flood Stories and the Great Mississippi River Flood of 1927: Social and Historical Backgrounds." *Southern Literary Journal* 16.2 (Spring 1984): 44–63. www.pipeline.com/~rougeforum/floodstories.html. Accessed 1 Sept 2008. Web.

Howe, Irving. "Faulkner and the Negroes." 1951. *Faulkner: New Perspectives.* Ed. Richard H. Brodhead. Englewood Cliffs, NJ: Prentice-Hall, Inc., 1983. 47–61. Print.

Howlin' Wolf. "Ain't Goin' Down That Dirt Road." 1968. *Chess Box.* Disc 3.

———. "Back Door Man." 1960. *Chess Box.* Disc 2.

———. *The Back Door Wolf.* 1973. Chess/MCA, 1995. CD.

———. "Can't Stay Here." 1973. *Back Door Wolf.*

———. *The Chess Box.* 3 CDs. Chess/MCA, 1991.

———. "Coon on the Moon." 1973. *Back Door Wolf.*

———. "Crying at Daybreak." *Moanin' at Midnight: The Memphis Recordings.* Varese Sarabande, 2002. CD.

———. "Forty-Four." 1954. *Chess Box.* Disc 1.

———. "How Many More Years." 1951. *Chess Box.* Disc 1.

———. "How Many More Years." *Shindig.* 20 May 1965. *YouTube.* www.youtube.com/watch?v=gWBS0GX1s90. Accessed 30 September 2013. Web.

———. "If I Were a Bird." 1971. *Message to the Young.*

———. "Killing Floor." 1964. *Chess Box.* Disc 3.

———. *Live and Cookin' at Alice's Revisited.* 1972. Raven, 2011. CD.

———. *The London Howlin' Wolf Sessions.* 1971. Chess, 1994. CD.

———. *Message to the Young.* 1971. Chess/Geffen, 2012. CD.

———. "Moanin' at Midnight." 1951. *Chess Box.* Disc 1.

———. "Moving." 1973. *Back Door Wolf.*

———. "The Natchez Burning." 1956. *Chess Box.* Disc 2.

———. "The Red Rooster." 1961. *Chess Box.* Disc 2.

———. "The Red Rooster." 1971. *London Howlin' Wolf Sessions.*

———. "Saddle My Pony." 1952. *Chess Box.* Disc 1..

———. "Sittin' on Top of the World." 1957. *Chess Box.* Disc 2.

———. "Sittin' on Top of the World." 1972. *Live and Cookin' at Alice's Revisited.* CD.

———. "Smokestack Lightnin.'" 1956.*Chess Box*. Disc 2.
———. "Trying to Forget You." 1973. *Back Door Wolf.*
———. "Wang Dang Doodle." 1960. *Chess Box*. Disc 2.
———. "Watergate Blues." 1973. *Back Door Wolf.*
Hudson, A. P. *Specimens of Mississippi Folk-Lore*. Ann Arbor, MI: Edwards Bros., 1928. Print.
Hughes, Langston. *Not Without Laughter*. 1930. New York: Macmillan, 1969. Print.
Humphrey, Mark. Liner notes. *The Back Door Wolf.* Chess, 1995. Print.
Hurston, Zora Neale. *Mules and Men*. 1935. New York: Harper, 1990. Print.
Hurt, Mississippi John. *Avalon Blues: The Complete 1928 Okeh Recordings*. Columbia/Legacy, 1996. CD.
———. "Frankie." 1928. *Avalon Blues*.
———. "Stack O'Lee." 1928. *Avalon Blues*.
Huston, John. *Frankie and Johnny*. 1930. New York: Benjamin Blom, 1968. Print.
Inge, M. Thomas, ed. *William Faulkner: The Contemporary Reviews*. Cambridge, UK: Cambridge UP, 1995. Print.
Irwin, John T. *Doubling and Incest/Repetition and Revenge: A Speculative Reading of Faulkner*. Rev. ed. Baltimore: Johns Hopkins UP, 1996. Print.
Jahn, Janheinz. "Blues: The Conflict of Cultures." 1961. Rpt. in Tracy, ed. 28–31. Print.
James, Skip. *The Complete Early Recordings*. Yazoo, 1994. CD.
———. "Devil Got My Woman." 1931. *Complete Early Recordings*.
———. "Hard Time Killin' Floor Blues." 1931. *Complete Early Recordings*.
Jefferson, Blind Lemon. "Match Box Blues." 1927. *Classic Sides*. Disc 2. JSP, 2003. CD.
Jenkins, Lee. *Faulkner and Black-White Relations*. New York: Columbia UP, 1981. Print.
Johnson, Blind Willie. "When the War Was On." 1929. *Complete Recordings of Blind Willie Johnson*. Disc 2. Sony, 1993. CD.
Johnson, Guy B. "Double Meaning in the Popular Negro Blues." 1927. Tracy, ed. 172–79. Print.
Johnson, James Weldon. *Black Manhattan*. 1930. New York: Arno P, 1968. Print.
Johnson, Lonnie. "Blue Ghost Blues." 1927. *Complete Recorded Works 1925–1932 in Chronological Order*, Vol. 3: *1927–1928*. Document, 1991. CD.
———. "Blues Is Only a Ghost." 1931. *Complete Recorded Works 1925–1932 in Chronological Order*, Vol. 6: *1930–1931*. Document, 1996. CD.
———. "Broken Levee Blues." 1928. *The Original Guitar Wizard*. Disc 2. Proper, 2004. CD.
Johnson, Robert. "Cross Road Blues." 1936. *Complete Recordings*. Disc 1.
———. "Dead Shrimp Blues." 1936. *Complete Recordings*. Disc 1.
———. "Hellhound on My Trail." 1937. *Complete Recordings*. Disc 2.
———. "Me and the Devil Blues." 1937. *Complete Recordings*. Disc 2.
———. "Phonograph Blues." 1936. *Complete Recordings*. Disc 1.
———. *Robert Johnson: The Complete Recordings*. 2 CDs. Columbia, 1990.

———. "Stones in My Passway." 1937. *Complete Recordings.* Disc 2.

———. "Stop Breakin' Down Blues." 1937. *Complete Recordings.* Disc 2.

———. "Sweet Home Chicago." 1936. *Complete Recordings.* Disc 1.

———. "Terraplane Blues." 1936. *Complete Recordings.* Disc 1.

———. "They're Red Hot." 1936. *Complete Recordings.* Disc 1.

———. "Traveling Riverside Blues." 1937. *Complete Recordings.* Disc 2.

Johnson, Tommy. "Big Road Blues." 1928. Patton, *Screamin' and Hollerin' the Blues.* Disc 6.

———. "Maggie Campbell Blues." 1928. Patton, *Screamin' and Hollerin' the Blues.* Disc 6.

Johnston, Kenneth G. "The Year of Jubilee: Faulkner's 'That Evening Sun.'" *American Literature* 46.1 (March 1974): 93–100. Print.

Jones, Anne Goodwyn. "'The Kotex Age': Women, Popular Culture, and *The Wild Palms.*" *Faulkner and Popular Culture.* Ed. Fowler and Abadie. 142–62. Print.

Jones, Diane Brown. "That Evening Sun." *A Reader's Guide to the Short Stories of William Faulkner.* New York: G. K. Hall & Co., 1994. 267–316. Print.

Keane-Temple, Rebecca. "The Sounds of *Sanctuary*: Horace Benbow's Consciousness." *Mississippi Quarterly* 50.3 (Summer 1997): 445–50. Print.

Kerr, Elizabeth M. "*The Reivers*: The Golden Book of Yoknapatawpha County." *Modern Fiction Studies* 13.1 (Spring 1967): 95–113. Print.

King, Vincent Allan. "Faulkner's Brazen Yoke: Pop Art, Modernism, and the Myth of the Great Divide." *A Companion to William Faulkner.* Ed. Richard C. Moreland. Malden, MA: Blackwell, 2007. 301–17. Print.

———. "The Wages of Pulp: The Use and Abuse of Fiction in William Faulkner's *The Wild Palms.*" *Mississippi Quarterly* 51.3 (Summer 1998): 503–25. Print.

Kinney, Arthur F. Go Down, Moses: *The Miscegenation of Time.* New York: Twayne, 1996. Print.

Koyama, Toshio. "Faulkner's Final Narrative Vision in *The Reivers*: Remembering and Knowing." Gresset and Ohashi, ed. 227–43. Print.

Krause, David. "Faulkner's Blues." *Studies in the Novel* 17.1 (Spring 1985): 80–94. Print.

Kreuger, Miles. Show Boat: *The Story of a Classic American Musical.* 1977. New York: Da Capo, 1990. Print.

Kubie, Lawrence S. "William Faulkner's *Sanctuary*: An Analysis" 1934. Rpt. in Canfield, ed. 25–31. Print.

Kuyk, Dirk, Jr.; Betty M. Kuyk; and James A. Miller. "Black Culture in William Faulkner's 'That Evening Sun.'" *Journal of American Studies* 20.1 (April 1986): 33–50. Print.

Lawson, R. A. "The First Century of Blues: One Hundred Years of Hearing and Interpreting the Music and the Musicians." *Southern Cultures* 13.3 (Fall 2007): 39–60. Print.

———. *Jim Crow's Counterculture: The Blues and Black Southerners 1890–1945.* Baton Rouge: Louisiana State UP, 2010. Print.

Lead Belly. "The Midnight Special." 1934. *Important Recordings, 1934–1949.* Disc A. JSP, 2006. CD.

———, and the Golden Gate Quartet. *The Midnight Special and Other Prison Songs.* Victor, 1941. Album.

Led Zeppelin. "The Lemon Song." 1969. *Led Zeppelin II.* Atlantic, 1994. CD.

Lee, Jim. "The Problem of Nancy in Faulkner's 'That Evening Sun.'" *South Central Bulletin* 21.4 (Winter 1961): 49–50. Print.

Lemann, Nicholas. *The Promised Land: The Great Black Migration and How It Changed America.* New York: Alfred A. Knopf, 1991. Print.

Lester, Cheryl. "*If I Forget Thee, Jerusalem* and the Great Migration: History in Black and White." *Faulkner in Context: Faulkner and Yoknapatawpha, 1995.* Ed. Donald M. Kartiganer and Ann J. Abadie. Jackson: UP of Mississippi, 1997. 191–217. Print.

———. "Make Room for Elvis." *Faulkner and Postmodernism: Faulkner and Yoknapatawpha, 1999.* Ed. John N. Duvall and Ann J. Abadie. Jackson: UP of Mississippi, 2002. 143–66. Print.

———. "Racial Awareness and Arrested Development: *The Sound and the Fury* and the Great Migration." *The Cambridge Companion to William Faulkner.* Ed. Philip M. Weinstein. Cambridge: Cambridge UP, 1995. 123–46. Print.

———. "'Same as a Nigger on an Excursion': Memphis, Black Migration, and White Flight in *Sanctuary.*" *Faulkner Journal* 26.1 (Spring 2012): 37–55. Print.

Lightweis-Goff, Jennie. *Blood at the Root: Lynching as American Cultural Nucleus.* Albany: SUNY P, 2011. Print.

Lipsitz, George. "White Desire: Remembering Robert Johnson." *The Possessive Investment in Whiteness: How White People Profit from Identity Politics.* Philadelphia: Temple UP, 1998. 118–38. Print.

Liston, Virginia. "You Don't Know My Mind Blues." 1923. *Complete Recorded Works in Chronological Order.* Vol. 1: *1923–1924.* Document, 1996. CD.

Lomax, Alan. *The Land Where the Blues Began.* New York: Dell, 1995. Print.

Lomax, John. *Adventures of a Ballad Hunter.* New York: Macmillan, 1947. Print.

———, and Alan Lomax, eds. *Negro Folk Songs as Sung by Lead Belly.* New York: Macmillan, 1936. Print.

Lott, Eric. "Back Door Man: Howlin' Wolf and the Sound of Jim Crow." *American Quarterly* 63.3 (September 2011): 697–710. Print.

———. *Love and Theft: Blackface Minstrelsy and the American Working Class.* New York: Oxford UP, 1993. Print.

Lurie, Peter. *Vision's Immanence: Faulkner, Film, and the Popular Imagination.* Baltimore: Johns Hopkins UP, 2004. Print.

Lynn, Kenneth S. *Hemingway: The Life and Work.* New York: Simon and Schuster, 1987. Print.

Madden, David. "Photographs in the 1929 Version of *Sanctuary*." *Faulkner and Popular Culture*. Ed. Fowler and Abadie. 93–109. Print.

Malone, Bill C. *Country Music, U.S.A.: A Fifty-Year History*. Austin: U of Texas P, 1974. Print.

Manglaviti, Leo J. "Faulkner's 'That Evening Sun' and Mencken's 'Best Editorial Judgment.'" *American Literature* 43.4 (Jan 1972): 649–54. Print.

Marcus, Greil. *Invisible Republic: Bob Dylan's Basement Tapes*. 1997. New York: Henry Holt & Co., 1998. Print.

———. *Mystery Train: Images of America in Rock 'n' Roll Music*. Rev. ed. New York: E. P. Dutton, 1982. Print.

Marquardt, Frederic S. "Shakespeare and American Slang." *American Speech* 4.2 (December 1928): 118–22. Print.

Matthews, John T. "The Elliptical Nature of *Sanctuary*." *Novel* 17.3 (Spring 1984): 246–65. Rpt. in Bleikasten and Moulinoux, ed. 105–23. Print.

———. "Faulkner and the Culture Industry." *The Cambridge Companion to William Faulkner*. Ed. Philip M. Weinstein. Cambridge, UK: Cambridge UP, 1995. 51–73. Print.

———. "Faulkner's Narrative Frames." *Faulkner and the Craft of Fiction: Faulkner and Yoknapatawpha, 1987*. Ed. Doreen Fowler and Ann J. Abadie. Jackson: UP of Mississippi, 1989. 71–91. Print.

Maurer, D. W. "Language and the Sex Revolution: World War I through World War II." *American Speech* 51.1–2 (Spring–Summer 1976): 5–24. Print.

McGeachy, M. G. *Lonesome Words: The Vocal Poetics of the Old English Lament and the African-American Blues Song*. New York: Palgrave Macmillan, 2006. Print.

McHaney, Thomas L. "*Sanctuary* and Frazer's Slain Kings." 1971. Rpt. in Canfield, ed. 79–92. Print.

———. *William Faulkner's* The Wild Palms: *A Study*. Jackson: UP of Mississippi, 1975. Print.

McHugh, Patrick. "The Birth of Tragedy from the Spirit of the Blues: Philosophy and History in *If I Forget Thee, Jerusalem*." *Faulkner Journal* 14.2 (Spring 1999): 57–74. Print.

———. "William Faulkner and the American New Jerusalem." *Arizona Quarterly* 48.1 (Spring 1992): 25–43. Print.

McMillen, Neil R. *Dark Journey: Black Mississippians in the Age of Jim Crow*. Urbana: U of Illinois P, 1989. Print.

———, and Noel Polk. "Faulkner on Lynching." *Faulkner Journal* 8.1 (Fall 1992): 3–14. Print.

McWhirter, Cameron. *Red Summer: The Summer of 1919 and the Awakening of Black America*. New York: Henry Holt & Co., 2011. Print.

Mellard, J. M. "Faulkner's 'Golden Book': *The Reivers* as Romantic Comedy." *Bucknell Review* 13.3 (1965): 19–31. Print.

Mencken, H. L. "The Sahara of the Bozart." 1917, 1920. *The Literature of the American South.* Eds. William L. Andrews et al. New York: W. W. Norton & Co., 1998. 369–78. Print.

Meriwether, James B. "The Novel Faulkner Never Wrote: His *Golden Book* or *Doomsday Book.*" *American Literature* 42 (March 1970): 93–96. Print.

Mesquita, Paula Pinto Elyseu. "Law(s) and Disorder(s): Male Trouble in Faulkner's *Sanctuary.*" *Atenea* 23.2 (December 2003): 153–75. Print.

Middleton, Richard. "O Brother, Let's Go Down Home: Loss, Nostalgia, and the Blues." *Popular Music* 26.1 (2007): 47–64. Print.

Millgate, Michael. *The Achievement of William Faulkner.* New York: Random House, 1966. Print.

———. "Faulkner's First Trilogy: *Sartoris, Sanctuary,* and *Requiem for a Nun.*" *Fifty Years of Yoknapatawpha: Faulkner and Yoknapatawpha, 1979.* Ed. Doreen Fowler and Ann J. Abadie. Jackson: U of Mississippi P, 1980. 90–109. Print.

Miner, Ward L. *The World of William Faulkner.* New York: Grove P, 1952. Print.

Mississippi Sheiks. "Sitting on Top of the World." *Stop and Listen.* Yazoo, 1992. CD.

———. "Stop and Listen Blues." 1930. *Stop and Listen.* Yazoo, 1992. CD.

Monge, Luigi. "Preachin' the Blues: A Textual Linguistic Analysis of Son House's 'Dry Spell Blues.'" *Ramblin' on My Mind: New Perspectives on the Blues.* Ed. David Evans. Urbana: U of Illinois P, 2008. Print.

Moreland, Richard C. *Faulkner and Modernism: Rereading and Rewriting.* Madison: U of Wisconsin P, 1990. Print.

Moses, W. R. "Water, Water Everywhere: 'Old Man' and A Farewell to Arms." *Modern Fiction Studies* 5 (Summer 1959): 172–74. Print.

Muhlenfeld, Elisabeth. "Bewildered Witness: Temple Drake in *Sanctuary.*" *Faulkner Journal* 1.2 (Spring 1986): 43–55. Rpt. in Bleikasten and Moulinoux, ed. 149–63. Print.

Murray, Charles Shaar. "Howlin' Wolf: 'The Legendary Sun Performers.'" 1977. *Shots from the Hip.* London: Penguin, 1991. 239–41. Print.

"Music: Spirituals to Swing." *Time* 33.1 (2 January 1939): 23. Print.

Näsström, Britt-Mari. "Freya—a goddess with many names." Billington and Green, eds. 68–77. Print.

Nilon, Charles H. *Faulkner and the Negro.* New York: Citadel P, 1965. Print.

Nunn, Erich. "'Dont Play No Blues': Race, Music, and Mourning in Faulkner's *Sanctuary.*" *Faulkner Journal* 24.2 (Spring 2009): 77–98. Print.

O Brother, Where Art Thou. Dir. Joel Coen. 2000. Perf. George Clooney, John Turturro, Tim Blake Nelson, John Goodman, Holly Hunter, and Chris Thomas King. Touchstone, 2001. DVD.

O'Connor, William Van. "Faulkner's One-Sided 'Dialogue' with Hemingway." *College English* 24.3 (December 1962): 212–15. Print.

———. *The Tangled Fire of William Faulkner.* Minneapolis: U of Minnesota P, 1954. Print.

Odum, Howard W. "Folk-Song and Folk-Poetry as Found in the Secular Songs of the Southern Negroes." *Journal of American Folklore* 24.93 (July-Sept 1911): 255–94. Print.

———. *Rainbow Round My Shoulder: The Blue Trail of Black Ulysses.* Indianapolis: Bobbs-Merrill, 1928. Print.

———, and Guy B. Johnson. *Negro Workaday Songs.* Chapel Hill: U of North Carolina P, 1926. Print.

Oliver, Paul. "Blues as an Art Form." *Blues World* 21 (Oct 1968): 1–7. Print.

———. *Blues Fell This Morning: Meaning in the Blues.* 1960. Cambridge, UK: Cambridge UP, 1990. Print.

———. *Screening the Blues: Aspects of the Blues Tradition.* 1968. New York: Da Capo, 1989. Print.

———. *The Story of the Blues.* 1969. Boston: Northeastern UP, 1997. Print.

"100 Greatest Singers of All Time." *Mojo* 59 (October 1998): 46–89. Print.

Online Discographical Project. Ed. Steven Abrams and Tyrone Settlemier. www.78discography.com/. Accessed 28 September 2012. Web.

Oshinsky, David M. *"Worse Than Slavery": Parchman Farm and the Ordeal of Jim Crow Justice.* New York: Free P, 1996. Print.

Ownby, Ted. *American Dreams in Mississippi: Consumers, Poverty, & Culture, 1830–1998.* Chapel Hill: U of North Carolina P, 1999. Print.

Palmer, Robert. *Deep Blues.* New York: Penguin, 1982. Print.

Parini, Jay. *One Matchless Time: A Life of William Faulkner.* New York: Harper, 2005. Print.

Parker, Robert Dale. *Faulkner and the Novelistic Imagination.* Urbana: U of Illinois P, 1985. Print.

Parrish, Susan Scott. "Faulkner and the Outer Weather of 1927." *American Literary History* 24.1 (Spring 2012): 34–58. Print.

Partridge, Eric. *A Dictionary of Slang and Unconventional English.* 7th ed. New York: Macmillan, 1970. Print.

Patton, Charley. "Down the Dirt Road Blues." 1929. *Screamin' and Hollerin' the Blues.* Disc 1.

———. "Frankie and Albert." 1930. *Screamin' and Hollerin' the Blues.* Disc 2.

———. "Green River Blues." 1930. *Screamin' and Hollerin' the Blues.* Disc 2.

———. "Hammer Blues." 1930. *Screamin' and Hollerin' the Blues.* Disc 2.

———. "High Water Everywhere, Parts I and II." 1930. *Screamin' and Hollerin' the Blues.* Disc 2.

———. "Jesus Is a Dying-Bed Maker." 1930. *Screamin' and Hollerin' the Blues.* Disc 3.

———. "Mississippi Boweavil Blues." 1929. *Screamin' and Hollerin' the Blues.* Disc 1.

———. "Moon Going Down." 1930. *Screamin' and Hollerin' the Blues.* Disc 5.

——. "Pony Blues." 1929. *Screamin' and Hollerin' the Blues.* Disc 1.

——. *Screamin' and Hollerin' the Blues: The Worlds of Charley Patton.* 7 CDs. Revenant, 2001.

——. "A Spoonful Blues." 1929. *Screamin' and Hollerin' the Blues.* Disc 1.

——. "Tom Rushen Blues." 1929. *Screamin' and Hollerin' the Blues.* Disc 1.

Pearson, Barry Lee. "Standing at the Crossroads between Vinyl and Compact Discs: Reissue Blues Recordings in the 1990s." *Journal of American Folklore* 105.416 (Spring 1992): 215–26. Print.

——, and Bill McCulloch. *Robert Johnson: Lost and Found.* Urbana: U of Illinois P, 2003. Print.

Pearson, Norman Holmes. "Faulkner's Three 'Evening Suns.'" *Yale University Library Gazette* 29 (1954): 61–70. Print.

Peavy, Charles D. *Go Slow Now: Faulkner and the Race Question.* Eugene: U of Oregon Books, 1971. Print.

Peek, Charles A. "'Handy' Ways to Teach 'That Evening Sun'" *Teaching Faulkner: Approaches and Methods.* Ed. Stephen Hahn and Robert W. Hamblin. Westport, CT: Greenwood P, 2001. 53–57. Print.

——. "'That Evening Sun(g)': Blues Inscribing Black Space in White Stories." *Southern Quarterly* 42.3 (Spring 2004): 130–50. Print.

Perkins, Hoke. "'Ah Just Cant Quit Thinking': Faulkner's Black Razor Murderers." *Faulkner and Race.* Ed. Fowler and Abadie. 222–35. Print.

Perrine, Laurence. "'That Evening Sun': A Skein of Uncertainties." *Studies in Short Fiction* 22.3 (Summer 1985): 295–307. Print.

Peters, Erskine. *William Faulkner: The Yoknapatawpha World and Black Being.* Darby, PA: Norwood, 1983. Print.

Phares, Dee Anna. "Downloaded Deck: Netflix's *House of Cards* and 21st-Century Tele-revision." Popular Culture Association/American Culture Association Conference. Chicago. 16 April 2014. Conference presentation.

Phillips, U. B. *American Negro Slavery: A Survey of the Supply, Employment and Control of Negro Labor as Determined by the Plantation Regime.* 1918. Baton Rouge: Louisiana State UP, 1966. Print.

Pilkington, John. *The Heart of Yoknapatawpha.* Jackson: UP of Mississippi, 1981. Print.

Pitcher, E. W. "Motive and Metaphor in Faulkner's 'That Evening Sun.'" *Studies in Short Fiction* 18.2 (Spring 1981): 131–35. Print.

Polchin, James. "Selling a Novel: Faulkner's *Sanctuary* as a Psychosexual Text." *Faulkner and Gender: Faulkner and Yoknapatawpha 1994.* Ed. Donald M. Kartiganer and Ann J. Abadie. Jackson: UP of Mississippi, 1996. 145–59. Print.

Polk, Noel. "Afterword." William Faulkner, *Sanctuary: The Original Text.* 293–306. Print.

——. *Children of the Dark House: Text and Context in Faulkner.* Jackson: UP of Mississippi, 1996. Print.

"Pony Blues" by Charley Patton. Advertisement. *Chicago Defender* 27 July 1929. Rpt. in *Screamin' and Hollerin' the Blues: The Worlds of Charley Patton*. Revenant, 2001. N.p. Print.

Poole, Charlie. "Leaving Home." 1926. *Essential Charlie Poole*. Disc 1. 101 Distribution, 2009. CD.

"Proceedings of the Modern Language Association of America." *PMLA* 49 (1934): 1295–1336. Print.

Pynchon, Thomas. *The Crying of Lot 49*. 1965. New York: Harper, 1999. Print.

Railey, Kevin. "The Social Psychology of Paternalism: *Sanctuary*'s Cultural Context." *Faulkner in Cultural Context: Faulkner and Yoknapatawpha 1995*. Ed. Donald M. Kartiganer and Ann J. Abadie. Jackson: UP of Mississippi, 1997. 75–98. Print.

Ramsey, Frederic, Jr. *Been Here and Gone*. New Brunswick, NJ: Rutgers UP, 1960. Print.

Rawson, Hugh. *Wicked Words: A Treasury of Curses, Insults, Put-Downs, and Other Formerly Unprintable Terms from Anglo-Saxon Times to the Present*. New York: Crown Publishers Inc., 1989. Print.

"Red Hot Ole Mose" [Moses Mason]. "Shrimp Man." 1928. *American Primitive 2*. Disc 2. Revenant, 2005. CD.

Rhodes, Pamela, and Richard Godden. "*The Wild Palms*: Degraded Culture, Devalued Texts." *Intertextuality in Faulkner*. Ed. Michael Gresset and Noel Polk. Jackson: UP of Mississippi, 1985. 87–113. Print.

Richardson, Edward H. "The 'Hemingwaves' in Faulkner's 'Wild Palms.'" *Modern Fiction Studies* 4 (Winter 1958–59): 357–60. Print.

Richter, Alan. *The Language of Sexuality*. Jefferson, NC: McFarland & Co., 1987. Print.

Robbins, Ben. "The Sexual Motivation of Flight: Transgressive Eroticism in William Faulkner's *If I Forget Thee, Jerusalem* and James Baldwin's *Another Country*." Faulkner and the Black Literatures of the Americas: Faulkner and Yoknapatawpha 2013. University of Mississippi. 22 July 2013. Conference Presentation.

Robeson, Paul. "Ol' Man River." 1928. *The Ultimate* Show Boat, *1928–1947*. Disc 1. Pearl, 1999. CD.

Rodgers, Jimmie. "Frankie and Johnnie." 1929. *The Essential Jimmie Rodgers*. RCA/BMG, 1997. CD.

Ross, Stephen M. *Fiction's Inexhaustible Voice: Speech and Writing in Faulkner*. Athens: U of Georgia P, 1989. Print.

Rossky, William. "*The Reivers*: Faulkner's 'Tempest.'" *Mississippi Quarterly* 18 (1965): 82–93. Print.

Roth, Philip. "Writing American Fiction." 1961. *The Novel Today: Contemporary Writers on Modern Fiction*. Ed. Malcolm Bradbury. Rev. ed. London: Fontana P, 1990. 27–43. Print.

Rothenbuhler, Eric W. "For-the-Record Aesthetics and Robert Johnson's Blues Style as a Product of Recorded Culture." *Popular Music* 26.1 (2007): 65–87. Print.

Rudat, Wolfgang E. H. "Bill Gorton and Jokes as Therapy." *Alchemy in* The Sun Also Rises: *Hidden Gold in Hemingway's Narrative.* Lewiston, NY: Edwin Mellen P, 1992. 173–206. Print.

Ryan, Tim A. *Calls and Responses: The American Novel of Slavery since* Gone with the Wind. Baton Rouge: Louisiana State UP, 2008. Print.

———. "'Go to Jail About This Spoonful': Narcotic Determinism and Human Agency in 'That Evening Sun' and 'A Spoonful Blues.'" *Faulkner and Black Literatures of the Americas: Faulkner and Yoknapatawpha 2013.* Ed. Jay Watson and James Thomas. Jackson: UP of Mississippi. 2015. Forthcoming.

———. "'A Little Music Aint About the Nicest Thing a Fellow Can Have': William Faulkner, *As I Lay Dying,* and Country Songs." *Mississippi Quarterly.* Forthcoming.

———. "'The Matter with Your Line': Gender, Sexual, and Racial Politics in Charley Patton's 'Pony Blues.'" *Journal of American Culture* 38.1 (March 2015): 27–38. Print.

Sackheim, Eric. *The Blues Line.* New York: Grossman, 1969. Print.

St. Louis Blues. Dir. Dudley Murphy, 1929. Perf. Bessie Smith, Jimmy Mordecai, and the Hall Johnson Choir. *Hollywood Rhythm.* Vol. 1: *The Best of Jazz & Blues.* Kino, 2001. DVD.

Samway, Patrick, S.J. "Narration and Naming in *The Reivers.*" *Faulkner's Discourse: An International Symposium.* Ed. Lothar Hónnighausen. Tübingen, Germany: Niemeyer, 1989. 254–62. Print.

Sandburg, Carl, ed. *The American Songbag.* New York: Harcourt, Brace & Co., 1927. Print.

Sanders, Barry. "Faulkner's Fire Imagery in 'That Evening Sun.'" *Studies in Short Fiction* 5.1 (Fall 1967): 69–71. Print.

Sanders, Lynn Moss. *Howard W. Odum's Folklore Odyssey: Transformation to Tolerance through African American Folk Studies.* Athens: U of Georgia P, 2003. Print.

Saxon, Lyle. *Father Mississippi.* 1927. Gretna, LA: Pelican, 2006. Print.

Schroeder, Patricia. *Robert Johnson, Mythmaking, and Contemporary American Culture.* Urbana: U of Illinois P, 2004. Print.

Segrest, James, and Mark Hoffman. *Moanin' at Midnight: The Life and Times of Howlin' Wolf.* New York: Pantheon, 2004. Print.

Sensibar, Judith L. *Faulkner and Love: The Women Who Shaped His Art.* New Haven, CT: Yale UP, 2009. Print.

———. *The Origins of Faulkner's Art.* Austin: U of Texas P, 1984. Print.

Shakespeare, William. *Complete Works.* Ed. Jonathan Bate and Eric Rasmussen. New York: Modern Library, 2007. Print.

Sharma, Bhesham R. "Poetic Devices in the Songs of Robert Johnson, King of the Delta Blues." *Revista Transcultural de Música* [*Transcultural Music Review*] 3 (November 1997). www.sibetrans.com/trans/trans3/sharma.htm Accessed 1 June 2009. Web.

Shay, Frank. *Judge Lynch: His First Hundred Years.* New York: Ives, Washburn, Inc., 1938. Print.

Shelton, Robert. *No Direction Home: The Life and Music of Bob Dylan.* New York: Ballantine, 1987. Print.

Shklovsky, Victor. "Art as Technique." 1917. *Modern Criticism and Theory: A Reader.* Ed. David Lodge. London: Longman, 1988. 15–30. Print.

Show Boat. 1936. Dir. James Whale. Perf. Irene Dunne, Allan Jones, Paul Robeson, Hattie McDaniel. Warner, 2014. DVD.

Singal, Daniel J. *The War Within: From Victorian to Modernist Thought in the South, 1919–1945.* Chapel Hill: U of North Carolina P, 1982. Print.

———. *William Faulkner: The Making of a Modernist.* Chapel Hill: U of North Carolina P, 1997. Print.

Singer, Nathan. *Chasing the Wolf.* Madison: Bleak House Books, 2006. Print.

Skei, Hans H. *Reading Faulkner's Best Short Stories.* Columbia: U of South Carolina P, 1999. Print.

Slabey, Robert M. "Faulkner's Nancy as 'Tragic Mulatto.'" *Studies in Short Fiction* 27.3 (Summer 1990): 409–13. Print.

———. "Quentin Compson's 'Lost Childhood.'" *Studies in Short Fiction* 1.3 (Spring 1964): 173–83. Print.

Smith, Bessie. "Backwater Blues." 1927. *Complete Columbia Recordings.* Vol. 3, Disc 1.

———. *The Complete Columbia Recordings.* 10 CDs. Sony, 2012.

———. "Empty Bed Blues." 1928. *Complete Columbia Recordings.* Vol. 4, Disc 1.

———. "Haunted House Blues." 1924. *Complete Columbia Recordings.* Vol. 1, Disc 2.

———. "Kitchen Man." 1929. *Complete Columbia Recordings.* Vol. 4, Disc 1.

Smith, Clara. "It Takes the Lawd (To Know What's On My Mind)." 1925. *Complete Recorded Works in Chronological Order.* Vol. 3: *1925.* Document, 1995. CD.

Smith, Jessica. "'Call Yourself a Man': Temple and Little Belle's Ephemeral Circumventions of Patriarchy." American Modernist Fiction & Gender Politics. Northern Illinois University. 21 April 2014. Conference Presentation.

Smith, Phil. "'The Megaphone's Bellowing and Bodiless Profanity': *If I Forget Thee, Jerusalem* and the Culture of Cacophony." *Faulkner Journal* 26.1 (Spring 2012): 75–96. Print.

Snell, George. *The Shapers of American Fiction 1798–1947.* New York: Cooper Square Publishers, Inc., 1961. Print.

Spears, Richard A. *Slang and Euphemism.* Middle Village, NY: Jonathan David Publishers, 1981. Print.

Spottswood, Dick. "Going Away to a World Unknown: Song Notes and Transcriptions. *Screamin' and Hollerin' the Blues: The Worlds of Charley Patton.* Revenant, 2001. Liner notes: 56–91. Print.

Springer, Robert. "On the Electronic Trail of Blues Formulas." Springer, ed. 164–86. Print.

———. ed. *Nobody Knows Where the Blues Come From: Lyrics and History.* Jackson: UP of Mississippi, 2006. Print.

Stafford, William T. "'Some Homer of the Cotton Fields': Faulkner's Use of the Mule Early and Late (*Sartoris* and *The Reivers*)." *Papers on Language and Literature* 5.2 (Spring 1969): 190–96. Print.

Stallman, R. W. *The House That James Built and Other Literary Studies.* East Lansing: Michigan State UP, 1961. Print.

Stephens, Robert O. *The Family Saga in the South: Generations and Destinies.* Baton Rouge: Louisiana State UP, 1995. Print.

Stepto, Robert B. *From Behind the Veil: A Study of Afro-American Narrative.* 2nd ed. Urbana: U of Illinois P, 1991. Print.

Stoneback, H. R. "Faulkner's Blues: 'Pantaloon in Black.'" *Modern Fiction Studies* 21.2 (Summer 1975): 241–45. Print.

Stonesifer, Richard J. "Faulkner's *Old Man* in the Classroom." *College English* 17.5 (February 1956): 254–57. Print.

Sullivan, John Jeremiah. "The Ballad of Geeshie and Elvie." *New York Times Magazine.* 13 April 2014. 24–31, 38, 44–46, 49. Print.

———. "Unknown Bards: The Blues Becomes Transparent About Itself." *Harper's Magazine,* November 2008, 85–94. Print.

Sunderman, Paula. "Speech Act Theory and Faulkner's 'That Evening Sun.'" *Language and Style* 14.4 (Fall 1981): 304–14. Print.

Sundquist, Eric J. *Faulkner: The House Divided.* Baltimore: Johns Hopkins UP, 1983. Print.

Sykes, Roosevelt. "44 Blues." 1929. *Complete Recorded Works in Chronological Order.* Vol. 1: *1929–1930.* Document, 1994. CD.

Szwed, John. *Alan Lomax: The Man Who Recorded the World.* New York: Viking, 2010. Print.

Taft, Michael. *The Blues Lyric Formula.* New York: Routledge, 2006. Print.

———. *Blues Lyric Poetry: A Concordance.* 3 vols. New York: Garland, 1984. Print.

———. *Talkin' to Myself: Blues Lyrics, 1921–1942.* New York: Routledge, 2005. Print.

Tanner, Gale. "Sentimentalism and *The Reivers*: A Reply to Ben Merchant Vorpahl." *Notes on Mississippi Writers* 9 (1976): 50–58. Print.

Taylor, Walter. *Faulkner's Search for a South.* Urbana: U of Illinois P, 1983. Print.

Tebbetts, Terrell. "*Sanctuary,* Marriage, and the Status of Women in 1920s America." *Faulkner Journal* 19.1 (2003): 47–60. Print.

Titon, Jeff Todd. "Autobiography and Blues Texts: A Reply to 'The Blues as Dramatic Monologues.'" *JEMF Quarterly* 6 (1970): 79–82. Print.

———. *Early Downhome Blues: A Musical and Cultural Analysis.* Urbana: U of Illinois P, 1977. Print.

Toker, Leona. "Rhetoric and Ethical Ambiguities in 'That Evening Sun.'" *Women's Studies* 22.4 (September 1993): 429–39. Print.

Tolnay, Stewart E., and E. M. Beck. *A Festival of Violence: An Analysis of Southern Lynchings, 1882–1930.* Urbana: U of Illinois P, 1995. Print.

Towner, Theresa. *Faulkner on the Color Line: The Later Novels*. Jackson: UP of Mississippi, 2000. Print.

———, and James B. Carothers. *Reading Faulkner: Collected Stories*. Jackson: UP of Mississippi, 2006. Print.

Tracy, Steven C. *Langston Hughes and the Blues*. Urbana: U of Illinois P, 1988. Print.

———, ed. *Write Me a Few of Your Lines: A Blues Reader*. Amherst: U of Massachusetts P, 1999. Print.

Trynka, Paul. "Deep Blue." *Mojo* 27 (Feb 1996): 40–51. Print.

Twelve Southerners. *I'll Take My Stand: The South and the Agrarian Tradition*. 1930. New York: Peter Smith, 1951. Print.

van der Tuuk, Alex. *Paramount's Rise and Fall: A History of the Wisconsin Chair Company and Its Recording Activities*. Littleton, CO: Mainspring P, 2003. Print.

van Rijn, Guido. "Imagery in the Lyrics: An Initial Approach." *The Cambridge Companion to Blues and Gospel Music*. Ed. Allan Moore. Cambridge: Cambridge UP, 2002. 141–57. Print.

———. *Roosevelt's Blues: African-American Blues and Gospel Songs on FDR*. Jackson: UP of Mississippi, 1997. Print.

Veeder, Toby. "Egalitarian Elixirs: Representations of Alcohol in American Literature, 1899–1932." PhD diss. Northern Illinois University, 2014. Print.

Vickery, Olga W. *The Novels of William Faulkner: A Critical Interpretation*. Rev. ed. 1964. Baton Rouge: Louisiana State UP, 1995. Print.

Volpe, Edmond L. *A Reader's Guide to William Faulkner: The Novels*. 1964. Syracuse: Syracuse UP, 2003. Print.

———. *A Reader's Guide to William Faulkner: The Short Stories*. Syracuse: Syracuse UP, 2004. Print.

Vorpahl, Ben Merchant. "Moonlight at Ballenbaugh's: Time and Imagination in *The Reivers*." *Southern Literary Journal* 1.2 (Spring 1969): 3–26. Print.

Voth, Danna. "*Ignis Fatuus* in Faulkner's *Sanctuary*." *Conflict in Southern Writing*. Ed. Ben P. Robertson. Troy, NY: Troy UP, 2006. 113–21. Print.

Wagner, Bryan. *Disturbing the Peace: Black Culture and the Police Power after Slavery*. Cambridge, MA: Harvard UP, 2009. Print.

Wald, Elijah. "Charlie Patton: Folksinger." 2002. www.elijahwald.com/patton.html. Accessed 3 March 2008. Web.

———. *Escaping the Delta: Robert Johnson and the Invention of the Blues*. New York: Amistad, 2005. Print.

Wardlow, Gayle Dean. *Chasin' That Devil Music: Searching for the Blues*. San Francisco: Miller Freeman, 1998. Print.

Waters, Muddy. "My Home Is in the Delta." 1963. *The Chess Box*. Chess, 1989. CD.

Watson, Jay. *Forensic Fictions: The Lawyer Figure in Faulkner*. Athens: U of Georgia P, 1993. Print.

Webster's New International Dictionary. 2nd ed. 3 vols. Ed. William Allan Neilson, Thomas A. Knott, and Paul W. Carhart. Springfield, MA: G & C Merriam Co., Publishers, 1938. Print.

Wells, Dean Faulkner. *Ghosts of Rowan Oak: William Faulkner's Ghost Stories for Children.* Oxford, MS: Yoknapatawpha P, 1981. Print.

Wenska, Walter. "'There's a Man with a Gun Over There': Faulkner's Hijackings of Masculine Popular Culture." *Faulkner Journal* 15.1–2 (Fall 1999–Winter 2000): 35–60. Print.

Werner, Craig. "'Tell Old Pharaoh': The Afro-American Response to Faulkner." *Southern Review* 19.4 (October 1983): 711–35. Print.

Weseen, Maurice H. *A Dictionary of American Slang.* New York: Thomas Y. Crowell Co., 1934. Print.

Wheatstraw, Peetie. "Don't Take a Chance." 1936. *Complete Recorded Works in Chronological Order.* Vol. 4: *1936–1937.* Document, 1994. CD.

———. "I Want Some Seafood." 1936. *The Essential Peetie Wheatstraw.* Classic Blues, 2003. CD.

"When the Dam Breaks." *Time* 33.4 (23 January 1939): 45–48. Print.

Whicher, Stephen E. "The Compsons' Nancies: A Note on *The Sound and the Fury* and 'That Evening Sun.'" *American Literature* 26.2 (May 1954): 253–55. Print.

Whitburn, Joel. *Joel Whitburn Presents Top R&B Singles 1942–1999.* Menomonee Falls, WI: Record Research Inc., 2000. Print.

———. *Joel Whitburn's Top Country Singles 1944–2001.* Menomonee Falls, WI: Record Research Inc., 2002. Print.

———. *Joel Whitburn's Top Pop Singles 1955–1999.* Menomonee Falls, WI: Record Research Inc., 2000. Print.

White, Bukka. *Aberdeen, Mississippi Blues.* CD. 101 Distribution, 2007.

———. "District Attorney Blues." 1940. *Aberdeen, Mississippi Blues.*

———. "Parchman Farm Blues." 1940. *Aberdeen, Mississippi Blues.*

———. "Shake 'Em On Down." 1937. *Aberdeen, Mississippi Blues.*

———. "When Can I Change My Clothes?" 1940. *Aberdeen, Mississippi Blues.*

White, Walter. *Rope and Faggot: A Biography of Judge Lynch.* 1929. Notre Dame, IN: U of Notre Dame P, 2001. Print.

The White Stripes. "Death Letter." *De Stijl.* Sympathy 4 the R.I., 2000. CD.

———. "Your Southern Can Is Mine." *De Stijl.* Sympathy 4 the R.I., 2000. CD.

Whiting, Nathaniel. "The Pleasing History of Albino and Bellama." 1637. *Minor Poets of the Caroline Period.* Vol. 3. Ed. George Saintsbury. 1921. Oxford: Clarendon P, 1968. Print.

Wilde, Meta Carpenter, and Orin Borsten. *A Loving Gentleman: The Love Story of William Faulkner and Meta Carpenter.* New York: Simon and Schuster, 1976. Print.

Wiley, Geeshie. "Last Kind Words Blues." 1930. *American Primitive 2.* Disc 2. Revenant, 2005. CD.

———. "Skinny Leg Blues." 1930. *American Primitive 2*. Disc 1. Revenant, 2005. CD.

Wilhelm, Randall. "Faulkner's Visual Blues and the Paintings of William H. Johnson." Faulkner and the Black Literatures of the Americas: Faulkner and Yoknapatawpha 2013. University of Mississippi. 24 July 2013. Conference Presentation.

Wilkerson, Isabel. *The Warmth of Other Suns: The Epic Story of America's Great Migration*. New York: Vintage, 2011. Print.

Williams, Chad L. *Torchbearers of Democracy: African American Soldiers in the World War I Era*. Chapel Hill: U of North Carolina P, 2010. Print.

Williams, David. "The Profaned Temple" 1977. Rpt. in Canfield, ed. 93–107. Print.

Williams, Gordon. *A Dictionary of Sexual Language and Imagery in Shakespearean and Stuart Literature*. Vol. 1, A–F. London: Athelone P, 1994. Print.

Williamson, Joel. *The Crucible of Race: Black-White Relations in the American South Since Emancipation*. New York: Oxford UP, 1984. Print.

———. *William Faulkner and Southern History*. New York: Oxford UP, 1993. Print.

Wittenberg, Judith Bryant. *Faulkner: The Transfiguration of Biography*. Lincoln: U of Nebraska P, 1979. Print.

———. "*The Reivers*: A Conservative Fable?" Gresset and Ohashi, ed. 211–26. Print.

Wolfe, Charles, and Kip Lornell. *The Life and Legend of Leadbelly*. New York: Harper, 1992. Print.

Wood, Amy Louise. *Lynching and Spectacle: Witnessing Racial Violence in America, 1890—1940*. Chapel Hill: U of North Carolina P, 2009. Print.

Woodson, Carter G. *The Negro in Our History*. Washington, DC: Associated Publishers Inc., 1922. Print.

Woodward, C. Vann. "Why the Southern Renaissance?" *Virginia Quarterly Review* 51.2 (Spring 1975): 222–39. Print.

Wright, Richard. *Black Boy: A Record of Childhood and Youth*. New York: Harper & Brothers, 1945. Print.

———. "Down by the Riverside." 1938. *Uncle Tom's Children*. New York: Harper, 2008. 62–124. Print.

———. "Silt." *New Masses* 24 (24 August 1937): 19–20. Print.

York, Jake Adam. "Before Knowing Remembers." *Persons Unknown*. Carbondale: Southern Illinois UP, 2010. 65–72. Print.

Yoshida, Michiko. "Faulkner's Comedy of Motion: *The Reivers*." Gresset and Ohashi, ed. 197–210. Print.

Young-Minor, Ethel. "'I Sees De Light En I Sees De Word': Black Female Transcendence of the Racial and Gendered Boundaries in *The Sound and the Fury* and 'That Evening Sun.'" *Faulkner and Formalism: Returns of the Text: Faulkner and Yoknapatawpha, 2008*. Ed. Annette Trefzer and Ann J. Abadie. Jackson: UP of Mississippi, 2012. 163–77. Print.

Zender, Karl F. *The Crossing of the Ways: William Faulkner, the South, and the Modern World*. New Brunswick, NJ: Rutgers UP, 1989. Print.

INDEX